Discipline Options:

Establishing a Positive School Climate

Discipline Options:

Establishing a Positive School Climate

Rita Coombs-Richardson and Charles H. Meisgeier

Credits

Every effort has been made to contact copyright holders for permission to reproduce borrowed material where necessary. We apologize for any oversights and would be happy to rectify them in future prints.

Excerpt from *Teacher Effectiveness Training by Thomas Gordon*, copyright 1974 by Thomas Gordon, used by permission of Random House, Inc.

Excerpt from *The Aggressive Child* adapted with permission of The Tree Press, a division of Simon & Schuster, Inc. by fritz Redl and David Wineman. Copyright 1957 by The Free Press.

Excerpts from the DSM-IV-TR are reprinted with permission from the Diagnostic and Statistical Manual of Mental Disorders, Fourth Edition, Text Revision. Copyright 2000 American Psychiatric Association.

Phi Delta Kappa Polls, used by permission of Phi Delta Kappa.

Example based on Multiple Intelligences by Howard Gardner, copyright 1993, used by permission of Perseus Book Group.

Pages 17–28 from *Schools Without Failure* by William Glasser, M.D. Copyright 1969 by William Glasser. Reprinted by permission of HarperCollins Publishers, Inc.

Emotional Quotient by Daniel Goleman, copyright 1995, used by permission of Bantam books, a division of Random House, Inc.

Excerpt from *Teaching Students to Read Through Their Individual Learning styles* by Marie Carbo, et al, copyright 1991. Used with permission Allyn & Bacon.

Father Flanagan's Boys Town, used by permission of Boys Town USA.

Christopher-Gordon Publishers, Inc.
1502 Providence Highway, Suite 12
Norwood, MA 02062
1-800-934-8322
781-762-5577

Copyright © 2001 by Christopher-Gordon Publishers, Inc.

Printed in the United States of America

10 9 8 7 6 5 4 3 2 1   06 05 04 03 02 01

Library of Congress Catalog Card Number: 00-111703

ISBN: 1-929024-29-0

Contents

Acknowledgments

The content of this book reflects the suggestions and feedback of dedicated teachers in special and general education. We are thankful for their input and for their commitment to students. In addition, we gratefully acknowledge the help, encouragement, and support of people close to us: Deborah Richardson and David Fuller, whose technological expertise in computers saved us from many potential disasters. A very special thank you to Constance Meisgeier, whose input and practical wisdom enriched the content of each chapter. She diligently worked with us, offering wise suggestions and ideas that we gratefully accepted. A special note of gratitude to Charles Meisgeier, Jr., Esq., for his contribution in chapter 9. He provided us with information on bullying in schools and shared many personal experiences on this topic.

We are forever grateful to Jodi Stuker, graduate assistant to Rita Coombs-Richardson at Southeastern Louisiana University. She helped to organize and edit the entire manuscript. Her youthful perspective helped us to focus on practical issues in developing topics. We wish to acknowledge the contribution of Sarah Al-Juraid and Allyson Broussard, graduate students at Southeastern Louisiana University. Sarah spent countless hours doing research on the Internet and organizing files for easy retrieval of information. Allyson was invaluable in assuming the responsibility of printing, duplicating, and assembling each chapter.

We are indebted to Dr. Carol Torrey for her chapter in applied behavioral analysis. Her expertise in this area gave a new meaning to behavior modification. Her proactive use of behavioral strategies focuses on increasing positive behaviors rather than just decreasing negative behaviors.

We would like to extend a thank you to Father Val J. Peter for his description of The Girls and Boys Town Program. Behaviorism can have a humanistic touch when properly applied.

We thank our very special editors and publishers at Christopher-Gordon for their expertise and patience.

Introduction

A common concern of teachers, parents, and school administrators revolves around discipline issues. Increasing acts of violence are becoming a public concern, and schools are instituting measures such as "no tolerance" and school uniforms in the hope of establishing a sense of order. Learning becomes extremely difficult when discipline problems interfere with the teaching process. Proficiency in teaching academic content certainly is required, but it is not enough; teachers must also be equipped with knowledge to help students increase social and emotional competence, leading eventually to self-discipline. Social competence is essential for developing self-management skills, and teachers can facilitate this process through proactive measures. Schools that promote positive and orderly climates secure students' right to learn in an atmosphere that is free of coercion and chaos.

Part I of this book presents the background of the issue. **Chapter 1** surveys the discipline problems that face public schools and how the public views them. It examines what teachers and students consider to be serious behavior problems. Lack of discipline in schools is the most frequently mentioned problem in public opinion polls. A second concern is the lack of financial support for the schools, but the public is not willing to personally bear that financial burden. Drug use, fighting, violence, and gangs combines to form a close third concern in public opinion polls. Parents continue to believe that drugs and weapons are problematic. Urban schools are perceived as more troublesome than nonurban schools, and a demand for more control over students is expressed in many communities. Teachers cite the following seven activities as the most serious discipline problems in public schools: alcohol abuse, violence (physical fights), theft, vandalism, teen pregnancy, drug abuse, and lack of parental support. The percentage of teachers who report students' possession of weapons as troublesome nearly doubled from 1988 to 1994. A survey of students' opinions and perceptions indicates a need for improvement in the social climate of the nation's public schools. One in four students, nationally, perceives that the most serious problems revolve around hostile or threatening remarks, physical fights, destructive acts, turf battles, and gang violence. Students voice a need for more personalized student-teacher interactions and a climate free of conflict among diverse groups of students. In response to the students' message, we have included suggestions for teachers to personalize discipline methods and to promote acceptance of diversity. We offer hope through the concept of resilience and suggest that even the most hardened student can "bounce back" with support and mentoring.

Chapter 2 discusses regularities, responsibility, and reinforcement: the three Rs of disipline. Classroom characteristics and antecedent conditions can help teachers to identify the regularities that govern classroom life and explain how they affect behavior management and discipline decisions. In particular, we examine the interconnectedness of the reinforcers that are offered, the responsible behaviors that are expected, and the classroom regularities that create a school's learning environment. In addition, we consider discipline practices, individual student differences, and classroom regularities in relation to one another in an attempt to determine how each may enhance or detract from the successful discipline of individual students. Although teachers and classrooms may differ from each other, the style and climate of any one teacher's classroom tends to remain much the same over time. Unless they have had special training, teachers' teaching styles reflect their own personalities and learning styles. Teachers teach the way they themselves learn best; thus, they accommodate the children whose learning style is most like their own. By the same token, their own differences in priorities and expectations strongly influence their selection of methods of discipline and the situations that require their use. *Regularities* are the qualities and characteristics that are consistently present in any given teacher's classroom. *System regularities* are the larger qualities and characteristics that are always present in a particular school or district. Systemwide and schoolwide regularities end up expressing themselves as classroom regularities. Classroom regularities provide the context for behavioral antecedents.

Chapter 3 describes and defines issues of classroom management and discipline as they relate to students' individual characteristics and overall school climate. Teachers learn the importance of personality or psychological types, learning style differences, and multiple intelligences in selecting and executing behavior management strategies and discipline options. We examine the terms *reinforcement* and *responsibility*. These words occur frequently in any discussion of discipline and may have different meanings for people of different psychological types. Therefore it is important to understand that individual personality differences, those of the student and those of the teacher, frequently dictate the selection of reinforcers used to produce responsible behaviors.

In **Chapter 4**, we discuss social and emotional growth and the process of socialization in relation to cognitive and affective development. Teachers are more adept at selecting discipline strategies when they understand how students develop socially and emotionally. Schoolchildren develop social sophistication as they become independent from their families and more interested in socializing with peers. The lack of social skills and peer acceptance frequently results in disruptive and destructive behaviors. *Emotional intelligence* is defined as developing self-awareness, delaying gratification, persisting in achieving goals, remaining motivated, and feeling and demonstrating empathy to others in adverse conditions. These qualities enable children to become part of a group, to lead fulfilling lives, and to develop into mature adults. Emotional intelligence is similar to *interpersonal intelligence* and *intrapersonal intelligence* in its importance to the development of self-awareness and awareness of others. An understanding of social development is an important prerequisite to teach socialization. Numerous schools are realizing the importance of teaching social skills and are adopting affective curricula in response to discipline problems. Schoolwide conflict resolution programs are used to teach students the skills of problem solving and peacemaking. Students are taught to control their impulses and resolve conflicts in a non-violent manner. Chapter 4 offers brief descriptions of several published social skills programs.

Part II introduces three paradigms of discipline: *discipline with loose boundaries, discipline with flexible boundaries,* and *discipline with tight boundaries.* These chapters explain how each establishes some type of parameter for children and youth, with a range from less restrictive to more restrictive.

Most of the strategies in **Chapter 5** are based on theories that encourage individuals to explore their emotions as well as their attitudes in their interactions with others. John Dewey's progressive movement gave rise to the democratization of the classroom. He believed that students should be given the freedom to make choices and that teachers should supply experiences that would lead to the correct choices. The emphasis of this model is to empower students and to give them control of their actions. Teachers are considered as facilitators, whose primary function is to direct students toward appropriate conduct. Miscommunication between individuals can lead to serious problems. Thomas Gordon and Hynam Ginott apply Carl Rogers' communication techniques for classroom use. Active listening and sending I- messages instead of you-messages can improve interpersonal relationships and deter discipline problems. Knowledge of Transactional Analysis (TA) can also teach students and teachers to become aware of how verbal and nonverbal behaviors affect the communication process. Students who constantly demonstrate mischievous "child" attitudes, and teachers who constantly demonstrate authoritarian "parent" attitudes, cannot achieve "OK" transactions. This chapter also includes strategies for managing classroom "surface" behavior as proposed by Redl, Morse, and Whineman and explores the "habits of the mind" to teach students persistence and impulsivity management.

In **Chapter 6** we discuss the origins of behavior modification and applied behavioral analysis. Most teachers use behavioral strategies in their classrooms on a daily basis. The behavior change model stresses proactive as well as reactive strategies. It requires teachers to specifically target and describe undesirable behaviors, collect baseline data, and plan an intervention. Strategies for increasing behaviors include positive and negative reinforcement. Teachers may use primary and secondary reinforcement to modify and change inappropriate student behaviors; however, the end goal should promote self-management. Negative reinforcement is unlike punishment because it increases a desired alternative behavior, whereas punishment decreases an undesired behavior. *Contracting, prompting,* and *shaping* are examples of negative reinforcement. Strategies for decreasing behaviors involve punishment as well as *differential reinforcement,* which reinforces a reduction of the targeted behavior. Extinction, response–cost, removal of a desired stimulus, time–out, and presentation of aversives can decrease disruptive behaviors. This chapter includes proactive strategies to prevent misbehaviors and increase appropriate behaviors.

In **Chapter 7**, we review various models that take into account the emotions and behavior of individuals as well as their democratic rights and the rights of others. The works of Abraham Maslow and Alfred Adler provide a foundation for several discipline procedures implemented in classrooms. Democratic approaches to discipline suggested by William Glasser and Rudolph Dreikurs teach students personal responsibility and accountability, realization of consequences, and respect and appreciation for other individuals. Dreikurs advises teachers to discover the cause of students' misconduct. He proposes four goals of misbehavior: attention getting, power, revenge, and helplessness, or inadequacy. Teachers must adapt their strategies to deal with each particular goal.

Donald Meichenbaum has pioneered strategies based on cognitive behavior modification. He suggests teaching students how to reflect on their behaviors, examine consequences, and develop alternative behaviors to produce winning outcomes. The work of Albert Ellis, founder of Rational Emotive Therapy (RET), also proposes a cognitive approach to achieve rational thinking and behavior. RET is based on the premise that your thoughts and beliefs about facts and events cause your emotions and feelings, which in turn cause your behavior. Forrest Gathercoal adapts the concept of constitutional rights into a discipline model he terms *judicious discipline*. This model elaborates on democratic ideals and presents a discipline approach based on a set of principles recognizing human rights. Milieu therapy is an ecological procedure that considers the needs of others in addition to the needs of the particular student. Strategies from this model stress open communication and students' involvement in their behavior management plan. Teachers should support formal and informal group activities to promote sharing, cooperation, compromise, and leadership.

Chapter 8 helps teachers to select a discipline strategy that considers the characteristics of individual students. It reviews the discipline strategies presented in Chapters 5, 6, and 7 and suggests discipline strategies to accommodate a student's variances. We discuss the importance of expanding a teacher's repertoire of discipline strategies to be able to match students' personality and learning differences. A teacher's own personality preferences may have the potential to cause conflict with students whose preferences are different. Many factors impact a teacher's ability to be successful in the use of particular discipline measures. Teachers' type preferences frequently influence their inclination and willingness to implement one discipline strategy over another.

In addition to personality type, two other variables must be considered in selecting a discipline procedure: the situation and the maturity level of the student. Situational leadership suggests seven power bases a teacher can use to obtain compliance and it describes four management styles: telling, selling, participating, and delegating. Teachers initially *tell* students of low maturity what to do. As students grow in maturity, teachers *sell* their expectations through discussions and explanations. When students accept responsibility, they are able to *participate* in decision making. Finally, teachers are able to *delegate* responsible tasks to those students who reach high maturity levels. This approach considers all the models of behavior management from different viewpoints.

Chapter 9 explores the increasing lethality of violent behavior in schools, which has accelerated to shooting sprees and mass killings of students. In addition to these isolated but extreme incidents, daily aggressive acts of students disrupt the learning environment. Violent acts in schools damage learning by stealing precious instruction time, thus promoting a culture of ignorance and illiteracy. The education field is losing teachers and failing to attract prospective dedicated ones because they are not willing to work in disruptive situations. In this chapter we examine the causes of violent and antisocial behavior and why some individuals appear to be desensitized to violence and aggression. Some of the risk factors leading to violence include coming from a family with a history of criminal violence, being abused (physically or psychologically), belonging to a gang, and abusing drugs or alcohol. Children are not born with a social conscience. They acquire the morality of their social environment. They must be taught the expectations of their society in order to be an accepted part of the larger community. When they do not internalize the traditional mores, they will seek acceptance from a smaller group, such as a gang. Bullying and teasing in schools often leads to disastrous outcomes. In this chapter we examine antisocial gangs from a multicultural perspective and conclude with special discipline procedures for students with disabilities.

Part I

Background

Chapter 1

Perception of Discipline Problems

Overview

Public's Perception
    Lack of financial support, funding
    Lack of discipline and need for more control
    Overcrowded schools
    Fighting, violence, gangs
    Use of drugs

Teachers' Perceptions
    Students' use of alcohol
    Physical fighting
    Theft
    Teenage pregnancy
    Vandalism
    Drug abuse
    Lack of parental support

Students' Perceptions
    Hostile and threatening remarks
    Physical fights
    Destructive acts
    Turf battles
    Gang violence
    Lack of teacher-student personalization

Response to Students' Message
    Personalizing discipline
    Teaching acceptance and respect for differences
    Resiliency: Students can "bounce back"

Summary

Activities

QUESTIONS

This chapter will help you to answer the following questions:

1. What are the general public's concerns regarding public schools?

2. What discipline problems do teachers perceive as the most problematic?

3. What discipline problems do students perceive as the most problematic?

4. How can teachers facilitate positive relationships between students from different backgrounds?

5. Do youth arrests account for the majority of violent crimes?

6. Are suspension and expulsion viable solutions for solving discipline violations?

7. How has the nature of discipline infractions changed over the years?

8. Is it possible to personalize education in large schools? Explain your answer.

9. How and why are schools structured according to an Anglo-Saxon configuration?

10. Why is it important to believe in the possibility of change and resiliency of students?

Overview

Schools must have a safe and orderly climate for teachers to teach and for students to learn. Learning cannot result in an atmosphere besieged with discipline problems. National polls have reported that discipline in schools has been perceived as a major concern for more than a quarter of a century. In addition, the media is swift in reporting students' misconduct, and violent incidents are often misinterpreted as the norm. Media reports are frequently distorted, and very often inaccurate reporting is repeated as factual. In fact, most public school districts have strict discipline codes and administrators do not hesitate to enforce them and swiftly suspend or expel students who present discipline problems. Educators often blame parents for lack of support and for not teaching their children to behave. In fact, most parents do care and want to support teachers. Traditional family structures have changed and will keep on changing, but the majority of parents want their children to be educated and disciplined.

Administrators have traditionally used suspension and expulsion to deal with students who violate school rules. Excluding students from school often positively reinforces the students who want to get out of school. In many cases suspension and expulsion places students out in the community to commit more mischief. Unless alternative placements are required by the school district, such punishment does not usually teach appropriate behaviors, it does not offer help and support, nor does it solve the underlying problem. Suspension and expulsion is not the answer to discipline problems when planned alternatives are not in place. In desperate efforts to maintain discipline, many high schools have implemented drastic measures, including students' ID bracelets, to keep outsiders from infiltrating schools. Increasing numbers of the nation's 100 largest school districts are using metal detectors, armed guards, drug-sniffing dogs, school uniforms, and zero tolerance policies. These measures may appear to be appropriate in some cases where expedient steps are necessary to protect teachers and students; however, these are not permanent solutions. Proactive, long-term interventions, such as teaching social skills and conflict resolution, usually yield more lasting results (Bailey, 1997). Students need more than just sound and consistent discipline intervention. They also need a school culture that allows them to develop emotionally as well as cognitively.

The large structure of many secondary schools, though cost efficient, is often impersonal and cold and lends itself to discipline problems. A solution to large schools may be the division into smaller units to personalize student-teacher relationships. This arrangement allows for effective management of smaller groups of students and facilitates implementation of measures to prevent potential problems. In addition, smaller classrooms allow teachers to give personal attention to students with learning or behavior problems. A democratic atmosphere empowers students and prepares them for a democratic society. An increasing number of schools are teaching peer mediation and peer mentoring and are involving students in developing discipline procedures (Johnson & Johnson, 1995). Students learn to avoid, ignore, diffuse, and work out acceptable resolutions to conflict. Establishing peer mediation teams places the responsibility on students for resolving conflicts. Facilitators are trained to teach students how to mediate, negotiate, and compromise to reach nonviolent solutions.

Discipline can be improved with changes in school structure and organization, in curriculum and assessment, and in establishing partnerships with parents and community leaders. Berliner and Biddle (1995), in the book *The Manufactured Crisis,* challenge the notion that American schools are failing. Their advice for school improvement includes the following: (a) bestow more dignity on parents and give hope to children, (b) provide fairness in funding to equalize opportunities in learning, (c) reduce the size of large schools to personalize the educational process, (d) emphasize and model the necessary skills for successful integration in a democratic society, (e) adopt innovative methods to teach competencies that will extend beyond the school curriculum, (f) strengthen the relationship between communities, homes and schools, and (g) strengthen the professional status of educators.

In an attempt to establish order, numerous school districts have adopted "canned" discipline programs to assist teachers. When such programs are introduced, teachers are typically trained in a 1-day workshop and are expected to be successful in implementing a profusion of information. Frequently, teachers are frustrated and disappointed and abandon the program. A possible explanation for the lack of success may be that most behavioral management systems offer homogeneous solutions and do not consider individual differences. Students have unique characteristics and experiences and often need special consideration. In addition, teachers have diverse personalities, teaching styles, and philosophies and respond differently to imposed discipline systems. A comprehensive behavioral model must include strategies from various paradigms of behavioral interventions. In addition to behavior modification approaches, teachers can use methods based on cognitive principles and humanistic and ecological techniques. Social skill training is also essential in a total behavior program. Strategies from all these areas can complement procedures from behavioral approaches and can focus on how emotional and interpersonal aspects of behavior impact on learning. Frequently, teachers expect children to be socially competent as they start school. Social skills training must be ongoing—modeled and reinforced at home and in school. Students' lack of social behaviors often contributes to rejection by the peer group, and failure to develop healthy relationships with peers and adults often results in antisocial behaviors and discipline problems.

We can frequently change the behavior of others by paying attention to the antecedents—namely, examining what happened before the occurrence of the behavior. We can also investigate our own behavior and the impact of our demeanor on students' responses. Seating arrangements, classroom organization, relevant instruction, and motivating activities are antecedents to learning. Conversely, a chaotic classroom and unplanned and repetitive "seat work" are antecedents to discipline problems. Teachers can often manipulate antecedents that cause the behavior. *Antecedent control* simply means becoming aware of what is precipitating the problem and devising a plan to change the antecedent. If a student is disruptive when seated close to a particular peer, the teacher can change the antecedent by assigning another seat and avoid disruptions until the two students learn to get along with each other. Teachers, parents, and administrators can assist and support one another through positive communication and collaboration. However, teachers also need skills to be self-sufficient instead of depending on administrators and parents to control every discipline problem. Teachers can use their skills to resolve routine disruptions and use proactive measures to establish an environment conducive to learning.

Public's Perceptions

Lack of discipline in schools is the most frequently mentioned problem in public opinion polls and has remained among the top five concerns for more than 25 years. In a recent poll by Rose & Gallup (2000), the public cited a lack of financial support or funding; a lack of discipline and the need for more control; overcrowded schools; fighting, violence, and gangs; and the use of drugs as the five most pressing problems facing public schools. Concern about standard quality and crime and vandalism were mentioned by only 5% of the public surveyed. In spite of their apprehensions, the respondents of the poll gave "good grades" to the schools in their own communities and the particular schools in which their children were enrolled. People tend to have higher regard for familiar public schools closer to them. The schools the public rated the lowest are the schools they do not know. A majority of the public (75%) is behind public education and would prefer to build up existing schools rather than introduce vouchers for private schools.

The public perception that more young people are arrested for serious criminal offenses than ever before is incorrect. In fact, children and teenagers are more often victims than aggressors. In 1994, the U.S. Department of Justice released a report indicating that the number of crimes against youth between 12 and 17 years old had risen 24% from 1988 to 1992. The public in urban districts believed that more must be done to contain this problem. Urban schools were believed to be more troublesome than nonurban schools (Snyder & Sikmund, 1995).

The recent report of violent incidents across the country has alarmed the nation. Although school shootings are extensively covered in the news media, the information available in news reports is not necessarily accurate. An FBI report (O'Toole, 2000) reviewed news reporting and concluded that the coverage presented and magnified a number of widespread but wrong impressions of violence in schools. Media reports often raise questions about the safety of children in schools. The issue of safety was examined in a national poll of people's attitudes toward public schools (Rose & Gallup, 2000). The respondents indicated that they perceived schools in their community as "very safe and orderly" (24%) to "somewhat safe and orderly" (62%). The response "very safe and orderly" rose to 42% in the schools attended by the respondents' oldest child. However, people asserted a need for stricter discipline to maintain a safe and secure school environment. The respondents strongly supported the zero tolerance policies adopted by numerous schools, and they believe that students carrying drugs, alcohol, and weapons should be suspended. They called for stricter rules and more control.

Punitive measures to establish discipline in schools are frequently counterproductive. Sautter (1995) proposed that dealing with youth violence requires more than a criminal justice approach, and that educators need to teach young people to consider the consequences of their actions and to develop alternatives to disruptive behaviors. Huntington Beach High School in Huntington Beach, California, is an example of how a typical high school can work to curb disruptive behaviors by personalizing teacher-student relationships. At first, administrators established a stricter dress code, increased the severity of punishment for misconduct, and discontinued extracurricular activities. Four unsuccessful years later, the administration decided to take a different approach. School officials launched a concentrated effort to personalize the school experience for that small percentage of students that engaged in disruptive behavior or indicated potential problems. The teaching staff, school officials, and the community outreach liaison worked together in identifying and providing assistance and support to targeted "problem" students. An Adopt-a-Kid program was initiated, matching adult volunteers with one or two students. The adults volunteered their time for personalized interactions with their protégés. In pairing students and teachers, administrators attempted to match students' learning styles and personalities with those of their adult mentors. The principal instituted "most improved student" awards, which were given every quarter. A student forum was held twice a month in the principal's conference room, open to any student who wished to discuss a school activity policy or to voice a complaint. In addition, administrators, school psychologists, the school nurse, the community outreach liaison, and selected staff members held weekly meetings to discuss the students' progress. During the first year, Huntington Beach saw a 47% decrease in suspensions over the previous year and an overall improved school climate (Shore, 1995).

Teachers' Perceptions

A representative sample of 4,000 teachers was polled by Phi Delta Kappa to compare the attitudes of the nation's public school teachers with those of the general public in the area of problems facing the public schools (Langdon, 1999). The largest percentage of teachers (69%) perceive alcohol to be a very serious problem, in contrast to parents, who cited lack of discipline and drugs as more severe than alcohol. Inner city teachers believe that discipline, drugs, fighting, gangs, and teenage pregnancy are more serious problems than do teachers in all other settings. Urban teachers see discipline, fighting, and gangs as more serious problems than do teachers in suburban, small town, and rural areas. Parents also viewed fighting, violence, and gangs as detrimental. Teachers in small towns express more concern with smoking than do their peers in other areas.

How do teachers perceive the support given to them by parents? The problem identified by teachers over several years was a lack of interest and support from parents, in contrast to a lack of discipline identified by parents. Nothing in the Rose & Gallup (2000) poll implies that there is public mistrust of teachers. The responses indicate that the public believes in the importance of qualified and competent teachers and that teachers are a key element in school improvement efforts. Teachers, on the other hand, believe that lack of parental support is the most serious problem (Langdon, 1999). A large percentage of teachers stated that parents were not supportive and would not back them when informed of their children's disruptive behavior or poor academic performance. More secondary teachers than elementary teachers expressed their concern that parents would not support them. In spite of differences, parents and teachers graded public schools higher than they did in past years. However, teachers' expectations of how much support they would receive from parents contradict parents' perceptions of their efforts to cooperate with teachers. This discrepancy certainly indicates that collaboration and communication between home and school is lacking and is an area that both parents and educators need to address.

Teachers give poor grades to the nation's public schools; only 28% gave the nation's schools a grade of A or B. However, like the parents, they gave high grades to the schools to which they were personally connected; 73% gave them a grade of A or B. The largest percentage of teachers expressed their belief that public schools have improved over the years, but more elementary teachers (45%) than secondary teachers (29%) believe that schools have improved (Langdon, 1999). Numerous teachers become discouraged with students when parents refuse to collaborate with schools. They feel helpless and burned out because their attempts to reach these students produce few or no results. They eventually come to believe that their efforts are futile because of the lack of continuity in the students' homes or because of an antisocial climate in their communities. This attitude is dangerous because it destroys hope. Hope is a virtue that enables us to reach our goals and to believe in the capacity of human beings to change.

Students' Perceptions

In a survey conducted for the Metropolitan Life Insurance Company (Harris, 1996), students voiced their opinions on social issues and policies. A majority of students did not feel confident that teachers, parents, and other adults in their community treat young people from different economic and racial or ethnic backgrounds equally. Are students from minority groups more often subjected to discipline procedures? Less than half of the students expressed much confidence that teachers (44%) and parents (39%) treat young people fairly regardless of their economic or ethnic background. Fewer students felt very confident that the police (31%), local shopkeepers (20%), and the courts (26%) treat students from different socioeconomic backgrounds equally. Significant improvements occur in students' perceptions of equality when they experience their teachers as respectful and encouraging and when their teachers help them to exhibit acceptance of each other. The responses in the survey indicated that students believe that teaching acceptance and understanding of diversity can improve race relations and discipline in schools and the community.

Students' opinions and perceptions of discipline problems in their schools reflect concerns with physical fights, hostile or threatening remarks, destructive acts, turf battles, and gang violence (Harris, 1996). These concerns appear to be more widespread in urban than in suburban or rural schools and among middle school students than high school students. Approximately 1 in 4 students reported having serious problems related to verbal remarks and physical confrontations. About 43% of students related that in their school only some students engage in friendly interactions, whereas 50% of students believe that most of their peers do get along with each other. The level of violence is undoubtedly a serious concern, yet the Harris poll indicates that, according to students' perceptions, violence had declined over the previous years.

Their view is supported by a Department of Education report that school violence continued to drop for 3 consecutive years (Ulloa, 2000). For students ages 12 to 18, overall school crime—including theft, rape, sexual assault, robbery, aggravated assault, and simple assault—decreased by nearly a third, from 144 school-related crimes per 1,000 students in 1992 to 101 crimes per 1,000 students in 1998. The decrease may be due to prevention programs specifically implemented in urban schools. Nevertheless, students in urban schools voiced greater concerns with problems of social tension than did students in nonurban schools. In addition, the recent gun violence incidents in schools have contributed to national fear and concern among students. The results of the poll suggested that students' perceptions of the level of violence changed over 3 years, from 1993 to 1996. From 1993 to 1994, violence in schools worsened, according to students' perceptions. In 1993 15% reported an increase in violence over the preceding year. This percent grew to 24% in 1994. By 1996 it dropped to 21% and the percentage reporting a decrease in violence grew. Together these changes indicate an overall improvement from 1994 to 1996 (Harris, 1996). Racial and ethnic groups differed in their perceptions. White students saw a slight increase in the level of violence from 1993 to 1994 and then a modest decline from 1994 to 1996. For African American students, the change was more substantial. After perceiving an increase from 1993 to 1994, they reported a significant decline from 1994 to 1996, exceeding the decline perceived by White students. Hispanic American students saw a steady decline over the years (Jones & Kirsberg, 1994).

Four important factors were identified in the Harris poll (1996) as important in promoting a positive climate free of social tension and in achieving meaningful learning outcomes:

1. Students believe that when the quality of teachers' relationships with students is high, positive social relations among peers are increased. Supportive teachers who demonstrate care, understanding, and interest in students' success are more likely to receive respect and compliance. In this type of atmosphere, students are also more likely to respect each other and interact positively.

2. Students believe that when the quality of their education is high, most students get along better and are more involved in the education process. Teachers who involve and empower students create a motivating and cooperating climate in which students

are actively learning from each other while forming beneficial relationships.

3. Students believe that when teachers model and teach social skills and tolerance, students from different economic, racial or ethnic, and religious backgrounds get along very well in their school.

4. Caucasian students were more likely than minority students to believe that teachers are fair in their treatment of students from diverse cultures, races, and religions. Teachers need to address diversity issues because intolerance and prejudice inevitably cause dissension among students and escalate to serious discipline problems. Societies are becoming increasingly multicultural and inclusive. Schools reflect this change, and educators must be prepared to deal with the problems of heterogeneous classrooms. The message that students are sending is a need for greater personalization in their treatment, increased participation in their learning, and fair treatment for all students.

Response to Students' Message

Personalizing Discipline

People are different, and a "one size fits all" approach does not work for most students. Schools have traditionally set rigid policies and procedures applicable to entire student populations. Special consideration and exceptions to school rules are difficult to apply in large schools, where teachers lack the time to get to know every student and establish supportive and caring relationships. Large schools are, by necessity, generally run like military operations and exceptions to the rules are viewed as disruptions to the organization. However, a push for personalizing learning is being felt in the education literature and in the media. Theodore Sizer, professor emeritus at Brown University and chairman of the Coalition of Essential Schools, advocates realistic student loads and time for teachers to get to know their students. This includes time for teachers, counselors, and family members to coordinate approaches to help each student. It also includes time to talk with students and to appreciate them as individuals (Sizer, 1999). Discipline problems are less likely to occur in classrooms in which everyone feels welcomed and empowered.

A decrease in class size has become a priority in educational reform, and this is gaining popularity with the public. A reduced number of students can bring about positive achievement gains and a decrease in the frequency of disciplinary action (Black, 1999). Class size reduction requires a substantial commitment of funds. Nevertheless, an increasing number of states are making serious budgetary commitments to reducing class size in an effort to increase test scores (Kirst, Bomstedt, & Stecher, 1998; Nye, 1992). Educators are under pressure to teach basic skills and to ensure that students are able to pass state-mandated tests. The students' social and emotional health ranks low on the list of priorities. Students come to school carrying all sorts of "baggage," such as poverty, homelessness, dysfunctional family life, and a myriad of psychological problems. In chapter 4, we examine the importance of social and emotional literacy. We believe that educators must join forces with related service personnel, such as school social workers and psychologists, and parents to implement social-emotional curricula as well as to raise students' cognitive skills. Learner-centered classrooms require teachers to teach first and foremost the students and then the academic content. Teachers have difficulty teaching content when students are disruptive and unmotivated to learn.

In addition to improving student achievement, lowering the teacher-student ratio should also result in other benefits. Class size reduction can enable teachers to recognize and diffuse potential discipline problems and personalize interactions with students by communicating more frequently with them (McPartland, Jordan, Legters, & Balfanz, 1997). Small-size classrooms and individualized education are not new for special educators. An individualized educational plan is mandated for every student receiving special services. The push to include students with disabilities in general classrooms may place students who are at risk at even greater risk, especially for students who have been classified as having a behavior or an emotional disorder. Many students are not eligible for receiving special education but nevertheless present discipline problems and require personalized attention.

Teaching Acceptance and Respect for Differences

There is an abundance of information on multicultural education in the literature (Bennett, 1996), yet teachers are hesitant to discuss issues dealing with race. Racial issues are perhaps too sensitive to discuss, and teachers may fear accusations of being politically incorrect. Student bodies are becoming increasingly diverse, and the demographic reality is that Euro-American teachers will enter classrooms filled with students of color (Kambon, 1995). Teaching for equity, justice, and peace is critical. The most frequent discipline encounters between students from different races or ethnic groups occur in secondary schools, where racial tension is often increased by levels of expectations. Lowering expectations negatively influences students' ability to reach their potential cognitively as well as socially. One of the authors of this book witnessed an incident in which a teacher reprimanded a student for being out of his seat by saying, "Get your f------ a-- back in your chair." When questioned, the teacher replied, "That's the only language these project kids understand." Both the teacher and the student were from the same race, however. When teachers teach students who are culturally or socially different from themselves, they must make the effort to learn and understand the culture of their students. This also holds true in cases of class differences.

Schools have traditionally failed to acknowledge the strengths of minority learners by adhering to practices such as tracking and the use of intelligence and norm-referenced testing to place minority students in special education. Native American students have the highest rate of dropouts, nearly 42%. Hispanic Americans are the most undereducated group, and their reading, writing, and math skills lag behind the national average. Their dropout rate is second to that of the Native American students, at 40% (Bennett, 1996). Although the scholastic achievement of African American students is improving, they still lag behind in the national average of scholastic achievement measures. The educational configuration of schools is still tailored to an Anglo-Saxon structure, and this holds true even when the students and faculty are predominantly from minority groups. Cultural compatibility can be achieved when educators address the learning styles, social organizations, and sociolinguistics of learners. In chapter 2, we discuss learning and personality differences. Although it is inconclusive, there is some evidence that students from minority cultures may have different learning-style preferences (Cushner, McClelland, & Stafford, 1992). The social organizations of many minority students differ significantly from the formal organization of an Anglo-Saxon–oriented school. Sitting for long periods listening to the teacher or doing "seat work" is incompatible with their less structured and informal social organization at home. *Sociolinguistics* is a term used to describe how cultural groups apply pragmatics or social language in their communication with adults and peers. This includes verbal and non-verbal communication (facial expressions, body language), tone of voice, proximity, and participation structure. Eye contact with an adult, for example, is considered impolite by Native American and Asian American students. Native American students also need more "wait time" to answer questions. Teachers who are unaware of this cultural sociolinguistic characteristic may interpret the extended pause as a lack of knowledge. African American mothers encourage their children to be assertive, which in turn can be viewed by teachers as impudence and noncompliance. Several minority cultures, such as Hispanic Americans, are more comfortable working in groups. They are less likely to be disruptive when they have the support of their peers in cooperative groups. Teachers must consider the social variances of their students when reading their behaviors. Understanding differences can avoid discipline problems and establish a climate conducive to learning (Cushner, McClelland & Stafford, 1992).

Resiliency

Studies of resiliency suggest that we all possess the capacity to change and to "bounce back" from adversity (Werner, 1999). This capacity transcends all social, economic, racial, and ethnic boundaries. Resiliency is inherent in humanity; it brings a message of hope. We are no longer chained to past experiences, such as a dysfunctional childhood or traumatic life events. We may bear the scars, but they no longer torment us because we are able to let go of negative and self-defeating thoughts. However, to overcome adversity, we may need help and support from others. We can stop viewing ourselves as victims when we are able to overcome adversity and claim our basic human needs and rights. One of these rights is the right to be happy and self-fulfilled. Many students come to school carrying emotional baggage. Teachers are not trained to implement clinical therapy in the classroom, but they can give students hope and direction to help them help themselves and to seek outside help when needed. Werner (1999) believes that it is crucial for caregivers, including teachers, to establish a close bond with children to help them develop resiliency. Teachers can make a difference, and as children reach adulthood they remember those teachers who made a difference in their lives.

Contrary to public perception, most adolescents who commit delinquent acts do not end up as toughened criminals. In Werner's study, 3 out of 4 delinquent males and 9 out of 10 delinquent females changed their lives as adults. The respondents in the study noted that the common denominator that made the difference was the support they received from someone who cared. That someone could have been a probation officer, a social worker, a member of the clergy, a family member, a friend, a foster parent, or a teacher. Many of the delinquents were discipline problems in school, and many had learning disabilities. Numerous adolescents rebel because they are passing through a normal identity crisis, and some rebel because of emotional problems. However, schools with rigid penalties and "three strikes and you're out" punishment policies drive students into deeper rebellion (Snyder & Sikmund, 1995).

A student in a middle school was classified as having a behavior disorder and placed in a self-contained classroom with five other students with similar problems. The student continued to present discipline problems, and the principal was determined to get rid of him. However, special education regulations prevented the principal from expelling the student. A committee had to decide whether the student's behavior was related to his exceptionality. This particular student, at the age of 5, discovered his father hanging at the end of a rope in the basement. His mother was seldom home, and he was responsible for caring for three younger siblings. His misbehavior in school consisted of skipping class, insubordination, and noncompliance. He had been involved in several fights during physical education classes. In all cases, the committee decided that the behavior was related to the exceptionality. Nevertheless, the principal set out to try to persuade members of the committee to expel the student. His reasoning was, "Let's throw him out, he will eventually get in trouble with the law and be declared a delinquent." The student's physical education coach resisted the principal's demands and reached out to this student. He obtained help through social services for the family and mentored the student throughout his school career. The student was able to bounce back, and with help he became resilient. He continued his education and became a success. Human beings are extremely resilient and with support can prosper even under adverse conditions. One can only wonder what would have happened if the principal had had his way?

Richardson and Gray (1999) have introduced a resiliency theory–based model for secondary schools. Their resiliency training includes strategies to enable students to increase many positive protective factors, such as self-esteem, self-efficacy, creativity, confidence, flexibility, and purpose in life. Their work with urban youth has been successful in replacing destructive gang activity and other "high risk" behaviors with more positive social behaviors. The Resilient Youth Program incorporates resilient school training, resilient family training, resilient youth clubs and organizations, and resilient youth curriculum.

Summary

The message derived from the general public, the teachers, and the students is that the nature of discipline problems in schools has changed. The general public is concerned but is not giving up on the public schools; it believes that with adequate funding the educational system can be improved. A qualified and competent teacher in every classroom was the number one choice for the most likely strategy to improve public education. Teachers indicated that fighting in schools and alcohol abuse were the most serious offenses, but they were also concerned with the lack of support from parents. Students believed that relations between peers can be improved when teacher-student interactions are personalized, when instruction is improved, and when the curriculum includes social skill and tolerance training. Teachers must believe that students are resilient and have the capacity to change. Studies on resiliency indicate that with support and caring, students can be helped. Many school districts are reacting to disciplinary problems by establishing stricter discipline measures. However, some educational systems are turning away from punitive procedures to more constructive and balanced programs that can address both intervention and prevention methods to curb discipline problems.

Activity 1: Role Play—Myths and Truths About Juvenile Violence

Mr. Scott and Mr. Powers are on their way to work on public transportation. They left their homes and families in the suburbs early in the morning to travel to the city. They are reading the morning paper, which carries somber news of youth violence in schools.

Mr. Scott: Young people today are criminals. They should all be tried as adults when they commit a crime. Most juvenile crime is violent crime.

Mr. Powers: No, Harry, you've got it all wrong. Look at these statistics, less than one half of 1% of all juveniles in the United States were arrested for violent offenses.

Mr. Scott: Come off it, Tom, don't be taken in by the media. It's a known fact that nowadays most youth are criminals. They have no morals. Look what's happening to family values.

Mr. Powers: Wrong again, Harry. Only about 5% of youth ages 10–17 were arrested for anything, and of that 5%, only 9% were arrested for a violent crime.

Mr. Scott: My barber told me that he heard that youth crime is spreading out of control and that there is a teenage crime menace.

Mr. Powers: Your barber is wrong. Youth crime rose significantly from 1987 to 1993, but since 1994 youth violent crime arrest rates have declined 12% and homicide rates among those youngsters ages 10 to 17 are down 31% since 1993. The decline in violent crime among teenagers from ages 13 and 15 accounted for 55% of the decline in juvenile arrests for violent crime from 1994 to 1995. In addition, remember that youngsters are at a much greater risk of being victims of violent crime than perpetrators of violent crime. Youths from ages 12 to 17 are 3 times more likely to be victimized than adults of all ages.

Mr. Scott: But Tom, look at the number of youth sitting in detention and correctional facilities. These kids are dangerous. We should lock them in maximum security and throw away the key.

Mr. Powers: Harry, Harry, Harry! The majority of kids in detention and correctional facilities are imprisoned for nonviolent crimes.

Mr. Scott: Tom, you must admit that when we were in our teens there was no youth violence. We respected the law. Our parents instilled fear in our minds, and we didn't dare disobey. These kids today have no fear. They are given too much freedom. I say let us go back to the good old days.

Mr. Powers: Harry, your good old days weren't so good. Violence has been a characteristic of teenage boys since time began. In a period of 50 years, youth crime rises and falls. It drops off dramatically when these young males reach the age of 25 or 30. The problem in today's society is that more young people are killing each other. Guns are easy to obtain and that's increasing youth homicide. After car accidents, guns are the second leading cause of death of young people.

Mr. Scott: Well, Tom, what can we as parents do to prevent such violence? What can schools do?

Sources for Mr. Powers' Statistics

Harris, L. (1996). *The metropolitan life survey of the American teacher: Students voice their opinions on violence, social tension, and equality among teens.* New York: Louis Harris and Associates.

Jones, M. A., & Kirsberg, B. (1994). *Images and reality: Juvenile crime, youth violence, and public policy.* Washington, DC: National Council on Crime and Delinquency.

Report of the Office of Juvenile Justice and Delinquency Prevention (1997). *Juvenile offenders and victims: 1997 update on violence.* Pittsburgh, PA: National Center for Juvenile Justice.

Snyder, H. N., & Sikmund, M. (1995). *Juvenile offenders and victims: A national report.* Washington, DC: Office of Juvenile Justice and Delinquency Prevention, U.S. Department of Justice.

Divide in groups and brainstorm solutions to Mr. Scott's questions.

Activity 2: Public Opinion Survey

The following are public school issues perceived by the general public to cause problems. Rank them according to the degree you believe the public would classify these problems in *your community*, with 1 being the most serious and 14 the least serious.

_____ Concerns about standards (quality of education)

_____ Teacher retention (keeping teachers in their teaching jobs)

_____ Lack of discipline (poor teacher and school control over students' inappropriate behaviors)

_____ Students' lack of motivation (poor attitudes, truancy, lack of value of education)

_____ Lack of financial support (not enough funding from local, state, and federal sources)

_____ Use of drugs and alcohol (using or selling drugs and alcohol)

_____ Overcrowded schools (large schools, too many students in a classroom)

_____ Poor teacher preparation (preservice college training, inservice on-the-job training)

_____ Difficulty getting good teachers (quality teachers, poor salary incentives)

_____ Lack of parental participation (indifference from parents, interference from parents)

_____ Poor administrative support (poor leadership, political administrative appointments)

_____ Violence in school (verbal abuse and physical fights)

_____ Inadequate teaching methods (methods old-fashioned or too progressive)

_____ Weapons in school (guns, knives, switchblades)

Activity 3: Teacher Survey

The following are school discipline problems that are considered disruptive to teaching and learning. Rank the issues that you believe are the most problematic in *your school*, with 1 being the most serious and 17 the least serious.

_____ Hyperactive behavior (running in halls, leaving seat, interrupting self and others)

_____ Verbal attacks (cursing, insults, racial and sexist slurs)

_____ Noncompliance (refusal to do work or to follow directions)

_____ Talking in class (talking when silence is required, interrupting)

_____ Physical fighting (physical contact, spitting, throwing objects)

_____ Eating in class (include chewing gum)

_____ Drug involvement (using or selling drugs)

_____ Hostile and threatening remarks (verbal assaults)

_____ Alcohol involvement (intake of alcohol, inebriated condition of student)

_____ Vandalism (destruction of peer property, vandalism of school property)

_____ Racial or ethnic confrontations (fights between racial or ethnic groups, prejudicial remarks)

_____ Violence (gang violence, rape, assault)

_____ Academic behaviors (being off-task, neglecting homework, poor academic achievement)

_____ Cheating (during exams or in homework, obtaining copies of exam)

_____ Theft (stealing on school grounds or outside school grounds)

_____ Possession of weapons (guns, knives, switchblades)

_____ Verbal abuse of teachers (disrespectful remarks, talking in inappropriate tone and manner)

Activity 4: Student Survey— Elementary Grades

Distribute this survey to your students and help them to rank the following, with 1 being the most serious and 17 the least serious. Use your students' responses to find out what they perceive as problematic and together develop a plan to correct deficiencies.

_____ Physical fighting (physical contact, spitting, throwing objects)

_____ Verbal abuse from students (racial slurs, cursing, insults, disrespecting teachers)

_____ Verbal abuse from teachers (name calling, racial slurs, insults)

_____ Schoolwork (too difficult, too much, not enough help)

_____ Poor teaching (teacher does not explain, teaches too fast, does not care)

_____ Homework (too much, too difficult, busy work)

_____ Crowded class (too many students)

_____ Cheating (during seat work, exams, homework)

_____ Theft (stealing on school grounds or outside school grounds)

_____ Lack of instructional materials (books, labs, computers)

_____ Vandalism (destruction of students' property, destruction of school property)

_____ Talking (speaking out and interrupting without permission)

_____ Disrespect (talking back to teacher, rude to peers)

_____ Off-task behavior (refusing to do work, getting out of seat, daydreaming)

_____ Truancy (skipping school, skipping class)

_____ Tardiness (late for school, late for class)

_____ Eating in class (include chewing gum)

Activity 5: Student Survey— Secondary Grades

Distribute the following survey to your students and ask them to rank the following, with number 1 being the most serious and 16 the least serious.

_____ Racial or ethnic confrontations (fights between racial or ethnic groups, prejudicial remarks)

_____ Physical fighting (physical contact, throwing objects, spitting, teacher attacks)

_____ Violence (gang violence, the use of weapons, rape, assault)

_____ Vandalism (destruction of students' property, destruction of school property)

_____ Use of drugs and alcohol (using or selling drugs and alcohol)

_____ Overcrowded schools (large schools, too many students in a classroom)

_____ Poor teaching (lack of knowledge, poor organization and planning skills)

_____ Poor teacher-student relationships (teacher lacks respects for students, uncaring)

_____ Verbal abuse of teachers (disrespectful remarks, talking in inappropriate tone and manner)

_____ Poor administration support (weak administrators or lack of counselors, nurses, librarians)

_____ Hostile and threatening remarks (serious threats, racial slurs, cursing, insulting remarks)

_____ Cheating (during exams or in homework, obtaining copies of exam)
_____ Theft (stealing on school grounds or outside school grounds)
_____ Lack of instructional materials (books, labs, computers)
_____ Truancy (skipping school, skipping class)
_____ Sexual activity (sexual harassment, pregnancy, sexual activity on school grounds)

Activity 6: Personalizing Quiz

Circle the number that indicates your agreement with the following statements, with 1 being "not at all" and 5 being "completely agree."

1. I take time to chat with every student at least once a week.

   1   2   3   4   5

2. I take time to analyze my feelings toward students who are discipline problems.

   1   2   3   4   5

3. I involve my students in their learning.

   1   2   3   4   5

4. I give my students choices

   1   2   3   4   5

5. I make exceptions to my discipline rules depending on the situation of the student.

   1   2   3   4   5

6. I ask my students for their input when I revise the classroom discipline rules.

   1   2   3   4   5

7. I make it a point to find out what motivates my students.

   1   2   3   4   5

8. I share information about myself with my students.

   1   2   3   4   5

9. I am concerned about my students' emotional well-being.

   1   2   3   4   5

10. My students seek my guidance when they have a problem.

   1   2   3   4   5

Activity 7: Collaborative Group Activities

1. Form groups of five or six. List the behaviors that were considered problematic in the elementary and secondary schools you attended. Next, list behaviors that are considered problematic in the school where you are presently teaching. Compare and discuss the lists.

2. In a group of three, examine the discipline practices used in your classroom and in your school. Are they effective? How can they be improved?

3. Discuss with your group and identify steps that could be taken to include proactive practices to avoid discipline problems.

4. Your new student has a strong regional accent. The other students imitate to make fun of her dialect. Problem solve with members in your group. What could you do to make your new student fit into her new environment? What could you do to stop the teasing and persuade her peers to accept her?

References

Bailey B. (1997). *There's got to be a better way: Discipline that works.* Oviedo, FL: Loving Guidance.

Bennett, C. (1996). *Comprehensive multicultural education: Theory and practice.* Boston: Allyn and Bacon.

Berliner, D., & Biddle, B. (1995). *The manufactured crisis: Myths, fraud and the attack on America's public schools.* Reading, MA: Addison-Wesley.

Black, S. (1999). Less is more. *American School Board Journal 186* (2), 38–41.

Cushner, K., McClelland, A., & Stafford, P. (1992). *Human diversity in education: An integrative approach.* New York: McGraw-Hill.

Harris, L. (1996). *The metropolitan life survey of the American teacher: Students voice their opinions on violence, social tension, and equality among teens.* New York: Louis Harris & Associates.

Johnson, D., & Johnson, R. (1995). *Reducing school violence through conflict resolution.* Alexandria, VA: Association for Supervision and Curriculum Development.

Jones, M. A., & Kirsberg, B. (1994). *Images and reality: Juvenile crime, youth violence, and public policy.* Washington, DC: National Council on Crime and Delinquency.

Kambon, A. (1995). Recruitment of minority teachers. *Future Teacher 2* (1), 4–8.

Kirst, M., Bomstedt, M., & Stecher, B. (1998, April). *A plan for the evaluation of California's class size reduction.* (Paper presented at the annual meeting of the American Research Association. San Diego, CA).

Langdon, C. (1999). The fifth Phi Delta Kappa poll of teachers' attitudes toward the public schools. *Phi Delta Kappan 80* (8), 611–618.

McPartland, J., Jordan, W., Legters, N., & Balfanz, R. (1997). Finding safety in small numbers. *Educational Leadership 55* (2), 14–17.

Nye, B. (1992). *Project Challenge preliminary report: An initial evaluation of the Tennessee Department of Education "at risk" student/teacher ratio reduction project in seventeen counties.* (ERIC Document Reproduction Services No. ED 352 180)

O'Neil, B. (1994, March 6). The history of a hoax. *New York Times Magazine*, pp. 46–49.

O'Toole, M. E. (2000). *The school shooter: A threat assessment perspective.* Quantico, VA: FBI.

Report of the Office of Juvenile Justice and Delinquency Prevention (1997). *Juvenile offenders and victims: 1997 update on violence.* Pittsburgh, PA: National Center for Juvenile Justice.

Richardson, G., & Gray, D. (1999). A resiliency-fostering curriculum for secondary schools. In N. Henderson, B. Benard, N. Sharp-Light (Eds.), *Resiliency in action.* Gorham, ME: Resiliency in Action.

Rose, L. C., & Gallup, A. (2000). The 32nd annual Phi Delta Kappan Gallup poll of the public's attitudes toward the public schools. *Phi Delta Kappan 82* (1), 41–58.

Sautter, R. C. (1995). Standing up to violence: Kappa special report. *Phi Delta Kappa 76* (5), K1–K12.

Shore, R. M. (1995). How one high school improved school climate. *Educational Leadership 52* (5), 362–363.

Sizer, T. (1999). No two alike. *Educational Leadership 57* (1), 6–11.

Snyder, H. N., & Sikmund, M. (1995). *Juvenile offenders and victims: A national report.* Washington, DC: Office of Juvenile Justice and Delinquency Prevention, U.S. Department of Justice.

Ulloa, M. (2000). *School violence drops for third straight year: Fewer students carrying weapons to school.* Washington, DC: U.S. Department of Education.

Werner, E. (1999). How children become resilient: Observations and cautions. In N. Henderson, B. Benard, N. Sharp-Light (Eds.), *Resiliency in action.* Gorham, ME: Resiliency in Action.

Chapter 2

The Three Rs: Regularities, Responsibility, and Reinforcement

Overview

Regularity Control
    Affecting classroom behavior
    Programmatic regularities and antecedent conditions
    Understanding regularities
    Examples of regularities
    Regularities associated with assessment
    The success/success–failure/failure cycle
    User friendly classrooms

Examples of Traditional and Alternative Regularities
    Regularity control
    Enhancing regularities
    Family and community regularities
    The "dry sock" approach
    The "eat your Wheaties" approach
    The "one size fits all" approach

Steps Toward Establishing Effective Discipline
    Seven steps
    Reinforcing regularities
    The sociological setting

Personalizing Discipline: Changing Regularities
    Gateways to achievement and responsible behavior
    Formal or informal settings
    The impact of special education on school regularities
    Class size regularities
    Regularities and personal recognition

Summary

QUESTIONS

This chapter will help you to answer the following questions:

1. What are classroom and school regularities?
2. What roles do school and classroom regularities play in managing student behavior?
3. Do differences in test and examination formats affect student behavior? performance?
4. Does fairness dictate that every child should be treated the same?
5. Do classroom regularities—the rules, routines, atmosphere, methods, and teacher expectations that shape classroom life— tend to create automatic discipline problems for some students?
6. What is the relationship of curriculum and teaching strategies to the behavior of students in a classroom?
7. Why should an analysis of consistently inappropriate student behavior include identification of the regularities that govern classroom activities and instruction?
8. What effect has special education had on school regularities?
9. Give an example of how changing a regularity can prevent a discipline problem.
10. Does reducing class size necessarily result in personalizing student learning?

Overview

Morning erupts into the day with an explosion of bright energy, and so do children. Teachers must have the "magic" to harness that energy to promote learning. Discipline can be described as the orderly way in which teachers quicken new understanding and channel a living flow of knowledge into each child's life. Teachers supervise the establishment of a miniature unit of society in their classrooms. The social interactions that occur there color every kind of learning experience for students and teachers alike. A teacher's wise direction may set the stage for responsible citizenship and hopefully for lifelong patterns of success in learning, growth, and human relationships.

When a teacher selects and applies a discipline procedure in the classroom, the question arises: What are its intended outcomes? What is it that the teacher's action is intended to accomplish? Teachers use various behavior management methods to obtain compliance from their students. Is a particular behavioral intervention intended to make the student comply with the class rules? It is important to learn to obey the rules. Is the intervention intended to reinforce or reestablish on-task behavior? That is also very important. Is the teacher's intervention designed to help the student master specific curriculum objectives? Is the intervention intended to prepare students for mandated tests? Is the intervention intended to increase the student's sense of personal achievement and love of learning? Is a particular discipline strategy designed to help the child learn to accept responsibility? Is it intended to help a child learn to behave appropriately, get along with others better, and lead a happier life? These questions must have answers in order to establish a rationale for the decisions that are made about discipline. The goal must be clear before the best strategies for achieving it can be identified.

Discipline options vary from classroom to classroom as much as student populations vary. To a large extent, teachers' behavior management objectives are a reflection of their own priorities. Differences in the expectations of teachers and others who establish school policies are numerous. They may vary nearly as much from teacher to teacher as they do from student to student.

The classroom environment, routines, rules, teaching methods, educational philosophy, physical arrangements, and the overall ambiance or climate of the classroom are unique expressions of a teacher's personality and philosophy of life. Coupled with the curriculum and general school policies, they form what can be viewed as *classroom regularities*. The term *regularities* was introduced in the educational arena by Seymour Sarason (1962). Regularities occur with consistency. They occur repeatedly in routine ways. They bring predictability to classroom happenings from day to day.

Chapter 2 will help teachers to identify the classroom regularities that govern school life and will discuss the impact those regularities have on behavior management and discipline. We will examine the interconnectedness between the responsible behaviors expected of students, the reinforcers offered in response to those behaviors, and the classroom regularities that create a school's learning environment. Finally, discipline practices, individual student differences, and classroom regularities will be considered in relation to one another in an attempt to determine how each may enhance or detract from the successful discipline of an individual student.

In this and subsequent chapters we consider the impact a teacher's own personality characteristics may have on his or her choice and establishment of classroom regularities. Also, we consider significant personality differences in students in order to show how the same regularities and daily routines may affect students in widely differing ways.

Classroom regularities establish antecedents or become antecedents to student behavior. When regularities are viewed in this way, it is possible to demonstrate that every aspect of classroom life is a stimulus for student behavior. The same regularity or antecedent may work to increase certain behaviors in one student and decrease them in another. With this recognition of the differences in student response to classroom regularities, the model presented in this chapter requires educators to ask a number of important questions. What can we do to help students succeed? What modifications in the learning environment will be necessary for students to be successful academically, personally, and socially? What reinforcement will increase the likelihood that a desired behavior will be repeated? The answers to these questions help us to identify supportive arrangements so that neither students nor teachers resort to inappropriate social or behavioral responses.

Regularity Control

Affecting Classroom Behavior

The most important variables in the management of appropriate classroom behavior seem to be associated with the following:

1. Establishing and reinforcing reasonable rules and routines that support the on-task behavior intended to master instructional objectives

2. A teacher's ability to develop and use a variety of interventions diverse enough to accommodate many kinds of situations and student personality types, interests, and intelligences

3. A teacher's ability to assess classroom climate, recognize potential problems in order to avoid them, modify classroom regularities, and have at their fingertips a wide array of behavioral interventions

4. Teachers who have positive interpersonal relationships with their students and a classroom where students feel physically and psychologically safe

5. Teachers who are themselves lifelong learners, who consistently strive to provide a healthy environment in which children can take risks and fail safely and can learn and grow physically, psychologically, socially, and academically

These variables are influenced by the conditions or regularities established in the classroom and throughout the school.

Programmatic Regularities and Antecedent Conditions

Classroom regularities include the curriculum; discipline and learning philosophies; instructional methods and arrangements; routines for assigning and collecting work; the establishment of schedules, rules, and goals; and the monitoring of the physical environment. Regularities have a powerful effect on students' learning and also on their behavior and attitudes. They influence the climate for learning in both positive and negative ways. Classroom regularities provide the context in which learning and social behavior take place. Regularities provide the foundation and the supportive infrastructure for everything that happens in the classroom, including the establishment and maintenance of orderly behavior.

The importance of controlling regularities so that they provide the supporting structure for accommodating individual differences in the classroom is part of what has been identified as behavioral diversity and regularity control (Meisgeier & Meisgeier, 2000). The Meisgeiers emphasize the importance of recognizing the behavioral diversity of students—psychological (personality) type, learning styles, and special interests and abilities—and establishing regularities that foster compatible learning experiences. When school and classroom regularities are flexible and supportive of individual differences, students will respond in positive ways. Discipline problems will be minimized, and student academic learning, personal development, and social behavior will be maximized.

The physical conditions in a classroom and the activities, procedures, and social interactions that occur there provide the context in which student behavior occurs. Classroom regularities become behavioral antecedents because they give birth to behavioral responses. *Antecedents* are arrangements or events in the environment that exist before a behavior occurs. They form conditions that may prompt a behavior in the first place, and they impact the probability that the behavior—appropriate or inappropriate—will occur again. Regularities and antecedents prompt social behavior as well as learning behavior.

Some antecedents to student behavior are outside classroom control. Divorcing parents may upset a student to the degree that both learning and behavior problems result. Victimization or neglect at home or bullying outside school clearly cause student distress and may serve as antecedents to problem behaviors. Social, emotional, economic, and health problems all affect learning. When these problems exist, interventions are necessary and referrals may have to be made. A teacher can provide help, but the antecedents that generate these kinds of behavioral problems are largely outside a teacher's control. However, regularities over which teachers do have control often serve as antecedents to student behaviors and misbehaviors in unanticipated ways. Schools may attribute student behavior problems to outside circumstances when in reality they occur in response to classroom regularities. They may be regularities that are not difficult to change once they are recognized.

The regularities in any social system in which we find ourselves will influence what we do, how we do it, when we do it, and how we think and feel while we are doing it. The regularities governing a classroom will be different from the regularities that govern a ball field, a library, a church, or a hospital. The learning environment in a school, the instructional strategies and arrangement, and the entire classroom structure may be viewed as regularities that have the potential to spawn antecedents to learning, personal growth, and social development. The design of an effective behavior management system must therefore include the indentification of the regularities that set it in place.

Once a sensitivity has been developed to the role of school and classroom regularities in prompting student behavior, it becomes important to develop a similar sensitivity to the differences among teachers that cause them to choose or establish certain regularities over others. Then it is important to ask why students may respond to school regularities in uniquely different ways. In our search for greater understanding of the individual differences that are clearly present among teachers and students in response to school regularities, we have found that psychological type theory offers the most helpful explanation. The differences described by psychological type theory may be referred to as personality *type differences* or simply as *type*. Psychological type will be explained in the next chapter.

Understanding Regularities

Sometimes regularities are embedded in daily life in ways that make them virtually invisible. They are so firmly established in a system—any system—that the idea of changing them is seldom considered. One clear illustration of this phenomenon might be found in a little ski village in the mountains of New England. The economy of the village is largely dependent on winter skiing, and the slopes above the village are so beautiful that the people of the area are thriving. One major problem, however, recurs each season. There have been far too many accidents and injuries on one of the more popular slopes.

The most enjoyable ski run edges around a lovely configuration of large rock outcroppings and ancient evergreen trees located about halfway down the mountain. Although the slope is beautiful, the turns are treacherous. Injuries at this point have been so frequent that concerned townspeople have collected money to provide ambulance service to transport injured skiers to the hospital in a nearby town. Soon after this was done, it was found that the ambulance had to be stationed permanently at the bottom of the mountain. A shelter was built for the ambulance and for the volunteers who staffed it. In time this service proved inadequate, so a small first-aid station was set up as well. Over a period of years, the first-aid station grew to become a fully staffed clinic that quickly wove itself into the fabric of village life. Everyone connected with the clinic worked to provide the finest, fastest care possible for injured skiers. The village justifiably took pride in the quality of its emergency medical care.

As the popularity of the little ski resort grew, measures to care for injured skiers were a constant focus of attention. Many ideas for improved care were studied and implemented. Although everyone worked to improve the care given to injured skiers, no one seemed to give much thought to prevention.

Seasons passed before a local teacher finally stood up at one of the town meetings with a rather tentative question. Instead of further clinic expansion, could steps be taken to remove the trees and boulders that formed the major hazard to the skiers? The suggestion prompted a brisk debate. Townspeople took sides and motions were made. Countermotions were proposed and argued about until the matter was finally tabled for future study. In the end, a decision was made to expand the clinic and leave the topology of the mountain unchanged. It was easier for the people of the village to invest effort and resources in coping with the problem of injured skiers—the outcome of the hazard created by the rocks and trees—than to cope with the idea of changing the landscape.

Sometimes the regularities in a school are such a part of its life that changing them is never considered, even though that might be the next effective solution to a problem. In this chapter we encourage educators to look for previously invisible program and system "outcroppings" that interfere with the smooth running of the operation. The rocks on that New England ski slope have been part of the landscape for as long as anyone can remember. That certainly qualifies them as regularities. For many "skiers," school regularities may contribute to the beauty of the "mountain," but for others they constitute a hazard and an obstacle with crippling potential. In schools, as in most social institutions, there is a tendency to pay more attention to the outcomes of system regularities than to address the regularities themselves.

Examples of Regularities

The following regularities may influence student behavior:

School Regularities

- Time of day when school begins and ends
- Length of time allotted for each class period
- Dress code—uniforms or choice
- Teacher-student ratio
- Teaching, learning, and discipline philosophy

Classroom Regularities

- Instructional arrangements and routines
- Styles of teaching
- Teacher and student modes of interaction
- Types of drill and review exercises
- Type and amount of homework
- Types of tests, evaluation procedures, and scoring methods

Modes of information presentation and assessment of mastery are regularities in most schools. Test taking is in itself a behavior and a performance apart from the mastery of the content being tested or the learning process designed to help the student learn it. The style, nature, and format of a test may have an impact on the potential for student success and be largely unrelated to the learning process. A student may respond positively or negatively to the test, based solely on the test format, in a way that has nothing to do with the quality or quantity of the learning that has taken place.

Regularities Associated With Assessment

Classroom regularities are usually associated with the physical environment, the emotional climate, the presentation of information, the assessment of the mastery of skills and retention of information, and behavior management. The classroom regularities that develop around testing and assessment activities in school form interesting examples of student success or failure rooted in factors that have little to do with mastery of the academic content involved. A quiet, studious, well-organized, well-prepared student may have consistent success on written examinations throughout the semester and then falter because the final grade depends on an oral presentation to the class. The individual differences found among students make it important to focus attention on the right antecedent when a student fails a test. It is as important to consider the goodness of fit of the characteristics of the test and student as it is to look at the quality of the teaching, the extent of student learning, and the adequacy of a student's study skills. Key questions include the following:

- Does the test require the student to transfer answers?
- Does it require complicated matching skills?
- Does it require handwriting or spelling skills?
- Does it require bubbling in tiny spaces?
- Is it an essay test?
- Do students circle answers?
- Does it require the use of a coding system?
- Does the test require high-level reading skills to come to a correct math solution?
- Is it untimed or timed?
- Does it demand high-level handwriting or reading skills despite the simplicity of the questions or the answers?
- Will it be graded on content, appearance, or format?
- Will information be assessed in a context different from the one in which it was presented or learned?

Knowing that a test will demand skills or abilities that are unrelated to the academic content being assessed allows the teacher to consider the test format itself as an antecedent to student failure, rather than poor instruction or lack of study or preparation on the part of the student. The outcome of the test may have very little to do with the student's mastery of the content material.

Teachers often develop a preference for a particular test design. When that occurs, test style becomes a regularity. If some students have problems with the test design, then it becomes an antecedent to failure for them. Some elements of test design that may become an antecedent to failure are the speed and legibility of a student's handwriting, spelling accuracy, reading speed, and the student's emotional state. A student may know the answers but perform poorly or give up because the test format presents major obstacles. Students' knowledge of history, science, math, or any other subject may be extensive, yet they may fail a test because its format requires strong eye-hand coordination, organizational ability, or other skills unrelated to the content material. Therefore, the design and format of a particular test may facilitate success for some students, cause frustration for a few, and ensure failure for others.

Everything that sets the stage for a student to succeed or fail in school is an antecedent. Thus, the characteristics of tests become precursors to success or failure. It could also be said that success itself is an antecedent to further learning. Success supports the learner and builds confidence for future learning or evaluation. By the same token, it could be said that failure is an antecedent—it can lead to further failure and to disciplinary problems. Viewed in a larger context, factors such as test characteristics that doom students to fail over time become regularities that in turn become antecedents to behavior problems. The kinds of regularities that form relentless antecedents to failure will almost certainly trigger discipline problems in any teacher's classroom.

There are many test modifications available to a teacher that will improve student performance while maintaining overall standards of mastery. The special accommodations that a teacher makes in assessment methods allow for profound individual differences in the ways students take in information and make judgments about organizing and retaining the information. Individualized assessment modifications include the following:

- Reading the test aloud to the student
- Putting questions on an audiotape to be used with a headset
- Employing a variety of questioning methods, such as multiple choice, matching, or true-false
- Limiting the number of options a student must read to select the answer
- Allowing extra time when necessary
- Allowing oral answers that are recorded by the teacher or an aide
- Interpreting concepts learned in role-plays, dramas, journaling, portfolios, tutoring others, or writing stories and essays
- Demonstrating skills in games and contests

With so many ways to determine the student's mastery of skills or information, the teacher is free to assess this in ways that accommodate individual differences.

The passage of the Individuals With Disabilities Education Act (IDEA) has resulted in greater teacher sensitivity to the test characteristics presented above and their impact on students with special needs. Most teachers understand that there is a need for special modifications to be made for students with disabilities. It is important to see that similar accommodations may be needed for other students as well.

The Success/Success–Failure/Failure Cycle

The greater the academic success that students experience, the better they will feel about themselves and the more their behavior will be desirable and appropriate. Failure or the fear of failure that students experienced in the past can diminish the quality of their current performance and produce failure regardless of their basic ability to master content material. The more students fail, the more teachers may find themselves applying strong discipline measures, sometimes in the mistaken belief that criticism, punishment, low grades, redoing work, shaming, or revoking privileges will motivate a student to work harder. For students accustomed to success in school, punishment for failure may spur greater effort; but for students caught in a cycle of constant school failure, punishment is very disheartening and seldom prompts greater effort. It serves, rather, to confirm expectations of further failure. In this instance, the learning that takes place is not about the subject matter.

Students who experience constant failure in school learn one grim lesson very well: They learn, rightly or wrongly, that they cannot learn and that they cannot be successful in school. When this occurs, tests can become recurring traps or "setups" for failure. The testing process itself represents a set of regularities that are antecedents to failure, shame, and discouragement for some students and to success and confidence for others.

Both students and teachers know that there are students who cannot succeed in taking a test and yet they are forced to try anyway because both students and teachers are locked into school testing regularities. They may also be locked into district- or state-mandated testing, which become powerful regularities affecting both student and teacher behavior. These regularities can place enormous stress on teachers as well as on their students, particularly when teacher performance is measured by the performance of the students. In some cases appropriate accommodations are made for students in special education inclusion programs, but similar steps are not taken to help other students who need accommodations.

This brief review of school testing as a regularity with far-reaching effects on student behavior is just one example of the need to examine school regularities when weighing questions related to student discipline.

User-Friendly Classrooms

We have seen that the regularities associated with assessment may become antecedents to student failure. Many students experience school as a stimulus for emotional pain and humiliation. It is easy to see how regularities that produce constant pain may become antecedents to aggressive responses. Emotional pain and reactions to failure, frustration, and shame often elicit aggression. When this occurs, the stage is set for major disciplinary problems. When a student's response is actively aggressive, strong and immediate behavioral interventions are required in the short term, but long-term changes in school regularities should be considered if permanent improvement in behavior is to occur.

Teachers and school personnel are acutely aware of students who respond aggressively to regularities that for them are antecedents to failure and shame. It is easy to be less aware of students who are passive or passive-aggressive in their responses. A band director in an inner city school reported that band members were enthusiastic and involved in the band until the first report card. Then the no pass–no play rule prohibited more than half of the band from playing at the height of the season. All were free to attend band practice, but attendance dropped dramatically and never recovered. There was a general perception in that school that students were lazy, undependable, and sometimes rather sullen. It would be much more accurate to see their behavior as a passive-aggressive response to a regularity that seemed arbitrary, unjust, and irrational. They saw the no pass–no play rule as punishing them in an area in which they were working hard and cooperating well, while it did nothing to help them in the areas in which they were struggling. Student responses in this situation were passive-aggressive and resulted directly from school regularities that were instituted to improve academic performance but instead punished effort and achievement in beneficial school programs.

Passive responses to failure are to be seen everywhere in schools. Recently a computer instructor expressed the frustration experienced by many teachers. Problems with schedules and budgets meant that there were not enough computers for every student to have a workstation. Absence or tardiness meant loss of access to a computer. Quickly a group of students fell behind, felt lost, became discouraged, and finally gave up. Some students expressed a willingness to do extra work to catch up; they seemed genuinely distressed to be failing. Yet each offer by the teacher to meet before or after school was met not with flat refusal or resistance but with sighs and comments like "I'm too tired today" or "I have a headache today." The teacher did not view these responses as evasive excuses but saw them as a genuine sense of discouragement that produced real depression and a desire to delay coming face-to-face with a confirmation of failure. The students' attitude was compared by the teacher to "the way I feel when I begin to prepare my income tax return—overwhelmed!" The passivity, depression, and hopelessness that these responses reflect is rooted as much in school-based antecedents and regularities as they are in broader sociological factors, family upbringing, or the students' fundamental attitudes toward school—factors frequently used to explain the behavior of students from lower socioeconomic backgrounds.

When a student's response to school failure is passive or passive-aggressive, withdrawal and disengagement are likely to occur, and discipline issues are more apt to revolve around inattentiveness, incomplete assignments, nonparticipation, and increased absences. Failure then becomes the antecedent to more failure, creating a cycle that leads to the need for escalating disciplinary measures. Intervention or remediation should focus first on an identification of the classroom regularities that set the stage for academic and social success or failure as well as on the student's inappropriate behavior.

Since teachers are primarily responsible for establishing classroom regularities, they can change them by working alone or in cooperation with other teachers and administrators. Changes that make schools more user-friendly provide increased potential for student success and may be expected to decrease the need for strong discipline measures. In the next section, Table 2-1 lists some traditional and alternative classroom regularities.

Examples of Traditional and Alternative Regularities

TABLE 2-1. CLASSROOM REGULARITIES

Traditional Classroom Regularities	Alternative Classroom Regularities
One teacher teaches all subjects.	Different teachers teach different subjects.
Each subject is taught in its own period. (*Time is a constant factor.*)	Longer block periods are offered in combinations of subjects. (*Time is a variable factor.*)
Students sit in orderly rows and work independently.	Students sit at tables or work in groups or at centers or stations.
Students raise hands to be recognized to speak.	Students monitor their own interactions.
Students speak only to answer questions.	Students may comment and ask questions as well as answer them.
Teacher does the talking and teaching and asks specific questions.	Teacher facilitates cooperative learning groups and uses Socratic or guided questioning techniques.
Primary learning activities involve texts, workbooks, and seat work.	Learning activities include a variety of resources, and experiential and hands-on activities and projects.
Students learn by listening and watching.	Students learn by doing, or in projects.
Standard lessons emphasize recall of factual data.	Emphasis is on global concepts, with freedom to pursue individual interests and applications of learning.
Students memorize facts: names, dates, times, places.	Students write stories, use role-play and cross-curricular activities.

Teacher assumes that some students want to learn and some do not or cannot.	Teacher assumes that all students can learn but that some need help with motivation.
Teacher expects dutiful obedience with assigned tasks.	Teacher permits some students to develop their own plans for completing some assignments.
Teacher relies on intimidation and punishment to obtain compliance.	Teacher works to create a friendly, supportive, cooperative, and safe climate.
Emphasis is on logical, rational, analytical instructional activities with competence expected in every area.	Recognition and support of individual differences, objectives, abilities, and achievement with special interests and intelligences honored.
Learning activities are orderly, regulated, and timed.	Student activities are flexible and changeable as a result of student response.
Schools in session from September through May, with vacation time in June, July, and August.	Schools in session year-round with vacations in December, April, and August, or at different times.
Students attend the same school every day.	Students may attend different schools for specialized activities.
Classrooms are coeducational.	Some classrooms may be restricted to all male or all female students.
School begins at 8 a.m. and ends at 4 p.m.	Some schools may have different beginning and ending times, eg, opens at 1 p.m. and close at 9 p.m.
School employs formal, traditional, norm-referenced testing.	Testing is more informal, curriculum based, and criterion referenced, or includes work samples (e.g., portfolios).
Students move from grade to grade year by year.	Students move within "families" houses or cohorts when ready.
All students wear approved clothing or uniforms.	Students choose their clothing with few or no restrictions.

Both traditional and alternative educational programs become classroom regularities. The lists of regularities in Table 2-1 establish conditions for schooling that may help some children but hinder others. These regularities could be called *programmatic regularities*—that is, they are global, basic, overarching, and fundamental. They have the potential to spawn other regularities at a behavioral level. *Behavioral regularities* are outcomes of the more comprehensive and global programmatic regularities.

Behavioral regularities act as antecedents that directly influence classroom behavior. Often the antecedents to a particular student's behavior can be modified so that the student's behavior will change. The behavioral regularities that function as antecedents change when programmatic regularities are changed. Thus, the modification of one programmatic regularity may change many behavioral regularities, which, in turn, have the potential for reducing the need for overt discipline interventions.

An example of the domino effect that programmatic and behavioral regularities have on students may be found in school systems that use a double shift (the first shift begins classes at 7 a.m.) as a way to cope with overcrowding. First-period classes find many students less than fully alert, and some students openly nap. Teachers may be less vivacious and dynamic than usual. As a result, they may lecture more and involve students less in discussions and hands-on activities. There may be an increased failure rate among students in first-period classes, so disciplinary measures come into play in response to failing grades. Students who play sports or participate in other extracurricular activities may be caught by the no pass–no play rule and have to withdraw from an activity that is the motivator that keeps them in school. This kind of punishment is a behavior management strategy that is designed to deal with failure in a particular class by withdrawing privileges. It is a strategy that attempts to solve the problem produced by classroom or family regularities, but it may ignore the regularity that may cause the problem in the first place.

Long-term management of many discipline problems has to begin with a clear focus on programmatic regularities even when they cannot be changed. In the example of early morning classes, instructional strategies and arrangements can be changed in ways that help the students to stay interested and alert. The inattentiveness of the students or ineffective teaching may not be the cause of student failure in early morning classes. It could be caused by sleep deprivation brought about by early morning class schedules—in other words, by overarching regularities, not bad behavior.

Not all students and teachers are adversely affected by early scheduling, of course. Some people are alert early in the morning and tend to be successful in classes that begin at 7 a.m. They like being through with their school day an hour earlier. Some are able to work at jobs they could not do if their classes ran later in the afternoon. Thus the programmatic regularity that adversely affects some students is a positive factor in the lives of others. As teachers grow increasingly alert to the effects of classroom regularities on individual students, there are many opportunities to be creative in making modifications that enhance learning for some without causing problems for others.

Regularity Control

Changing a regularity may be done to improve academic learning, student behavior, or both. Academic success may resolve inappropriate behavior. In either case, many regularities are under the control of the teacher, principal, or parents. When an action is taken to change or manipulate an antecedent, it is called *regularity control*. When an action is taken to change or manipulate an antecedent, it is called *antecedent control*. Existing regularities or antecedents are always candidates for modification or replacement. New ones may be added to help make the classroom run more smoothly, to help more children achieve academically and behave according to an established standard.

Enhancing Regularities

Teachers can lay a foundation for effective discipline practices by establishing a harmony of classroom regularities and individual differences. Enhancing regularities are expansive and inclusive. They should respect, encourage, and support the individual differences found in students and teachers. Enhancing regularities impact the behavior of students and positively affect their school performance, self-concept, motivation, and social behavior. We emphasize again that the same regularity or antecedent may affect one student quite differently from the way it affects another student.

Family and Community Regularities

Children's behavior in school is affected by classroom regularities, but it is also affected by established regularities at home and in the community. There are individuals, including teachers and those who set test standards, who still persist in the notion that all students are alike, should be treated as such, and must be disciplined in the same way to ensure consistency. This view is held despite contrary information that students walk into the classroom with significant advantages or disadvantages resulting from the many regularities that impact their lives outside school. Regularities at home are influenced by factors such as income level, educational level of the parent(s), housing, and parenting practices and beliefs.

It has been known for decades that home and family environments greatly influence children's performance in school. Parents who are critical, abusive, hostile, or inconsistent with their discipline put their children at risk for developing aggressive behavior problems or conduct disorders (Webster-Stratton, 1998). In an analysis of a mother-child data set from the National Longitudinal Survey of Youth, Mary Eamon (2000) reports that children who live in poverty are more likely to experience low self-esteem, lower levels of sociability and initiative, and more aggression, hyperactivity, and depression than children in families with greater financial resources. As the years in poverty increase, the child is more likely to experience sadness, anxiety, and dependency. Acting-out behaviors such as aggression, bullying, and tantrums also predict poor school performance and delinquency.

Eamon also found that stress-related parenting practices—such as emotional unresponsiveness, inability to provide stimulating experiences, harsh physical discipline, and an unsafe home environment—directly influence a child's socioemotional adjustment. Children whose socioemotional adjustment is retarded or interrupted may not behave in appropriate ways. There is a readiness for learning in the social-behavioral arena that is just as real as readiness in any academic subject. Students may not be prepared to address the growth tasks that schools and teachers ask of them. It is unproductive to punish students if they have not been taught appropriate behavior. There are times when the most fundamental behaviors must be explained. Social skills deficits can be considered as errors in learning and taught like any other skill.

Social and behavioral remediation or direct instruction are expected to precede the accomplishment of a social-behavioral learning task. Just as remediation for math or reading problems may involve going back and filling in learning gaps, remediation in the normal sequence of social learning is often necessary for students with behavior problems. The school's behavorial expectations may have to be adjusted to accommodate the student during the time when remediation is undertaken and before a student is disciplined for failure to comply with those expectations. If the child has social skills but does not use them consistently, a performance deficit exists that can usually be remediated by the careful use of positive reinforcement of the appropriate skills (ERIC Clearinghouse, 1993). For example, many young children just do not know that it is wrong to take something they need or want without permission. They may have no training whatsoever in behaviors related to respect for boundaries. There are many similar behaviors that children may not have been taught. Discipline practices need to provide the means not only for correction or remediation but also for teaching the initial concept. It is important for teachers to look beyond the presenting misbehavior to determine and remediate the cause of the problem.

The "Dry Sock" Approach

One elementary school student may start the day with wet shoes and socks because she walked to school in the rain. She may exhibit very different behavior from that of her classmates who are dry and comfortable because they were driven to the school door by their parents. In this instance it is more advantageous to provide the child with dry socks than to give her detention or time-out for the disruptive behavior caused by the physical discomfort of sticky socks and wet shoes. The "dry sock" approach is more likely to resolve the problem. A time-out approach may tend to create anger and further problems, all of which result from an antecedent over which the student had little or no control.

The "Eat Your Wheaties" Approach

Educators and health care professionals have known for years that children who do not eat breakfast are less efficient and less productive. Whether a child eats breakfast on a daily basis is a regularity. Teachers are confronted by the outcomes of home-based regularities every day. Researchers at Massachusetts General Hospital (Murphy et al.,1998) who studied inner city elementary school children found that students who ate breakfast earned higher grades in math. They were less likely to be described by their parents or teachers as hyperactive, anxious, or depressed. Hyperactive, anxious, and depressed students tend to exhibit problematic behaviors in the classroom and often require some type of intervention by the teacher.

Researchers found that eating a well-balanced breakfast helps children to think more quickly and clearly, solve problems more easily, and be less irritable. Conversely, students who do not eat breakfast have difficulty selecting the information they need for problem solving and are impaired in verbal fluency, attentiveness, and the ability to recall and use new information. Children who skip breakfast are less productive, handle tasks less efficiently, and exhibit impaired mental and memory performance. All of the negative consequences of home and family regularities that result in the failure to eat breakfast set the stage for possible discipline problems.

Many other studies also indicate that children who eat breakfast have an advantage in school over those who do not. No matter what a teacher does to deal with hyperactivity, inattentiveness, or poor recall in a child who has not had breakfast, it will be far less effective than establishing a new regularity. Ensuring that a child eats breakfast at home or at school changes the regular practice of omitting breakfast and results in fewer offending behaviors and patterns of failure.

In the past teachers have been compelled to draw upon a whole repertoire of behavior management strategies that may or may not be successful in motivating a hungry student or alleviating poor concentration or irritability. As an alternative, many schools serve a nutritious breakfast and so have eliminated the need for disciplinary interventions associated with this issue.

In the same way that problems are created in school because a child fails to eat at home, a child who comes to school without enough sleep may have behavior and performance problems that discipline interventions cannot solve. Writing a child's name on the board, taking away points, using time-out, scolding, sending a child to the principal's office, giving demerits, using detention, lowering grades, or even using positive reinforcement will not remedy the problem of sleep deprivation, wet socks, or an empty stomach. Instead, such discipline measures may have unanticipated and undesired consequences. Punishing students for behaviors that stem from strongly negative family system regularities may create more severe behavior problems. Allowing a student to take time out for a nap when conditions at home make a normal night's sleep impossible may eliminate the problem behaviors more effectively than any kind of punishment or reinforcement. Such an intervention addresses a problem by remedying the root cause rather than addressing the behavioral outcomes of system regularities.

Family regularities like sleep deprivation and skipping breakfast may not be something that a teacher can change, but classroom regularities are under the teacher's control. Teachers and administrators often find that there are more options open to them than they realized. Making changes in classroom regularities can produce changes in student behavior that are as dramatic as those produced by permitting naps and providing breakfast programs. Why focus on changing the unwanted outcomes of a regularity with withdrawal of privileges or restrictive punishment? Changing the regularity itself may have a long-term effect on the child and diminish the need for escalating behavioral interventions on the part of the teacher.

The "One Size Fits All" Approach

Traditionally, discipline practices have been applied more or less uniformly with all students. Behavior management strategies have addressed an entire school as though every student would respond to those strategies in a similar way. Our understanding of research findings on behavior management and individual differences as well as years of observation leads us to reject this notion. Under the banner of consistency, firmness, and fairness, many schools institute a "one size fits all" approach to discipline that disregards the causes of student misbehavior. One size fits few! Inappropriate instructional and behavior management strategies evolve from models that assume that students are all alike. Despite increased research on and understanding of individual differences, students within a given grade level or classroom too often are viewed as a homogeneous group and are therefore treated the same way.

Schools, teachers, and parents have bought into the myth that students are like all the others in their grade or class. Nothing could be further from the truth. Even schools that recognize differences in the way children learn may not recognize the need to acknowledge differences in the way children should be disciplined. Historically, the expectation has been that all children will respond to discipline in a similar way. Any parent of more than one child knows that discipline practices that work with one child may not work—and may even exacerbate the problem—with a younger or older sibling. All children may be held to a certain standard of behavior, but the route to compliance may vary significantly.

It has been well established that any classroom will have students who differ markedly in size, physical development, and skill. They will also differ in age, intellectual ability, level of achievement, style of learning, personality type, and strength of interests and abilities. They will differ in the amount of time it takes to complete a learning task and achieve mastery of new skills. The instructional strategies and the learning and social climate created by the school will affect each student differently. The methods, strategies, and climate of every classroom make up the regularities that describe it, not the homogeneity of the students. Many schools remain static, with teachers employing traditional means of instruction and arrangements, passive learning, and an overabundance of direct teaching and seat work.

At the elementary level, the reading achievement within any given classroom can cover a span roughly equal to twice the grade level of the class in first through third grades. For students from fourth through sixth grades, the span of reading levels within the class may be one and a half to two times the grade level or more. A sixth-grade class might include students whose reading levels range from second grade to tenth grade—a span of nine levels. By the time students reach high school, the span continues to be very large. When students' differences in learning style, personality, socioeconomic status, cultural background, and other variables are factored in with the differences in academic achievement, the diversity becomes so great that a teacher's brain beeps "overload" and may simply shut down or ignore the differences. However, many school districts and individual schools have demonstrated that they and their classes can be organized to accommodate and support the tremendous diversity that confronts every teacher.

Variance in students and classrooms is a given; it goes with the territory. It is a regularity that will not change. Therefore, every teacher must establish a learning environment that accommodates variance.

Steps Toward Establishing Effective Discipline

We have identified seven steps to help teachers develop effective discipline practices.

Step 1: Establish Regularity Control

As soon as a class of students is established, the regularities that influence classroom operations should be identified. Identify which regularities are controllable (changeable) by teachers or school officials and which are uncontrollable (unchangeable). Identify the controllable variables that influence instruction and academic performance and those that might influence personal and social behavior in the classroom. Based upon studies that establish the efficacy of differentiated instruction and the individual and unique characteristics of learners, determine which regularities must be changed to establish user-friendly classrooms. Establish immediate and long-range priorities for change. Continually monitor performance, personal development, and social interaction to identify additional areas in which regularities or antecedents need to be changed or deleted and new ones established.

Step 2: Help Students (and Teachers) to Accept Responsibility

A vital step in establishing effective discipline practices is to help students to see themselves as ultimately in charge of their own learning and success. Students must accept responsibility for their own social behavior and for developing a positive image of themselves as learners and as people. Many positive strategies support students as independent learners. Acquisition of skills such as metacognition, cognitive behavior modification, self-reinforcement, self-monitoring, self-management, and problem solving help students to increase self-control and assume responsibility for their own learning and behavior. At the same time, the teacher has to accept responsibility for restructuring the regularities in a classroom so that each student has the best possible chance to learn. This can be done by modifying regularities in ways that accommodate the students' personality differences (psychological types), multiple intelligences, learning styles, and personal interests. Learning to do this is a major task for a teacher.

Step 3: Provide a Variety of Instructional Arrangements

The neurosensory literature (Wolfe & Brandt, 1998) suggests that students' ability to concentrate on new and difficult learning tasks in a direct teaching situation may be more limited than we previously realized. Neuroscience suggests that the amount of time a student is able to focus intently on the teacher may be related to the student's age. For example, normal 5-year-olds are probably able to focus solely and intently on the teacher and the task for approximately 5 minutes. A 15-year-old may be able to focus intently on the teacher's instruction and directions for about 15 minutes. Because of social norms, most adults are able to remain quietly attentive in outward demeanor well past the time when they are able to learn and absorb new material well, but everyone has limits. For example, many people are involved in learning new things about their personal computers. Most of them find that they are able to listen intently to instructions and remember the directions for operating a new program for brief spurts of time before turning their attention elsewhere. Classroom regularities that require students to focus for 30 to 40 minutes without a change of format tend to leave many children far behind; this sets the stage for behavioral difficulties. Providing a variety of learning activities is necessary to supplement direct instruction from the teacher. The literature abounds with studies that support the efficacy of differentiated instructional arrangements, including mastery learning, continuous progress learning, personalized instruction, families, cohorts, or programs such as schools within schools.

Step 4: Expect Good Behavior With Good Performance

Students with discipline problems are seldom enjoying success in learning. The relationship between good performance and good behavior is so striking that it cannot be ignored. Indeed, it is so strong that it may be said that the best strategy for many discipline problems is a good healthy dose of academic success. Because poor performance and poor behavior are so inseparable, an attempt to provide learning success must be at the forefront of every attempt to deal with discipline. When students are experiencing academic and social success and like school, then the need for discipline interventions will usually be minimal. It is useful for teachers to employ a variety of discipline methods. Talking with the student, jointly identifying ways to handle the situation better the next time, using logical consequences, and giving positive reinforcement will usually be enough.

There are, of course, students who get straight As who also have behavior problems. When that occurs, it may be that they are not learning or achieving their full potential in spite of their good grades. They may be bored, unhappy, unchallenged, or achieving to satisfy someone other than themselves. These students may not enjoy their learning success. In such a situation, it is also appropriate to consider changes in instructional regularities. The student may be the best source of suggestions in determining the nature of the changes. Students will respond positively to a teacher who is sincerely interested in their views on how to encourage joy in learning and improved behavior.

A teacher who genuinely enjoys the process of learning new ways to structure a classroom to support student learning usually finds that the students make helpful partners. The wonderful thing about the classroom is that it is an environment dedicated to learning, growth, and discovery. When teachers see their classrooms as providing rich opportunities for their own acquisition of new skills and insights, then consultations between student and teacher become something that both can enjoy.

Step 5: Adopt a Positive Attitude

It is important for teachers to adopt a positive attitude toward working with students who require attention for their behavior. Student failure is not the only kind of failure experienced in a classroom. When a student meets with constant failure in school, interest in learning fades; the same is true for a teacher. When teachers are unable to help students overcome academic failure, they may feel that they have failed. A teacher who sees little improvement in student behavior may also feel failure. Such teachers understandably become disappointed and discouraged. Students and teachers cannot afford to settle into passive acceptance of failure. They can acquire additional skills that lead to success and increase the satisfaction they find in the classroom. Both must make a decision to maintain a positive attitude.

Teachers should not give up on students with behavior problems, yet sometimes it happens. Despite an increase in team teaching and teacher mentoring throughout the country, a lone teacher coping with student behavior problems in the classroom is still common in American schools. It is a regularity in education that a class has one teacher, yet few teachers have the necessary training to proactively adapt their behavior management strategies to accommodate different personality types and learning styles.

Many teachers find that they do best with students who are most like themselves in style and personality. Few teachers are naturally able to handle the behavior problems of all kinds of children equally well. It requires time and experience for teachers to learn to understand students who are not like themselves. The fresh perspective offered by an understanding of psychological types and other models for individualizing instruction are helpful in dealing with problem behaviors as well as instructional ones. Just as teachers tend to be more successful in teaching children who are like themselves, they tend to be most successful in managing behavior problems and discipline with children who are like themselves.

It is important to remember that difficulty in managing a student is not a sign of teacher failure, rather, it is simply a problem waiting to be solved— a learning opportunity for the teacher and student. It also is important to maintain an upbeat attitude. As teachers acquire additional skills in behavior management, they will enjoy more success and satisfaction in their work.

Step 6: Establish Positive Emotional Regularities

The role of emotion in learning cannot be ignored. Students who have healthy self-concepts—who feel safe, supported, and respected in school— behave differently from children under great stress who feel threatened, shamed, or anxious. Distressed students often downshift or experience a fight-or-flight response that results in the need for strong discipline and diminishes learning as well.

No matter how completely schools focus on the development of the mind, emotional learning is happening in every classroom all the time. Most of it is incidental learning, since it is neither planned nor monitored. Some of it is counterproductive to healthy emotional, social, and intellectual development. The emotional climate in a classroom is often the most invisible school regularity. It is seldom examined, planned for, or changed. When the emotional regularities in a classroom are ignored, they are no less strong and their impact on student learning and behavior is no less powerful; they are simply uncontrolled.

When a classroom activity evokes positive emotions, it causes a chemical response in the brain that increases retention. Therefore, learning experiences that are exciting and meaningful stir positive emotions that cause the brain to remember the material better. Both positive and negative feelings are important. Joseph LeDoux (Wolfe & Brandt, 1998) has pointed out that when an emotion is strongly negative, learning is decreased. In a situation that is perceived by a student as threatening, shaming, or stressful, the ability to master new material and perform well may be lessened.

Behavioral problems that result from negative emotional regularities in school are much more common than educators previously believed. Because the negative and the positive effects of emotion on learning are so strong, it is important to pay close attention to the regularities that contribute to both. For positive academic and social behavior to occur, the classroom must be a place in which enhancing regularities ensure that students feel safe and supported.

Step 7: Plan for Effective Management

Kounin (1970) describes effective teachers as having orderly classrooms, high levels of time on task, and a minimum of student misbehavior. Effective teachers prevent disruptions from occurring by careful planning and prepare in advance to deal with problems that arise. They have high expectations for student learning and behavior that are supported by behavioral rules. Effective teachers are warm and encouraging to students. They maintain a brisk and continuous pace of instruction and they respond quickly to misbehavior by enforcing classroom rules promptly, consistently, and equitably. Effective teachers emphasize, teach, and model self-discipline and share with students the responsibility for classroom management.

Reinforcing Regularities

Over time teachers have learned to employ positive reinforcement as a means to correct inappropriate behavior. Rewards are selected from an array of reinforcers to influence a student's behavior and make it acceptable. A *reinforcer* is an object that is given or an event that occurs when a desired behavior is exhibited; it increases the likelihood that the desired behavior will occur again. A reinforcer may also be given when an alternative behavior replaces an undesired behavior.

For most children, the use of reinforcers works very well when the reinforcer is something valued by the student. However, there are times when individual students become inattentive, fidgety, restless, and noncompliant despite the use of reinforcement. They may make inappropriate comments or become defiant when asked to do a simple task. Merely asking them to do something like copy and complete math problems at the blackboard can become a major power struggle. The reinforcer may have lost its power, but the problem might be more complex. Too often a teacher's common response is to resort to threats or various forms of punishment. In many instances, it is more productive to widen the arena in which action is taken by considering the larger realm of classroom regularities than to use specific reinforcers, or other similar methods, alone.

Classroom regularities that support individual student personality types, learning styles, and interests may be thought of as *reinforcing regularities*. Reinforcing regularities set the stage for a student to be successful academically and socially. Regularities that allow a student to operate in his or her "comfort zone" become reinforcing in and of themselves. A comfort zone is created when a student is in an environment that respects his or her personality type, learning style, and individual interests and abilities. Regularities that affect learning and behavior may have to be carefully analyzed and modified to accommodate individual differences among students.

With highly resistant students, better outcomes are achieved by the establishment of reinforcing regularities than by employing punishment in the form of detentions, suspensions, low grades, or isolation. Academic success increases self-esteem, which in turn tends to reduce the need for strong behavioral interventions. By contrast, low self-esteem is compounded by academic failure, and together they set the stage for strong discipline interventions.

The Sociological Setting

At times most teachers have changed the physical arrangement of a classroom by moving a student to a different seat. Changing the sociological setting in which learning occurs may also be a good solution to a student's inappropriate behavior. For example, changing from large-group to small-group instruction can change student attitudes. Allowing some students to work alone or in pairs or to talk with one another also helps some students to work and learn better. Modification of the social regularities in which students work allows teachers to implement more individualized strategies and methods. These changes may be the best and easiest kinds of interventions, despite the fact that they represent changes in the realm of instructional practices rather than traditional behavior management strategies. Such interventions change the climate and can reduce tension in the classroom to such a degree that additional disciplinary action is unnecessary.

The classroom is a physical, social, emotional, and intellectual environment. Considering it solely in terms of its intellectual happenings ignores powerful forces at work within it all the time. Intellectual growth does not occur in isolation from other developmental issues. Isolating discipline and behavior management from the whole classroom experience is impossible. Problems that occur in one area of classroom life often have their antecedents in another. Changing the antecedents that are associated with difficulties in learning is related to change in personal behavior as well.

Changes in the social settings in which learning occurs often necessitates increased personal responsibility on the part of students to behave appropriately toward one another without continual supervision. Such changes require respectful behavior, and this must be taught, clearly explained, modeled, practiced, supported by rules and routines, and reinforced. A teacher who treats all students with respect establishes respectful interactions as a regularity in the classroom. Insisting on respectful behavior by all students toward one another reinforces that regularity and supports the successful use of various kinds of individual and small-group learning experiences.

A study of the classroom as a sociological system and of its regularities allows a teacher to examine a variety of social factors that impact student behavior. For example, engaging the class as a whole in the task of establishing rules for respectful and courteous behavior sets the stage for involving them in responsible enforcement of the agreed-upon rules.

Classrooms that are troubled by disruptive behavior are often governed by regularities that include disrespectful social interchanges. Introducing students to the concept of regularities involves them in the process of analyzing the classroom and generating the rules by which it will be governed. Students generally behave toward one another in ways that are expected. Once those behaviors are understood to be regularities that are subject to change, and students are allowed a measure of power to determine the course of that change, they will participate in the process.

Students who experience success in learning that is accompanied by positive social interactions will generally exhibit appropriate behavior and will follow the rules that make sense to them. Lapses in following the rules can then be dealt with quickly and reasonably without escalation of inappropriate behavior by using predetermined logical consequences that have been agreed upon by everyone. Students are more likely to respond appropriately to rules of conduct when they have participated in formulating them. Reminders not to interrupt, to walk slowly, to treat others respectfully, or to begin working may then result in compliance without escalation of teacher threats or punishments.

Personalizing Discipline: Changing Regularities

Gateways to Achievement and Responsible Behavior

Everything about classroom life is subject to analysis when a teacher is on the lookout for the regularities or antecedents that will support learning and good behavior for a particular student. The teacher has control of the instructional arrangements, the opportunities for practice, the hands-on experiences, the quality and nature of interactions, the selection of tasks and materials, and the use of behavior management strategies. An important goal is to elicit and support the students' sense of responsibility for their own learning. Everything within a classroom is structured toward that end. To achieve it, students must find enough flexibility and adaptability in the classroom to allow them to succeed. Helping students to develop responsible behavior requires an individualized approach to discipline—and, indeed, to everything else.

The teacher is the gatekeeper for the learning arena of the classroom. Regularities that serve as an open gate for one student may act as a closed one for another. For example, reading is not a gateway to learning for all children. Even today that concept is startling to many people. The ability to read serves different learners in different ways, but even those who never become proficient in reading can be helped to learn by other means. For years students with reading disabilities or visual impairments have used audiotaped books, readers, computer voice readers, highlighted materials, and other techniques to obtain information. Reading is only one antecedent to learning, yet in many schools, if a student fails to learn to read there is little effort to find an alternative. Instead of being given alternative methods for acquiring information, students are subjected to the repetitive use of methods and procedures that do not work for them.

There are few students who are so disadvantaged that no gateways to learning can be found for them—even for nonreaders. In a classroom environment that is friendly to all students, the regularities are flexible enough to accommodate many differences that have an impact on student learning and social or personal behavior. To a large extent, the degree of individualized instruction and attention children will receive depends on the understanding that teachers have of the regularities that affect learning and behavior.

Formal or Informal Settings

One rather vivid example of a classroom regularity that is considered sacred by some but subject to change by others is the formality of the setting in which students work. There are some educators who fervently believe that no learning can take place unless a student is in a chair with "every seat on a seat and all feet on the floor"—and all attention focused on the teacher.

Some students thrive in such a formal work setting, but others work better with materials spread out on the floor, with the freedom to discuss the topic with their peers, or in some other more flexible arrangement. There is often a mismatch between seating and other instructional arrangements and the type of work assigned. For instance, when grouping students for collaborative assignments, the clustering of desks, the use of tables, or the use of circles may be appropriate. For some students, these arrangements can be distracting when they are completing individual assignments. Students work best when learning and working styles are considered. For certain kinds of assignments and for some types of students, seating in rows can result in increased amounts of work. For other assignments there may be a need for enough flexibility to permit some students to sit in rows with clearly defined boundaries around their workstations while permitting others to work with a partner or group in an informal setting or to read independently in a beanbag chair or while lying on a rug. It is reasonable to match seating arrangement with the goal of the lesson, the nature of the task, and the learning style of the student. If the regularities in a school or classroom preclude the flexibility of antecedents such as seating arrangements, there will always be a mismatch between some students and their learning environment.

Teachers who themselves need the support of a formal work setting naturally assume that others need the same thing. Teachers who work better in informal settings have had the opportunity to see the success of those who prefer formal settings; they also have observed work styles in operation that are unlike their own preferences. They have seen demonstrations of the fact that people who prefer to work in different conditions succeed very well. They tend to be more flexible in considering different work settings for their students. However, students and teachers who have worked only in schools in which the "stand and deliver" model prevails—where rigid regularities permit no one to spread out their work, use centers, stations, or talk through problems with a classmate or small group—may have difficulty seeing its possible benefits.

Another widespread attitude about school regularities deserves to be considered. Many teachers are adamantly opposed to individual accommodations for students because they consider them unfair. They believe that making changes to help one student gives him or her an unfair advantage over the others. They find it difficult to grasp the idea that students whose learning styles match the existing classroom regularities already have a built in advantage over other children. Similarly, students whose learning preferences do not match existing regularities have a built-in disadvantage. It is important for all teachers to realize that some school regularities operate like special accommodations that favor some students while hindering success for others.

The Impact of Special Education on School Regularities

Good teachers do not buy into the myth that all children should be treated the same way. They have given up the idea that consistency is more important than appropriateness. They are no longer troubled by the idea that it is unfair to give special attention or accommodation to individual students who do not learn as the others do. Each student needs school to provide an environment in which success is possible. Special education has demonstrated that students with serious problems can learn in a regular classroom when adaptations are made to its regularities and antecedents. In the past, it was not unusual for a student to be referred to special education because of behavior problems in a regular classroom. The use of traditional discipline practices, which focused only on interventions after the behavior problems appeared, proved largely ineffective. When flexible adaptations are made that involve changes in classroom regularities and antecedents, students begin to experience success in learning, and behavior problems become manageable as well.

There is one more point to consider in this matter of flexible versus rigid regularities. Recently there has been an increasing emphasis on the need to hold schools and teachers accountable through an individual education plan (IEP) and the development of goals, objectives, and annual reviews that measure the success of the student. Can teachers be held responsible for teaching some students differently if different teaching options are not open to them? Should teachers be held responsible for grade or behavior improvement if they are not given the freedom to change the regularities associated with instruction and behavior?

Inclusion programs for students with disabilities often provide the impetus for change in school regularities. Nothing is sacred in terms of school regularities, according to the Individuals With Disabilities Education Act (IDEA) and similar laws, which demand that school systems make whatever changes are necessary to facilitate learning and foster appropriate behavior for children with disabilities. This strong legal requirement for accommodation in schools has produced a whole body of information on individualized instruction that was not previously available. It has been found that the techniques developed for special education students often work just as well, and in many cases better, for students in general education. If the requirement for individual accommodation is considered by Congress to be absolutely essential for special education children, should it not be provided for all children? Shouldn't every student have an IEP? Every child needs to be accommodated in areas of special difficulty and provided with a learning environment that maximizes his or her development and achievement.

Class Size Regularities

In recent years the regularity of class size has been changed by state law or by local school boards. The purpose in changing this regularity is to solve many problems. Although class size is a significant regularity to change, it is not a panacea for school problems. There is a widespread belief that reducing class size will produce greater student success in school. This belief is based on the idea that a teacher will be free to offer more individual attention to each student in a smaller class, but there is no cause-and-effect relationship that ensures that students will receive more individual attention. Many teachers continue to teach small classes in the same "stand and deliver" style they used with larger classes. How is the individual attention in a small class expected to differ from the attention in a large class if the teacher does nothing different? There is a need to implement strategies that accommodate individual needs and differences even in reduced-size classes.

Regularities and Personal Recognition

Stationing teachers at each school entrance and at classroom doors with instructions to welcome students by name is an example of a regularity designed to reduce student anonymity and increase personal contact. Reducing anonymity, and similar practices, can reduce inappropriate student behavior throughout a school. The need for personalizing education has led many school districts throughout the United States to develop atypical regularities in education.

Summary

Every aspect of classroom life is a potential tool with which a teacher may be able to help a student to succeed. Reinforcement may be combined with regularity or antecedent changes to bring about the desired behavior. The physical arrangement of libraries, for instance, supports quiet reading and study. Personalizing the businesslike atmosphere created by some very dedicated and competent teachers may be critical to success for some relationally sensitive students. Similarly, tightening the organizational structure for individual students may be critical to their success in a warm, relaxed, unstructured classroom in which other students do very well.

When all students and teachers are performing satisfactorily, no action is required. If behavior or achievement falls short of expectations, then changes must be made. Traditionally, schools have assumed that academic failure or inappropriate conduct required changes (improvements) in student behavior. School discipline policies have therefore focused on ways to motivate or control individual students. Too little recognition has been given to the power of programmatic regularities to shape student behavior.

Inappropriate behavior has a cause. When only the behavioral outworkings are treated, the root of the problem—regularities and behavioral anteced-ents—may be missed. Both must be addressed. Developing behavior plans without addressing the core issues may result in short-term improvement, but the basic issues will undoubtedly continue to trigger problems. Programmatic regularities may exist because they are expected to produce desired instructional or behavioral outcomes, or they may exist because of something like architectural requirements or factors unrelated to educational issues. When unanticipated consequences occur, it must be recognized that they are outcomes of the existing regularities. The unintended outcomes will probably continue until the regularities that produce them are changed. Efforts to change the outcomes can be better focused on changing the regularity that spawned them.

Meisgeier's theory of behavioral diversity and regularity control stresses the importance of recognizing psychological types, learning styles, and special interests and abilities. Individual students must be supported by regularities that accommodate behavioral diversity. All classroom regularities should be examined for intended and unintended outcomes. Classroom regularities include instructional methods and materials, the physical arrangement of the classroom, the emotional climate, teacher procedures for acknowledging individual differences, the policies and practices that make up classroom discipline, and the ways in which teachers interact with students. Discipline and behavior management strategies are among the most important programmatic regularities to monitor for intended outcomes and actual outcomes. Discrepancies between these two may signal a need for change in the regularities. Current practices and the classroom regularities established by them will have to give way to alternatives, which are always available.

Sarason (1962) has concluded from his research that failure to consider alternatives is an obstacle to change in any system, including a school. Freedom to explore alternative strategies and policies must undergird attempts to establish effective discipline practices in school settings. School change efforts traditionally focus on outcomes and leave the overarching programmatic regularities virtually untouched. Instructional and discipline regularities form the heart of the school experience. They should be considered central to any study of children's behavior in school.

Activity 1: Identifying Regularities

1. In groups of three, identify and discuss regularities that were present in your school for the earliest grades you remember. Compile a list of specific regularities and discuss those that have changed over the years.

   Examples: Was the teacher always addressed as "Ma'am"? Did recess occur at the same time every day? Were children silent walking through the halls?

2. Discuss how the regularities you identify affected your academic performance.

Activity 2: Changing Regularities

1. With your group compile a list of regularities that exist in your school today and identify those that establish either positive or negative conditions in schools. Apply Meisgeier's concept of behavioral diversity and regularity control in making your list.

2. Select regularities that should be changed immediately, those that could be changed in a semester, and those that would require more time to change.

Activity 3: Control of Regularities

Identify regularities that are under the control of the individual teacher, those that are controlled by the administration or school board, and those controlled by federal, state, or local laws.

Under the control of teacher:

Under the control of administration or school board:

Under the control of federal, state, or local laws:

Activity 4: Planning for Change

Each small group joins with another small group to devise a plan that includes a time line, the resources, and the activities that would be required to change the items on the list of regularities identified in Activity 2.

References

Briggs, K., & Myers, I. (1987). *The Myers-Briggs Type Indicator.* Palo Alto, CA: Consulting Psychologists Press.

Eamon, M. (2000). A structured model of the effects of poverty on the externalizing and internalizing behavior of 4- and 5-year old children. *Social Work Research 24* (3), 143–154.

ERIC Clearinghouse on Disabilities and Gifted Education. (1993). Behavioral Disorders Focus on Change. (ERIC Digest #518)

Kounin, J. S. (1970). *Discipline and group management in the classroom.* New York: Holt, Rinehart, & Winston.

Meisgeier, C., & Meisgeier, C. S. (2000). Behavior management, individual differences and psychological type. *Proceedings of the 4th biennial education conference, creating collaborative learning communities: The role of type in education* (pp. 225–234). Gainesville, FL: Center for Applications of Psychological Type.

Meisgeier, C., & Murphy, E., (1987). *Murphy-Meisgeier Type Indicator for Children Manual.* Palo Alto, CA: Consulting Psychologists Press.

Meisgeier, C., Richardson, R., & Meisgeier, C. S. (1995). Preparing teachers to accommodate behavioral diversity: A unique perspective. Reston, VA: Council for Exceptional Children.

Meisgeier, C., Swank, P., Richardson, R., & Meisgeier, C. S. (1994). Implications and applications of psychological type to educational reform and renewal. In M. Fields (Ed.), *Orchestrating educational change in the '90s: The role of psychological type.* Gainesville, FL: Center for Applications of Psychological Type.

Murphy, J. M., Pagano, M., Nachmani, J., Sperling, P., Kane, S., & Kleinman, R. (1998). The relationship of school breakfast to psychosocial and academic functioning: cross-sectional and longitudinal observations of inner-city school sample. *Archives of Pediatric Adolescent Medicine. 152* (9), 899–907.

Sarason, S. (1962). *The culture of the school and the problem of change.* Boston: Allyn & Bacon.

Webster-Stratton, C. (1998). Preventing conduct problems in Head Start children: Strengthening parents' competencies. *Consulting and Clinical Psychology 66* (5), 715–730.

Wolfe, C., & Brandt, R. (1998). What do we know from brain research? *Educational Leadership 56* (3), 8–13.

Chapter 3

Implications of Behavioral Diversity for Discipline Practices: Psychological Types, Learning Styles, and Multiple Intelligences

Overview

Behavioral Diversity
    Defining behavioral diversity
    Personality, psychological type, and learning style
    Goodness of fit

Learning Styles
    Elements of learning style

Psychological Types
    Where the energy flows
    How we perceive
    How we make decisions
    How we prefer to live

The Significance of Psychological Type Characteristics in the Classroom
    Extraversion and Introversion
    Sensing and Intuition
    Thinking and Feeling
    Judging and Perceiving
    Psychological type and discipline
    Psychological type combinations

Multiple Intelligences
    Linguistic Intelligence
    Logical-mathematical Intelligence
    Spatial Intelligence
    Bodily-kinesthetic Intelligence

cont.

Musical Intelligence
Interpersonal Intelligence
Intrapersonal Intelligence
Naturalist Intelligence
Other Intelligences
Comparison of psychological types, learning styles,
and multiple intelligences

Examining a Mismatch of Psychological Types
José: A case history
Discipline problems embedded in school life
Interaction of regularities, type, and discipline

Summary

Activities

QUESTIONS

This chapter will help you to answer the following questions:

1. Why do discipline measures that work well with some children seem to have little positive effect with others?

2. How can understanding differences in students' personalities guide a teacher in selecting classroom management strategies?

3. Why does the behavioral diversity of students demand diversity in teaching styles?

4. What are the outcomes of mismatches between student learning styles and a teacher's discipline practices?

5. Do teachers need to become warm, friendly, and personal in relating to students to help them be successful?

6. How can the accommodation of individual learning styles be expected to affect behavioral and discipline problems?

7. Can a student-teacher personality mismatch create discipline problems?

8. Why is a "one size fits all" approach to discipline inappropriate?

Overview

Chapter 3 describes issues of classroom management and discipline related to personality differences and school climate. Teachers will learn the importance of personality or psychological types, learning style differences, and multiple intelligences in successfully executing behavior management strategies. Teachers will become familiar with reinforcement and responsibility and will learn that these words have different meanings for people of different psychological types. They will understand that identifying desirable behaviors for children and choosing the reinforcers that produce them are decisions to be made in light of individual students' personalities. Traditional discipline theories and practices will be reviewed in terms of new perspectives about classroom regularities and individual student differences.

Common discipline practices, individual student differences, and classroom regularities will be considered in relation to one another; the relationship among psychological types, learning styles, and multiple intelligences is probably the least understood but most significant factor in understanding why discipline strategies fail or succeed. Additional understanding increases the ability to accommodate these differences in the instructional process and expands the teacher's ability to select appropriate individually focused discipline strategies.

Unless specific instruction is offered to the contrary, teachers instinctively believe that their students learn as they themselves learn and respond to discipline strategies as they themselves respond. It is an entirely understandable belief, but it is incorrect. Students learn in remarkably different ways and respond to discipline interventions very differently. They may exhibit similar behavior in response to specific circumstances, but the motivation for the response may be quite different from one student to another. It is important to involve the students themselves in the search for an understanding of the best ways to support their learning efforts. Educators must teach students to take responsibility for their own learning and allow them to participate in structuring their own discipline strategies and consequences. In addition, educators must permit a measure of flexibility in which students can make their own adaptations to discipline policies. Students become an integral part of an inclusive philosophy of discipline and behavior management. This kind of carefully structured freedom can reduce the frustration level of those students who are the least matched to their school's regularities and this in turn reduces discipline problems.

Students must accept responsibility for their learning and also for their behavior and its consequences, both good and bad. The teacher provides a learning environment that establishes regularities that reinforce the best gifts and abilities that each learner brings to the classroom. Students can learn to work with the teacher to develop the classroom accommodations that will allow them to succeed without offending others and to eliminate self-destructive classroom patterns.

Behavior management involves more than a reaction to interruptions, misbehaviors, and off-task activities in a classroom. It is not incidental to the teachers' work of instruction; rather, behavioral management is an integral part of all the systems and programs that make up classroom life. Being able to correct inappropriate behavior and reinforce appropriate behavior are essential skills for every teacher. Effective teachers utilize a variety of interventions of the types described in subsequent chapters. They use positive reinforcement to obtain appropriate behavior and teach students how to accept responsibility for their own learning and behavior; they value the importance of collaboration with students in the development of classroom rules and routines; they develop an awareness and sensitivity to their classrooms, are able to anticipate problems, and they make modifications in their behavior management plans as necessary. When teachers have a broad understanding of the behavioral diversity in the classroom, the application of these essential skills will create a healthy climate for learning.

Much of this chapter is based on Meisgeier's (1995) theory of Behavioral Diversity and Regularity Control. This concept emphasizes the importance of establishing school regularities that accommodate individual differences. According to Meisgeier, school regularities must be structured to accommodate students' psychological (personality) types, learning styles, special interests, and abilities. When this is accomplished, Meisgeier believes, students' academic, social, and personal behaviors will develop steadily and require minimal discipline. Students must be taught in the way they learn best in a safe, supportive classroom.

Behavioral Diversity

Behavioral diversity means that people are different in what they do, what they can do, and how they do it. These differences show up in every area of life. No single theory explains all the differences in the ways children learn, but a growing body of research is revealing more all the time. How can knowledge of behavioral diversity help a teacher? What is *psychological type*? What is *learning style* and its relation to psychological type? What are *multiple intelligences*? How are they identified and what are the ways to accommodate them in students? How can a teacher use information about these concepts to reduce negative behavior and the need for discipline in the classroom?

When a child's behavior is consistently inappropriate or unresponsive, the first step should be to look for a match or a mismatch between the classroom regularities and the child's psychological type or learning style. In the previous chapter we pointed out that regularities include everything in the school and the community that affects the teaching and learning process— everything that occurs in school on a regular basis. Regularities include such things as teacher-pupil interactions, methods and materials, and the physical environment of the classroom. Teachers establish and maintain the regularities in their classrooms to match their own psychological type preferences and learning styles. Why would they do anything else? Without special instruction of some kind, what other guide would a teacher have in organizing and arranging the classroom? Classroom regularities are influenced by the psychological type of the teacher. It is one of the most important variables affecting both instruction and behavior management.

Defining Behavioral Diversity

Most teachers today understand the need to address cultural, ethnic, racial, and social differences in cognitive learning. Schools have made a good start in this area, but additional methods to accommodate diverse learners are still needed. Although educators have some understanding of the above-mentioned kinds of diversity and their relation to instruction, there is less understanding of the concept of behavioral diversity and its influence on nearly everything that occurs in schools. Behavioral diversity may transcend all other diversity issues. *Behavioral diversity*, as used by Meisgeier (1995), describes normal differences in the ways that children behave as a result of their psychological (personality) types, and/or temperament differences.

Meisgeier (1995) has found that psychological type differences have profound impact upon the behavior of children across age, gender, racial, ethnic, and cultural differences and across intellectual, physical, and emotional abilities. Predictable patterns of behavior result from the psychological type preferences of both teachers and children. They influence social patterns, learning styles, decision making, and the need for structure or freedom. Many behavioral differences once thought to reflect cultural or gender differences or learning disabilities may be more accurately understood as behavioral diversity and therefore explained by psychological type and learning style differences.

Personality, Psychological Type, and Learning Style

Personality type and *psychological type* are interchangeable terms in this context. The preferred term is *psychological type*; it encompasses most learning style differences and is also correlated with several of the multiple intelligences (Meisgeier et al., 1996). Schools seldom consider psychological type differences in either teachers or students in selecting curriculum or behavioral management strategies, yet type preferences drive both teacher and student behaviors in significant ways. Normal behavioral expressions of personality by either teachers or students may be ignored or punished or may be viewed as hostile.

Although the behavior differences produced by the various psychological types present themselves every day in every classroom, schools are often not aware of the tremendous variance that exists or why it should be considered in the teaching and learning equation. Schools may exhibit a cursory acknowledgment of basic auditory, visual, and tactile differences but seldom do much with that knowledge. Observations throughout the nation indicate that many schools continue to employ the traditional "stand and deliver" model of teaching, in which the teacher presents information to an entire class of students with little adaptation to individual needs and differences. In this model, few students are challenged; many are underchallenged and many are overchallenged. The attitudes of students toward school, learning, success, and failure in this kind of setting can be negative and are usually very predictable.

In the day-to-day business of the classroom, teachers do not acknowledge or make modifications for student differences in concrete versus abstract perception or in global versus sequential thinking. They may not recognize the need in some students for social interaction and the need in others for quiet reflection. Classrooms do not always accommodate the factors that influence the ways students make judgments and decisions. Teachers may not differentiate between a student's preference for order and closure or spontaneity and change. Yet these personality differences are well researched among adults and are found in students and teachers. All have been identified as psychological type differences.

Multiple Intelligences, defined later in this chapter, are also helpful in identifying differences. Understanding the relation of Multiple Intelligences to individual learning styles and psychological type differences adds to an understanding of how students learn.

Goodness of Fit

Traditionally, beginning teachers either replicate the way they were taught as students, or they teach the way their supervising teacher modeled while they were student teaching. Student teachers are under considerable pressure to employ the methods and strategies of the supervising teacher and the policies of the particular school. In either case, the modeled behavior often compromises what they may have learned in college education courses. As teachers gain experience, they begin to move past these tendencies and make organizational and curricular changes in the classroom. At that point, the changes teachers make are likely to reflect their own personalities and learning style preferences rather than the needs of particular students. Their preferences for particular teaching models tend to reflect their own personalities, learning styles, interests, and intelligences rather than a rational choice of pedagogical theories. If a student has a personality profile unlike the teacher's, the "fit" is not good and gives rise to pressure points of discomfort. A good fit, or match, occurs when students and their teachers have similar preferences. A good fit can be obtained, regardless of the personality characteristics involved, if the teacher understands behavioral diversity and is willing to accommodate it. Students in a classroom with a good fit respond and interact more positively, with minimal need for discipline interventions. Conversely, discipline problems often abound where an unacknowledged mismatch exists.

Educators create a comfort zone by establishing regularities congruent with both student and teacher styles. Good teaching and good learning occur in an easy and natural way under such circumstances, and the problems that do arise usually can be addressed with standard and positive discipline practices. Theorists who espouse an ecological model of behavior stress the importance of the interaction between students and the ecosystem of which they are a part. The ecological model, milieu therapy, therapeutic environment, establishing operations, and antecedent control are examples of the importance of looking at behavior in the context in which it occurs. These approaches address behavior by manipulating the environment or antecedents so that a goodness-of-fit interaction occurs between the child and the environment. The Meisgeier model of Behavioral Diversity and Regularity Control is based on the principles of an ecological model. This model specifically calls for a goodness-of-fit interaction of classroom and school regularities with individual characteristics of personality type, learning style, special interests and abilities, and family issues. Reinforcing regularities encourage brain-friendly teaching and learning techniques. They provide choice and accommodation of differences in the classroom.

Learning Styles

Learning styles is a broad term that people define differently. It may be associated with theories such as brain-based learning, metacognition, cognitive style, and personality styles. Fisher and Fisher (1979) define learning style as "a pervasive quality in the behavior of an individual, a quality that persists though the context may change" (p. 157). Lawrence (1984) refers to "cognitive style in the sense of preferred or habitual patterns of mental functioning: information processing, formation of ideas and judgments." He indicates that students' learning styles are reflected by what they attend to and the kinds of learning tools they use or avoid. According to Lawrence, students seek out learning environments that are compatible with their cognitive styles, attitudes, and interests, and they avoid environments that are not congenial. Learning style can be measured by instruments such as the Learning Style Inventory (Dunn, Dunn, & Price, 1989) and the Murphy-Meisgeier Type Indicator for Children (Meisgeier & Murphy, 1987).

The following section focuses on learning styles as defined by Rita Dunn (1983) and Dunn and Dunn (1975, 1978). Dunn (1983) defines learning style as the way in which individuals concentrate on, absorb, and retain new information or skills. Early in her career, Rita Dunn was awarded a grant to explore innovative new methods for helping students who were failing in school. Her goal was to find the most helpful methods for students who were having learning difficulties in a regular school program. She and her staff tried to offer the richest variety of learning experiences they could assemble with the idea that the novelty and excitement of new and different experiences would engage students who had shut down in school. As one example, Dunn and her group translated the essential learning objectives identified by the state of New York into various kinds of games. They also used a variety of alternative methods to teach the objectives, and failing students were presented with choices to accomplish their individual objectives in an array of options—a "smorgasbord" of choices. Dunn's expectation was that students would come to school looking for something new and different every day. That did not turn out to be the case.

Dunn reported that the students in the project did indeed try one method after another for learning *until* they found the one that worked *for them*. The students were different from one another in the ways they were enticed into the learning process, but they were quite consistent within themselves in the choices they made. Surprised by the realization that students experimented with new and novel learning methods only until they found one that worked, Dunn began an exhaustive study of the research available at that time. It confirmed what she was seeing in her own project. Students have preferences for learning that are as fundamental as their preferences for using the right hand or the left. Compelling them to learn in ways contrary to their natural preferences led to difficulty or defeat. This same tendency occurs with behavioral diversity.

In her research, Dunn found that children had marked differences in their preferences for temperature and in the degree to which a quiet learning environment was important. Some worked well with the hubbub of life happening around them, some liked the controlled sound provided by music, and still others required silence for peak performance.

Elements of Learning Style

Twenty-one elements of learning style have been specifically identified by the Dunns, which they arranged in five strands or stimuli (Carbo, Dunn, & Dunn, 1991; Dunn & Dunn, 1978; Dunn et al., 1989).

The environmental Strand identifies preferences related to the following:
- Sound (the absence or presence of music or environmental noise)
- Light (bright or low)
- Temperature (warm or cool)
- Design (formality of the work setting)

The Emotional Strand identifies preferences related to the following:
- Motivation (causing students to engage in learning)
- Persistence (helping students to complete tasks)
- Responsibility (nurturing inner locus of control and self-starting)
- Structure (personal organizing and scheduling)

The Sociological Strand identifies the following preferences in groupings for learning:
- Colleague (friends & contemporaries)
- Self (alone)

- Pair (tutor or one learning partner)
- Team (study groups that share tasks and responsibilities)
- Authority (an "expert" or authority figure to direct)
- Varied (variety and change in groupings)

The Physical Strand describes the following preferences in bodily factors that impact learning:

- Perception (sense modality—eyes, ears, etc.)
- Intake (a need to snack while learning)
- Time (a particular time of day for learning)
- Mobility (a need to be physically active while learning)

The Psychological Strand notes the following simultaneous or successive processing:

- Analytical or global ("forests or trees")
- Cerebral preference (preference for right or left brain thinking)
- Reflective & impulsive (preferring to think before or after action)

What Rita Dunn was uncovering in her pioneering work was the magnitude of diversity in learning style present in any group of students. It became clear that the differences found among students cause them to be affected differently by classroom and school regularities. Even more important, she was learning that changing regularities—controlling them—made the difference between success and failure for her students.

Most students appear to have strong preferences, one way or the other, for some of the learning style elements Dunn identified and little preference either way for others; however when strong preferences were identified, she found it was essential to consider ways to accommodate them.

Dunn's work invariably strikes a chord in those who hear of it because we are all aware of the differences she describes. We may not have understood their importance to learning, but we have encountered the differences in people that she identified. The idea that is empowering to teachers is this: By controlling regularities identified in learning style research, a teacher may transform a student's experience in school from one of struggle to one of satisfying achievement. The relation of success in school to student behavior is apparent. Successful students feel better about themselves, have less need to break the rules, and are more apt to develop self-discipline and accept responsibility for their own learning.

Psychological Types

Over the years the authors have greeted the steady flow of information about learning style with great interest. The light shed on individual differences and upon behavioral diversity by the additional concept of psychological type is comprehensive and significant. An understanding of differences revealed by psychological type may be as fundamental as understanding brain-based learning. The idea that mismatches of teaching style and learning style create problems is well documented (Dunn & Dunn, 1975). The same principle is applicable to student-teacher mismatches resulting from psychological type differences. Much material presented in this book relates to type theory. A mismatch between student and teacher that is not accommodated accounts for many troublesome classroom discipline problems. Although no theory explains all behaviors, psychological type theory provides a rationale for understanding the behavioral diversity that sets the stage for discipline problems.

Carl Jung (1971) developed the theory of psychological type. Jung identified three of the four indexes shown in Table 3-1: Extraversion-Introversion, Sensing-Intuition, and Thinking-Feeling. His work was extended by Isabel Myers and Katharine Briggs. The mother-daughter team added the Judging-Perceiving index and provided a structure for understanding similarities and differences in human beings. Together they developed the Myers-Briggs Type Indicator®, (Myers & Myers, 1985).

TABLE 3-1. PSYCHOLOGICAL TYPE DIFFERENCES

Energy Flow	Perceiving	Deciding	Lifestyle
Extraversion **E**	Sensing **S**	Thinking **T**	Judging **J**
Introversion **I**	Intuition **N**	Feeling **F**	Perceiving **P**

One preference from each of the four indexes is identified to determine an individual's psychological type; for example, ESTJ or INFP. There are a total of 16 possible psychological type profiles. Table 3-2 gives a brief description of some of the type characteristics of each of the four pairs of preferences (Meisgeier & Meisgeier, 1987; Meisgeier, Meisgeier, & Weisenfelder, 1995; Meisgeier, Murphy, & Meisgeier, 1987).

TABLE 3-2. TYPE CHARACTERISTICS

Where the energy flows:	
Extraversion (E)	**Introversion (I)**
Extraverts focus on the outer world of action, objects, concepts, and persons. They relate to others, cooperate, are sociable, people oriented, outgoing, and respond well to peer and cross-age interaction and cooperative learning.	Introverts focus on the inner world of ideas. They are reflective, quiet, preferring independent study and projects. Interpersonal relationships tend to be fewer and have greater depth; privacy and alone time are energizing. They tend to respond

cont.

They act and speak more impulsively and are energized by intensity.	more slowly and avoid high-energy social situations.

How people perceive:

Sensing (S)	Intuition (N)
Sensing types attend to the immediate, real, and practical. Sensing types focus on factors, like data and tasks, to be sequential. They learn through repetition, handle details well, and tend to be realists. They avoid theoretical subjects and focus on practical applications.	Intuitive types focus on future possibilities. They seek a broad understanding of relationships and meaning in life experiences. They need a global, theoretical intro-duction to new material. They neglect details and factual information in favor of synthesizing old and new concepts.

How people make decisions:

Thinking (T)	Feeling (F)
Thinking types view life and learning objectively and consider causes and consequences in logical, analytical ways. They are task oriented and demanding of self and others. They suppress feelings in favor of logical analysis, and they respect competence.	Feeling types view life and learning subjectively and consider the impact of events on people and relationships. They are empathetic, require harmony, and strive to create a warm and accepting environment. Their values are important and will be defended.

How individuals prefer to live:

Judging (J)	Perceiving (P)
Judging types strive to be decisive and orderly, aiming to regulate and control events. Tasks are structured and alternatives minimized in favor of the bottom line. They dislike surprises and tend to resist change in well-established regularities.	Perceiving types are spontaneous and flexible, aiming to understand life and adapt to it. They are curious and creative problem solvers in crisis situations. Free spirits, they hate routine. They like surprises. Existing regularities are not considered sacred. Change is often welcome.

The Significance of Psychological Type Characteristics in the Classroom

Extraversion and Introversion

The differences described above touch every area of life and have a significant role in the education of children. The following examples underscore that importance:

- Extraverts learn well in interactive experiences and by being involved in activities.
- Introverts gather data during such activities, but they do their learning inside their own heads by thinking about their experiences later.

Extraverts share the progress of their learning in an open and verbal way. The teacher and everyone else probably has a good idea of what they are thinking and learning while it is actually occurring. In contrast, the conclusions drawn by Introverts may not be as evident to the teacher or anyone else by the completion of a classroom activity or even by the end of the day. Any assessment of learning during or immediately after an activity may give a less than accurate indication of the quality of learning that occurs for the Introverted student. An Extravert is actually learning, thinking, and developing ideas while speaking and interacting—*while the happening is happening.* An Introvert likes to answer when the work of thinking it all through is complete. An Extravert participates outwardly to facilitate his or her own learning, whereas Introverts wait until they have thought things through before entering the discussion. Even then, they may not say what they are thinking, depending on their comfort level, the size of the group, and other factors. Both Introverted and Extraverted preferences support excellent and valid ways to learn, but they can look quite different to a teacher or classmates.

The quiet Introvert who can be doing wonderful work internally may appear to be very intent in one situation but mildly distracted and not fully engaged in another. The Introvert may go inside his or her own head to accomplish the most creative work of the day. When asked by the teacher to recite or perform in front of the class, an Introvert may experience a degree of anxiety that seriously interferes with the quality of the performance. This method may precipitate a negative, uncooperative, or belligerent response. Measuring the quality of a performance in front of the class may not be an accurate way to assess learning for Introverted types. Written reports, tests, and one-to-one or small-group reporting may be a more appropriate way to assess the performance of Introverted types and their mastery of the material.

Extraverts prefer a high-energy-level classroom in which a dynamic sense of group is present and the intensity of interactions increases. Extraverted teachers facilitate group classroom activities by generating enthusiasm and excitement and by speaking rapidly and with intensity. Rising intensity levels alarm Introverts, who see themselves as serving the group by attempting to restore calm. An Introverted teacher may dampen the Extraverted students' energetic drive to create a high-energy learning experience. Introverted teachers may employ methods, rules, or routines that punish many normal Extraverted learning behaviors. When this type of mismatch occurs repeatedly, students who prefer Extraversion tend to feel constrained and may talk out to the class or resort to other outgoing behaviors that may be punished by the teacher.

Sensing and Intuition

Teachers who prefer Sensing work to reduce theories and broad concepts to doable rules and concrete tasks. In contrast, intuitive teachers naturally seek to expand students' grasp of reality, and so they broaden data from specifics to more global concepts. Sensing teachers and learners prefer to talk and learn about the "trees" but may have difficulty describing the "forest." Intuitive teachers and learners think and talk in terms of the "forest" but may have difficulty describing the "trees." An Intuitive teacher or learner will work toward discarding rules and facts as soon as overarching concepts can replace them. Sensing teachers and students work to set aside theory as soon as a rule can be set in place. Sensing types live in the concrete world of the here and now. Intuitive types live in an abstract world more occupied with possibilities.

The concrete and practical approach of the Sensing teacher suits a Sensing student very well. Sensing students like a realistic account of the facts of the matter. Sensing students tend to pay little attention to theory, and Sensing teachers tend to be much more practical than theoretical. In a Sensing teacher's classroom, Intuitive students may feel bombarded by facts and examples not tied together by a global theory. Intuitive students look for the integration of broad concepts with previous learning. Intuitive types are not able to make sense of facts that are not given an umbrella of theoretical coherence. Intuitive students need a global introduction and a global summary of the material that has been presented. Sensing students do not pay much attention to either one but focus on the facts themselves and their practical application. Sensing students prefer detailed and specific instructions. In contrast, Intuitive students like an assignment that allows them wide latitude and opportunities to do things "their way." Sensing students are out of their comfort zone when given broad, general directions without specifics or examples. The reactions of Intuitive students to the regularities of a Sensing type of classroom, or sensing students to the regularities of an Intuitive type of classroom, may result in frustration, withdrawal, anxiety, anger, failure, and various kinds of negative behaviors.

Thinking and Feeling

Thinking types operate in a world of profound respect for fairness, logic, and competence. To them, personal issues interfere with the flow of productivity. Thinking teachers and students strive to rid a learning task of any feeling content. They look and listen for the logic of the argument or activity. For them anything having to do with another's feelings will tend to be ignored or resisted—and punished, if necessary. Feeling students and teachers, on the other hand, cannot engage in a learning task when there is conflict or lack of harmony. Heated arguments or loud and intense contentiousness may be stimulating to thinking students, but it is upsetting and even frightening for students who prefer feeling. In an argumentative free-for-all, students who prefer Thinking may thrive, whereas students with a Feeling preference may become defended, withdraw, or focus on ways to establish a harmonious climate rather than on the content being discussed.

Feeling types scan the groups they are in to take a reading on everyone's feeling state. When signals indicate antagonism, suspicion, criticism, or hurt feelings, Feeling types will redirect their attention to reconciling the differences in the group until harmony is restored. They will resist engaging in the assigned group task until they are satisfied that conflict has been resolved.

Very little learning takes place in a classroom when students with a feeling preference experience criticism or conflict with their teachers. This emphasis on harmony makes Thinking types impatient and may increase the tension bothering the Feeling types. Awareness of this paradox improves the smooth functioning of any group that includes Feeling types, and this includes groups of teachers as well as students.

Even when task deadlines loom with urgency, a Feeling preference person will take the necessary time to address relational issues or to honor other high-priority interpersonal values. Indeed, they will sacrifice the task to the relationships. Thinking types, on the other hand, find this attitude baffling and will more readily sacrifice the relationships to the task and the goal. They appear at times to ride roughshod over the Feelings and sensibilities of others when the pressures of the task begin to build. Most human endeavors are best served by a healthy representation of both groups.

An exception to the Feeling type's aversion to conflict can arise when their values are challenged. The fundamental values they hold are largely unspoken forces that govern their choices and drive their lives and behavior without much outward discussion. Conflict in a group arises when unspoken fundamental values are stepped on or challenged or when they differ sharply from those held by others. Feeling types are fervent in their commitment to their values; when a deeply held value is challenged, they become fierce defenders of their views.

Judging and Perceiving

Both Judging and Perceiving students encounter difficulties in a class with teachers of the opposite preference. Teachers with a Judging preference strive for order and feel supported by clearly stated and firmly enforced rules. Students with a Perceiving preference tend to resist rigid structure and numerous rules. Students with a strong preference for Perceiving may shift their focus from the assignment to looking for ways to "beat the system" or "get around the rules" when the sense of constraint becomes too strong. Such behaviors prove as punishing to a teacher as his or her efforts at discipline may prove punishing to the student. Judging types are supported by clearly defined schedules and strive for early closure to clean up all the loose ends that may exist. Perceiving types prefer situations in which options are open and feel a sense of loss when forced to make a choice and sacrifice the options not chosen.

The very idea of settling at last on the topic for a paper or project produces different responses in Judging and Perceiving types. Judging types are uneasy until things are decided and concluded; Perceiving types are uneasy after the decision is made and other options are closed. These differences do not necessarily represent a character defect or a disciplinary problem. They are type-related differences.

In summary, a classroom is a more user-friendly place when both student and teacher understand and honor the differences present between them. The explanations above highlight the importance for teachers and schools of developing the power to accommodate psychological type differences in the classroom. When this is done, children are free to address the learning tasks that are unique to each personality type and develop personal responsibility and respectful social behaviors. A wide variety of personality factors come together to form a child's preferred learning style. Psychological type indicators for both adults and children provide one very helpful system for identifying learning style differences in ways that allow for accommodations in school.

Two psychological instruments—the Myers-Briggs Type Indicator[®1] (MBTI) (Briggs & Myers, 1987), used for adults, and the Murphy-Meisgeier Type Indicator for Children (MMTIC) (Meisgeier & Murphy, 1987)—identify individual preferences on each of the four psychological type preference scales just described. The MMTIC also includes for each set of preferences a "U-band" on each side of the mean designed to allow for undetermined preferences. Everyone is a mixture of all eight preferences, but the four strongest preferences determine a person's type. There are 16 possible combinations of the eight preferences measured by the indicators.

Psychological Type and Discipline

Discipline problems occur when strong but contrasting preferences are present between teacher and student. A Sensing-Judging combination tends to be more prevalent among teachers than in the population at large. Sensing-Judging combinations are predominant among public school teachers at every level. According to a national data base teachers with each of the eight psychological types that include Judging are represented in the teaching profession at or above the frequency with which they occur in the population at large. All of the eight perceiving types are underrepresented in teaching, with the exception of ENTPs, who are present as 4% of the population and 4% of teachers. A further indication of the prevalence of the judging preference in public education was found in a recent study of school board members, showing that nearly 80% had a Judging preference (Isenberg & Cassel, 2000).

Understanding the different priorities and attitudes of psychological types is of benefit in areas such as team building in business, or resolution of conflicts in family counseling. This understanding is also helpful in the selection, planning, and execution of instructional strategies and behavior management practices in schools. It is important to stress that the goal is not to eliminate all nonpreferred learning experiences. That would not be possible and is probably not even desirable. Rather, the goal is to ensure that enough accommodation of behavioral diversity (psychological type) is made for each child to be successful. Children can also be taught to "type adapt" (Meisgeier et al., 1995) and learn to be more accommodating to teachers, other adults, and peers who are of a dissimilar type. They can learn the give and take of interacting in positive and constructive ways with those who are different.

Is it realistic, feasible, or appropriate to punish a child for reacting to a negative environment in which the regularities establish conditions that are stacked against them? Is it appropriate to use strong behavioral measures to force children to comply with methods, routines, or teacher–pupil interactions that are antithetical to their fundamental learning style? To do so requires very hard work, offers limited hope of success, and may be unethical. Instead of employing stronger measures to make individual students conform to nonsupportive regularities that interfere with learning and social interaction, we suggest changing regularities to accommodate the psychological type of the child.

Psychological Type Combinations

The eight type preferences are combined to form four indexes (EI, SN, TF, JP). When they are combined, they form the 16 individual psychological types that are listed in Table 3-3.

TABLE 3-3. THE 16 PSYCHOLOGICAL TYPES

ISTJ	ISFJ	INFJ	INTJ
ISTP	ISFP	INFP	INTP
ESTP	ESFP	ENFP	ENTP
ESTJ	ESFJ	ENFJ	ENTJ

By gathering the 16 possible types into groups that have two preferences in common, the number of differences being studied and accommodated can be reduced from 16 to 4. For example, the combinations that include SJ will be contained in the four type profiles ESTJ, ESFJ, ISTJ, ISFJ. Researchers may select any pair of preferences to study different aspects of type, but teachers normally begin to accommodate different types by reducing the number of variations they attempt to accommodate in their classrooms from 16 to 4. They may accommodate other preferences over time as they grow in their understanding of type differences and the strategies that are useful in working with them.

Temperament. When planning lessons, teachers may find it useful to look at combinations of personality preferences. Temperament theory (Table 3-4) reduces the number of possible personality groupings from 16 to 4. David Keirsey and Marilyn Bates (1978) and Keirsey (1998) identify the four temperament groups as SJ, SP, NT, and NF.

TABLE 3-4. TEMPERAMENT GROUPS

SJ	Sensing Judging	Stabilizers, Guardians (ESTJ, ESFJ, ISTJ, ISFJ)
		Responsible, dependable, dutiful
SP	Sensing Perceiving	Artisans (ESTP, ESFP, ISTP, ISFP)
		Performer, adventurer, playful
NT	Intuitive Thinking	Innovators, Rationals (ENTJ, ENTP, INTJ, INTP)
		Competent, objective, logical
NF	Intuitive Feeling	Idealists (ENFJ, ENFP, INFJ, INFP)
		Empathetic, subjective, harmonizing

Other combinations. Another way for teachers to plan for student differences is to look at the combinations ES (Extraverted Sensing), IS (Introverted-Sensing), EN (Extraverted-Intuitive), or IN (Introverted-Intuition). A third alternative to accommodate differences is to plan for ST (Sensing-Thinking), SF (Sensing-Feeling), NT (Intuitive-Thinking), or NF (Intuitive-Feeling) preferences.

Multiple Intelligences

Brain research establishes that multiple complex and concrete experiences are necessary for purposeful learning to occur (Caine & Caine, 1991). Our brain is organized to respond to a great variety of challenges and explore new avenues in our search for knowledge. Robert Sylwester (1995) reminds us that everything is connected to everything else and that learning does not occur in isolation in our environment or in our brain. Our brain is designed to process many distinct types of intelligences in addition to scholastic intelligence. Until recently, educators have had inflexible expectations about children who performed poorly on standardized measures of ability and intelligence. With the idea that there are many ways to know, to understand,

and to learn about life and the world, stereotypical thinking about IQ, the traditional measure of scholastic intelligence, is changing. It is no longer regarded as the defining measure of a child's potential in school or in life.

Howard Gardner (1983, 1999) has suggested that there are many forms of intelligence. While Gardner has expressed a belief that there are probably even more intelligences that he and his team have not identified, the eight "ways of knowing" he has studied correlate with functions of the brain. His conclusions are called the "Theory of Multiple Intelligences." The unique abilities associated with a particular intelligence are employed in an individualized educational program to accomplish learning objectives. Individual intelligences and the strengths they represent are recognized, enhanced, and applied to the activities of daily living in an instructional program designed to serve all children well. Multiple Intelligences provide useful ways to help children understand differences in themselves and others. They help children to grow in their respect for one another and strengthen their ability to collaborate effectively in a group. This theory of Multiple Intelligences provides teachers with a model to guide them in developing opportunities for students to reach their potential in one or all of the eight intelligences.

The following descriptions are based primarily on David Lazear's (1991, 1999, 2000) definitions of Multiple Intelligences. For a detailed explanation of each one, refer to Howard Gardner (1983, 1999).

Verbal Linguistic Intelligence involves language and how it is produced. Membership in the human family depends largely on the ability to communicate. Communication results from the ability to produce language, the function of Linguistic Intelligence. Language is the basis of oral and written expression. From their earliest words spoken as young babies, children are involved in the work of developing and using their Linguistic Intelligence. Authors, playwrights, poets, public speakers, comedians, and news and media figures have highly developed verbal and Linguistic Intelligence. As students address tasks related to metaphors, similes, grammar, abstract reasoning, conceptual patterning, and symbolic thinking, they are working in the realm of Linguistic Intelligence. This wonderful intelligence enables people of every age to enjoy reading and writing and talking.

Logical-Mathematical Intelligence is employed in what is called "scientific thinking." It is involved in both inductive and deductive reasoning. The ability to recognize patterns, perceive relationships, grasp such abstract concepts as geometric shapes and numbers, and synthesize abstract pieces of information all represent Logical-Mathematical Intelligence at work. Bankers, accountants, computer programmers, and mathematicians all utilize this intelligence. Traditional testing programs typically measure this intelligence.

Spatial Intelligence expresses itself through the beauty of the visual arts. Painters and photographers rely heavily on Spatial Intelligence. Architecture, with its management and control of space, is another example of spatial Intelligence at work. The ability to perceive and interpret visual information quickly and accurately is a vital skill in many sports, which requires players to visualize the outcomes of actions taken in play rapidly and well. A ball carrier on the football field may be running while he considers throwing a ball to another player who also is running; hitting the mark when he throws requires Spatial Intelligence. Many sports skills are expressions of Spatial Intelligence. Special giftedness in this intelligence is also present in engineers, sculptors, graphic designers, pilots and dentists.

Bodily-Kinesthetic Intelligence is expressed through the use of the body. Both fine motor and gross motor activities employ this intelligence. Working skillfully with objects of any kind utilizes Bodily-Kinesthetic Intelligence. It is seen in the work of artisans as they wield their tools and handle their materials. Using the body as a means of expression and communication employs this intelligence in nonverbal ways. Bodily-Kinesthetic Intelligence encompasses both the movement itself and the physical dexterity required for performance or production of objects. Teachers who find themselves having to break up a fist fight are witnesses to an example of a Bodily-Kinesthetic dialogue. The fight constitutes a contest between two individuals taking place in the arena of bodily-kinesthetic intelligence. A fight demonstrates vigorous physical effort and specific bodily skills. It uses Bodily-Kinesthetic Intelligence to express feelings and exchange information and opinions. Dancers, actors, acrobats, and athletes possess a high degree of Bodily-Kinesthetic Intelligence.

Musical Intelligence is particularly interesting because its power and influence go largely unnoticed in the busy world of daily commerce. Few of us pause to realize that every presentation on radio and television is embedded in music. Stores influence the pace of their shoppers by playing brisk music when traffic is heavy and leisurely music when it is light. Virtually every kind of business and office setting, down to and including elevators, creates a controlled background of music designed to improve morale and increase efficiency. Music influences the climate in which work is done, business is transacted, and life is lived in ways that are powerful and yet subliminal. The recognition of rhythmic and tonal patterns, sensitivity to sounds from the environment, and variations in the human voice are processed through Musical Intelligence. Since much of the affective content of speech is communicated through tonal differences and inflection, a large part of the data received and processed depends on this intelligence working with verbal and linguistic functions. The singsong rhymes children use to memorize the alphabet demonstrate one role of this intelligence in learning. Experiments in the use of music to teach foreign languages are having a profound effect. In recent years an array of methods have been developed that use music as an adjunct to learning in the classroom, but music may still be underutilized. Researchers in the field of Multiple Intelligences suggest that, of all forms of intelligence, Musical Intelligence produces the most consciousness-altering effect in the brain. Instrumental musicians, composers, and singers demonstrate this intelligence. Musical Intelligence is one of the earliest intelligences to emerge.

Interpersonal Intelligence describes the ability to interact with another individual or with a group. All of society's collegial and collaborative efforts are expressions of Interpersonal Intelligence in action. Satisfying family life and friendships rely on this intelligence for their success. It includes the ability to communicate with and relate to others. Sensitivity to the nuances and currents of thought and feeling involved in human interactions is an indication of Interpersonal Intelligence at work. Empathy and sensitivity to the moods and needs of others engage Interpersonal Intelligence. The ability to discern the underlying motives in the actions of others is another aspect of this intelligence. Psychiatrists, psychologists, and counselors demonstrate this intelligence, and wise parenting and teaching require its constant use.

Intrapersonal Intelligence is the form of intelligence that enables an individual to be self-aware. Recognition of the emotional, intellectual, spiritual, and motivational aspects of one's inner self demonstrates intrapersonal intelligence. The sense of being alive and the conscious conduct of one's inner life involve the use of one's Intrapersonal Intelligence. It includes self-examination and the development of self-responsibility as well as setting goals, activating one's will, and planning for the future. Any inner motivation strong enough to compel behavior—such as that seen in students who are "self-starters"—is an expression of Intrapersonal Intelligence. Individuals who are described as "centered" within themselves demonstrate Intrapersonal Intelligence. The lack of Intrapersonal Intelligence is evident in individuals who have virtually no self-awareness, little self-control, and little self-responsibility. Introspection activates and develops this intelligence.

Naturalist Intelligence is referred to as a "nature-smart" kind of ability. In an interview with Howard Gardner conducted by Ronnie Durie (1998), the editor of *Mind Shift Connection*, Gardner said, "The core of the Naturalist Intelligence is the human ability to recognize plants, animals, and other parts of the natural environment, like clouds or rocks" (p. 1). In an earlier interview with Kathy Checkley (1997), Gardner said the following:

> Naturalist Intelligence designates the human ability to discriminate among living things. . . . This ability was clearly of value in our evolutionary past as hunters, gatherers, and farmers; it continues to be central in such roles as botanist or chef. I also speculate that much of our consumer society exploits the Naturalist Intelligences, which can be mobilized in the discrimination among cars, sneakers, kinds of makeup, and the like. The kind of pattern recognition valued in certain of the sciences may also draw upon Naturalist Intelligence. (p. 12)

Naturalist Intelligence is related to the ability to categorize, classify, and explain the things encountered in the world of nature. Ranchers, farmers, hunters, gardeners, and animal handlers may exhibit this intelligence. Naturalist intelligence adds a dimension that is unique but is apparent in people everywhere.

Other Intelligences are being considered and explored. For example, Wilson (1998) identifies *Cosmic Intelligence* as

> the recognition and ability to discern subtle and overt patterns in the activity of natural elements, other species, and humans. Cosmic Intelligence would also include the ability to recognize universal connections and patterns. Or it might include an acute awareness of universal changes and the possibility of spiritual or cosmic links in which one is both aware and respectful of the interconnectedness of all life forces. (p. 2)

Other intelligences that Gardner (1999) is investigating include *Spiritual Intelligence*, *Existential Intelligence*, and *Moral Intelligence*. Gardner believes:

> there may be an Existential Intelligence that refers to the human inclination to ask very basic questions about existence. Who are we? Where do we come from? What's it all about? Why do we die? We might say that Existential Intelligence allows us to know the invisible, outside world. (Checkley 1997, p. 9)

Armstrong (1994) explains that each intelligence has been valued across time and cultures. Each has a historical context; certain intelligences may have been more important in certain times in history. The intelligences have roots embedded in the history of human development. Each intelligence is located in a section of our brain and can work in isolation. A person who has had stroke damage in the brain's language section may not be able to talk but be able to sing. Each intelligence can be symbolized. Linguistic Intelligence has a number of spoken and written languages. Spatial Intelligence includes graphic language used by architects. Musical Intelligence has a scale of notes as its symbols.

Lazear (1999) has identified four stages of teaching as a guide for using multiple intelligences in the classroom: (a) awakening the intelligence, (b) amplifying the intelligence, (c) teaching for or with the intelligence, and (d) transferring the intelligence. The senses are activated in the awakening stage. How intelligences work and can be used is addressed in the amplifying stage. Increasing knowledge and accessing and demonstrating learning is the teaching stage. Integrating the intelligences into the daily lives of students is the transferring stage.

In response to a question about his hope for the Multiple Intelligences movement in education, Gardner has expressed the idea that Multiple Intelligences would become a powerful tool for two educational ends (Durie, 1998, p. 2):

1. To support educational programs that will enable children to realize a desired end state (e.g., musician, scientist, civic-minded person)

2. To help teachers reach more children who are trying to understand important theories and concepts in the disciplines

The educational ends mentioned by Gardner are similar to those discussed previously regarding psychological types and learning styles. When children are measured by their proficiency in scholastic intelligence—only one of many possible intelligences—then some children who may rank very high in other intelligences will be labeled as having low intelligence across the board.

Education has come a long way since the Stanford–Binet intelligence test caused immigrants to be deported because their IQ test results labeled them as "feeble-minded morons." The intent of the original intelligence test was to separate "the wheat from the chaff," and it has consequently segregated many minority children in institutions and, more recently, in special education. Before discussing intelligence, we need to ask, "Who was the greater genius, Beethoven or Einstein? Mother Teresa or Christopher Columbus? Darwin or Picasso?" They each excelled in their own intelligence.

Comparison of Psychological Types, Learning Styles, and Multiple Intelligences

Gardner (1999) views the theory of Multiple Intelligences as being different from the theories of psychological types and learning styles, but many of the intelligences appear to be related to the psychological type preferences. Meisgeier et al., (1996) discovered a correlation between certain multiple intelligences and psychological types. These are shown in Table 3-5.

TABLE 3-5. SIGNIFICANT CORRELATIONS OF THE MURPHY-MEISGEIER TYPE INDICATOR FOR CHILDREN (MMTIC) AND THE TEELE INVENTORY OF MULTIPLE INTELLIGENCES (TIMI) WITH 161 SECONDARY STUDENTS

MMTIC	TIMI
Extraversion	Bodily-Kinesthetic
Perceiving	Bodily-Kinesthetic
Sensing	Logical-Mathematical
Judging	Logical-Mathematical
Thinking	Logical-Mathematical
Extraversion	Interpersonal
Perceiving	Interpersonal
Feeling	Interpersonal
Introversion	Intrapersonal

Fourqurean, Meisgeier, and Swank (1990) also found significant correlations between Dunn and Dunn's (1975, 1978) learning styles elements and psychological type. Lawrence (1984) reviewed studies linking MBTI preferences and various measures of learning style, producing the following results:

Extraversion: activity level, talkativeness, and a carefree attitude

Introversion: need for solitude

Sensing: need for order, field dependence, and step-by-step procedures

Intuition: autonomy, field independence, imagination, theoretical orientation

Thinking: endurance, logical organization

Feeling: need for affiliation, nurturance, social interests

Judging: order, formalized instruction

Perceiving: change, autonomy, impulsiveness

The results of an analysis of the Dunn Learning Style Inventory (DLSI), and the MMTIC by Fourqurean, Meisgeier, and Swank indicate that they can be collapsed into three bipolar dimensions, represented essentially by the MMTIC's Extraversion-Introversion index, the Sensing-Intuition index, and the Judging-Perceiving index. The E-I and J-P dimensions of the MMTIC relate to specific learning preferences measured by the DLSI and the RSLSI. The MMTIC E-I and J-P indexes may be seen as useful measures of learning style. In this study, two bipolar learning preferences, characterized by a "reflective learner–active learner" dimension and a "structured motivated–unstructured casual" dimension, were identified. Ferrell's (1983) factor analysis of the Kolb Learning Style Inventory (1976) supports a passive-active learner dimension and a structured motivated–unstructured casual dimension. Holland (1982) also cites the need for structure as a crucial element of learning style for some students. The above dimensions suggest a need for some students to learn independently and by reflection while others need to work collaboratively and interact during the learning process. A third group requires a realistic, practical, and concrete approach in contrast to those who prefer a global, theoretical presentation. Table 3-6 illustrates these relationships.

TABLE 3-6. THREE BIPOLAR PREFERENCES OF LEARNING STYLE

Factor 1	Active Learner (Extraversion)	Reflective Learner (Introversion)
Factor 2	Structured Motivated (Judging)	Unstructured Casual (Perceiving)
Factor 3	Concrete Realistic (Sensing)	Global Imaginative (Intuition)

The application of psychological type theory may be a practical and powerful way to provide a structure for basic school and classroom change and reform. The applications of psychological type theory along with multiple intelligences and learning styles provide a powerful rationale for basic school reform. Applications of these theories along with recent brain research can become a powerful stimulus for changing or establishing new regularities that support student learning and user-friendly classrooms.

Examining a Mismatch of Psychological Types

José: A Case History

The following is an example of what we call the *cycle of regularities*. The teacher establishes regularities based on his or her psychological type preferences. Students are required to operate within the context of the teacher-determined regularities whether or not they are compatible with each student's psychological type preferences. The students respond in ways consistent with their own type profile, which, when there is a mismatch, has the potential to produce problem behavior.

José was a fourth-grade student who had a good school record in both academics and behavior until he was put into a classroom with Miss Rose, a beginning teacher. Very soon he became a behavior problem. He stopped doing his homework, he didn't want to go to school, and he was late for class. He refused to begin his class work and would not answer the teacher. In a short time, he began to withdraw and become aggressive with other students when they interacted with him. José's parents were troubled by what was happening. They contacted a counselor, and a behavioral consultant was assigned to them.

Initially a behavioral plan was developed that included opportunities for José to earn points for turning in homework and completed class work. Scolding and fault finding were to be reduced to a minimum. Rewards were offered that could be earned for good behavior at school and at home and were lost when José did not conform to the teacher's expectations. José made no effort to earn the rewards. The plan failed and his behavior grew worse.

The consultant and José's teacher continued to work together on José's problem. They explored ideas for enlarging the reward menu and for removing more or different privileges at home and at school. Their efforts produced no change in José's attitude or behavior. Their focus was on behavior management strategies only. The methods they employed to deal with José were designed to change his behavior in isolation from his school experience as a whole. When José's behavior did not improve, it became clear that the teacher and consultant had not considered the regularities or antecedents that might be causing José's unacceptable behavior.

A second behavioral analysis was done. This time it included a review of the classroom regularities and the way they were operating as antecedents to José's misbehavior. The assessment identified regularities that needed to be altered to accommodate both José's learning style and his personality type. The teacher completed the MBTI and José completed the MMTIC.

Differences were identified in the teaching style of Miss Rose and the learning style of José. For example, José was found to be a reflective child. He needed a period of time to observe an activity and consider the nature of his participation in it before being compelled to perform. When wait time was not provided, José became embarrassed and resistant, then belligerent, and finally totally noncompliant. A substantial number of children (40%-50%) possess José's reflective personality characteristics. For them, any demand to perform without allowing the required time for reflection—called "wait time"—is stressful. Students with a preference for Introversion require a period of time to gather their thoughts and establish a strategy for what they are about to do. Most of them want to think their way through to the conclusion of any problem before undertaking it. Other children may be very satisfied allowing the process to unfold as they go along, but José was not like that. He grew sullen and stubborn if pushed to do something before he felt ready. He also was uncomfortable with conflict. His Introverted Intuitive Feeling Perceiving (INFP) type was completely opposite to Miss Rose's Extroverted Sensing Thinking Judging (ESTJ) type.

Miss Rose was an efficient and well-organized teacher. She had a rather high-pitched, full-voiced, and rapid-fire manner of speaking. Things moved along briskly in her classroom, and many of the children enjoyed the bright and interesting pace she maintained in her presentations. She worked hard to hold the students' attention, so when she asked one of them a question and did not get a prompt and enthusiastic response, she felt she was failing in her goal of keeping the classroom lively and fast moving. She also felt that any student who failed to respond energetically and immediately was not paying full attention. Her own outgoing personality made it difficult for her to understand that José's reflective style of response was not an indication that he was less than completely on-task. While he was carefully considering his answer, he looked like he had disappeared somewhere inside his own head. His face would grow still and he would be silent for a number of seconds. When he began to speak, his words were slow and deliberate. All of that meant that José was making a special effort to answer well, but to Miss Rose it spelled uninterest and inattention.

In reality, José's outward behavior when he was asked a question masked a quick-moving mind and complete concentration on the subject at hand, so it was very hurtful and punishing to him when his slow-moving answers were curtly interrupted with a clear attitude of censure and his question was offered to another student to answer. He felt he was not given a chance and that he was unfairly punished and embarrassed in front of his friends. He believed that they would view him as failing to measure up and, to a large extent, he was right. The sense of shame this perception of failure produced in José prompted him to act out inappropriately—in most cases to withdraw and be passive—on many occasions throughout the day. Other aspects of his personality were likewise ignored. After a time he grew so resistant to all participation in classroom activities that he virtually shut down in school.

One of the most important things to recognize about Miss Rose is that she was a very creative, hard-working teacher. She employed direct instructional methods of teaching with presentations and explanations directed to the entire class as a group. She often asked questions herself, but she was not comfortable with student-initiated questions. She was a novice in handling a class and required a great deal of preparation. It was difficult for her to consider making alterations in a classroom program that she was just learning to pull together. Her desire to maintain a relatively intense, fast-paced atmosphere in her classroom was fundamental to her teaching style, and the idea of allowing "dead air" to accommodate José's reflective learning style did not occur to her. Miss Rose was a good teacher for children who mirrored her personality type, and José was a good learner for teachers who understood, mirrored, or accommodated his personality type. It just happened that the mismatch between them resulted in a deadlock.

With experienced teachers many accommodations occur routinely and quickly. Sometimes they require major effort, and sometimes they just never happen. Even when counselors or school consultants strongly recommend changing certain regularities or antecedents, change may not occur for many reasons. A student may become a serious behavior problem as a result.

In José's case, the teacher resisted making any of the suggested changes in her routines, in the way she presented information, or in the way she organized the class for instruction, and she expected José to participate in classroom activities without allowing for the wait time an introverted child requires. The consultant did persuade the teacher to reward José for turning in homework and completed class work by using a point system. The program allowed José to trade in points earned for free time to read. However José never earned quite enough points to receive free time, and his behavior continued to deteriorate.

The consultant believed that over time José's teacher would try some additional modifications. She informed his parents, however, that further modifications would require much effort, an extended period of time, and special training for the teacher. Meanwhile, José's behavior and attitude were deteriorating, and it began to seem possible that a whole year might be lost before the necessary changes occurred.

José's parents were familiar with personality differences and the theory of psychological type. They had some experience in dealing with strong psychological type differences in their own family. They noticed the strong type differences between José and his teacher and understood the problems those differences could cause. There were additional personality type issues that went beyond the issue of Extraversion and Introversion. José had a preference for a flexible, global Intuitive ways of taking in information. Miss Rose presented information in sequential, factual, practical ways. When it became apparent that José's teacher was unable or unwilling to consider making changes, the parents urged immediate action. They requested that he be placed with another teacher without waiting for an extended period of time during which José's negative attitude might harden against the school and perhaps have long-lasting effects.

The request to transfer José to another class was supported by the counselor, the consultant, Miss Rose, and eventually the assistant principal. At first the principal refused. The reasons she gave for her refusal were familiar: The schedule would have to be changed and it would set a precedent. Other parents would pressure her to have their children moved to their favorite teachers; therefore, policy prohibited it. She believed that no situation is ever perfect and that children must learn to cope with reality. She was concerned that the change might make José's teacher feel that she had failed with José, and she had observed Miss Rose's success with other children and believed her to be a good teacher. She believed that José's parents didn't have enough facts to make a clear judgment.

After an informal meeting of the parents with the superintendent of schools, the principal changed her mind. José was moved into the classroom of a more experienced teacher, one whose personality type more nearly mirrored his own. The new teacher was more flexible and made a special effort to make accommodations in her plans, organization, and discipline methods as needed for José. Within 3 weeks, there were remarkable, visible changes in José's behavior, and soon after his behavior was back to normal. In a short time, his parents reported that he was "back to his old self" at home as well.

Once José was comfortably settled with his new teacher, the counselor met with him several times and gave him the results of the MMTIC. She helped him to understand his own psychological type and how it affected his learning style. She explained that he would always find that his personality preferences differed in some ways from his classmates and teachers. Using information she had about Miss Rose, the counselor pointed out many of the ways in which José and his former teacher were dissimilar in personality characteristics. In particular, they discussed the contrasts in the highly energetic, intense, enthusiastic, rapid-fire manner of speaking characterizing Miss Rose's teaching style, which was upsetting, intrusive, and punishing to José, and the more reflective, controlled, and understated manner of his new teacher with whom he was more comfortable. The counselor helped José to understand ways that he could adapt to the rules, routines, teaching methods, and the curriculum of teachers whose personalities were unlike his own. He learned that while he was different, it is normal and OK to be different.

Discipline Problems Embedded in School Life

José's problem was not simply a refusal to complete his homework assignment or engage in the assigned classroom tasks. Those issues were problems embedded in the total picture of José's life in Miss Rose's classroom. The differences between Miss Rose and José's new teacher went far beyond the manner in which they assigned homework or even the way they handled a student who rebelled against following directions. The conditions necessary for glowing success for some students were present in Miss Rose's class, but they were not present for José. The conditions for success or failure were related to the fundamental psychological mismatch between José and Miss Rose.

Psychological type differences influenced a whole range of regularities and antecedent conditions that created a mismatch between José's learning style and Miss Rose's teaching style and classroom norms. They will be explored in depth in chapter 8. For now, it is important to understand that regularities must complement and support the learning styles and psychological type patterns of individual students in every classroom. Awareness of personality type differences helps to establish a healthy classroom environment in which good discipline and behavior management usually can be established with few problems.

Discipline problems will not end by simply removing a student and placing him or her with another teacher. Problems with other children will arise to take the place of a child who is moved to another classroom. Teachers should have an understanding and acceptance of individual differences in students and a willingness to change regularities to accommodate their students. A knowledge of individual differences and a repertoire of techniques to deal with them are essential if long-term solutions for discipline problems are to be found. Psychological type in teachers can be identified by the MBTI; in children, the MMTIC may be used. This is a good place to begin planning for instruction in any classroom. Many teachers respond to type theory and learning style differences without formal measurement or identification and enjoy the challenge of developing accommodations that honor the behavioral diversity present in their classrooms.

Interaction of Regularities, Type, and Discipline

Simple factors in a classroom that we all may take for granted, such as the arrangement of chairs or desks in neat rows, are regularities that are rewarding to some children because they contribute to their comfort zone. They are punishing to other students because they are made uncomfortable by rigid structure and lack of movement. Almost everything in a classroom can be expected to enhance the school experience for some children and detract from it for others.

Teachers tend to consider factors that are the most fundamental to their own comfort zones as universal reality or a kind of ultimate truth. It is natural for a teacher to believe that his or her own learning preferences—the kinds of things that best support the teacher's own learning—will support learning for every student as well. Unconsciously a teacher's own preferences shape the classroom regularities that structure their teaching. The importance of those regularities as part of a good learning environment is so taken for granted that they become invisible as regularities that can be changed. Once understood, the differences between student preferences and classroom regularities may be relatively easy to modify, but until insight is gained, the power they exert remains a strong force in a student's life, and little change is possible.

A student may have a strong learning style need to spread out a project informally on the floor, and though that student may be acutely uncomfortable sitting in a straight row on a straight chair, the student's discomfort may be misunderstood. If a rule for the class requires all feet on the floor and every seat in a seat, a child who needs more flexible space or movement may come to be viewed as a discipline problem. Often such students shame themselves with self-accusations of laziness or some other idea with which they have explained their own out-of-step responses to themselves. Students themselves may not feel justified in having preferences that differ from classroom norms until they are taught to understand behavioral diversity and learn about their own psychological type. The self-perception that something is wrong with them can upset a student enough to interfere with normal learning—and certainly enough to spawn behavior problems. When students understand the psychological type underpinnings of classroom antecedents such as rules, teacher's type preferences, and classroom routines, they can be expected to adapt more readily to those that would normally grate on them or elicit a negative response. This is especially true when there is an avenue of appeal or negotiation open to a student when specific problems arise.

Each of the three approaches to identifying behavioral diversity described in this chapter—Psychological Types, Learning Styles, and Multiple Intelligences—provides strong support for the recognition of individual differences in the classroom. The differences in interests and abilities present in a learner require differences in the methodologies used by the teacher. In every instance in which a match can be achieved, or the disparity reduced, between the teaching style and the student's preferred style of learning, the potential for success in both teaching and learning improves. There is no single factor that contributes more to the probability that a student will behave well in school than engagement in interesting learning and social experiences that lead to academic success. There is no single factor that more accurately predicts that a student will misbehave than boredom, frustration, and academic failure.

Regularities that encourage, establish, and promote positive reinforcement, good interpersonal relations, the use of proactive strategies, logical consequences, and alternatives to punishment that reinforce success are discussed in later chapters.

Summary

Educational researchers have long recognized the importance of implementing teaching and learning strategies that accommodate individual differences and unique needs of children. In recent years, information and research about psychological types, learning styles, and special interests and abilities have supported the rationale for individualized, personalized, differentiated curriculum and teaching strategies. Brain research confirms the validity of educational efforts that are personalized and individualized. According to Diamond & Hopson (1998), this information does the following:

- Supports the concept of "learning by doing"
- Recognizes the importance of a healthy emotional and social climate free of undue stress
- Encourages social interaction and collaboration in the learning process
- Provides challenges that are appropriate to each child's level of understanding and performance
- Provides opportunities for education and development of the whole child—socially, emotionally, physically, intellectually, and aesthetically
- Involves students as active and responsible learners

The traditional "one size fits all" approach to education cannot effectively address these findings. The traditional classroom does not accommodate the many differences of children found in every class. Many schools and districts persist in adopting and employing educational programs that ignore the above learning requirements. The regularities that support traditional teacher-focused, whole-class instruction should be available as an option only for those children who learn best in an authoritative, teacher-directed setting. It should not be imposed on all students as the primary instructional delivery system. According to Jensen (2000), multiple learning opportunities and making choices is compatible with healthy brain function.

It must be emphasized that knowledge of learning styles, psychological types, and multiple intelligences should not be used to label individuals but rather to understand them. Results obtained by administering any psychological instrument—including measures of type, intelligence, and style—must be used with caution. It is appropriate for teachers to consider the results of the individual measures as a guide only. There is no "best" type, learning style, or intelligence. Everyone has individual gifts.

At times everyone behaves in a manner contrary to his or her preferences. As we mature, we learn to adapt our preferences and working styles when we must to accommodate to situations outside our comfort zones. When our differences are honored some of the time, then it is easier for us to adapt the rest of the time. Knowledge and understanding of differences can help to raise self-awareness and awareness of others. Teachers who consider students' learning styles, psychological type differences, and multiple intelligences are in a better position to individualize the learning process. When this occurs and students are on-task, teachers are free to devote more time to teaching and less to managing inappropriate behavior.

Reinforcing Regularities that support individual strengths and preferred modes of learning are very different from traditional regularities that support the "one size fits all" approach to schooling. Both reinforcing and negative regularities have significant implications for behavior management in the classroom and will have an impact not only on student behavior but also on the teacher's selection and use of discipline interventions.

Activity 1: Identify Your Psychological Type

1. Obtain a copy of *Please Understand Me* by David Keirsey and Marilyn Bates, and complete the temperament sorter instrument to determine psychological type.

2. Obtain the MBTI and complete and score the instrument as directed to determine your psychological type.

3. Engage in an Internet search on "personality type" or "psychological type" and complete a given quiz to determine your personality preference.

4. Take the color code survey on line at: www. enol.com/~meridamx /color.htm.

5. Search the Web for information on an alternative personality quiz.

Conduct a self-analysis to determine whether you agree or disagree with the results.

Activity 2: Group Type Work

Once the psychological type of each individual has been determined, form type-alike groups of five to seven individuals who are either Extraverts or introverts. Each group of Extraverts and each group of Introverts will plan an enjoyable outing for the group. Have a scribe in each group jot down the day's plan.

While the groups are working, appoint an observer to notice the differences in the energy level and noise level between the Extraverts and the Introverts. Call it to the attention of the group at an appropriate time.

Give each group an opportunity to share their plans. Ask each group how they react to the plans of opposite type groups. Discuss how the type characteristics are reflected in the plans each group has devised.

Activity 3: Teaching Strategies

In groups of three, each person identifies his or her own most preferred teaching strategies.

Teaching strategy 1:

Teaching strategy 2:

Teaching strategy 3:

Consider how those strategies reflect the psychological type of the person with the type of strategy. Share conclusions with the larger group.

Activity 4: Lesson Plan

Form type-alike groups (Sensing and Intuitive) of five people each. Plan a short lesson and modify it to accommodate both sensing students and intuitive students. Discuss the strategies to be used in each lesson and how they reflect type characteristics.

Report back to the larger group. Discuss.

Original lesson:

Modified lesson:

Activity 5: Learning Style and Personality Type

Search the Web for a learning style inventory or log in at the following addresses and complete the inventory.

http://www2.ncsu.edu/unity/lockers/users/f/felder/public/ILSdir/ilsweb.html

http://www.merexcorp.com

Compare your learning style with your personality type.

My learning style is:

My personality type is:

Characteristics common to my learning style and personality type are:

Activity 6: Multiple Intelligences

Search the Web for a multiple intelligence test for adults.

Complete the inventory in Thomas Armstrong's book, *Multiple Intelligences in the Classroom.*

Compare your learning style, personality type, and multiple intelligence characteristics.

My learning style is:

_____

_____

My personality type is:

_____

_____

My strongest intelligence(s) is/are:

_____

_____

Characteristics common to my learning style, personality type, and strongest intelligence(s) are:

_____

_____

References

Armstrong, T. (1994). *Multiple intelligences in the classroom.* Alexandria, VA: Association for Supervision and Curriculum Development.

Briggs, K., & Myers, I. (1987). *The Myers-Brigg Type Indicator.* Palo Alto, CA: Consulting Psychologists Press.

Caine, R., & Caine, G. (1991). *Teaching and the human brain.* Alexandria, VA: Association for Supervision and Curriculum Development.

Carbo, M., Dunn, R., & Dunn, K. (1991). *Teaching students to read through their individual learning styles.* Needham Heights, MA: Allyn & Bacon.

Checkley, K. (1997). The first seven . . . and the eighth: A conversation with Howard Gardner. *Educational Leadership 55* (1), 8–13.

Diamond, M., & Hopson, J. (1998). *Magic trees of the mind: How to nurture your child's intelligence, creativity, and healthy emotions from birth through adolescence.* New York: Penguin Putnam.

Dunn, R. (1983). Learning style and its relation to exceptionality at both ends of the spectrum. *Exceptional Children 49* (6), 469–506.

Dunn, R. (1990). Rita Dunn answers question on learning styles. *Educational Leadership. 48* (2), 15–19.

Dunn, R., & Dunn, K. (1975). *Educator's self-teaching guide to individualizing instructional programs.* West Nyack, NY: Parker.

Dunn, R., & Dunn, K. (1978). *Teaching students through their individual learning styles.* Reston, VA: Reston.

Dunn, R., Dunn, K., & Price, G. E. (1989). *Learning Style Inventory.* Lawrence, KS: Price Systems.

Durie, R. (1998). An interview with Howard Gardner. *Mind Shift Connection.*

Ferrell, B. (1983). A factor analytic comparison of four learning-styles instruments. *Journal of Educational Psychology 75* (1), 33–39.

Fisher, B., & Fisher, L. (1979). Styles in teaching and learning. *Educational Leadership 36* (4), 235–254.

Fourqurean, J., Meisgeier, C., & Swank, P. (1990). The link between learning style and Jungian psychological type: A finding of two bipolar preference dimensions. *Journal of Experimental Education 58* (3), 225–237.

Gardner, H. (1983). *Frames of mind: The theory of multiple intelligences.* New York: Basic Books.

Gardner, H. (1999). *Intelligence reframed: Multiple intelligences for the 21st century.* New York: Basic Books.

Goleman, D. (1995). *Emotional intelligence: Why it can matter more than IQ.* New York: Bantam.

Holland, R. (1982). Learner characteristics and learner performance: Implications for instructional placement decisions. *Journal of Special Education 16* (1), 9–20.

Isenberg, J., & Cassel, J. (2000). Using the MBTI with school boards to enhance the governance process. In J. Reid, M. Fields, & S. Hencin (Eds.), *Creating collaborative learning communities: The role of type in education*. Gainesville, FL: Center for Applications of Psychological Type.

Jensen, E. (2000). *Brain-based learning*. San Diego: Brain Store.

Jung, C. (1971). *Psychological types*. New Jersey: Princeton University Press.

Keirsey, D. (1998). *Please understand me II: Temperament, character, intelligences*. Del Mar, CA: Prometheus Nemesis Books.

Keirsey, D., & Bates, M., (1978). *Please understand me*. Del Mar, CA: Prometheus Nemesis Books.

Kolb, D. (1976). *Learning style inventory: Technical manual*. Boston: McBer.

Lawrence, G. (1984). A synthesis of learning style research involving the MBTI. *Journal of Psychological Type 8*, 2–15.

Lazear, D. (1991). *Seven ways of knowing: Teaching for multiple intelligences*. Palatine, IL: Skylight Training and Publications.

Lazear, D. (1999). *Eight ways of teaching: The artistry of teaching with multiple intelligences*. Arlington Heights, IL: Skylight Training and Publications.

Lazear, D. (2000). *Pathways of learning*. Palatine, IL: Skylight Training and Publications.

Lowry, D. (1988). True colors. Corona, CA: Communications Companies International.

Meisgeier, C. (1995). *Preparing teachers to accommodate behavioral diversity: A unique perspective*. Reston, VA: Council for Exceptional Children.

Meisgeier, C., Dahl, R., & Meisgeier, C. S. (1998). A multiple intelligences/psychological type initiative to increase school performance and parent-teacher communication. In M. Fields (Ed.), *Counter attack: Rising to the challenge to education* (pp. 253-260). Gainesville, FL: Center for Applications of Psychological Type.

Meisgeier, C., Meisgeier, C. S., Dahl, R., Johnson, P., Davidson, L., Cuff, T., Rodriquez, R., Valent, E., & Johnson, N. (1996). Integration of the theories of psychological type and multiple intelligences and application to the instructional process with at-risk students. In M. Fields (Ed.), *Quality education: Evolution and revolution—The role of psychological type*. Gainesville, FL: Center for Applications of Psychological Type.

Meisgeier, C., & Meisgeier, C. S. (1987). *A parent's guide to type: Individual difference at home and in school*. Palo Alto, CA: Consulting Psychologists Press.

Meisgeier, C. & Meisgeier, C. S. (2000). Behavior management, individual differences and psychological type. In *Proceedings of the 4th biennial education conference, creating collaborative learning communities: The role of type in education*, (pp. 225–234). Gainesville, FL: Center for Applications of Psychological Type.

Meisgeier, C., Meisgeier, C. S., & Weisenfelder, C. (1995). *Exploring differences*. Houston, TX: Synergistic Education Associates.

Meisgeier, C., & Murphy, E. (1987). *Murphy-Meisgeier Type Indicator for Children*. Palo Alto, CA: Consulting Psychologists Press.

Meisgeier, C., Murphy, E., & Meisgeier, C. S. (1987). *A teacher's guide to type: A new perspective on individual differences in the classroom*. Palo Alto, CA: Consulting Psychologists Press.

Meisgeier, C., Swank, P., Richardson, R., & Meisgeier, C. S. (1994). Implications and applications of psychological type to educational reform and renewal. In M. Fields (Ed.), *Orchestrating educational change in the 90s: The role of psychological type*. Gainesville, FL: Center for Applications of Psychological Type.

Myers, I. B., & Myers, P. (1985). *Gifts differing*. Palo Alto, CA: Consulting Psychologists Press.

Rogers, J. K. (1999). *Resources in teaching: Introduction to multiple intelligence theory, naturalistic intelligence*. [On-line]. Available: http://www.harding.edu/-chr/midemo/nat.html.

Sylwester, R. (1995). *A celebration of neurons: An educator's guide to the human brain*. Alexandria, VA: Association for Supervision and Curriculum Development.

Wilson, L. (1998). The eighth intelligence: Naturalistic intelligence. [On-line]. Available: http://www.lwilson@uwsp.edu.

Wolfe, C., & Brandt, R. (1998). What do we know from brain research? *Educational Leadership 56* (3), 8–13.

Footnote

[1] Myers-Briggs Type Indicator and MBTI are registered trademarks of Consulting Psychologists Press of Palo Alto, CA.

Chapter 4

Developing Social and Emotional Competence

QUESTIONS

This chapter will help you to answer the following questions:

1. How can brain research help educators to develop behavior management strategies?

2. In what ways is emotional intelligence similar to intrapersonal intelligence and interpersonal intelligence?

3. Joey's motivation in anything is short-lived. He cannot get along with peers and adults. In which of the intelligences does Joey need strengthening? (a) Interpersonal intelligence, (b) intrapersonal intelligence, (c) both.

4. Is an understanding of child development theory necessary for generating behavior management plans?

5. Dafka always expects something in return for her services. At what stage of moral reasoning is Dafka functioning?

6. At which stage of friendship development do students begin to develop mutual understanding, support, loyalty, and problem solving? (a) Adolescence, (b) middle childhood, (c) early childhood.

7. What area of social skills deals with coping with various situations and attention to social cues?

8. How does the lack of social and emotional competence influence behavior?

9. What strategies would you use to teach social and emotional competence?

10. What would you look for in a social skills program for children or adolescents?

Overview

Educational systems place great importance and emphasis on academic accomplishments. We should value and recognize academic success, but we must also pay attention to students' emotional needs. Individuals need to develop a stable level of emotional intelligence as well as cognitive intelligence to function adequately in society. Most disruptive students are deficient in coping with their emotional responses, and in many cases their behaviors prevent them from achieving intellectually. Educators in general have assumed a behaviorist position and have given little attention to variables they cannot control. Since education is not in the business of understanding internal processes such as emotions and brain function, educators have concentrated on what is observable and quantifiable—that is, students' behaviors. This has served the profession well, and teachers have learned to be observant and to reach out to their students.

However, just observing behavior can lead to generalizations about gender and certain groups of students. It does not consider individual differences and tends to mechanize the educational process. Uniform standards of behavior are expected to be maintained at all costs. Teacher training programs generally do not include the natural sciences, cognitive psychology, or research on emotions to understand the whole child. Training programs for teachers in special education revolve around a generic type of program. The curriculum is geared to students with either moderate or severe disabilities. We cannot revert to the "factory model" of schooling in the information age. Students are presenting increasingly difficult challenges, and teachers must be educated in more areas than just education to meet these challenges.

The 1990s saw a renewed interest in brain research. This interest has filtered down to educators, who are beginning to look beyond behaviorism. Brain research is still controversial; nonetheless, it has awakened possibilities for teachers to set the stage for providing "chicken soup for the brain." Teachers can set up activities to release chemicals in the brain that will allow students to "feel good." Positive feedback is essential to combat unhealthy feelings toward oneself and others. Many students misbehave to get attention, to get even, to gain power, or because they lack the emotional maturity necessary to solve problems in a socialized manner. Teachers can provide opportunities for students to grow and mature in emotional intelligence. A large number of discipline problems can be attributed to students' lack of social and emotional competence. Students who lack these qualities experience difficulty in discrimination and generalization. They are unable to distinguish the types of behaviors that are appropriate for different times, places, persons, and situations. In addition, they are unable to maintain these skills over time and require external control to remind them to behave appropriately. Many factors are responsible for causing students to behave according to social norms. Certainly, caregivers bear a great influence on children's ability to develop emotional stability and social responsibility. However, parents and teachers frequently observe that siblings raised in similar conditions do behave differently. Parents comment, "It seems that Kendra was always an easy child, she hardly gave us any problems," or "Kim was difficult to handle the minute she was born." What other variables are therefore responsible for causing children to achieve social and emotional competence? Socioeconomic and physical conditions, gender, community expectations, peer influence, permissive or authoritarian discipline, and even birth order can impact a child's emotional state. There are no simplistic explanations; complex interactions of numerous conditions are responsible for our character development and for our behavior.

In this chapter, teachers will become familiar with the concept of emotional intelligence and the importance of social skills training. They will come to understand that social and emotional competencies are as important as cognitive competencies. Blaming and constantly punishing students for their immature and inappropriate behavior is not a viable solution. The "blame game" must stop and be replaced by more constructive action. We will present the constructs of emotional intelligence ("EQ"), and their importance as predictors of success in life and school. Educators can help students to achieve higher stages of moral growth in their developmental process. Individuals sequentially attain different levels of social and moral achievement regardless of chronological age, and their behavior will consequently reflect various proficiency levels of emotional intelligence. The lack of social and emotional competencies influences the moral development of students. Children develop emotionally, socially, and morally as a result of what they learn and experience. Numerous social skills programs are commercially available, but teachers need to understand what constitutes social and emotional competence. Teachers can incorporate an affective curriculum when they understand the areas of a social skills program; these are social cognition, social interaction, social acceptance, social insight, and social accommodation.

The Decade of the Brain

The 1990s is frequently referred as the "Decade of the Brain." During this period, government agencies, private foundations, advocacy groups, politicians, and the media pursued various avenues to raise the public's interest in brain research. Brain-based educators supported this movement because they interpreted the outcome of brain studies as progressive and constructive. Brain-compatible education strategies, such as experiential learning and thematic instruction, involve students in a global and holistic fashion. Thematic units are designed to engage students in complex activities containing several content areas. The brain-compatible learning literature addresses cognitive, emotional, and behavioral understanding related to the neurochemistry of the brain. Although brain science has a special attraction to certain educators, it has received a warning of caution from leading authorities. Joseph LeDoux (1994), an expert on the neuroscience of emotion, has cautioned educators not to misinterpret the literature on the brain and education. He warns of the dangers of taking brain research literature beyond its actual basis in science. Robert Sylwester (1995) has written extensively on how the brain affects learning. He explains that some people may misuse brain theories to support racist, sexist, and other elitist beliefs. Nonetheless, educators should be involved in learning how brain research can contribute to advance in their professional practice. Educators must explore every avenue to help students grow emotionally as well as cognitively. It is not our intention to provide detailed descriptions of brain-based learning. We will briefly summarize how the brain works in learning and examine how educators can provide activities to stimulate students' brain power and redirect students' emotions toward constructive behaviors. Further information on the brain and learning can be found in the works of Sylwester (1995), Sprenger (1999), and Caine and Caine (1994).

Learning occurs when the *neurons*, or nerve cells in our brain, develop connections and produce enriched *dendrites* (branches). Each neuron is composed of a cell body, the dendrites, and an *axon*, or stem that conducts impulses away from the cell body. Sprenger (1999) describes a neuron as similar to the configuration of a hand and a forearm; the cell body represents the palm, the dendrites the fingers, and the axon the arm. Dendrites are the major receptive surface of the neuron. Each neuron acts like a relay station, receiving signals from other neurons across tiny gaps called *synapses*. The neurons do not connect but produce chemicals called *neurotransmitters,* which carry information from one neuron to another via certain chemicals that are necessary to transmit messages easily and quickly.

Neurotransmitters: Chicken Soup for the Brain

Dendrites have receptor sites designed for particular neurotransmitters. Cortisol, norepinephrine, seratonin, dopamine, and endorphins are chemicals that can affect students' behavior in educational situations. Low levels of cortisol can make us euphoric when we feel in control; high levels of cortisol can lead to feelings of despair and failure when stress turns into distress. Teachers can reduce stressful school environments by becoming aware of students' abilities to handle stress and by organizing assignments to decrease stressful situations. They can allow students to stretch occasionally and to become actively involved in the lesson. They can lend a sympathetic ear when students feel overwhelmed and burdened by schoolwork, home responsibilities, and outside employment. They can help students to organize their schedules and their time while also holding them responsible in their roles as students. Many behavior problems occur as a result of uninterest and a feeling of helplessness. High levels of norepinephrine can cause aggression. Seratonin, dopamine, and endorphines can, in many instances, control aggressive behaviors; they cause us to "feel good." Teachers can help students to release their natural chemicals by developing a personal relationship with the students, by providing positive reinforcement and supportive comments, and by allowing students to "shine." Music and exercise have been recommended for the release of these positive chemical; yet traditional classrooms are expected to be quiet and sedentary. We do not suggest constant motion and chaos, but a motionless group of students engaged in constant seat work is certainly not brain challenging and frequently results in boredom, hostility, and noncompliance.

Classrooms may be the only safe haven for children who are constantly stressed at home. Sylwester (1995) notes that emotionally stressful school environments are counterproductive because they can reduce the students' ability to learn. Stressful environments are also a breeding ground for discipline problems. Teachers cannot help students to grow emotionally when they do not empower them to develop a positive self-concept and positive relationships with others. Teachers can make "chicken soup for the brain" by providing an enriched classroom environment, a meaningful curriculum, and relevant activities. Conversely, an irrelevant or punitive learning environment can cause downshifting. When students "tune out" they switch from the neocortex—where they think, plan, remember, organize, and solve problems—to their limbic system, which regulates emotions such as frustration, fear, apathy, or despair. Overreliance on instructional methods such as lecturing, seat work, and standardized testing prevent students from developing self-efficacy and complex learning.

Constant punishment, lack of positive feedback, and a feeling of powerlessness can produce stress chemicals that obstruct the helpful neurotransmitters that make logical connections in the brain. Our challenge in education is to produce an enriched classroom environment where students can assume an active role in their instruction. Teachers can affect brain chemistry in the classroom by including experiential activities, by empowering students to make decisions, and by implementing cross-curricular thematic instruction. Additional procedures may include the following:

- Teaching self-regulation skills
- Reducing stressful experiences as much as possible
- Playing soothing music
- Teaching relaxation techniques
- Allowing movement like stretching and role-playing
- Providing an outlet for individual expression such as journal writing, art, and music
- Empowering students by giving options and a feeling of some control
- Applying what students learn in meaningful and real-world contexts

Many students start school with "impoverished dendrites" as a result of neglect or poverty in their early years. Marian Diamond (1988) conducted an extensive study with rats to study brain development by placing rats in either enriched or impoverished conditions. The rats in enriched environments were given toys, food, and the companionship of other rats. She also housed an isolated rat (with no companionship) in an enriched cage. The rats in impoverished environments had food only, no toys or companionship. The results indicated that the rats in the enriched environments grew more dendrite connections than the rats in the impoverished environments. In addition, the rats with toys and companions learned more than the isolated rat in the enriched environment. Diamond concluded that rats learn more through interaction and in an enriched environment and that dendritic growth is more likely to occur as the result of such a condition.

Emotional Intelligence

John Dewey (1938) commented on the absurdity of mature adults who educate immature students but do not guide them to rise in emotional maturity. *Emotional intelligence* is defined as the ability to develop self-awareness, to delay gratification, and to be persistent, motivated, and empathetic. Emotional intelligence also includes self-discipline and the ability to control impulses (Goleman, 1995). When students are unable to control their actions and behave according to social expectations, teachers need to consider the emotional characteristics and maturity development of the students in this context. Psychological type, learning style, and multiple intelligences all bear a great influence on teaching and learning. Many students are still resistant and noncompliant in spite of modifications to accommodate their variances in learning. They have difficulty controlling their emotions and often respond impulsively, without consideration for others or for the consequences they must face as a result of their behavior. Students lacking emotional intelligence often feel unhappy and unsatisfied. They may withdraw from their peers, exhibit depression, or psychosomatic illnesses, or lash out with aggressive behavior. An extreme lack of emotional intelligence is frequently demonstrated in incidents of suicide or violent acts toward others. John Mayer and Peter Salovey (1993) explain the model of emotional intelligence by proposing that emotionally competent persons generally display abilities in the following five domains. We will track the progression of two teenage girls, Kerina and Katya, through these domains.

Domain 1: Understanding One's Emotions

Individuals who are introspective, insightful, and in touch with their feelings are better equipped to manage their behaviors and their lives. Kerina and Katya are from different families. The parents of both girls have relocated from a large city to a small town, and they have enrolled their daughters in a small rural middle school. Katya is not pleased with the move and is very unhappy but does not truly understand her feelings. Instead, she projects blame onto that "dumb" school and those "hick" students. She perceives her peers as unsophisticated, unfriendly, and unworthy of her company. In addition, she blames her parents for the move, and her relationship with her family is belligerent and hostile. She feels a gnawing pain in her stomach, and that feeling festers as time goes by. Kerina is also not pleased with the move and feels uncomfortable in her new environment. However, she understands her own feelings as well as why her parents moved. She feels lonely and unhappy but does not project blame onto her new peers. She accepts that coping with new situations is sometimes painful and requires readjusting and accommodation.

Domain 2: Managing One's Emotions

Understanding one's feelings leads to a better management of them and, consequently, to happier situations. Kerina understands the cause of her unhappiness and accepts responsibility for her feelings. She reasons that if she reaches out to her peers, she will be able to make friends and will eventually change her feelings. She manages her emotions and does not give in to self-pity or aggression. She initiates friendly overtures and volunteers for school projects. Katya, on the other hand, is burning with self-pity that eventually turns into anger. She is unable to control her behavior and becomes a discipline problem in school and at home. Many youngsters experience difficulty in handling their own pain. Over the years, there have been detractors who discount the importance of emotional issues in the education of children—some to the point of mocking efforts to come to grips with the affective issues that are so apparent in the lives of troubled children. Schools can no longer afford to ignore the plight of children whose level of pain has risen above their ability to cope. If this plight is not addressed, it will carry on into their adult lives. Adults must provide instruction to help children discuss their feelings of sadness, disappointment, fear, and rejection. Children need help and concrete experiences that offer insight into their own feelings, as well as practical strategies for how to handle their feelings. Children who are running on empty all the time emotionally have no reserves to carry them through times of special stress. In the Littleton, Colorado, high school shooting, for example, one of the boys had been rejected by the military. In the Conyers, Georgia, shooting the perpetrator had been rejected by his girlfriend. What may be a transient crisis for one child can become insurmountable pain for another—the straw that breaks the camel's back. What may be seen as a passing problem for a healthy child can be a serious overload for a child who is habitually distressed and like a loose cannon eventually explodes.

Domain 3: Motivating Oneself

Individuals who are able to manage their feelings in a positive direction are able to control their impulses. They are in charge of their behavior and feel empowered to change their destiny. Kerina took hold of her unhappy feelings and was able to guide her emotions toward a specific goal—to make friends and accommodate to her new environment. Realization of her goals did not happen overnight; several peers recognized Kerina's plight and efforts and initiated friendly overtures. Katya could not delay gratification or stifle her impulsivity. Her aggression and criticism of "this stupid small-town school" increased, and she was soon the ultimate outcast. Her peers increased her feelings of rejection by ridiculing and belittling her.

Domain 4: Recognizing Emotions in Others— Empathy Must Be Learned

Is it possible to teach children in such a way that aggression is diminished and gentler responses are encouraged? Kaplan (1995) explains that aggression can be decreased by teaching them how to recognize their feelings and the feelings of others and the importance of being empathetic in response to those feelings. Programs to develop empathy and control aggression were developed and implemented in several California elementary schools. There was an astonishing decrease in aggressive behaviors by the students who participated in the program's exercises. Empathy is a quality that is crucial in maintaining a civilized social order. It negates the "every person for him- or herself" mentality and causes people to abide by certain moral principles. Empathetic individuals are sensitive to the feelings of others and are able to put themselves in "another's shoes." Kerina realized why her peers were awkward at first; they did not know her and were suspicious of her "big city" background. Therefore, she reached out to them. Consequently, her peers responded and became empathetic to Kerina, feeling her initial sense of isolation. Katya, on the other hand, was unable to empathize with her parents or her peers, and her attitude made it difficult for her peers to empathize with her and see beyond her obnoxious behavior.

Domain 5: Handling Relationships

The art of influencing people requires skill in managing the emotions of others. Katya lacked the social skills to influence her peers, but Kerina established a synchrony between herself and her peers through friendly overtures. Handling relationships requires the ability to set the emotional tone of an interaction. Frank, a student in Katya's math class, approached her after class. She rudely said, "Get off my back, country boy." He smiled and said, "I take it you prefer the big city. What is it like living in a big city?" Katya started to talk about the city she left behind and how she felt isolated in such a small rural town. Frank listened and nodded, and then invited her to a movie that had been filmed in Katya's big city. After the movie, she reminisced about the places they saw in it and her attitude gradually began to change.

Daniel Goleman (1995) explains that emotional intelligence, even more than IQ, is the most reliable predictor of success in school and in life. He describes predictors of success as follows:

> It is being self-assured and interested; knowing what kind of
> behavior is expected and how to control the impulse to misbehave;
> being able to wait and delay gratification, to follow directions, to
> turn to teachers for help, and to express needs while getting along
> with other children. (p.193)

He describes the famous marshmallow study conducted at Stanford University on the relationship between emotional maturity and academic success. Preschool children were individually brought into a room and given a marshmallow. They were told that they could immediately eat the marshmallow; however, if they delayed eating it while the researcher ran an errand, they could have two marshmallows. Approximately one third of the children ate the single marshmallow right away, and some waited a little longer. One third were able to wait 15 or 20 minutes until the researcher returned. The researchers tracked the children 14 years later and found out that the children who were able to postpone eating the marshmallow were less likely to engage in antisocial behaviors. They were better liked by their teachers and peers and were still able to delay gratification in pursuit of their goals. The children who instantly ate the marshmallow were prone to pick fights and fall apart under stressful conditions. In addition, it was discovered that the children who waited scored an average of 210 points higher on the SAT.

Temperament and psychological type can influence development, as do environment and individual needs. The people in our lives also shape our character in one way or another. Goleman (1995) explains that emotional intelligence is not fixed at birth; and it can be nurtured and strengthened by parents and teachers. Children can be taught appropriate emotional responses; they can learn to handle frustration, disappointment, daily aggravation, and anger. They can be taught to handle stressful situations, to peacefully resolve conflicts, and to behave appropriately in various situations. When children learn empathy, they become sensitive and caring and are able to take the perspective of others; empathetic children and youth are less likely to adopt prejudices and stereotypes. Emotionally competent children are able to recognize the difference between feelings and behavior, and they feel positive about themselves, their environment, and their experiences. Interventions aimed at increasing emotional competence can prevent numerous discipline problems. Emotional illiteracy causes intrapersonal problems such as poor self-confidence, lack of motivation, apathy, and an inflated ego. Emotional illiteracy also causes interpersonal problems such as noncompliance, uncooperativeness, aggressiveness, and lack of social skills. The cost of emotional illiteracy on society takes its toll in the form of prejudice, fanaticism, and violence.

Interpersonal and Intrapersonal Intelligences

Howard Gardner's (1993) theory on multiple intelligences was explained in chapter 3. In this section we will reexamine two of the intelligences, interpersonal and intrapersonal intelligences, as they relate to social and emotional competence. Gardner believes that these are the most important intelligences for achieving self-awareness, social adjustment, and happiness. Proficiency in these two intelligences is an excellent predictor for self-fulfillment and peaceful coexistence. Teachers can help students cognitively as well as affectively by teaching them to employ several intelligences in completing their assignments. For example, a teacher may assign an academic project such as a social studies activity in which students must work collaboratively in small groups to achieve a goal. Each group member contributes his or her special talent and establishes interdependence among team members.

Interpersonal Intelligence: Predictor for Peaceful Coexistence

Interpersonal intelligence is described as "a core capacity to notice distinctions among others; in particular, contrasts in their moods, temperaments, motivations, and intentions" (Gardner, 1993, p. 23). In more advanced forms, this intelligence permits an adult to read the intentions and desires of others. People with high interpersonal intelligence are successful in their interactions with people, whether they are like or unlike them. They are able to deal effectively with diversity and are attuned to problems caused by bigotry. They accept differences and reach decisions based on appropriate information rather than on stereotypes or hearsay. They are able to work cooperatively and contribute to a group. They behave responsibly and respect different opinions and beliefs. They are able to resolve conflicts peacefully and refrain from animosity or resentment. People with high interpersonal intelligence are also very persuasive and convincing; they are able to influence others to accept their beliefs and opinions. Leaders attuned to interpersonal intelligence can charm and redirect individuals or groups to follow them. They do not dominate but rather motivate their followers to willingly engage in highly productive work. In addition to the ability to relate to others, people with high interpersonal intelligence are able to self-examine and be true and honest to themselves. They are also competent in intrapersonal intelligence.

Intrapersonal Intelligence: Predictor for Self-Realization

Gardner (1993) describes intrapersonal intelligence as knowing who you are, understanding your strengths and limitations, and knowing what you can and want to do. Self-awareness guides a person in reacting to situations and people and in judging what to avoid and what to confront. Individuals who develop self-understanding are able to deal with their strengths and their weaknesses in positive and constructive ways. They do not feel threatened by the success of others, and, as Stephen Covey (1990) explains in his book *The Seven Habits of Highly Effective People*, they function with an abundant mentality rather than a scarcity mentality. Such people welcome collaboration because they feel secure within themselves. People with high intrapersonal intelligence are able to self-assess and share their feelings with others. They display a high level of confidence and are adept in taking a position different from that of the peer group. They are comfortable in selecting calculated risks and at assuming the role of leader or follower. They are self-motivated and actively engage in their own learning and goal setting. They work through their activities carefully and thoroughly to accomplish their objectives. When they attempt to solve a problem they show good decision making and independence; however, they do not hesitate to ask for help when they need it. They are able to generate several possible hypotheses and solutions and accept and learn from feedback. Most of all, people with high intrapersonal intelligence accept responsibility for their actions and possessions. They practice self-control and delayed gratification and are able to handle frustration and stress. In addition to valuing self-realization, they attach importance to realizing the potential of others, because they understand that in unity there is strength. Discipline problems can be avoided when children are active learners and are taught through their strengths—that is, their most developed intelligence, psychological type, and learning style. Let us examine Thatya's problem.

Thatya is strong in musical, linguistic, and spatial intelligences but weak in interpersonal and intrapersonal intelligences. She often disrupts the class and is very critical of her peers. Her teacher employs music, art, and creative writing as antecedents to encourage Thatya to demonstrate and share her skills with her peers. If Thatya responds positively, she is likely to receive approval from her peers and teacher, which in turn causes Thatya to continue to behave appropriately.

Both Gardner and Goleman refer to the neurochemistry of emotion. Gardner explains the function of the frontal lobes in interpersonal intelligence; damage to this area can cause profound personality changes while leaving other forms of problem solving intact. Goleman explains the research on the neurobiology of our emotions. He refers to the "anatomy of emotional hijacking" and explains how the amygdala, in the limbic system of the brain, can react to an emotional situation before the neocortex, our thinking brain, has time to process it rationally. Gardner's and Goleman's messages are hopeful, and we are inclined to believe that physical impairment, temperament, harsh circumstances, and austere environments do not necessarily dictate our destiny. The social skills required to develop emotional, interpersonal, and intrapersonal intelligences must be taught early, and they are essential for maintaining a safe and orderly climate in homes, schools, and the community. These intelligences develop most successfully as a result of the interaction of learning and maturation. It is therefore important that teachers become aware of socialization development processes.

Stages of Affective Development

Prior to teaching interpersonal and intrapersonal skills, we must understand how children develop in moral and character growth. The works of numerous developmental and educational psychologists, such as Martin Hoffman (1970), Robert Selman (1976), and Lawrence Kohlberg (1976), suggest that affective education for students should precede academic learning. A wholesome education should include training to develop empathy, interpersonal skills, and moral growth. These qualities are essential in acquiring the democratic ideals of equality, fairness, and commitment to social justice.

Empathy Development: "I Know How You Feel, I've Been There"

Martin Hoffman's (1970) perspective on empathy is approximately parallel to the developmental stages of Jean Piaget. Learners' capacity to feel empathy improves with age, experience, and teaching. In the first stage of empathy development, *Global Empathy*, infants may experience distress when they are around someone who is expressing a strong painful feeling. For instance, a baby may start crying when hearing another baby crying. In the second stage, *Egocentric Empathy*, children may attempt to comfort someone in distress by offering something that is comforting to them, such as their blanket or their mother's help. The third stage, *Empathy for Others*, may begin in the early childhood years and extend throughout the elementary school years. At this stage children can partially identify with the pain of others and respond in a nonegocentric manner. In the fourth stage, *Empathy for Other's Life Condition*, empathy and sensitivity are fully developed. Individuals are able to understand a more generalized view of what the other person is feeling. Their personal experiences and/or developed social cognition allow them to experience a deeper appreciation for another's condition. They may demonstrate their empathy through attempts of assistance and comfort.

Interpersonal Development: "A Friend in Need Is a Friend Indeed"

Robert Selman (1976) describes three stages of friendship development, which he calls "levels of interpersonal understanding." At the first stage, the *egocentric level*, preschool children's understanding of friendship is concrete and reflects selfish perspectives. A friend is someone who can entertain and play with them, and interpersonal feelings are not considered in a quarrel or in an attempt to resolve a conflict. At the second stage, *reciprocal trust*, elementary school children develop empathy, trust, altruism, and helpfulness. They realize that friendship is a mutual relationship that involves acceptance of differences and tolerance. The third stage, *mutual perspective taking*, occurs in adolescence. Teenagers begin to develop mutual understanding, support, loyalty, and problem solving. They begin to appreciate the value of cooperation, collaboration, and friendship. They also start to understand the necessity and process for peacefully resolving conflicts.

Moral Reasoning Development: Learning to Do Good Because Good Is Good to Do

Lawrence Kohlberg's (1976) analysis of the acquisition of judgment and morals remains influential in the developmental literature. Children's acquisition of morals is a developmental process. Teachers who are sensitive to Kohlberg's stages of moral readiness can plan appropriate learning steps for their students. A brief review of his levels of moral reasoning explains the evolution of morals and the importance of providing students with instructional strategies to assist them in developing universal ethics and values.

Preconventional Level

Stage 1: "It's got to be good if I can get away with it," or *the punishment/obedience orientation.* Individuals at this level view cultural rules as good or bad depending on personal satisfaction and gratification. Consequences are judged according to reward or punishment. These people are not concerned with others but reason in terms of their own needs. They believe that whatever they can get away with is good. A child will avoid hitting others because of previously experienced punishment. An adult will avoid running a red light because of a previous expensive ticket.

Stage 2: "You scratch my back and I'll scratch yours," or *instrumental relativist orientation.* Self-interest and an exchange philosophy motivate individuals at this stage. They are driven by a naive hedonism and believe that people should look out for their own interests and gain. They won't do anything for nothing, but will give only if they can get something in return. Nevertheless, progress is evident, and these people are just beginning to acquire a vague sense of fairness and equity.

Conventional Level

Stage 3: The Golden Rule, "Do to others as you would want others to do to you," or *interpersonal concordance orientation.* In addition to believing in the philosophy of the Golden Rule, these individuals think that goodness should always be rewarded. The saying "What goes around comes around" is typical of what people believe at this stage. Being good means having good motives, showing concern, and giving to others. Being good also means following the standards and regulations of a chosen organization, such as a religious group or a political system. What people think of you is important, as is the need to maintain rules that support stereotypical good behavior.

Stage 4: "Your country [society, religion, or organization], love it or leave it," or *authority-maintaining orientation.* Adherence to a social system and a patriotic conscience strongly identifies this stage. Laws are important and should be upheld regardless of individual needs. People at this stage do not believe in challenging established authority or changing the status quo. The individual's responsibility is to contribute to the group's welfare, as determined by existing standards. This stage, though legalistic and inflexible, is considered important in keeping the social order from breaking down.

Postconventional Level

Stage 5: "The greatest good for the greatest number," or social-contract legalistic orientation. Democratic values are important at this stage. Contractual commitments to families, friends, employers, and employees should be maintained and honored. Laws decided upon by the majority must be obeyed to keep up the social order; however, rights such as life and liberty must be upheld regardless of majority opinion.

Stage 6: "We are the world," or universal ethical orientation. Universal ethics characterize this highest stage of moral development. Its principles are universal ethics of justice, and a personal commitment is made toward human rights and human dignity. A sense of human interconnectedness is evident at this stage.

An understanding of child development is essential in helping students to mature and handle transitions from a punishment/obedience orientation to a universal ethical orientation. Teachers need to consider the students' readiness skills, including their emotional and cognitive abilities. Affective education as a component of a total discipline program can teach students the importance of developing a social conscience and the consequences of antisocial behaviors at home, in school, and in their community. Polls indicate that a majority of parents would agree to nonsectarian programs in public schools that teach ethics, values, community responsibility, and citizenship (Nazario, 1990). However, controversy over which skills should be taught and whose responsibility is it to teach them often surfaces in many communities. We believe that parents are their children's first teachers but that schoolteachers are also responsible for teaching social skills to facilitate student growth in moral development. It is never too early or too late to teach social behavior through directive or nondirective approaches. We propose a directive approach, which means teaching the skill, involving students in their learning, and demonstrating and modeling desired behavior. Learning is a two-way street, and teachers and students influence each other's behaviors every day. Teachers can take advantage of "teachable moments" throughout the day to reinforce the skills and to model appropriate social behaviors.

Social Skills Training

You don't teach a new mathematical concept while students are taking an exam. Competent teachers provide instruction prior to testing for knowledge and comprehension. Likewise, you don't teach social skills in the middle of a controversy. Teaching social skills is a proactive and ongoing process that can serve as a deterrent to many behavior problems. Students who are deficient in these skills are often defiant, oppositional, and noncompliant, and they will not listen to the "you should," "you ought," and "you need to" of parents and teachers. Social skills instruction involves more than teaching conflict resolution; it involves understanding oneself, others, and society. It includes learning to respect one another, the environment, and the relationship between values and behavior. Goleman (1995) believes in "schooling the emotions."

In the 1970s Charles Meisgeier developed a social skills curriculum for children based on his research (Meisgeier, Meisgeier, & Weisenfelder, 1982). It was designed to provide tools necessary to (a) accept responsibility for personal behavior, (b) deal appropriately with feelings, (c) communicate effectively, (d) develop workable problem-solving strategies, (e) cope with life's stress, (f) resolve conflict, and (g) understand and cope with problems that occur in relationships.

A study investigating the program indicated that students showed marked progress. Teachers who taught the program found it personally helpful to themselves as well. Similar programs were being established in schools all over the nation until the "back-to-basics" movement began to dominate education in the 1980s. That movement—and all the new forms it has taken since—discounts psychology and social behavior courses in schools, as well as other nonacademic activities; it views them as an unnecessary financial burden. Today special-interest groups continue to work through legislatures and local school boards to eliminate the expense of psychological counseling and related services.

Many schools have outstanding counseling and mental health initiatives; however, other schools have very limited counseling, and some have none at all. Clerical duties, such as scheduling, and vocational counseling occupy their time. They are rarely involved in crisis situations and hardly ever help in the resolution of students' personal conflicts. In many districts, a school counselor's primary responsibilities involve working out class schedules and related clerical tasks. Much of what these counselors do could be assigned to counseling aides or clerical personnel. School counselors should be brought up to date in their counseling skills, and they should be selected for their abilities in counseling and small-group leadership. School counselors should actively intervene in school situations involving cliques, bullying, ridicule, abuse, bigotry, intimidation, and aggression. Counselors must be proactive in identifying and working with troubled children.

Serious thought should also be given to expanding the role of psychologists and related personnel who now spend most of their time testing and labeling children rather than intervening in critical situations involving troubled individuals, gangs, cliques, and other serious behavioral problems. They need to be trained to offer expert consultation services to teachers who are dealing with severe behavior management problems in their class-rooms. In addition, teachers must be reeducated to take on many of the roles currently assumed by counselors, school psychologists, and social workers. Teachers may feel overwhelmed by their present duties, but whether they realize it or not, they are daily imparting and modeling values and social skills to their students, and they could do a better job with support and training.

Social behavioral programs and extracurricular activities should be expanded. The back-to-basics movement, at its inception, was motivated by a refusal to fund anything but the basics in the schools. It still is, in many public schools across the nation. The aftermath of that refusal is funding for prison construction at an unprecedented rate. It should be apparent to everyone by now that neither the back-to-basics philosophy nor any of its current mutations should be the guide for educational decisions or programming. Another outcome of the emphasis on "academics only" instruction in many states is a preoccupation with standardized testing. Principals are threatened with removal from their jobs if test scores do not improve. Benefits or rewards, if they exist, are given to teachers for improvement of test scores. Thus, a great deal of additional pressure is put upon teachers to prepare their children for these tests. Schools expend enormous energy, resources, and time preparing for these tests. A school's priority should be the development of emotionally healthy, socially mature, and academically proficient young people, with strong characters and an understanding of civic responsibility as well as academic proficiency.

Domains of a Social Skills Curriculum

Academic proficiency is attained through a planned curriculum of study. Likewise, social and emotional competence can be realized through programmed instruction. We have identified five broad areas of a social program: social cognition, social interchange, social acceptance, social insight, and social accommodation. In addition to these areas, teachers can identify other categories that they consider important in the socialization process of their particular group of students. Each category is divided into specific skills necessary to master the broader goal. Many skills are not exclusive and often overlap. Several skills can be combined and instructed simultaneously, and care must be given to guide students to transfer what they learn to other settings and with various people.

Social Cognition

Social cognition is a process that involves how individuals perceive and interpret the actions and feelings of others. It also involves being able to share experiences and show compassion. The following skills are necessary to achieve social cognition (Bee, 1992; Gardner, 1993; Goleman, 1995, Kohlberg, 1976):

- *Perception*: to accurately perceive the intentions conveyed through the verbal and nonverbal messages of others.
- *Empathy*: to be able to "put oneself in another's shoes" and to empathize and show concern.a.
- *Interpretation*: To accurately interpret the intentions, feelings, and verbal and nonverbal messages of others.
- *Understanding*: To accurately understand the intentions conveyed through the verbal and nonverbal messages of others.

Social Interchange

Social interchange explains how students interact with others in public and private situations. The following skills are necessary to achieve effective social interchanges (Bee, 1992; Gardner, 1993; Goleman, 1995):

- *Collaboration*: to cooperate, share, and work in harmony with others.
- *Communication*: to communicate verbally and nonverbally, exchange ideas, and listen when others are speaking.
- *Social amenities*: to use social amenities, including socially approved manners and respect for adults and peers.
- *Generalization*: to generalize social behavior across settings and when interacting with different persons.

Social Acceptance

Students are socially proficient when they are in sync with their social circle. However, some students may be socially effective with their peer group but not with the expectations of the broader society. Teachers need to provide the students with various situations that require effective behavior for success outside the peer-group milieu. The following skills are necessary to achieve social acceptance (Eisenberg, 1990):

- *Tolerance*: to accept differences in oneself and in others.
- *Appearance*: to present an accepted appearance in various social situations.
- *Assertiveness*: to be assertive in interactions and to distinguish between assertiveness and aggressiveness.
- *Compliance*: to comply with social demands when appropriate.
- *Peaceful coexistence*: to be able to come together and agree on behaviors that encourage compatibility.

Social Insight

Individuals with social insight are able to predict consequences and make decisions based on calculated risks. Teachers can facilitate the process of decision making by allowing students to learn from actual or contrived problems. The following skills are necessary to achieve social insight (Bloom, 1981; Gagne & Briggs, 1992):

- *Prediction*: to predict consequences and appraise various situations.
- *Reflection*: to reflect on the consequences of one's behavior.
- *Reasoning*: to reason and examine one's impulsive behavior and select alternative behaviors.
- *Problem solving*: to solve problems individually and in groups.

Social Accommodation

Students need to be taught that certain behaviors may or may not be tolerated by individuals. In addition, certain behaviors may or may not be appropriate in specific settings or situations. For instance, some teachers are more accepting of noise or informality than are other teachers. Nevertheless, students must adapt to various situations and experiences. They must learn to appraise their position and assess and modify their behavior accordingly. The following skills are necessary to achieve social accommodation (Bandura, 1977; Meichenbaum, 1975):

- *Coping*: to select and use coping skills such as stress management and relaxation procedures.
- *Self-control*: to control impulsive behaviors and demonstrate self-management, including self-recording and self-reinforcement.
- *Discrimination*: to discriminate between situations and adjust behavior to fit the situation.
- *Imitation:* to be able to imitate a modeled behavior.
- *Attention to social cues*: to attend to social cues and adapt to environmental expectations.

Strategies for Teaching Social Skills

In the home, parents frequently teach social skills incidentally or nondirectively. The lessons are not structured and skills are learned as they are needed. When a child is given a gift, the child is reminded to say "thank you," and parents will require that toys and candy be shared with friends or siblings. Children will often imitate the behavior of adults, who have power and control the reinforcers. Children will imitate appropriate behavior as well as antisocial and aggressive behavior by observing the actions of other people in their environment. In addition to modeling appropriate behavior throughout the day, teachers can provide specific structured strategies such as coaching, role-play, and guided discussions. In subsequent chapters we review strategies adapted from various models of discipline. Here we discuss strategies to reinforce proficiency in the five domains of social development described in the previous section of this chapter. To these we have added a sixth, social motivation.

Social Cognition

Kohlberg (1976) presented children with hypothetical dilemmas and analyzed their responses to determine their level of moral reasoning. In responding to these dilemmas, the children considered the actions and intentions of the characters. They also proposed solutions, and gave reasons for their opinions. Teachers can present students with similar hypothetical dilemmas to help students think critically and analytically. Moral dilemmas similar to Kohlberg's can be adapted to fit the experiences and problems of a specific group of students. Numerous stories in children's and adolescent literature are excellent sources for developing social cognition. In addition, teachers can coach students in composing particular dilemmas that incorporate real-life situations. Prior to the presentation of the dilemmas, teachers should develop six questions for each dilemma: two questions to discuss each of the three skills; perception, empathy, and understanding. Students should be encouraged to present diverse opinions in reaching and interpreting solutions to the dilemmas. They may be reminded that the way they perceive the problem often is the problem.

To achieve social cognition, students need a new level of thinking. We suggest strategies such as brainstorming, prioritizing choices, role-playing, and exercises in inductive thinking to help students reflect on and come up with solutions for each dilemma. After a general discussion, small groups of students can continue to discuss the issues and consequences, summarize the group consensus, and present it to the class. Throughout the process, teachers should assume a coaching role and probe the students' understanding and knowledge of concepts.

Social Interchange

Egocentrism limits children in their interactions with others. Younger children believe that other people view the world as they do. Many older students and adults continue to hold that belief. Egocentrism decreases as a result of children's social experiences. As children relate to peers and adults, they discover the diverse perceptions and beliefs of others.

Mutual cooperation, communication, collaboration, and sharing of ideas are necessary to increase social interactions. It is important to create experiences and environments where children choose to interact and cooperate. Teachers are in an excellent position to foster an atmosphere of cooperation while providing structure. Structuring, especially in the early grades, supplies physical as well as emotional safety. Effective teachers plan ahead and organize activities to promote sharing and collaboration.

Teaching communication skills is important for elementary school students as well as for secondary school students. Strategies such as rehearsing—practicing what to say and do—can be used to help the impulsive youngster and the awkward adolescent. Pragmatic activities enable students to relate to peers, adults and to the entire school experience. The ability to use social language relates to successful achievements in adult life. Play-acting, video portrayal, journal writing, and book reports are motivating strategies to increase pragmatic skills. In addition, students working in small cooperative groups can develop and enact scripts on a given topic.

The lack of socially approved manners interferes with relationships and often causes discipline problems. Instruction in social amenities is important at any age. The influence of parents in this type of training cannot be minimized; however, teachers are also influential. Teachers and students can simulate certain social situations, such as a birthday party, a prom, or a job interview, and role-play designated parts. Students can create helpful reminders on posters, using their artistic abilities or computer software designed to create posters.

Generalization refers to the ability of students to transfer a learned behavior across different settings, situations, and individuals. Many students will behave appropriately in certain classrooms but not in others. In addition, many students will comply with the requests of only certain teachers. Teachers can help students to generalize appropriate behaviors by collaborating with colleagues and parents in encouraging students to apply social skills across different settings.

Social Acceptance

Peers exert a tremendous influence during the middle childhood years and throughout adolescence, and acceptance by a peer group becomes an important factor. Students must learn to accept themselves in order to be genuinely able to be accepted and to accept others.

Strategies to increase positive self-concept and self-acceptance are built around a cooperative and cohesive classroom climate. Teachers must minimize competition and build goals around the common good of all students. Teachers can encourage friendships between students by arranging situations in which individual students get to know each other. Peer tutoring is an example of a strategy that allows a pair of students to use their strengths to help each other. The roles of the tutor and the tutee should be reversed to encourage acceptance and minimize rivalry.

Nonconforming dress and appearance is a healthy way for adolescents to communicate self-expression and identity formation; physical appearance is an important factor in peer-group acceptance. However, appearances considered "outrageous"—such as tattoos, pierced facial appendages (eyebrows, tongue, nose, and lips), and revealing apparel—have caused much consternation in schools as well as in many homes. There are more benefits for physically presentable students than for those who do not fit the mainstream social stereotype. Many schools are adopting school uniforms to deal with dress code violations, theft, and physical fighting over clothes. Although this approach may prove to be effective in some schools, it may inhibit certain students from building relationships with peers and cause them to resist complying with authority figures. The benefits of acceptable appearance and hygiene can be taught through structured instruction in a health education or social skills class. Visualization and imagery are effective strategies to help students realize how they will look and what they will wear 10, 15, or 20 years from now. Students can role-play job interviews or formal events that require certain attire. Teachers should be sensitive to the students' socioeconomic status and the family's ability to provide certain luxuries. Acquisition of "props" for role-playing exercises can avoid embarrassing situations. The probability of success is more likely to occur and become permanent when teachers employ strategies that focus on increasing positive behaviors rather than focusing on punishing negative behaviors.

Richardson (1996) includes assertiveness training in her social skills program. Assertiveness training empowers students and teaches them to become self-advocates, a skill that will benefit them as they mature into adulthood. Assertiveness training teaches students to express themselves in socially acceptable ways. It teaches the difference between aggressiveness and assertiveness as well as how students can respect their own rights along with the rights of others. Empathetic assertiveness is an important skill in dealing with friends and authority figures. It requires understanding the feelings of others and verbally expressing this understanding. For example: "Mr. Jones, I know you want to help, and I appreciate it, but I would rather handle this myself," as opposed to a comment such as, "Please, Mr. Jones, I can do this myself."

Noncompliant and disruptive students are more likely to cooperate when they are involved in establishing classroom rules and taking part in conflict resolution teams. Teaching children self-regulation skills increases the probability of compliant behavior and reduces the occurrences of noncompliant behavior. Interventions include teaching students to record instances of noncompliance, to think of the consequences of their behavior, and to select, implement, and evaluate alternative behaviors. Parents and teachers can reinforce compliance and gradually fade the reinforcers to help the child internalize appropriate behaviors.

Peaceful coexistence is necessary for a civilized society to prosper. Aggression is counter to peace and harmful to both the aggressors and their targets. Aggressive children carry anger, frustration, humiliation, and other destructive emotions. Teaching peace should begin with prevention. Teachers should start the school year by building a cohesive classroom community through activities that involve the entire student body. In addition, we suggest that teachers instruct students in interpersonal skills such as communication, negotiation, mediation, compromise, and peacemaking. Aggressive children are placed at further risk when peers and adults reject them. Interventions for aggression follow a continuum, from least restrictive to more restrictive. Social skills training, self-regulation training, and positive reinforcements are effective in teaching children alternative behaviors to aggression.

Social Insight

Students with behavior problems lack the ability to predict consequences or to foresee future social opportunities. They are impulsive and rarely stop to think before they act. They are disorganized in their thinking as well as in social situations. They often disrupt play activities and are unable to delay gratification.

Teachers can directly teach students to predict and appraise situations by presenting "cliff-hanger" stories and asking students to predict consequences and find solutions. Journal writing is another strategy that can be used to examine and compare behaviors and consequences.

A "stop, think, plan, check" strategy is used in cognitive behavior management to teach self-management and to increase reflective reasoning (Richardson, 1996). Verbal mediation, or thinking aloud, has been described as critically talking to oneself when confronted with a problem or a new situation. In verbal mediation, the students are taught to define problems, to examine their initial impulsive response, to choose alternatives, and to evaluate their decisions. Training in problem solving has also been effective in reducing and eliminating problem behaviors.

Social Accommodation

Accommodation refers to dealing effectively with the environment. To successfully adapt to new situations, children must assimilate and interact with the new environment and fit new experiences into their existing understanding and abilities. When children are unable to assimilate new experiences, they must modify or accommodate their personal responses to fit the new experiences. Students with behavior problems need assistance to cope with new experiences. They need to be able to control impulsive behaviors, learn to discriminate between situations, and behave accordingly. These students often have difficulty attending to social cues and thus fall short of societal expectations. Paying attention to social cues comes naturally to most students; however, students with attention and/or behavior problems have difficulty picking up cues to adapt to social expectations. Teachers can use modeling of desired behaviors, puppets, and videotapes to teach young children strategies to attend to social prompts and cues. Role-playing can also reinforce focusing attention and imitating the appropriate behaviors of others.

Teachers can help students to cope with difficult situations through stress reduction strategies. We suggest the following technique to teach students to relax and to cope with frustration. The following script is an example of a relaxation exercise developed by Charles Meisgeier. One way of relaxing both mentally and physically is to tighten and relax the muscles of the body. This is a good way to deal with stress when one has to do things that make one feel uptight (e. g., taking a test, giving a report in class, asking someone for a date). In the Olympic games, for instance, before the athletes jump from the diving board or get ready to go down the ski slope they stop, relax, and get their bodies tuned to the activity. In this way they take control of their bodily reactions.

The following exercises can be used any time in any tense situation.

Breathing: Take three deep breaths slowly. Hold the last breath for a minute, and then exhale slowly. After each breath, relax your entire body.

1. Inhale, 2, 3, hold.
2. Exhale, 2, 3, 4.
3. Pause and say, "Notice yourself becoming more relaxed."
4. Repeat three times.

Legs: Now we are going to tighten and relax our feet, toes, and leg muscles.

1. Sit in a comfortable position, legs stretched out in front and slightly off the floor.
2. Tighten toes, feet and legs, 2, 3, 4, 5.
3. Relax, 2, 3, 4, 5.
4. Notice the relaxation in your legs and feet (pause).
5. Repeat three times.

Arms: Now we are going to tighten all the muscles in our arms. Tighten the muscles in the upper arm, in the forearm, and in the wrist and hand. Make a tight fist.

1. First stretch arms out in front of the body.
2. Tighten the fist and the muscles of the arms, 2, 3, 4, 5.
3. Put your arms down and relax your arms and hands at your sides, 2, 3, 4, 5.
4. Note the relaxation in your arms and shoulders (pause).
5. Repeat three times.

Face: Now we are going to tighten and relax our face muscles.

1. Look straight ahead.
2. Close your eyes tightly (remind contact wearers not to close too tightly), tighten face muscles, make a face, bite down and tighten jaw, 2, 3, 4, 5.
3. Relax, 2, 3, 4, 5.
4. Repeat three times.

Summary: Now we are going to breathe deeply again. Sense how relaxed you are in your legs, in your arms, in your face.

Explain the purpose of this activity to the students. Tell them that by relaxing they can become more in tune with themselves, reduce stress, and concentrate their thoughts and energy on the day's activities. Reexplain the purpose and importance of relaxation. Impress the students with the idea that they can use these techniques to help them before taking a test, when tackling a difficult problem, or when they feel they may be losing self-control (Meisgeier, Meisgeier, & Weisenfelder, 1982).

Social Motivation

In addition to the above areas, we have included social motivation be-cause most misbehaving students experience difficulty in being motivated to learn. In many cases their misbehavior is a result of apathy, boredom, and detachment. Nobody is born motivated. Learned motivational states results from the person's interaction with the social environment or culture. We often refer to motivation as being intrinsic. However, teachers can manipu-late the environment to create a drive within students to want to learn and behave. This is evident when students are involved in a project that they perceive as interesting and relevant. Extrinsic motivation can eventually be internalized; however, caution should be exercised in the constant use of reinforcers such as tokens, candy, or stars. This can have drawbacks, for in-stead of doing something because it's fun or has its own value, students will comply because there is something "in it for them." Teachers should keep the following in mind to increase students' motivation:

1. Involve the students in decision making.
2. Use examples that are relevant to the students.
3. Involve the students in the practical application of concepts.
4. When a student misbehaves, find out how you can individualize the activity to meet his or her interests.
5. Show enthusiasm while teaching, and don't do all the talking. Allow students to question and discuss.
6. Remember that motivated students are less likely to misbehave.

Lack of motivation often produces a behavior known as *learned helpless-ness*. Students with this condition feel unable to help themselves or to allow anyone to help them. Students who believe that they are controlled by their environment are more likely to fail in school. Their feelings of inadequacy can translate into passive or passive-aggressive behaviors. A procedure to counteract learned helplessness is to gradually teach students to control their destiny. Teachers can assist students in developing self-management skills. This must be systematically taught and reinforced. During the preintervention stage, the teacher and the student together set the goals of the intervention.

Self-reinforcement is more effective and longer lasting than external reinforcement. Teachers can show students how to examine their feelings upon achieving even small approximations of their goal. The teacher may assume the role of coach or facilitator during the implementation of the intervention and periodically monitor the procedure, providing assistance when necessary. Self-evaluation is an important step of the intervention; the teacher may guide the student in a careful and honest analysis of the results. With the teacher's help, the student can design and implement necessary adjustments and modifications when the goals are not achieved. Additional information on self-management is included in chapter 6. Ken's story illus-trates how his teacher, Mrs. Ford, helped him to develop self-discipline.

Ken had a learning disability in reading and was included in Mrs. Ford's English class. The motivation he experienced in the first year of his schooling completely evaporated by the fifth grade, and he developed learned helplessness. He eventually became disruptive in class in order to avoid any reading assignments. Most of his teachers would send him to the office when he started to misbehave. Mrs. Ford was the exception. She and Ken set a goal to decrease his annoying classroom behavior and increase his reading skills. Every morning before class, Mrs. Ford tutored Ken for 5 minutes and taught him to read the last line of a story. In addition, Ken would keep a record every time he started to interrupt or cause a disturbance. At the end of the day they would chart his progress. It was agreed that Mrs. Ford would not provide a tangible reinforcer, but instead Ken would examine his chart and determine his own progress. Ken started to memorize the last line of the story to build up his confidence; later he learned additional lines and eventually an entire paragraph. Gradually, his confidence increased and his interruptions decreased. He was not embarrassed to read aloud or ask questions. His motivation became intrinsic as he learned to reinforce himself.

Character Education

The goal of social skills training is to guide students in developing a responsible and sensitive character. Few discussions about character education occur without sharp differences of opinion, many of which seem to end in a deadlock that has resulted in a public policy stalemate. Educators must affirm their conviction that young people need caring adults to take an interest in the formation of their characters. People who live in lovely homes and enjoy a measure of privilege, often have no idea of the deprivation and neglect that teachers see in the lives of their students every single day. We do not deny that deprived and neglected children have an opportunity to develop values; on the contrary, they develop values all through their lives—values based on the most fundamental issues of survival and self-interest. However, these values may bear little resemblance to the values that society wants them to have. When there is little care and nurturance in the life of a child, then no one is teaching or modeling empathy or caring for others. Many children are raised by caring parents who teach and model social values, but many other children do not have that advantage.

A problem in teaching social values lies in the definition of the term. Consider the following: There are many people for whom the most important values are kindness, consideration, and graciousness. Some people think honesty and meticulous care in the handling of the property and money of others is the highest value in life. Still others value justice and fairness above all. Another segment of society may hold that speaking the truth and avoiding hypocrisy, falsehood, and sham is of paramount importance. Many people have religious value systems that are of prime importance in their lives. Freedom of religion has been a fundamental value in this country from its earliest days, and no educator wishes to weaken the determination to up-hold it. However, all of these diverse opinions make the possibility of agreement on the content of social and emotional education seem remote.

What is needed, then, is to help students develop the character to maintain values that are important in a civilized society. Some people will say that a person of good character is always on time, performs to the letter what is expected by society, complies with the stated rules of behavior, and does not contribute to the chaotic nature of the world by rebelling. Others believe that excellence of character is found in the absolute refusal to succumb to peer pressure or to the demands of others to violate our principles. There is real truth and value in both positions, but these two groups would not agree on the content of a character education or a social skills program because they differ so sharply in their respective definitions of the nature of good character. A simple answer is to expect to be treated as one wants to be treated, but this is more easily said than done. To reach this goal, teachers must consider each individual student's experiences, strengths, and weaknesses. Several social skills programs have attempted to address the skills that would predispose students to follow the Golden Rule.

Social Skills Programs

Teachers inadvertently teach social skills; however, there are numerous published curricula and programs that address general and specific social behaviors. Teachers must develop a needs assessment and consider their students' learning characteristics and social deficits in selecting a program. In addition, the activities and strategies should be relevant to the target population. The following is a brief summary of programs designed to promote social behavior.

Connecting With Others: Lessons for Teaching Social and Emotional Competence. Champaign, IL: Research Press.

The first two volumes, for Grades K–2 and 3–5, are authored by Rita Coombs Richardson. The lessons are designed to teach self-awareness based on the principles of transactional analysis. The ego states are referred to as "me" attitudes; the adult attitude is the "thinking me"; the parent and the child states each assume two attitudes—the parent's "bossy me" and "caring me" and the child's "enthusiastic me" and "impulsive me." Skills for attaining social competence and social cognition are taught through the principles of cognitive behavior modification and lessons for developing social effectiveness are based on assertiveness training.

Rita C. Richardson and Elizabeth Evans produced a similar program for middle school students based on the same theoretical framework. The goals and objectives were rewritten to correlate with the needs of this specific age group. Rita Coombs-Richardson and Charles Meisgeier (2000) extended the program for high school students and added rational emotive therapy (RET) to the theoretical foundation.

The Skillstreaming Series: Champaign, IL: Research Press.

Arnold Goldstein (1999) and other authors provide training programs that address the social skills of young children and adolescents. The programs are intended to help students increase self-esteem, deal with interpersonal conflicts, and interact with peers, family, and authority figures.

The Prepare Curriculum, also by Arnold Goldstein (1988), seeks to teach interpersonal skills to aggressive, antisocial youth as well as to those who are withdrawn and socially isolated. It teaches empathy, cooperation, problem solving, conflict resolution, anger control, stress management, and social perceptiveness.

Creating the Peaceable School. Champaign, IL Research Press.

Richard Bodine, Donna Crawford, and Fred Schrumpf (1996) developed this program for upper elementary and middle school students. It presents a plan to achieve a peaceful climate in schools. Central to this plan is the creation of a cooperative school environment, achieved through the institution of a rights-and-responsibilities approach to discipline and the liberal use of cooperative learning. Through conflict resolution strategies of mediation, negotiation, and group problem solving, students learn to recognize, manage, and resolve conflicts in peaceful, noncoercive ways.

Learning the Skills of Peacemaking. Rolling Hills, CA: Jalmar Press.

This program by Naomi Drew, which offers an activity guide for elementary-age children on communication, cooperation, and resolving conflict (Drew, 1987), teaches children the necessary skills for developing social competence. These include problem solving, social reasoning, and self-control. The program offers 56 lessons that include activities to achieve positive interpersonal relationships, peacefully resolve conflicts, and develop responsibility.

Cooperative Discipline. Circle Pines: MN: American Guidance Service.

This program by Linda Albert is based on the causes for misbehavior cited by Rudolph Dreikurs (1982). Albert proposes four major causes for misbehavior: attention getting, power struggles, revenge, and helplessness. *Cooperative Discipline* includes a staff development component consisting of an overview videotape, transparencies, activities, and handouts. The program emphasizes teaching students responsibility for their behavior and offers suggestions for dealing with angry, aggressive, and difficult students. It incorporates a conflict resolution process intended to resolve teacher-student problems as well as student-student problems. The parents are involved through a parent-teacher partnership action plan.

Teaching Social Skills to Youth. Boys Town, NE: Father Flanagan's Boys Home.

The program was developed by Tom Dowd and Jeff Tierney (1995) and is part of the Boys Town behavior management curriculum. It is primarily based on the theory of social learning and behavioral analysis that emphasizes direct instruction, modeling, and reinforcement of appropriate behavior. Improvements in behavior as well as gains in social skills are accomplished through manipulation of antecedent events. Individuals using this program are taught functional analysis to record detailed accounts of the youths' behaviors. By analyzing each ABC component, (antecedent, behavior, onsequence), adults can determine what appropriate social skill should be taught to replace students' current problem behavior. Each lesson is structured and teacher directed.

Solving the Violence Problem: Teens, Crime, and the Community. Eagan, MN: West Publishing Company.

This program is a joint publication of the National Institute for Citizen Education in the Law and the National Crime Prevention Council. It is part of kit entitled *Making Life Choices*, which also includes programs in social interactions, career and employment decisions, and health education. The program addresses such topics as teens and crime prevention, victims of crime, property crime and violence, criminal and juvenile justice, conflict management, child abuse, acquaintance rape, substance abuse and drug trafficking, drunk driving and shoplifting. The activities are designed to enable students to understand civic problems of crime and to take action to prevent it.

The Think Aloud Program. Champaign, IL: Research Press.

Bonnie Camp and Mary Ann Bash developed this program, based on the concepts of cognitive behavior modification, to teach students self-instruction through verbal mediation. The students are taught to identify a problem, generate solutions, monitor their solutions, and assess their performance by answering the following questions: What is my problem? What is my plan? Am I using my plan? How did I do? The program provides activities to increase self-management skills.

The Discover Skills for Life. Educational Assessment Publishing Company, Inc.

This series includes a program for students in elementary and secondary grades. It is built on the belief that drug abuse and its related problems result primarily from high-risk or unhealthy lifestyle choices. The program is intended to create safe and drug-free schools by presenting decision-making and relationship skills as well as drug information and ways to prevent violence and build self-esteem. In addition, it offers 24 videos—4 per grade—organized around the unit themes. The program also offers a Spanish version and a parent-child learning library.

Scripting: Social Communication for Adolescents. Eau Claire, WI: Thinking.

The goal of this book by Patty Mayo and Patti Waldo (1986) is to increase social communication skills and to teach positive interpersonal skills in the home, school, and community. Many discipline problems occur because of students' deficits in social language. Students may have difficulty in conversing in a socially acceptable fashion and may interrupt or monopolize a conversation. The use of profanities and inappropriate facial expressions, gestures, and body posture are frequent reasons for punishment. Difficulties with communication competence can persist into adulthood and affect students' academic, vocational, and social performance. The scripts, the situations, and the activities of this program help to promote a unit approach to teaching social skills.

A Sourcebook of Pragmatic Activities (Grades pre-K–6) and *A Sourcebook of Adolescent Pragmatic Activities* (Grades 7–12). Tucson, AZ: Communication Skill Builder.

Barbara Weinrich, Ann Glasser, & Elizabeth Johnston (1986) offer activities to address social communication. The program contains an organized series of lesson plans for remediating pragmatic problems. The programs include lessons to teach social-linguistic rules and roles that create successful experiences in school and to provide students with effective social communication skills.

Thinking, Feeling, Behaving. Champaign, IL: Research Press.

Ann Vernon (1989) developed an emotional education curriculum for students in Grades 1–6 and 7–12. She based her program on RET in order to provide professionals working in schools with a curriculum to help youngsters develop positive mental health concepts. Each volume contains 90 activities arranged by grade levels and grouped into the following areas: self-acceptance, feelings, beliefs and behaviors, problem solving and decision making, and interpersonal relationships.

Guidelines for Selecting a Social Skills Program

Numerous projects involving social skills training in public schools have had encouraging results. The New Haven Social Competence Program in the New Haven public schools, Grades 5–8, was assessed by independent observers. Compared to a control group, the experimental group revealed better impulse control, improved problem-solving skills, and improved interpersonal effectiveness and popularity (Weissberg & Shriver, 1996).

When selecting a social skills program, ask the following questions:

1. Does the program address the needs of particular groups of students in my school? If violence and/or drugs are pressing problems, does the curriculum include these problems?
2. Does the program address the needs of diverse cultures reflected in the student body, or does it appeal to a single culture?
3. Are the social skills universal? Do they teach values for good

citizenship, or are they biased and oriented toward a specific philosophy or religion?

4. Do the strategies involve students in relevant and motivating activities?

5. Is the program based on sound theory?

6. Do the activities consider individual differences and aptitudes?

7. Are the activities feasible and practical for my situation?

8. Will the parents and administrators support the program?

9. Is the program flexible, and will I be able to adapt it to my teaching schedule?

10. Is the program adaptable, and will I be able to correlate other activities to the goals and objectives?

Summary

John Dewey (1938) believed in educating the whole child. Nearly a century later, educators are still predominantly concerned with standardized testing and teaching basic skills. Emotional, interpersonal, and intrapersonal intelligences are essential to a holistic approach to education. Lack of these intelligences frequently results in antisocial behavior, such as withdrawal, aggression, and violence. The research on brain-compatible learning is opening new avenues to understanding why children behave the way they do and what is needed to help them behave and learn. Educators can enrich brain potential by providing a warm and nurturing environment. Emotional intelligence means having the ability to understand one's emotions, to manage one's emotions, to motivate oneself, to recognize emotions in others, and to handle relationships. Similar to emotional intelligence, interpersonal and intrapersonal intelligences are important for achieving self-realization and for getting along with others. An understanding of how children develop in moral and character growth is essential to help children grow in emotional intelligence and develop social behavior. A wholesome education should include affective as well as cognitive instruction. Social and emotional skills can be taught and learned. Social skills interventions can have positive effects on students with behavior problems. Teachers can manipulate the environment to create a drive within students to learn and behave. Students who lack motivation eventually give up and experience a state referred to as learned helplessness. They feel like victims manipulated by their environment. Teachers can help such students by teaching self-management procedures and by showing care and concern.

Numerous programs are available to teach social skills to students in elementary and secondary schools. Teachers must consider several factors when selecting a social skills curriculum, such as learners' needs, parental support, school needs, objectivity in teaching good citizenship values, and relevant and motivating activities.

Activity 1: What Is Your Emotional Quotient (EQ)?

Answer (1) yes, (2) no, or (3) sometimes to the following questions.

1. Can you wait for a positive reinforcement (reward or praise) for at least 8 hours?____
2. Do you identify with people in trouble to understand how they feel? ____
3. Do you persist in completing a difficult task? ____
4. Can you motivate yourself, even if the task is boring or difficult? ____
5. Can you control your temper in a difficult situation? ____
6. Would you complete a household task without getting paid or rewarded? ____
7. Do you find it difficult to wait for your turn to speak without interrupting? ____
8. Can you work cooperatively in a group? ____
9. When you are in a bad mood, can you continue with your life without taking it out on others? ____
10. Can you think things through (analyze) when you feel frustrated or angry? ____

Total number of "yes" answers:

9 or 10 = a very high EQ	3 or 4 = a low EQ
7 or 8 = a fairly high EQ	1 or 2 = a very low EQ
5 or 6 = an average EQ	0 or 1 = danger zone

Activity 2: Strategies for Moral Development

Organize in small groups and read the following scenario. Determine Sophia's level of moral development, and develop three strategies to help Sophia improve her behavior and progress in her development.

Sophia, a 10-year-old fifth grader, has a problem keeping friends. At home she is constantly fighting with her 4-year-old sister. In school she frequently instigates arguments, disrupts instruction, and projects blame onto others. She is manipulative and uses others to satisfy her own needs. Her behavior has improved somewhat only because her teacher and her parents decided to deny her privileges and implement a time-out system of punishment whenever Sophia acts out. However, she resumes her obnoxious behavior whenever the adults relax the punishment.

Strategy 1:

Strategy 2:

Strategy 3:

Activity 3: Writing Goals and Objectives

1. Divide workshop participants into five small groups. Assign a different social skill area to each group and direct participants to write a major goal and an objective for each sub-goal.

2. Direct them to develop one activity for each objective.

3. Tape each group's poster paper in view of everyone and direct a spokesperson from each small group to discuss their group's goal, objectives, and activities.

References and Suggested Readings

Albert, L. (1982). *Cooperative discipline.* Circle Pines, MN: American Guidance Service.

Bandura, A. (1977). Self-efficacy: Toward a unified theory of behavioral change. *Psychological Review 84,* 191–215.

Bee, H. (1992). *The developing child* (6th ed.). New York: HarperCollins.

Bloom, B. (1981). *All children learning.* New York: Pergamon.

Bodine, R., Crawford, D., & Schrumpf, F. (1996). *Creating the peaceable school.* Champaign, IL: Research Press.

Caine, R., & Caine, G. (1994). *Making connections: Teaching and the human brain.* Menlo Park, CA: Addison-Wesley.

Coombs-Richardson, R., & Meisgeier, C. (2000). *Connecting with others: Lessons for teaching social and emotional competence.* Champaign, IL: Research Press. (For Grades 9–12)

Covey, S. (1990). *The seven habits of highly effective people: Powerful lessons in personal change.* New York: Simon & Schuster.

Dewey, J. (1938). *Experience and education.* New York: Collier.

Diamond. M. (1988). *Enriching heredity: The impact of the environment on the anatomy of the brain.* New York: Free Press.

Dowd, T., & Tierney, J. (1995). *Teaching social skills to youth.* Boys Town, NE: Father Flanagan's Boys Home.

Dreikurs, R. (1982). *Maintaining sanity in the classroom* (2nd ed.). New York: Harper & Row.

Drew, N. (1987). *Learning the Skills of Peacemaking.* Rolling Hills, CA: Jalmar Press.

Eisenberg, E. (1990). Prosocial development in early and mid-adolescence. In R. Montemayor, G. S. Adams, & T. P. Gullotta (Eds.), *From childhood to adolescence: A transitional period?* (pp. 240–268). Newberry Park, CA:

Gagne, R., & Briggs, L. (1992). *Principles of instructional design.* New York: Holt, Rinehart, & Winston.

Gardner, H. (1993). *Multiple intelligences: Theory into practice.* New York: Basic Books.

Goldstein, A. (1988). *The prepare curriculum.* Champaign, IL: Research Press.

Goldstein, A. (1999). *The skillstreaming series.* Champaign, IL: Research Press.

Goleman, D. (1995). *Emotional intelligence: Why it can matter more than IQ.* New York: Bantam Books.

Hoffman, M. (1970). Moral development. In P. H. Mussen (Ed.), *Carmichael's manual of child psychology* (Vol. 2). New York: Wiley.

Kaplan, J. S. (1995). *Beyond behavior modification: A cognitive-behavioral approach to behavior management in the school* (3rd ed.). Austin, TX: Pro-Ed.

Kohlberg, L. (1976). Stage and sequence: The cognitive-development approach to socialization. In D. A. Goslin (Ed.), *Handbook of socialization theory and research.* Chicago: Rand McNally.

LeDoux, J. (1994). *Mind and the brain: Dialogues in cognitive neurosciences.* New York: Cambridge University Press.

Mayer, J. D., & Salovey, P. (1993). The intelligence of emotional intelligence. *Intelligence* 17, 433–442.

Mayo, P., & Waldo, P. (1986). *Scripting: Social communication for adolescents.* Eau Claire, WI: Thinking.

Meichenbaum, D. (1975). Self-instructional methods. In F. H. Kanfer & A. P. Goldstein (Eds.). *Helping people change.* New York: Pergamon Press.

Meisgeier, C., Meisgeier, C., & Weisenfelder, C. (1982). *Exploring differences.* Houston, TX: Synergistic Education Associates.

Nazario, S. L. (1990, April 6). Schoolteachers say it's wrongheaded to try to teach students what's right. *The Wall Street Journal,* p. B8.

Richardson, R. C. (1996). *Connecting with others: Lessons for teaching social and emotional competence.* Champaign, IL: Research Press. (For K–5)

Richardson, R. C., & Evans, E. (1998). *Connecting with others: Lessons for teaching social and emotional competence.* Champaign, IL: Research Press. (For Grades 6–8)

Selman, R. (1976). Social-cognitive understanding: A guide to educational and clinical Practice. In T. Lickona (Ed.), *Moral development and behavior.* New York: Holt, Rinehart, & Winston.

Sprenger, M. (1999). *Learning and memory: The brain in action.* Alexandria, VA: Association for Supervision and Curriculum Development.

Sylwester, R. (1995). *A celebration of neurons: An educator's guide to the human brain.* Alexandria, VA: Association for Supervision and Curriculum Development.

Vernon, A. (1989). *Thinking, feeling, behaving.* Champaign, IL: Research Press.

Weinrich, B., Glasser, A., & Johnson, E. (1986). *A sourcebook of pragmatic activities.* Tucson, AZ: Communication Skill Builder.

Weissberg, R., & Shriver, T. (1996). *School-based prevention programs: A comprehensive strategy.* Philadelphia: Mid-Atlantic Laboratory for Student Success. (ERIC Document Reproduction Services No. ED 403 338).

Part II

Discipline Models

Chapter

Discipline With Loose Bounderies

Overview

Progressivism: Child-Centered Education
    John Dewey

Communication
    Teacher effectiveness training (TET): Thomas Gordon
    Sane messages, labeling, correcting, and expressing
        feelings: Haim Ginott

Transactional Analysis
    Examining interactions: Eric Berne, Thomas Harris
    The different states: The parent, the child, the adult

Creative Emotional Expression
    Music, art, free play, role-play, sociodramatic play,
        puppetry, bibliotherapy

Influencing and Supporting Techniques
    Managing surface behaviors
    Life-space interviews

Habits of the Mind
    Managing impulsivity
    Understanding and empathy

Summary

Activities

Q U E S T I O N S

This chapter will help you to answer the following questions:

1. How did John Dewey's progressivism beliefs influence behavior management in today's schools?

2. How did Thomas Gordon adapt Dewey's scientific problem solving in the "no lose" approach?

3. How would you change the following you-message to an I-message? "Stop talking now, you are such a problem in this class, you are the worst chatterbox in this entire school."

4. Which procedure (active listening or an I-message) should the teacher use when the student owns the problem?

5. Which procedure (active listening or an I-message) should the teacher use when the teacher owns the problem?

6. What are some of the roadblocks to communication as identified by Thomas Gordon?

7. What actions exemplify your enthusiastic child? Your manipulative child? Your bossy parent? Your caring parent?

8. How would your adult state respond to this bossy parent statement? "You must turn in your homework first thing in the morning, or else I will have to call your parents."

9. What creative expression techniques can you use to establish cooperation and collaboration in your classroom?

10. Which habits of the mind contribute to social behaviors?

Overview

Is it the teacher's role to counsel students and address their psychological needs? Do teachers require intense training in psychology to implement discipline strategies that focus on students' unconscious responses and emotional processes? Or are guidance counselors, school social workers, and psychologists the most appropriate professionals to assume this function? In the best of possible worlds, these specially trained professionals should shoulder such responsibilities. However, in the real world, teachers are expected to teach the "whole" student, cognitively and affectively. The "discipline with loose boundaries" model suggests a variety of strategies within the affective domain, focusing on emotional concerns. Although several of the strategies may appear to be impractical to the classroom teacher, we believe that many are worthwhile and can be modified to fit individual needs.

The study of psychiatry and psychology has focused on the inner nature of human beings. The cause of behavior (*why* students behave they way they do) must first be established in order to determine the best intervention or cure. Education methods based on such models endorse strategies that allow students to examine and express their feelings in relation to their behavior. These models advocate placing limited boundaries and emphasize guiding students to achieve unmet psychological needs. Followers of this model believe that coercive tactics can actually increase resistance, hostility, and aggression. In addition to a caring environment, teachers must be proactive in preventing disruptions in the classroom.

This chapter gives a brief history of child–centered education as advocated by Plato, Jean-Jacques Rousseau, and John Dewey. Their influence is evident in the discipline methods recommended by Thomas Gordon and Haim Ginott. Gordon believes that too many adults use roadblocks such as threats, sarcasm, and preaching when communicating with youngsters. He considers this method of communication to be ineffective and believes that it results in more harm than good. Gordon suggests a "no-lose" conflict resolution approach in which both parties can emerge as winners. Gordon's active listening and I-messages contribute to an ongoing developmental discipline method in which the teacher's role is to facilitate. Ginott's method is also based on positive interactions with students. Teachers and students must be able to communicate and express their feelings in a controlled manner. He advises teachers to model social behaviors and to direct students toward positive outcomes.

An understanding of transactional analysis (TA), proposed by Eric Berne and Thomas Harris, is helpful to increase self-awareness and awareness of others as well as to examine messages contained in various interactions. Berne describes three ego states, or attitudes, that people assume when dealing with others: the parent, the child, and the adult. The parent can be bossy or caring, the child can be manipulative and rebellious or enthusiastic and creative. The adult is the referee between the parent and the child; this is our rational state, our thinking self. TA describes positive "OK" interactions and negative "not OK" interactions and explains how "OK" and "not OK" feelings can be permanently recorded in a person's memory and lead to positive or negative behaviors. TA provides an understanding of attitudes and attitudinal changes that can lead to more mature behaviors and outcomes.

Art and play are used extensively in therapeutic settings to help individuals get in touch with their feelings. Creative expression—which includes, art, music, drama, play, and role-playing—is an effective way to teach cooperation and self-awareness. In addition, the chapter reviews simple interventions to restore order in the classroom. Influencing and supporting techniques are quick interventions that teachers may use to manage surface or potential behaviors. Teachers can diffuse potential problems by changing their own behaviors—for instance, standing close to the misbehaving student (proximity control), sending a potential problem student on an errand (antiseptic bouncing), offering individual assistance (hurdle helping), or using a nonverbal sign (signal interference).

Teachers can discover underlying problems by applying a technique known as life-space interviews, in which the teacher listens and poses guided questions. Another method we describe is called habits of the mind, which teaches students to manage impulsivity and develop empathy.

Progressivism: Child-Centered Education

Individuals who advocate discipline with loose boundaries believe in placing limited adult control around children. Children are empowered and given choices in order to develop self-discipline. The adherents of this philosophy believe that discipline problems are more likely to occur when school personnel control, manipulate, and shape the behavior of students. The opponents of this philosophy consider it to be too permissive and unconventional. They lament that students in "the good old days" did not dare to pose discipline problems because of strict, imposed, and controlling methods. Actually, discipline with loose boundaries can be traced back to the time of Plato, who recommended that education be compatible with each child's aptitudes. Plato suggested a noncoercive approach, using gentle probing to discover each child's natural talents (Hale, 1971). In the 18th century, Rousseau believed in the innate goodness of children and in their ability to find the right path with little adult supervision or direction (Gorman, 1980).

The 20th century witnessed different and competing values regarding public education. Some educators believed that schools could best serve society by socializing and controlling students through scientific manipulation based on behavioral techniques. Others believed in the progressive ideas of Jean Piaget, Maria Montessori, and John Dewey, who espoused reforms that would personalize and democratize education. Dewey (1938) intended education to be the channel to a more egalitarian and democratic society. His ideas of progressive education did not reach the majority of students, however, but were practiced only in schools serving the elite. Instead, the public schools chose the "factory model" of structuring schools to educate the masses. The emphasis was once again placed on content and standardized practices. In addition, the discipline of psychology was struggling to be accepted as a "science" so it applied B. F. Skinner's behavioral methods in empirical research. Education followed psychology in this regard and adopted behavioral procedures rather than a child-centered approach to discipline. Teachers were trained to observe, count, and chart behaviors and to apply positive and negative reinforcement and punishment to modify behavior. Dewey, on the other hand, believed that imposed control did not teach students to resolve problems. He believed that guiding students to use the scientific problem-solving method could help them to develop rational responses to the conflicts and dilemmas they would encounter throughout life (Borich & Tombari, 1995).

The progressive philosophy of Dewey is felt within the discipline with loose boundaries model. Progressivism views human beings as basically good and that when students are allowed freedom, they will generally choose the best course of action. Contrary to some misinterpretations of this approach, Dewey did see the need for teachers to provide guidance in the learning environment for meaningful learning to take place. Dewey placed a heavy emphasis on developing students' problem-solving skills, and many of his followers believed that inductive teaching could help students to resolve their conflicts with limited adult interference. *Inductive teaching* requires students to develop their own solutions rather than depend on some already established reasoning. Dewey believed that students can learn from experience; therefore, teachers must use students' experiences and exploratory methods to guide them in finding effective solutions. Followers of Dewey's ideas believed that students could be motivated to learn and would be less inclined to misbehave when they were given autonomy and choices in their learning and treated with respect and empathy (Karges-Bone, 1997).

The ideals of progressive education are resurfacing in the 21st century. Educators are seeking and using models to personalize and democratize learning. Dewey's egalitarian vision inspired reformers to support an inclusive education in which students could learn together regardless of race, gender, ethnicity, or disability. Teachers in numerous schools are implementing strategies such as whole language, cooperative learning, cross-curriculum thematic instruction, and attention to individual learning styles. On the other hand, educators are caught between the push to personalize learning and the demand for a uniform curriculum, scripted teaching, and mandated testing. Deborah Meier (2000) describes this dichotomy as "the factory model school redesigned for the 21st century workplace—and considered the latest in progressive thinking." Teachers who are trying to implement Dewey's vision need skills to reach out to students through effective and meaningful communication.

Communication

Teacher Effectiveness Training (TET)

Thomas Gordon (1974) emphasized communication as crucial in establishing positive interactions and in avoiding and resolving conflict. He was influenced by the teachings of John Dewey (1938), Abraham Maslow (1968), and Carl Rogers (1961). Maslow and Rogers agreed that nature and nurture have great influence on the individual, but they emphasized that people have the capacity to move forward in personal development in spite of genetics and past experiences. They believed that self-concept, attitudes, and beliefs make up our true identity. We develop our self-concept based on our experiences with the world and our interactions with others. However, we are also free to choose what to believe and which direction to take. Maslow maintained that every human being is directed toward self-actualization; however, unmet basic needs interfere with personal achievement. Maslow proposed a hierarchy of human needs that must be met in ascending order. That is, we are unable to meet our highest need, that of self-actualization, when our physiological needs, social needs, belonging needs, and esteem needs remain unfulfilled. Individuals become maladjusted when their sense of self is in opposition to their expectations. Rogers believed that we can achieve our potential only when the needs for love and self-esteem are actualized. Teachers can help students to achieve their potential by trusting them to take control of their lives and by guiding them in this process.

Thomas Gordon (1974) incorporated Rogerian concepts into teacher practices. He took his cues from Maslow and Rogers and believed that control and coercive methods prevent students from achieving their full potential. He advised teachers to become active listeners: to "listen" to the students' feelings as well as their words and to refrain from using roadblocks to communication such as threats, sarcasm, criticism, orders, admonishments, lectures, shame, and moralizing. The following scenario illustrates listening to words but not to feelings:

> *Student:* This work is dumb, why do I have to know how to figure out percent, I have a calculator that can do it for me.
>
> *Teacher:* Roy, what if you lost your calculator? Settle down and do your work, or else I'll double your homework assignment.
>
> *Student:* I don't care. (*Tears up his worksheet, puts his head on the desk and pretends to nap*)

The next scenario illustrates listening to Roy's feelings as well as to his words.

> *Student:* This work is dumb, I can't figure this out. Why do I have to know how to do percentages, I have a calculator that can do it for me.
>
> *Teacher:* (*thinks*) Roy is usually good in math, he must be feeling frustrated working with percentages. (*responds*) Roy, I hear you say that you are having difficulties figuring out percentages, and that really frustrates you.
>
> *Roy:* Yeah, this has really got me. I was good with fractions.
>
> *Teacher:* Let me show you an easy way to do it. I always had a hard time with decimals myself, once upon a time. Thank goodness for calculators, but it's good to know how to do it yourself.

In the second scenario, the student is more likely to continue the conversation and to avoid a confrontation.

Gordon explained two techniques that, when properly used, could deter many discipline problems and produce a positive teacher-student relationship: *active listening* and *I-messages*. Teachers must first analyze each individual situation to determine which of the two techniques to use. Active listening is used when students own the problem, and I-messages are used when the teacher owns the problem. In the Roy scenario, the student owned the problem because he was unable to do the assignment. The teacher listened actively: "I hear you say that you are having difficulties figuring out percentages." In active listening, a person listens attentively, tuning in to subtle verbal and nonverbal cues such as body language and tone of voice. The listener encourages communication by feeding back the message to the speaker. The listener may paraphrase the message or describe the feeling.

Gordon suggested using *door openers* or *communication leads* after listening carefully. Communication leads may start with supportive phrases: "you feel . . . ," "What I hear you saying . . . ," "Where you're coming from . . . ," "It seems to you. . . ." Teachers may use door openers such as "Go on" or "That's interesting, tell me more" to encourage students to continue the conversation. Sometimes passive listening is required. In some circumstances silence communicates acceptance. However, one may use occasional acknowledgment expressions to show that one is tuned in to what is being said. These cues my be verbal or nonverbal but should not cause interruptions to the student's message. The listener may nod, smile, lean forward, frown, or use other body movements to indicate attention. Verbal cues such as "Oh, wow," "You don't say," "Gee," or "Yikes" also indicate that the listener is attentive.

Teacher-owned problems occur when students' behaviors prevent the teacher or others from functioning. For example: If Roy accelerated his behavior and threw a temper tantrum, cursed, and interfered with the other students' right to learn, then the teacher and his classmates would have a problem. I-messages are used when the teacher owns the problem; they involve the willingness of teachers to disclose their feelings about the students' misbehavior. I-messages do not attack the person but are directed at the behavior. As a result, students do not feel personally threatened; they realize that authority figures are human and subject to the same feelings as everyone else. On the other hand, a you-message attacks the person: "You are so lazy and irresponsible." It is demeaning and humiliating and provokes anger and retaliation. Gordon suggests the following guidelines to forming effective I-messages:

1. Describe the student's behavior. In the event of Roy's temper tantrum, the teacher could say: "Roy, throwing a temper tantrum and cursing . . ."

2. Describe the effect of the behavior on the teacher: ". . . prevents me from teaching, and prevents students from learning. We have a problem."

3. Describe the feeling: ". . . and that makes me feel very upset."

Active listening and I-messages are certainly useful techniques in many situations. However, it is sometimes difficult to determine who "owns" the problem. In addition, many hostile youngsters feel victorious when they manage to upset the teacher. A positive teacher-student relationship must first be established in order for the students to care about how the teacher feels. Gordon believes that such a relationship can be achieved by providing a democratic climate in which students are empowered and are given certain rights. He describes three methods of resolving conflicts. The first two are win-lose methods. Method 1 is an authoritarian approach in which teachers use their power to win and the students lose (I win–you lose). When this method is consistently used, students feel powerless, hostile, and resentful. Method 2 is a permissive approach described as "Okay, you win, I give up." The teacher who uses this method allows students to do what they want until the situation become so chaotic that the teacher switches to method 1, and the conflict continues. Gordon proposes method 3, which he labels "no-lose." Prior to using this method, teachers must have acquired some competence in active listening and in using I-messages. Method 3 is also a further application of Dewey's scientific method of problem solving. It has six separate steps:

1. Defining the problem: My problem is I am constantly interrupting the teacher.
2. Generating possible solutions: I could count to 10 before talking. I could bite my tongue as a reminder. I could put my head on my desk when I get the urge to interrupt.
3. Evaluating the solutions: Biting my tongue hurts, and putting my head on my desk will appear as if I am not listening. Counting to 10 may help, but 10 seconds isn't much.
4. Deciding which solution is best: I guess I could count to 10 twice at first and gradually decrease the count.
5. Determining how to implement the decision: I could keep a written tally of my counting and let the teacher in on my plan.
6. Assessing how well the solution works: This is great. I don't even need to count anymore, and the teacher listens to my comments whenever I speak.

Gordon believed that a principal cause of antisocial behavior is an over-reliance on punitive discipline for the purpose of control. Guiding students to solve their own problems promotes self-discipline. Gordon's techniques, though effective for relationship building, do not offer solutions for serious discipline problems, but, they are excellent proactive measures to prevent discipline problems and to build caring teacher-student relationships.

Sane Messages, Labeling, Correcting, and Expressing Feelings

Haim Ginott (1972) extended the work of Carl Rogers by emphasizing the art of effective communication between students and teachers. He believed that teachers are able to achieve meaningful communication with their students when they use effective alternatives to punishment. Ginott advocated setting boundaries on certain behaviors; however, no limits should be set on feelings. All feelings are to be accepted, no matter how inappropriate they might seem. For example: Tom is angry, so he punches Don and gives him a bloody nose. Ginott would ask Tom to verbally express his angry, jealous, frustrated feelings, but would place limits on his behavior. "Tom, I understand your feelings of anger, but people are not for punching." The next step would be to provide a symbolic outlet for the feeling: "If you feel like you have to punch to express your feelings, there's a punching bag in the gym."

Ginott advised teachers to regard discipline as a developmental process to be accomplished over time. Disruptive students can change their behaviors in the long run when teachers are "at their best" in working with them. Teachers "at their worst" are caustic, sarcastic, and demeaning. They attack students' characters, deny their feelings, label them, and demand cooperation. They use praise and tangible reinforcement to elicit compliance and often use grades to manipulate students. Teachers "at their best" invite cooperation. They accept and acknowledge feelings, avoid labeling, correct by directing, and convey "sane messages" that address the behavior rather than the students' characters. Teachers must provide appropriate models of behavior for their students.

Ginott's concepts of sane messages, labeling, correcting, and expressing feelings merit close attention. The following is a brief explanation of these concepts.

Sane messages: Ginott warns against personal attacks on the student's character: "You are such a chatterbox" or "You have a filthy garbage mouth." Instead, Ginott's sane message would attack the situation: " No talking" or "No cursing or swearing—cursing is against the rules."

Labeling: Calling a student "lazy," "chatterbox," "garbage mouth," or "troublemaker" sends a self-fulfilling message, and students will live up to the label. Instead, Ginott suggests that teachers remind students how they are expected to behave.

Correcting: Correction should not dwell on the inappropriate behavior but should teach the appropriate behavior. Teachers must show the student how to behave and, if necessary, repeat the lesson until the student can demonstrate the desired behavior. For example, the teacher should not say, "How many times must I tell you to stop talking? This is your fifth warning, now stop it." Instead, the teacher can say, "No talking while working."

Expressing feelings: Teachers and students alike should be able to express their feelings in a controlled manner. The tone of voice and the verbal and nonverbal communication should be free of attack. Teachers should not belittle the offending student, nor should the student use offensive language. Ginott urges teachers to acknowledge students' feelings: "Tom, I understand your feelings of anger, but people are not for punching."

Effective communication is essential to help students get in touch with their emotions as well as their behaviors. In many cases, students are unable to define what they feel. An understanding of what is happening in various transactions can be helpful in increasing self-awareness and awareness of others. Students then become more analytic and adept in resolving their daily dilemmas.

Transactional Analysis

Transactional analysis (TA) has its roots in Freudian psychology and stresses the influence of early experiences and traumatic events on emotions and behavior. It has even been used in defensive driving courses to teach drivers the dangers of persevering in childlike behaviors behind the wheel.

Sigmund Freud (1924/1952) advanced the theory that the psyche has three parts: the id, the ego, and the superego. The id is the instinctual part and is dominated by a tendency for self-gratification. The ego, the reality-oriented part of the psyche, tries to direct the id to find satisfaction in appropriate ways. The superego is the conscience, the rules that tell a person what to do or not do.

The following example illustrates how these three parts of the psyche work.

Paul, a middle school adolescent, is taking a final history exam. He did not study for the exam and is having difficulty figuring out the answers. He looks at Ken's paper to copy his answers. In Freudian terms, his id is telling his ego to copy Ken's work so that he will not receive a failing grade. His teacher catches him cheating and gives him an F. Paul also tries to cheat in his Math and English classes, but his teachers are wise to his cheating, and he fails at every attempt. After a number of such encounters, Paul develops a superego (a set of rules to avoid getting an F), which guides his ego in choosing a different behavior. In Freudian psychology, all behaviors are the outcome of the id, the ego, and the superego, with the ego mediating between the other two. Education professionals have simplified and applied Freudian concepts to their practices, and they are frequently used by psychologists, school counselors, social workers, and teachers.

Examining Interactions

TA is a method to develop awareness of our attitudes and behaviors when interacting and communicating with others. Children often perceive teachers as bossy and authoritarian; teachers are constantly giving orders and telling students when they should and should not do. TA originated in Eric Berne's book *Games People Play* (1964) and was further developed by Thomas Harris in *I'm OK, you're OK* (1969). Berne describes three states that are roughly equivalent to Freud's three parts of the psyche: the child (id), the adult (ego), and the parent (superego). Horizontal transactions from adult to adult indicate healthy interactions. Diagonal transactions, in which someone takes the parent role and someone takes the child role, may not be healthy. Very often teachers assume a parent (bossy) attitude when confronting misbehaving students. This in turn often increases students' hostility and results in further misbehavior. Understanding the parent, the child, and the adult is helpful in evaluating and changing our behavior to facilitate interactions.

The Different States

The parent state can assume two attitudes: a caring and nurturing attitude or a domineering and controlling attitude. We often "rewind and play" our bossy parent tapes when we make statements such as "You ought to be ashamed of yourself, you should know better" or "Don't you lie to me." The parent attitude is often used to evoke obedience or to instill social values; however, an excessively controlling attitude can intimidate and alienate students. This state relies on the use of guilt, fear, and control. The parent tells others what they should and should not do. Body language such as pointing and shaking the index finger reveals the bossy parent. The nurturing parent, on the other hand, shows care, concern, and consideration. Teachers show this side of the parent state when they tell their students to get plenty of rest before an exam, for instance. The caring parent's body language is open and inviting: a pat on the back, a hug, or another sign of approval.

The child state can also assume two attitudes: irresponsible, hedonistic, irrational, and impulsive or enthusiastic, fun loving, and creative. The positive child feels OK because of nurturing experiences in the formative years. Whenever we let down our inhibitions and have fun, we are showing our pleasure-seeking child. Daydreaming is a childlike activity that allows us to be creative; it offers a retreat and creates possibilities. Misbehaving students allow their negative child to be in control when they conflict with parents, teachers, or peers. Students may carry a "wounded inner child" who suffered painful experiences, causing them not to feel OK. Teachers who recognize this attitude can change their own attitude from a bossy parent to a caring parent or switch to the adult state.

The adult state is rational. Children who have been exposed to adults modeling this state are more likely to become insightful and logical. They are able to examine their behavior and its consequences and can make decisions based on careful deliberation. They demonstrate a high level of intrapersonal and interpersonal intelligences. They seek information and process the data rationally and realistically. The adult state is the "referee" between the child and the parent; it is wise to the game playing of both the parent and the child. The adult gives the parent permission to give sound advice: "You should study for the test and make an outline of the events from 1860–1864." The adult also allows the expression of the enthusiastic child: "Let us cheer our team loudly at the game." However, the adult state knows how to discriminate and behave in different situations. The adult is sensible and knows when to be assertive and when to keep a low profile.

Subsequent authors have applied TA concepts in developing discipline and social skills programs. Alvyn Freed adapted the TA concept for children of all ages: *TA for Tots* (1971), *TA for Kids* (1973), and *TA for Teens* (1988). Ken Ernest (1973) authored a student version of Berne's book, and Rita C. Richardson (1996) incorporated the three states in her social skills program.

TA provides tools to learn interaction skills to cope with dilemmas and to grow in maturity and understanding. It does not, however, provide a definite plan for teaching self-discipline and behavior change. Teachers and students need structured training, along with school administration and parental support, to effectively implement a TA program.

Creative Emotional Expression

Music, art, free play, role-play and sociodramatic play, puppetry, and bibliotherapy are excellent channels for expressing personal feelings. Numerous students come to school with hurtful experiences and act out their negative emotions in acts of defiance, noncompliance, and aggression. Other students withdraw and disengage from school-related tasks and activities and develop learned helplessness; they feel powerless, apathetic, and discouraged because of repeated failures and lack of a positive self-concept. Teaching through the expressive media can influence students to be motivated to learn. This method also addresses the concept of multiple intelligences and is especially appealing to students with strong musical, spatial, kinesthetic, and verbal-linguistic intelligences. Social motivation can be a powerful force through which to engage students in their learning and can consequently decrease discipline problems. Teachers can use various media that allow students to express their feelings in constructive ways. Discipline within a loose boundary framework offers strategies to help students express their anger, stress, and frustrations in socially acceptable ways. Many of the expressive media strategies offer acceptable pathways to vent emotions and provide channels to communicate, interrelate, and find solutions to problems.

Traditionally, schools have given a great deal of attention to the cognitive side of learning. Subjects such as art, music, and even physical education are often thought to be "extras." When money is unavailable, these subjects are the first to be cut back. However, the arts are important vehicles for teaching academic and emotional competence. They include: composing and reciting poetry, playing a musical instrument, composing melodies, singing, writing lyrics, writing and acting out scripts, clay manipulations and sculpture, photography and videotaping, free drawing, and computer graphics. Brain research makes us realize that emotions, creativity, and cognitive learning cannot be separated. Brain-compatible teaching and learning stimulates the brain and builds creativity, concentration, problem solving, coordination, motivation, and a positive self-concept. The arts promote an affective curriculum of social behavior leading to self-discipline and social interactions and encourage a sense of belonging to the school community. In a 1990 Florida study, researchers documented the role of fine and performing arts in dropout prevention, improving student motivation, and decreasing discipline problems. The report noted that teachers were amazed at the intensity of student interest and involvement in their learning when they participated in creative activities (Florida State University, 1990). The enthusiasm for expressing oneself through various art forms seemed to be a motivating force for attending classes and for the development of both academic and artistic skills.

Music

Music education has positive and lasting academic and social benefits. Of all the disciplines in the curriculum, music has the most success in fostering cooperative learning. Music significantly affects the moods of the learners. It also enhances abstract reasoning, social interactions, stress management, and memory retention. Young children learn to recite the letters of the alphabet through melody long before they begin their formal education. A few television programs have presented social skills through musical presentations; many children have learned social skills from songs featured in *Captain Kangaroo* and by Barney, the purple dinosaur. Youth values are often expressed in music. In the past four decades, popular music has been characterized by themes of social and political rebellion, friendship, narcissism, patriotism, love, and self-esteem. Many adults frown at numerous rap music lyrics, yet many "raps" also express messages that adults need to hear: hope, defiance, despair, and anger.

Art

Art is more than a symbolic representation of form. It is also the expression of emotion, moods, fantasies, and balance. Students enjoy manipulating substances in their art; finger paints, clay, sand, and even soapsuds provide opportunities to experiment with a multitude of new shapes, colors, and textures. Students learn to cooperate and experience success; perfection and real-life representation are not criteria for judging performance. Teachers may include artistic activities in an integrated thematic unit or use art as a problem-solving process. Young students in primary grades can draw pictures in their journals of a conflict incident and a conflict resolution and verbally explain what their drawings represent. Students can express feelings in a finger painting and explain their choice of colors to express various feelings, such as anger, love, happiness, sadness, jealousy, fear, courage, pride, and pain.

The following suggested activity illustrates an art project for secondary school students. Mr. Boudreaux, an English teacher, has a problem with gangs in his classroom. The gang members are discreet in their membership because of school regulations, but Mr. Boudreaux knows who belongs to certain gangs. Although the gangs have not yet engaged in violent acts, there is much antagonism between students. Mr. Boudreaux decides that he will use an art activity to create a more peaceful climate. He begins by forming heterogeneous cooperative groups, placing students from different gangs in each group. He directs each group to compose a "peace" art collage. The students are given some instruction and limitations but are allowed to use their graffiti talents to demonstrate the negative effects of war, violence, and hate on poster boards. Another group is instructed to compose poems or raps on peace and the consequences of the lack of peace. In addition, they may use graphic designs or hand drawings to illustrate their poetry. A third group is instructed to design a comic strip illustrating a conflict and a peaceful resolution.

Free Play

Young children are seldom able to talk about what is bothering them in a direct and effective way. Their natural medium is play; Sigmund Freud referred to play as a child's first cultural and psychological achievement. Through play children have the opportunity to express their thoughts and emotions. As young children interact, they begin to learn to cooperate and to understand what is socially acceptable and not acceptable. Inappropriate social roles are often the root of children's discipline problems. Through play activities, the teacher can guide young children to examine the consequences of their behaviors and can provide appropriate modeling. Virginia Axline (1947) and Haim Ginott (1972) suggest that teachers can gain valuable insight by observing children in play situations. Certain guidelines must be observed to facilitate this strategy. Defining play spaces is the first step in eliminating and avoiding undesirable behaviors. The classroom area must be clearly defined and explained. Teachers should avoid large open spaces within the room to eliminate running and chasing. These physical activities are appropriate for outdoor areas or in a gym. Teachers should also avoid complicated games and include group games, sandboxes, water tables, dollhouses, toy animals, trucks, cars, and other such play objects to stimulate expression of feelings and promote social interaction. Today's children have more toys that encourage solitary play than did children of earlier generations. In addition, children spend many hours watching television, which is likely to reduce the amount of time they have to develop their social skills in free-play situations. In free-play sessions, children are invited to use the play objects but are not directed or forced to use them. Teachers can teach organizational skills by labeling boxes with pictures for the various materials. Students learn where materials are stored and develop responsibility, organizational skills, and independence by putting things in their place when playtime is over. Many emerging social skills, such as sharing, taking turns, and conflict resolution, can be taught in a play atmosphere. Many behavior problems occur because of the lack of these competencies.

Role-Play and Sociodramatic Play

Role-playing is another form of play often used with students in primary and secondary grades. It allows students to experiment with a variety of behaviors and experience the reactions and consequences of behaviors in a safe and nonthreatening situation. Role-playing can enable students to clarify their feelings as they relate to their world. In reversing roles, students learn to experience the feelings of another character and thus to identify and empathize with the feelings of others. Role-playing allows children to express strong feelings, resolve conflicts, and associate these feelings and conflicts with experiences they can understand. Many students with behavior problems have difficulty expressing strong feelings such as anger and frustration. Role-play activities are safe avenues for such emotional manifestations without the fear of retribution or shame. Cecil and Ann Mercer (1997) suggest four steps in the role-playing process. We have amended the steps as follows:

1. Students, guided by the teacher, identify a specific problem that affects the entire classroom or a conflict between certain individuals (student-student or teacher-student).

2. The students and the teacher establish roles and assign these roles to various students. It is preferable for students to volunteer; students should not be forced to role-play.

3. Students enact the situation, and the role-play is brief. The same situation may be repeated with different actors to present different solutions.

4. A general class discussion follows, or separate cooperative groups can discuss and bring their solutions to the entire class. The discussion should focus on the behavior and not on the students' role-playing.

Puppetry

Puppets are usually used with young children to help them experience different emotions or to teach social skills and values. Basic values such as honesty, fairness, love, and loyalty are popular themes for puppet shows. Children will remember what happened to Pinocchio's nose when he told a lie. Puppets can increase students' awareness of the consequences of inappropriate behaviors in a nonthreatening atmosphere. Primary school teachers often engage in providing puppet theaters that involve students in developing puppets, topics, and scripts. Teachers may guide students to examine pressing social problems in the classroom; social problems may vary, from disruptiveness to shyness, peer rejection, stealing, cheating, and cursing. After the problem is identified, a general script is developed, characters are chosen, and the puppet show is implemented. After the show, the teacher engages the group in brainstorming several solutions to the puppets' problem. Five basic rules should be followed to protect students and to establish a democratic climate:

1. Ridicule and put-downs are not allowed.
2. The similarity of the puppets' behaviors to that of certain classmates must not be accentuated.
3. Avoid threatening issues.
4. Involve all students in the production, whether the task is creating the puppets, developing the scripts, or role-playing the characters.
5. Involve all students in the problem-solving discussion.

Elaborate commercial puppets can be purchased, but these are unnecessary; simple hand puppets are just as effective, and students enjoy creating them. In addition, students develop a sense of ownership when they are involved in the construction of the characters. They can be made out of paper sacks, paper mache, cloth, socks, and other materials.

Students in secondary schools can also engage in creating puppet shows to express personal dilemmas and to find solutions to school-related problems. In addition, they can be guided to produce a puppet show for younger students. English and art teachers may coordinate their teaching by including puppet script training and puppet construction in their programs. Life-size body puppets have been used in role-playing situations to facilitate conflict resolution and social skills learning.

Bibliotherapy

Bibliotherapy is a technique that uses literature to help students develop self-awareness and understanding of problems. The characters in a book learn to cope with difficulties similar to an existing one within a classroom or with individual students. In addition, the characteristics, attitudes, and behaviors of story characters can serve as models. When targeting a specific problem in a classroom, the teacher must do the following:

1. Clearly identify the problem
2. Select a story in literature that focuses on a similar problem
3. Read the story to the students, or direct the students to read the story
4. Ask questions that will cause the students to examine the emotional content of the literature

Example: How do you think the main character felt when he was not accepted in the group? Why did the members of the group reject him or her? How could they solve the problem? What can the main character do if the group refuses to change? For bibliotherapy to be effective, students must experience three phases (Gladding & Gladding, 1991):

1. Identification: Students must identify with the problems encountered by the main character.

2. Catharsis: Students must relate and release their feelings about the problems.

3. Insight: Students must empathize with the character or the plot and develop plans to solve their problems.

The books chosen for bibliotherapy should focus on a particular need and should be written at the students' independent reading level. The selection should depict a realistic approach and have lifelike characters. For bibliotherapy to be effective, students must become personally involved and identify with the situation in the story. They should be able to release emotional tension and empathize with the characters in the story. The teacher should guide the students in their discoveries but must allow the students to reach their own conclusions. When stories correlating to specific problems are not available, teachers and students can generate a story and "publish" it for discussion.

Influencing and Supporting Techniques

Teachers are responsible for setting the tone and for providing a healthy classroom atmosphere. They must be on guard against counteracting a student's aggression and anger. Otherwise, the student succeeds in perpetuating a self-fulfilling prophecy of life: "I make you angry because I'm no good; everybody hates me." School personnel must involve students' home and community life when considering interventions. However, if that is not possible, the school then becomes the major source of support for students. Teachers assume the role of influencing and supporting agents for many students who require it. Educators bear a tremendous responsibility as role models to students, and students quickly learn to distinguish between the "do as I say" and the "do as I do" teachers. Students from kindergarten to graduate school inevitably seek out teachers who are supportive and caring. The following strategies in managing surface behaviors are designed to prevent or decelerate disruptive behaviors. Life-space interviewing is a counseling technique traditionally used by psychologists, psychiatrists, counselors, and social workers. However, teachers can apply the basic elements of this interview to students with behavior problems.

Managing Surface Behaviors

Redl and Wineman (1957), suggest 12 behavior management techniques to prevent, diffuse, and correct inappropriate behaviors in the classroom. Teachers regularly implement many of these techniques. A main advantage is that they prevent incidents from developing into more difficult situations. Such incidents are less difficult to handle when they are "nipped in the bud." Another advantage revolves around two crucial rules for behavior management: Do not intervene unnecessarily and "pick your battles." The influencing techniques involve minimal interference and are therefore less likely to arouse counter hostility from students. Once applied, these supportive methods can assist students to regulate their own behaviors in an acceptable manner.

Planned ignoring. Some behaviors will decrease in frequency or disappear altogether when they are ignored. Paying attention to an inappropriate behavior is rewarding to an attention-seeking student, even if the attention is negative. Although this technique works well with certain students and certain behaviors, it is subject to limitations. The teacher must decide when to use planned ignoring and determine if the behavior is detrimental to others or to the teaching situation. For example, a child who is constantly raising his or her hand to answer questions can be intermittently ignored. A student who utters an unflattering comment under his or her breath may also be ignored. It is difficult if not impossible to ignore aggressive behavior.

Signal interference. Teachers learn to use their intuitive and prediction powers and know when there is a potential problem. Cues from the teacher—such as turning off the light, giving a stern stare, or tapping the chalk or a pencil—are often sufficient to restore order and prevent the acceleration of misbehavior.

Proximity control. What would you do if you were driving over the speed limit and you suddenly noticed a police car down the road? You would start slowing down. Frequently, the proximity of an authority figure (teacher, parent, or police officer) causes us to change our behavior. Teachers can move closer to students when they notice potential disruptive behaviors. The proximity of the teacher can also sometimes eliminate certain behaviors, such as talking, cheating, or daydreaming. In some cases, the teacher's closeness may help students who are experiencing anxiety and frustration to calm down and feel secure. The teacher's movement in the classroom helps to keep students on-task and sends them a message: "I am interested and involved with you in the task at hand." Shores, Gunter, and Jack (1993) recommend that teachers move about the room during seat-work activities instead of remaining isolated behind their desks.

Interest boosting. This is a technique used by teachers in drawing students' wandering attention back to work without scoldings, criticism, or sarcasm. This can be done by offering help, by offering a positive comment on the completed work, or by asking students for suggestions on how to make the work more interesting. This procedure serves to renew the students' interest in the task; the teacher must be assured that students have the necessary skills for successful completion.

Tension decontamination through humor. Humor can be used in a friendly way to handle behavior problems. A joke or funny remark will frequently reduce tension and increase the positive relationship with the teacher. Students will perceive the teacher as human and secure enough to be able to joke. However, humor must be used wisely and not at the expense of another. Sarcasm is not funny and can increase tension, aggression, and hostility. Many students, especially at the preadolescent stage, are very sensitive;

therefore, teachers must consider their particular group of students when they use humor.

Hurdle helping. Students sometimes misbehave because they cannot understand the work at hand. Rather than losing face in the eyes of their peers, they refuse to ask for help or announce that "this work is dumb." The sense of frustration and anxiety that results from their inability to do the work is further accelerated upon seeing their peers working and succeeding at the task. This frustration is often demonstrated in misbehavior such as interrupting and hackling the working classmates. In such situations, concerned teachers can enable the misbehaving students to develop skills by offering individual instruction instead of focusing on the misbehavior.

Program restructuring. It is easy to become inflexible with a classroom curriculum, especially when school administrators are very concerned with completing it. The traditional way of teaching can be boring and meaningless to many students and cause them to become restless and misbehave. Teachers need to be flexible and restructure classroom activities when they perceive that students are not learning. For example, instead of writing a traditional book report, students can be allowed to role-play or recount a story they read.

Support from routines. Flexibility is important, but students also need routine and a predictable environment. Routine does not imply regimentation; however, an unstructured environment is an invitation to discipline problems. Acting-out and withdrawn students in particular benefit from structure. The environmental stability resulting from routine offers students guidelines and a sense of security; they know what to expect. Routinizing classroom activities at the start of the school day offers balance and a good start. Students know what is required and are less likely to misbehave. Teachers should consider the various personality types of students and work toward providing an arrangement to help students follow schedules, rules, and routines. The list may be easier to enforce when students and parents are asked for their input.

Direct appeal. Teachers frequently behave with an authoritarian mindset and tell students what to do and what not to do. This comes naturally, because teachers are expected to be in control. However, students will often respond to a direct appeal from teachers. Direct appeals are successful when teachers have established a positive relationship with the students. In the direct appeal approach, teachers can appeal to the students' sense of fair play and remind them of the consequences in a nonthreatening manner. However, the impact of the reference to theconsequences depends on how the students interpret these consequences (e.g., students welcome suspension). Teachers must consider the reaction of the entire class when making the appeal. Some students feel that respecting a teacher's appeal will cause them to lose face with their peers. Using Gordon's I-messages instead of you-messages in the appeal is very important. Teachers must have the authority to follow through with consequences when students do not respond to direct appeals.

Removing seductive objects. Wise parents remove valuable and harmful objects when their toddlers begin to walk and explore their environment. Likewise, teachers should remove seductive objects to avoid confrontation. Some students, especially those who lack behavioral control, are attracted to objects that will get them in trouble. Thus, leaving personal valuables, science equipment, shop tools, athletic gear, and other such objects in plain view invites trouble. Students may be distracted by certain toys, combs, boom boxes, or magazines. Whatever keeps the students from the assigned task should not be permitted. Teachers can avoid potential problems by providing a list of prohibited objects to students and parents at the beginning of the school year.

Antiseptic bouncing. Teachers can prevent a disruptive behavior from escalating by removing the student from the environment in a nonpunitive manner; this is called *antiseptic bouncing*. For example, Mr. Smith notices that Iris and Christy are snapping at each other in the back of the classroom. Mr. Smith casually calls Christy to him and asks her to return a book to the library. He has therefore diffused the incident by removing Christy while sparing her embarrassment and providing her with an opportunity to calm down. When she returns, Mr. Smith again separates the girls by assigning them tasks on opposite sides of the room. He plans to teach a unit on conflict resolution in the very near future.

Diversion. Many parents and teachers use diversion to interrupt annoying behaviors. They distract the misbehaving children from their inappropriate pursuits by directing attention toward more appropriate activities. Changing the topic of conversation or asking a question may often be enough to break the pattern. These interruptions serve to discontinue or suspend the undesirable behavior and channel energies along more acceptable lines.

We did not include physical restraint in the influencing and supportive techniques; however, in some cases restraining students is necessary. Physical restraint is recommended *only* when someone's safety is at stake and when verbal or nonverbal interference does not work. Physical restraint should not be used unless the student becomes agitated and poses a danger to self or others. The student is held in a firm but kind hold until calm, and the teacher communicates concern until the student relaxes: "Relax, I will protect you, I will not let you harm others or yourself because I care about you." Physical restraint is surrounded by controversy because this practice has been abused in the past, and teachers are subject to a lawsuit or a reprimand if the student is injured in the course of the restraint. Teachers should also be concerned about their own safety, especially if they are physically unable to restrain a stronger student. They should know the school district's policy on restraining an out-of-control student. Parental permission must be obtained in case restraint becomes a necessity. When students are classified as having a disability, the option of using physical restraint when necessary should be included in the individualized education plan (IEP). Several school districts offer restraining instruction workshops and provide support personnel to implement this practice when needed.

Life-Space Interviews

Teachers often counsel students to help them cope with a crisis or to manage an everyday problem. An additional supporting technique is life-space interviewing, suggested by Fitz Redl (1959). The life-space interview attempts to use a troublesome situation to guide students in developing problem-solving skills and working out solutions independently. During the process, teachers must be nonjudgmental and assume the role of listener and facilitator. The life-space interview may be employed for two purposes: clinical exploitation of life events and immediate emotional first-aid.

In the first purpose, clinical exploitation of life events, the teacher refers to a student's troublesome behavior, and together they explore more acceptable behaviors. Example: Yvonne's problem behavior was tripping other students when they would pass her on the way to the teacher's desk. Whenever she was reprimanded, she acted as though it was an accident and that her feet just "got in the way." With the help of the school counselor, the teacher decided to try a life-space interview. Whenever Yvonne tripped anyone, her teacher took her aside and verbally reconstructed the incident. The teacher listened to Yvonne's excuses and eventually led her to realize that the tripping was indeed intentional. Together they designed a plan to remind Yvonne to keep her feet under the desk.

In the second case, immediate emotional first-aid, support is provided in times of emotional distress. The purpose is to help students regain stability and the ability to continue the activity at hand. Example: Tyrone was usually friendly and polite. However, when something upset him, he would lose his temper and scream out obscenities and insults. One day, while playing basketball in the school gym, Joe stepped on his toe, making him drop the ball. Tyrone was furious and began punching Joe. The coach realized that immediate emotional first-aid was needed. He stopped the fight, took both students aside, and listened as each student reconstructed the incident as he perceived it. The coach listened nonjudgmentally and then offered his version as he perceived it. He guided the students in making a plan to at least tolerate each other. The boys agreed and continued playing basketball.

Morse (1971) outlines the steps of life-space interviewing:

1. Each student involved in the specific incident is allowed to give his or her own impression of the occurrence without interruption.

2. The teacher listens and, without passing judgment, asks questions to determine the accuracy of each student's perception.

3. In the event that the students cannot solve the problem constructively, the teacher may have to propose an acceptable plan to resolve the conflict.

4. The students and the teacher work together to develop a plan for solving similar problems in the future.

Habits of the Mind

A group of teachers was discussing the violent episodes occurring in schools. One teacher commented, "If parents would just learn to teach their children to feel empathy, we would not have these violent outbursts." Another teacher replied, "If students would just learn to think before they act, they would realize the seriousness of their behavior." "I agree," interjected the assistant principal. "We need to teach students the habits of the mind as well as preparing them academically." The habits of the mind are based on a humanistic philosophy of respect for others and acknowledge an intellect that is based on reason and appropriate emotion. Arthur Costa and Bena Kallick (2000) have identified 16 habits of the mind necessary for human beings to live productively in an increasingly chaotic world:

1. *Persisting*: Remaining focused, not "giving up," and obtaining closure to tasks.

2. *Managing impulsivity*: Thinking before acting; acting calmly and deliberately.

3. *Listening with understanding and empathy*: Using active listening to understand the other person's point of view.

4. *Thinking flexibly*: Considering the other person's opinions and ideas; changing perceptions.

5. *Thinking about thinking (metacognition)*: Reflecting on one's thoughts, feelings, and actions and reflecting on the impact of one's actions.

6. *Striving for accuracy*: Having a desire for accuracy; the ability to check and make corrections.

7. *Questioning and posing problems*: Inquiring, searching for data, and solving problems.

8. *Applying past knowledge to new situations*: Merging past experiences with new experiences; learning from one's mistakes.

9. *Thinking and communicating with clarity and precision*: Striving for clarity in communicating with others; avoiding twisting facts and events.

10. *Gathering data through all the senses*: Using taste, smell, touch, sight, and sound to obtain information.

11. *Creating, imagining, and innovating*: Being willing to try different ways and ideas.

12. *Responding with wonder and awe*: Showing interest in differences in the environment and in people.

13. *Taking responsible risks*: Seeking challenges and venturing out.

14. *Finding humor:* Seeing the humor in situations and in the unexpected; laughing at oneself.

15. *Thinking interdependently:* Collaborating with others and showing a willingness to depend and be dependent on others.

16. *Remaining open to continuous learning:* Admitting that one doesn't know it all but is willing to find out.

Two important habits necessary to develop social competence are managing impulsivity and listening with understanding and empathy. The ability to manage impulsivity enables individuals to develop intrapersonal intelligence. Many students today are on medication to help them control hyperactivity and inattention. In some cases, medication is appropriate and should be decided upon by a physician and the parents. However, in addition to taking the medication, impulsive students should learn to control their impulsivity through guided instruction by adults. They should be taught to become effective problem solvers and to think before acting. Teachers can lead students to establish a vision, goals, or an action plan and to measure their behavior one step at a time. Many students will use their medication as a crutch and blame their behavior on "I didn't take my medicine, that is why I acted this way."

Listening with empathy and understanding is a habit that increases interpersonal intelligence. Using active listening involves being able to paraphrase another person's ideas and to identify the speaker's feelings and emotions. The listener is able to empathize and to offer comfort and support. Piaget (1975) called this ability "overcoming egocentrism," a quality lacking in many students with behavior disorders. It is important that teachers model this habit in their interactions with students by listening with empathy and understanding to them. It is also important that students become aware of their interactions with peers and adults. Costa and Kallick (2000) describe competence in this area as being able to direct our mental energies to others and to invest ourselves in their ideas. When students develop empathy and understanding, they are able to refrain from imposing their own values, judgment, opinions, and prejudices and listen to and consider another person's perspective. Students become introspective and insightful and refrain from ridiculing and putting down others.

To develop these habits of the mind, teachers refuse to accept excuses and remind the students to accept responsibility and the consequences of their actions. In teaching these habits, teachers employ Socratic dialogue, bibliotherapy, journaling, student self-evaluation, humor, and repeated practice. When teaching the habits of the mind, teachers must adhere to the following guidelines (Cohen, 1994, p. 48):

- New behaviors must be labeled and discussed.
- Students must be able to use labels and discuss behavior in an objective way.

- Students must have a chance to practice new behaviors.
- New behaviors must be acknowledged and reinforced when they occur.

Summary

In this chapter we presented several discipline methods proposed by followers of a behavior management philosophy that relies on discipline with loose boundaries. The primary belief of this philosophy is that students are less likely to develop an internal locus of control when adults place tight controls and restrictions on their behaviors. Conversely, students are more likely to attain self-discipline when they are guided and taught to take responsibility for their actions. Students are given opportunities to make decisions, to make mistakes, and to learn from their mistakes.

John Dewey's progressivism gave educators a democratic approach to managing students' behaviors. He emphasized guiding students to think critically and to find solutions to their problems by scientifically examining the cause. Dewey believed that students should be provided with relevant experiences to explore and understand their environment and to help them establish positive interpersonal relationships. Dewey's contributions were so powerful that his idea of allowing students democratic rights continues to shape much of educational practice to this day.

Effective communication is essential in improving student-teacher relationships. Thomas Gordon offers specific steps to active listening, giving I-messages, and resolving conflicts in ways that everyone is the winner. Gordon's techniques, though effective for relationship building, do not offer specific solutions to deal with serious discipline problems. Nonetheless, his techniques are useful in making teachers aware of the way they communicate with students and how students communicate with each other.

Transactional analysis, which was proposed more than 30 years ago, is still useful for increasing growth in interpersonal and intrapersonal intelligences. Three states (the parent, the child, and the adult) describe the attitudes we use in our interaction with others. Referring to these states is helpful in analyzing the messages we send to one another. The attitudes we bring to a relationship can either strengthen or weaken that relationship. Teachers who constantly behave in an authoritarian parent state cannot win the confidence of students. Students who regularly behave in an impulsive and mischievous child state find themselves in constant conflict. TA does not provide definite plans to teach self-discipline and behavior change, so teachers and students also need structured training and administration and parental support to effectively implement a TA program.

Procedures within the creative emotional expression framework media can influence students to be motivated to succeed cognitively and affectively. Students who are engaged in their learning are motivated and less likely to become discipline problems. Teachers can use various media that allow students to express their feelings in constructive ways. Creative emotional expression strategies assist students in expressing their anger, stress, and frustrations in socially acceptable ways. Many of these strategies offer acceptable pathways to vent emotions and provide channels to communicate, interrelate, and find solutions to problems. Although teachers in the classroom can apply these strategies, several are time consuming and are regarded as the work of therapists and counselors. Curricular changes are also difficult to implement by classroom teachers without the sanction of school and school-district administrators.

Teachers are frequently placed in positions similar to the roles of parents, psychologists, and counselors. Next to parents, they are the primary influencing and supporting agents for many students. Students know and seek out teachers who are supportive and caring. Strategies to manage surface behaviors are designed to prevent or decelerate disruptive behaviors. A stern stare, a tap on the desk, a hand on the shoulder, or even moving closer to the student may prevent a behavior from accelerating. Teachers can use the life-space interview to enable students to solve immediate problems and to consider different perspectives in finding solutions to problems.

The habits of the mind philosophy endorses specific habits as essential lifespan learning. This philosophy proposes 16 habits as dispositions responding to problems, dilemmas, and enigmas. We have concentrated on two particular habits in this chapter, managing impulsivity and listening with empathy and understanding. These two habits are important in developing interpersonal and intrapersonal intelligences. They are instrumental in overcoming egocentrism and gaining personal insight into other people's ideas and feelings.

Activity 1: Determining Problem Ownership

Read each situation carefully. If the teacher owns the problem, write T in the blank on the left. If the student owns the problem, write S in the blank on the left.

_____ 1. Wally uses profanity out loud in the library.

_____ 2. Jody sleeps in class and is off-task.

_____ 3. Lakisha is frequently tardy and misses the first 20 minutes of instruction.

_____ 4. Mason refuses to cooperate and makes jokes during cooperative group activities.

_____ 5. Tyrone is unmotivated and is failing. He is influential among his peers, and they are beginning to imitate his unproductive behavior.

_____ 6. Georgio has a slight undetected hearing problem. When he cannot understand instruction, he becomes frustrated and walks out of the classroom.

_____ 7. Tara is in need of constant attention. She constantly interrupts her teachers and her classmates during class discussion.

_____ 8. Shaheen is embarrassed by her parents because of a language barrier and does not want to involve them in school activities. She is having difficulties relating to her peers.

_____ 9. Don poured paint over the teacher's desk because he failed math and was dismissed from the football team. You know it was Don who did it because someone saw him do it and told you.

_____ 10. Roberta is disorganized and is constantly losing her homework and classwork.

Activity 2: Active Listening

Pair with a colleague and initiate a conversation. For 3 minutes, listen actively to what your partner is saying. Switch roles, and for another 3 minutes your partner should listen actively to you. Discuss the activity with your partner.

Useful Phrases for Active Listening

You feel . . .	From your point of view . . .	It seems to you . . .
From where you stand . . .	Where you're coming from . . .	You think . . .
You believe . . .	What I hear you say . . .	You mean . . .
In your opinion . . .	I'm picking up that you . . .	As you see it . . .
Are you suggesting that . . .	Do you suppose you thought . . .	You perceive that . . .

You're . . . (Identify the feeling—angry, sad, annoyed, frustrated, overjoyed, lonely, hurt, etc.)

Phrases to Use When You Are Not Perceiving Clearly or When the Sender Is Not Receptive to Your Active Listening

Could it be that . . .	I'm not sure that I'm with you, but . . .	I wonder if . . .
Would you buy this idea . . .	Correct me if I'm wrong, but . . .	Is it possible that . . .
From where I stand . . .	Could this be what's going on, you . . .	It appears that you . . .
I think you're saying . . .	Does it sound reasonable that you . . .	Maybe you feel . . .

Perhaps you are
feeling . . .

If I understand you
right . . .

You appear to be
feeling . . .

Is there any chance that
you . . .

Let me see if I'm with
you, you . . .

This is what I think I hear
you saying . . .

Let's look at it
again . . .

It looks as if you . . .

It seems as if . . .

Activity 3: Sending I-Messages

Read each vignette, examine the you-message, and change it to an I-message. Write it in the blank column.

SITUATION	YOU-MESSAGE	I-MESSAGE
Ms. Simpson, the librarian, is talking with the assistant principal, Mr. Legree. Tauny, a student, cannot find a book she desperately needs. She stands close by, waiting for the conversation to end so that she can get help from Ms. Simpson. Suddenly Ms. Simpson turns around, faces her and says:	You are so rude young lady, can't you realize that I am having an important and private conversation with Mr. Legree? Haven't you learned that it is poor manners to mind other people's business? Go wait in the carrel over there.	
John and Mario are on opposing teams. Mario trips John during a ballgame, causing him to drop the ball. John punches Mario and they start to struggle. The coach separates them and screams out:	You two are animals. You ought to be locked up in cages. You are not fit to play in civilized sports. You are out of the game permanently.	

cont.

Mr. Jason is teaching a unit in American history on the early settlers and refers to the early inhabitants as "American Indians." Souki, a Native American student, corrects him, and he blurts out:	You are ignorant, that's what the early settlers called them. I should know, I am the teacher.	

Activity 4: TA States

Complete the following exercise individually and discuss your responses in small groups.

1. Write down two parental attitudes that you are imitating in your interactions with others.

   a.

   b.

   Are these attitudes negative or positive?

   Do they still influence your behavior in any way? Where? With whom?

2. Describe two situations, one in which you behave like a natural carefree child and one in which you behave like a manipulative mischievous child.

   a.

   b.

   Describe your feelings in each situation.

3. How do you use your adult state at work, at meetings, at home, and in social gatherings?

Activity 5: Art Projects

Divide into groups of five. Distribute a situation to each group. Group 2 will need markers and poster boards or butcher paper. Direct participants to use their artistic abilities to illustrate a solution to their situation.

1. You bought a lovely house in a lovely neighborhood. Your neighbors are all lovely as well, until your next-door neighbor moves out and a family with five children, ranging from ages 6 to 16, moves in. The father frequently parks his employment vehicle in front of your house. The young children dump litter in your yard, and when the parents aren't home the teenagers entertain their friends with loud music, and you suspect they drink alcohol. You have asked them nicely to be quiet several times but your requests have not been heeded so far. Write a script to role-play a solution.

2. Many of your students are unkind to students from other cultures or races. You have overhead them using derogatory names and observed the separation in the lunch hall and on the playground. Create a mural that depicts unity, understanding, and cooperation.

3. A negative attitude permeates the faculty, and teachers often yell at each other at faculty meetings. You would like to improve morale. Develop illustrated bookmarks with special sayings.

Examples:

When spiders unite, they can tie up a lion.

Great minds think alike.   We're in this together.

You are a reflection of me.   It takes less effort to smile than
   I like you.   to frown.

Laughter is good for the soul and the health. Let's laugh.

References

Axline, V. (1947). *Play therapy.* Boston: Houghton Mifflin.

Berne, E. (1964). *Games people play: The psychology of human behavior.* New York: Grove Press.

Borich, G., & Tombari, M. (1995). *Educational psychology: A contemporary approach.* New York: HarperCollins.

Cohen, E. (1994). *Designing groupwork: Strategies for the heterogeneous classroom* (2nd ed.). New York: Teachers College Press.

Costa, A., & Kallick, B. (2000). *Discovering and exploring habits of the mind.* Alexandria, VA: Association for Supervision and Curriculum Development.

Dewey, J. (1938). *Experience and education.* New York: Collier.

Ernest, K. (1973). *Games students play and what to do about them.* Mellbrae, CA: Celestial Arts.

Florida State University. (1990). *Role of the fine and performing arts in high school drop out prevention.* Tallahassee, FL: Tallahassee: FSU Center for Music Research.

Freed, A. (1971). *TA for tots—and other important people.* Sacramento, CA: Jalmar Press.

Freed, A. (1973). *TA for kids—and grow- ups too.* Sacramento, CA: Jalmar Press.

Freed, A. (1988). *TA for teens—and other important people.* Sacramento, CA: Jalmar Press.

Freud, S. (1952). *A general introduction to psychoanalysis* (J. Strachey, Trans.). New York: Washington Square Press. (Original work published 1924)

Ginott, H. (1972). *Teacher and child.* New York: Macmillan.

Gladding, S., & Gladding, C. (1991). The ABC's of bibliotherapy for school counselors. *The School Counselor 31,* 7–13.

Gordon, T. (1974). *T.E.T.: Teacher effectiveness training.* New York: Davis McKay.

Gorman, A. R. (1980). *Developmental psychology.* New York: Van Nostrand.

Hale, J. (1971). *Renaissance Europe: Individual and society, 1480–1520.* New York: Harper & Row.

Harris, T. (1969). *I'm OK, you're OK: A practical guide to transactional analysis.* New York: Harper & Row.

Karges-Bone, L. (1997). Wanted: Idealist, intellectual, prophet—John Dewey as a teacher educator for the new millennium. *The Educational Forum, 62,* 53–59.

Maslow, A. (1968). *Toward a psychology of being* (2nd ed.) New York: Van Nostrand.

Meier, D. (2000). Progressive education in the 21st century: A work in progress. In R. Brandt (Ed.), *Education in a new era.* Alexandria, VA: Association for Supervision and Curriculum Development.

Mercer, C., & Mercer, A. (1997). *Teaching students with learning problems.* (5th ed.). New York: Merill-Macmillan.

Morse, M. (1971). Worksheet on life space interviewing for teachers. In N. J. Long, W. C. Morse, & R. G. Newman (Eds.), *Conflict in the classroom: The education of emotionally disturbed children* (2nd ed.). Belmont, CA: Wadsworth.

Piaget, J. (1975). *The development of thought: Equilibration of cognitive structures.* New York: Viking Press.

Redl, F. (1959). The concept of the life-space interview. *American Journal of Orthopsychiatry 29,* 1–18.

Redl, F., & Wineman, D. (1957). *The aggressive child.* New York: Free Press.

Richardson, R., (1996). *Connecting with others: Lessons for teaching social and emotional competence.* Champaign, IL: Research Press.

Rogers, C. (1961). *On becoming a person.* Boston: Houghton Mifflin.

Shores, R., Gunter, P., & Jack, S. (1993). Classroom management strategies: Are they setting events for coercion? *Behavioral Disorders 18,* 92–102.

Chapter 6

Discipline With Tight Boundaries
Carol Cheselka Torrey

Overview
    Influential contributors

The Behavior Change Process
    The importance of proactive behavior management
    Steps in the behavior change process

Strategies for Increasing Behaviors
    Positive reinforcement: Primary and
      secondary reinforcers

Negative Reinforcement
    Contracting
    Prompting
    Shaping

Strategies for Decreasing Behaviors
    Differential reinforcement
    Extinction
    Removal of a desired stimulus
    Response-cost
    Time-out
    Presentation of aversives
    Overcorrection

Punishment Versus Discipline

Application of Behaviorist Principles

Summary

Activities

QUESTIONS

This chapter will help you to answer the following questions:

1. What is applied behavior analysis, and how does it differ from behavior modification?
2. What are several components of proactive behavior management?
3. What are the five steps in the behavior change process? When do we implement this behavior change model?
4. How do we record baseline data?
5. How can teachers determine what is reinforcing to a child?
6. What interventions can be used to increase student behavior?
7. How is negative reinforcement different from punishment?
8. What interventions should be used by teachers to decrease behavior?
9. How do we evaluate if the behavior management program is successful?
10. Give two examples of the proactive use of behavioral analysis strategies.

Overview

At the turn of the 20th century, the discipline of psychology sought to be accepted as a science in its own right. However, the study of psychology was not regarded as precise and empirical enough by the other sciences. J. B. Watson (1926) was instrumental in developing a theory of human development called *learning theory*, which could produce methodical research in psychology. It includes three components: classical conditioning, operant conditioning, and social learning theory. All three flow from a school of thought called *behaviorism*. The central belief of behaviorism is that conclusions about human development must be based on scientific observation of quantifiable behaviors and the events that strengthen or weaken the behaviors.

Behavior modification and applied behavior analysis have been used throughout the 20th century as a viable means of managing the inappropriate behavior of students with and without disabilities. It is, however, a system that is used by many other systems and components in society. Through environmental manipulation and adult-teacher application of a specific five-step process, inappropriate behaviors can be decreased and appropriate behaviors increased. Through this process we learn behaviors that enable us to abide by societal rules and to reach for goals that promise reinforcing rewards.

This chapter details strategies that can be used to either increase or decrease behaviors. Several of these strategies can be applied to groups of students or to modify the behavior of an entire class. When choosing which techniques to use, we want to consider attempting to increase behaviors rather than decrease behaviors. It is a more positive approach to working with and teaching individuals and allows us to emphasize the student's strengths—that is, what the student can do. Positive reinforcement, a strategy to increase behavior, is very easy to implement. Positive reinforcement increases the probability that an appropriate behavior will recur. Those who give the reinforcer and those who receive it feel good. On the other hand, punishment is frequently taxing for both the punisher and the punished. Other strategies to increase behavior that are discussed in this chapter include negative reinforcement and its techniques of contracting, prompting, and shaping.

Teachers often seek to decrease behaviors because these are easily identified and recognized; they are often aggravating to teachers and peers and truly disrupt the instructional process. Because of the disruption, teachers seek to immediately stop those behaviors and restore order. To eliminate an unwanted behavior, teachers frequently resort to some form of punishment. In this chapter, several procedures are recommended prior to the use of punishment. Teachers are encouraged to follow a hierarchy of less intrusive strategies, which include differential reinforcement and extinction. The more intrusive procedures of response cost, time-out, presentation of aversives, and overcorrection are also discussed; however, we recommend that these be used sparingly.

This chapter is defined as discipline with tight boundaries because the teacher is in control. He or she manipulates the reinforcements to control the behaviors of students. We wish to emphasize that many of the principles of behavior modification and applied behavior can be used proactively and in a nonpunitive manner. This chapter will introduce the reader to a general understanding of behavioral strategies that can be used to modify the inappropriate behaviors of students in the classroom.

When we implement strategies with tight boundaries to manage or change behaviors, we are referring to utilizing techniques of applied behavior analysis. *Applied behavior analysis*, a more current term for behavior modification, highlights the application of behavior modification principles in everyday situations and settings, outside highly controlled psychological laboratory settings. Although applied behavior analysis has its roots in behavior modification, it is viewed as a more humane application of behavioral principles. The intent is to help individuals change socially significant behaviors and, ultimately to improve the quality of life for the individual. The applied behavior analysis framework establishes a more restrictive perimeter, and increased teacher control is evident in the management of behaviors.

Behavior modification is the field of psychology concerned with "the analysis and modification of human behavior" (Miltenberger, 1997, p. 5). Various scientists and events have contributed to its development. Through the work of major figures such as Ivan P. Pavlov, Edward L. Thorndike, John B. Watson, and B. F. Skinner, a shift from the psychoanalytic approach of Sigmund Freud (1856–1939) to the behavioral approach allowed us to better understand behavior. The work of these individuals was instrumental in the development of behavior modification. The focus shifted from the individual's internal psychological forces (i.e., drives, impulses, motives, internal conflicts) to the individual's overt behaviors and environmental events related to the behaviors.

Pavlov (1849–1936), an animal psychologist, conducted studies during 1927 demonstrating that a dog could be conditioned to salivate with the introduction of a ringing bell. Subsequently the dog learned to salivate when the bell was repeatedly rung without the presentation of food. *Classical conditioning* refers to the relationship between the stimulus (ringing bell) and the reflex response (salivating).

Watson (1878–1958) was influenced by the classical conditioning studies of Pavlov and conducted experiments with a child named Albert. Albert was scared by the sound of a loud noise while he was petting a white rat. He was conditioned to fear the white rat even when the sound was omitted. The child's behavior was controlled by the environmental event. Watson's behaviorist manifesto gave strength to American school psychology. He declared:

> Give me a dozen healthy children, well formed, and my own specified world to bring them up in and I'll guarantee to take any one of them at random and train him to become any type of specialist I might select: doctor, lawyer, artist, merchant, chief, and yes, beggar man, and thief, regardless of his talents, penchants, tendencies, vocations, and race of his ancestors (Watson, 1926, p. 10).

Watson believed that an infant's mind was a blank slate that could be manipulated by stimuli from the environment.

Thorndike (1874–1949) studied the relationship between animal behavior and environmental conditions. Working with a cat in a cage, Thorndike placed food outside the cage but in the cat's view. The cat learned to hit a lever with its paw to gain access to the food. This *law of effect* describes the relationship between actions that produce satisfaction and the increased likelihood of the behavior to recur. The association between responses and consequences may be referred to as *associationism*.

Skinner (1904–1990) was influenced by the work of Thorndike and expanded the research on relationships between consequences and behavior. In his work with laboratory animals, he concluded that when a behavior has a consequence that is reinforcing, it will be more likely to recur: A positive reinforcer strengthens a particular behavior. He also clarified the difference between operant conditioning and classical conditioning. *Operant conditioning* refers to the relationship between overt events in the environment (e.g., antecedents and consequences) and changes in specific target behaviors.

The study of operant behavior continued in laboratory settings until the 1950s, when behavioral principles were increasingly utilized with people. Subsequently, thousands of studies have established the effectiveness of behavior modification principles and procedures. Applied behavior analysis extends behavior modification to include socially significant behaviors in real-life settings. The following is an example of operant conditioning that often occurs in the school setting:

Antecedent: Ray and the class members are working on math problems, but Ray is unable to read and complete the problems.

Behavior: Ray becomes frustrated and throws the paper on the floor.

Consequence: The teacher sends Ray to the office to be punished.

This scenario teaches Ray that when he engages in this inappropriate behavior, he does not have to complete the work.

The Behavior Change Process

The behavior change process is integral to applied behavior analysis. The behavior change process involves significant and time-consuming efforts by the individual (teacher) initiating the behavior change. The teacher should not begin this process with all children or all behaviors. It should be initiated for significant problem behaviors after the child has not responded to general techniques of management control. General management techniques include changing the physical environment (e.g., child's seat, visual instruction cues), changing social environmental variables (e.g., providing peer models, changing the classroom work groups), providing intermittent positive reinforcement, and implementing general class management procedures. As indicated in these examples, both the physical and social environment are important components in proactive behavior management. A further explanation of peer modeling is provided in the following example.

Fred is noncompliant and defiant. His teacher, Mr. Berry, has tried several procedures to obtain his cooperation, but to no avail. Mr. Berry decides to change the antecedent by working with Fred's friend, Paul. He reinforces Paul for modeling the desired behavior, and Fred gradually imitates Paul's behavior.

Manipulating factors in the environment can prevent the occurrence of significant inappropriate behaviors. The physical environmental factors of temperature, lighting, amount of space, and closeness of furniture can either hinder or enhance one's behavior. Social environmental factors—such as being in the presence of peers and/or adults with whom you get along, whom you do not like, or who don't like you; being around people who are happy versus grumpy; receiving praise; or simply having a content physical affect—also positively or negatively affect one's behavior. These environmental factors may subtly or dramatically affect an individual's behavior, depending on one's specific personality characteristics.

In addition, the curriculum and the teacher's behavior can affect student behavior. The curriculum should be at a level at which the child can be successful, it should be engaging and interesting, and it should be age-appropriate. There should be an adequate amount of materials, and the materials and teaching styles should be appropriate for or match the child's learning style. Instructional time should be structured according to the child's needs (not too long or too short) and should involve active engagement, regardless of the child's age. Child-teacher interactions should also be monitored; the teacher should consider the type of interaction and the number of positive interactions. Children need a variety of positive interactions with adults. Adults may respond when a child needs assistance, relays information to an adult, or behaves appropriately or inappropriately, or when the adult needs to provide information about a procedure. Throughout the day, a teacher should respond to every child in each of these ways. However, with a child who has a behavior problem, we sometimes find that the teacher engages in only one type of interaction (i.e., responding to inappropriate behaviors), and the interaction is often negative. Teachers and other adults generally don't consider the type or number of interactions with children or students. With monitoring, we can often change the child's behavior without much individual effort.

When environmental, proactive procedures are not as effective as we might like, and a change in the student's behavior is warranted, five steps can be followed to result in optimal outcomes. The same basic process should be followed regardless of the individual's specific characteristics or circumstances. Although there are necessary modifications that might be made in the process, the steps typically remain the same:

1. Identify the behavior that is to be changed.
2. Collect baseline data.
3. Identify the reinforcers.
4. Develop and implement the intervention.
5. Evaluate the intervention.

Step 1: Identify the Behavior That Is to Be Changed

A child often exhibits many behaviors that need to be changed. Too often a child exhibits many behaviors that teachers finds offensive or aggravating, and the teachers become overwhelmed when attempting to bring the students' behaviors under control. It is unrealistic for a student to change all of the inappropriate behaviors at one time. Prioritizing should be based on the following: Does the behavior harm the health or well-being of the individual or of others? Will the behavior prohibit the individual from living with the family? Will it affect the individual staying in the community? How will the behavior affect school placement—remaining in the public school or in a general education program (Alberto & Troutman, 1999)? It is critical that the teacher prioritize behaviors, debating which ones are most critical to the successful functioning of the child in the present or most optimum environment.

Changing behavior can involve increasing, decreasing, or maintaining behavior. Increasing a behavior allows the adult to provide positive reinforcement; it is a more positive approach than decreasing behavior. If we choose to decrease a behavior, a major consideration is that we must decide what behavior will replace that which we decrease. We must identify a replacement behavior, or a *fair pair*. For example, Corinne frequently calls out during science class discussions, interrupting other students who are attempting to answer the teacher's questions. The teacher wants to decrease the number of these call-outs. Rather than using a technique to decrease the behavior, we might identify the fair pair as "hand raising." The teacher could then reinforce Corinne every time she raises her hand to answer the question. If Emilio hits other students during recess (and we want to decrease this behavior), we might identify the fair pair as "asking peers to play." The teacher, paraprofessional, or other adult could reinforce Emilio every time he asks his peers to play with him.

Once we have determined which behavior to change (the target behavior), we must clearly define and describe the behavior so that anyone who observes the child can determine whether it is occurring. The behavior must be observable and measurable. For example, the target behavior of "reducing the occurrence of a tantrum" does not clearly describe the tantrum behavior. Does a tantrum involve sitting and crying, or head banging and screaming, or throwing oneself down on the floor and yelling? Two observers might have very different definitions; therefore, it would be difficult to consistently identify and measure the occurrence of tantrums. The following are examples of adequate observable and measurable definitions of various activities:

- Correct computation of two-digit addition and subtraction (without regrouping) problems
- Head oriented and eyes focused toward teacher
- Walking down hall with hands touching sides of body
- Call-outs during class discussion
- Mumbling that is audible to anyone within arm's length
- Uttering curse words

Once the behavior is specifically defined, the conditions and criteria must also be established. Conditions under which the behavior will occur (e.g., during a spelling test, independent seat work, eating in the cafeteria, at recess on the playground), and the criteria for acceptable performance (e.g., with 80% accuracy, in four out of five store purchases, in 85% of the opportunities) must be determined. The criteria will be determined after baseline data have been collected. Criteria are determined by the type of behavior, the type of recording system, and in accord with the need for accuracy in displaying the skill. For example, crossing the street successfully means 100% accuracy; one incorrect display of the skill could result in a serious accident; while 80% accuracy in tying shoes for a second-grade child might be acceptable.

Step 2: Collect Baseline Data

Teachers and parents are often overheard saying, "The student always does_____" (e.g., "Johnny always picks fights on the playground.") When students exhibit undesirable behaviors, it seems as if they occur all the time. In reality, when we measure them, they usually do not occur nearly as often as we had thought. When we collect baseline data, we get a more accurate picture of some dimensions of the behavior. Baseline data also help us to develop the intervention and evaluate whether it has been successful in changing the child's behavior. Various dimensions of behavior, methods for recording behavior, and the components of a functional behavior assessment are aspects of collecting baseline data that are discussed in this section.

Dimensions of Behavior

There are several dimensions of behavior that can be measured; these are described below. The specific behavior, as well as one's behavior objective, will provide an indicator as to which dimension will be measured.

Frequency is a measure of how often the behavior occurs. If a child leaves the classroom seat to walk around the room, frequency measures how often the child leaves the seat and walks around the room. To measure this dimension, the behavior should have a clear beginning and ending.

Duration is a measure of how long the behavior continues. If a child leaves the classroom seat to walk around the room, duration measures how long the child is out of the seat walking around the room.

Latency is a measure of the time that elapses after a direction is given and the child begins the task. When it is time for a spelling test, the teacher could measure how long from the time the teacher provided the directive "Let's get ready for our spelling test" until the student begins to clear the desk and get out a blank sheet of paper for the test.

Force is a measure of the strength of the behavior. If a child bites him- or herself, the force of the bite might be a concern of the observer when the bite breaks the skin but not when teeth simply touch the skin. When measuring force, a rubric or scale must be established to "grade" the force.

Topography is a measure of the different environments in which the behavior occurs. We might choose to measure the call-outs of a child in a special education class compared to a general education inclusion class, the cafeteria, or the bus. After determining the dimension of the behavior, the teacher must decide which method he or she will use to collect and record the behavior. Methods to collect data are discussed below.

Methods for Recording Behavior

Anecdotal recording occurs when the observer describes all the actions of the target child and interactions with anyone else in the environment. A scripting of the environment occurs and a thorough narrative description is written. The setting needs to be thoroughly described, and this is often accomplished before to the actual observation. This method of recording is very time consuming and is difficult to complete while a teacher is teaching. To accomplish anecdotal recording, teachers often use their paraprofessional (aide), an evaluator from the assessment team, an administrator, a psychologist, or a peer teacher. This buddy can either be taught to complete the scripting or can engage in an activity with the children while the teacher records the data. Once the recording is completed, a *sequence analysis* is necessary to help "make sense" of the data. The observer designs an "ABC" sheet to determine what behaviors (B) occurred, what was the antecedent (A) for each behavior, and what was the consequence (C) for each behavior. The observer will list all desirable and undesirable behaviors. Then the observer will determine what action occurred immediately before the behavior (the antecedent) and what occurred immediately after the behavior (the consequence). The antecedent and consequence may be something that occurred by the teacher, other students, or any individual in the room, or it may be an environmental event (e.g., a bolt of thunder, a fire alarm). Antecedents and consequences may be planned or unplanned. Often anecdotal recording and sequence analysis is completed because the student is exhibiting inappropriate or undesirable behaviors, and the teacher is not quite sure of the specific behavior to target.

Event recording describes the number of times (frequency) the target behavior occurs. Each time the behavior occurs, it is counted. The observer or teacher designs a tally sheet, establishes a code for occurrence and nonoccurrence of the behavior, and determines the length of the observation. Event recording is easy to design; however, the teacher must continually monitor and observe the student for the entire length of the observation. The frequency of the behavior and other tasks and responsibilities that the teacher must engage in will determine the feasibility of using this recording method. It is difficult to use event recording if the frequency of the behavior is high, if the behavior occurs quickly, if the teacher has a large class to monitor, and if the teacher is actively involved in direct teaching activities. Data can be summarized by discussing the number of times that the behavior occurs within a given time period.

Interval recording is a method that provides us with an index of the number of occurrences of the target behavior. However, it describes the number of intervals in which the target behavior is exhibited rather than the specific number of times the behavior occurred. Therefore, this method of recording is not as exact as event recording. To conduct interval recording, the observer needs to predetermine the length of the observation and divide the time period into shorter time segments (intervals). Intervals are typically not longer than 2 minutes. The observer marks whether the behavior occurs during each interval of time. Interval recording is useful when the behavior occurs at a high frequency, and it also provides an index of the continuity of the behavior. Interval recording is often impractical for busy teachers.

Time sampling measures whether the target behavior is occurring at the end of an interval (whether the behavior is occurring at a specific point in time). Once the length of the observation is determined, intervals of any time length are established. Often intervals range from 2 to 15 minutes. This method of recording is less exact than other data recording methods because the observer is required to watch the student only at the end of the interval. It is therefore much easier to teach while using this method rather than either event recording or interval recording. However, if the behavior does not occur at the end of the time sample interval, we will not be able to get a reliable measure of the occurrence of the behavior.

Duration recording measures the length of time that the target behavior continues. Once the behavior begins, how long does it persist? (E.g., how long does a student persist with a writing composition task?) When using duration recording, the observer must mark the time that the behavior begins and then mark when the behavior stops. The difference between starting and stopping time is a measure of duration.

Latency recording is used to measure how much time elapses from when directions are provided to when an individual begins a task. How long does it take an individual to begin a task once directions are provided? For example, the teacher tells a student to line up at the door. How long before Suzanne gets up from her desk and begins to move to line up? The observer marks down the time that directions were provided and the time that the student begins the task, and then finds the difference.

Functional Behavior Assessment

A functional behavior assessment is another form of baseline data that can be collected. This will assist in determining the method of intervention. A functional behavior assessment determines the function that the inappropriate behavior is serving for the individual, and it provides information about the physiological and environmental factors that contribute to an individual's inappropriate behaviors. Through this assessment process, several outcomes are determined: the times that the behavior does and does not occur, antecedents and consequences of the behavior, environmental stimuli that are evident when the behavior occurs, and identification of behaviors that may occur together. Additionally, hypotheses that describe the behaviors, situations and reinforcers that maintain the behavior in those situations, and a collection of data that support the hypotheses are developed (O'Neill, et al., 1997). To assess the function of inappropriate behaviors, teachers must consider the antecedent of the behavior (Burke, 1992). Table 6-1 shows a functional assessment.

TABLE 6-1. ABC TABLE

A = ANTECEDENT	B = BEHAVIOR	C = CONSEQUENCE
Tom (a C student) sits close behind Milly (an A student) during a math test.	Tom can see over Milly's shoulder and copies her answers.	Tom gets an A on the test. Or Tom is caught cheating and gets an F.

Tom's behavior is the result of his need to acquire, or have access to, a good grade. All behavior is a result of four functions: escape, access, attention, or sensory fulfillment. For example:

- Edmund has difficulty doing math computation. Every time the teacher assigns a math work sheet, he repeatedly breaks his pencil point and has to get up to sharpen his pencil. He never completes the class work. The function of his behavior is *escape*: He escapes doing and completing the math work sheet.

- John and Emile want to type their written compositions on the computer, but only one student can work at that station at a time. John trips Emile as he moves to the computer, therefore arriving first at the computer. The function of the behavior is *access*: John wants and gets to use the computer.

- Almost every morning during the pledge of allegiance, Elsie giggles, fidgets, sings the pledge, and goofs off. The teacher often sneers at Elsie, and the class pays attention to Elsie, snickering and giggling along with her. The function of the behavior is *attention*: Elsie want and gets attention from class peers and the teacher.

- Leslie drums her fingers on the desktop and slaps her hand against her leg during seat work. Sometimes the teacher ignores her, and sometimes she reprimands Leslie, but Leslie continues with the behavior. The function of the behavior is *sensory*: She enjoys the tactile sensation of the fingers drumming and her hand hitting her leg.

Functional behavior assessment can be conducted by informant procedures, direct observation, or functional analysis manipulations. Informant procedures involve parents, teachers, or other significant individuals who participate in an interview (O'Neill et al., 1997) or complete a questionnaire such as the Motivation Assessment Scale (Durand, 1988). Direct observation involves a professional directly observing the target individual in the natural environment engaging in inappropriate behaviors. An Antecedent Behavior Consequence analysis can be conducted, or more systematic forms can be completed (e.g., scatter plot, explained in Touchette, MacDonald, & Langer, 1985; functional assessment observation form by O'Neill et al., 1997). In functional analysis manipulation, the teacher hypothesizes the function and sets up a test situation. The test situation involves the manipulation of specific variables (e.g., structural variables such as level of attention provided to an individual during an activity, task length, or task difficulty) or manipulation of consequences to determine if they are associated with the inappropriate behaviors. Each of these methods requires time and additional work for the teacher. Sometimes, after conducting a functional assessment, the function of the behavior is quite clear; however, sometimes the behavior is serving various functions. Although time consuming, use of these techniques is recommended so that the intervention can be more appropriately designed and will be more effective. This is further explained in Step 4.

Step 3: Identify the Reinforcer

A principle of reinforcement dictates that it increases the likelihood of the recurrence of a specified behavior. Reinforcers are specific to an individual: What is reinforcing for one individual will not necessarily be reinforcing for another. Often teachers think that a particular item may be reinforcing to a student; however, if the behavior does not increase, the item is not a reinforcer.

Several methods can be used to determine reinforcers for an individual. The simplest procedure is to ask the individual what he or she likes. However, many teachers prefer to provide students with a menu of reinforcers and request that the student either mark all that they like or rank the items from most to least desirable. Words or pictures can be placed on the menu, depending on the ability levels and ages of the students. In another method, individuals with more significant cognitive disabilities may be given repetitive choices involving two or three actual items. Their choices are recorded and systematically paired with other chosen items to determine which items are most highly valued. This process of *reinforcement sampling* is time consuming but sometimes necessary to determine an individual's preferences. Teachers can also ask family members for suggestions of reinforcers for their child, or observation of peer preferences may also suggest reinforcers. The easiest and simplest method for determining reinforcers should be used first. Redetermination should be done periodically, as reinforcers lose their value due to satiation or change in child preferences.

Step 4: Develop and Implement the Intervention

The intervention will be most effective when developed as a result of determining the function of the behavior. Refer to the examples identified in Step 2.

- After the function of Edmund's behavior is identified as escape, an intervention might involve the teacher placing many pencils or pens or a pencil sharpener on Edmund's desk so he would not have to waste time getting up and moving around the room. Another intervention could involve reinforcement for work completion. An inappropriate method would be to time-out Edmund, because he *wants* to escape the task and it would function as a reinforcer.

- When John trips Emile, the teacher might choose one of the following as an intervention: Establish rules for determining who can use the computer, establish times for computer use for each student, or determine that if aggressive incidents occur, the noninitiator receives access to the computer. An inappropriate method would be to allow John access (by default) because he gets to the station first, or because Emile says, "Oh, it's OK."

- When incidents occur during the pledge of allegiance, the teacher can choose to verbally prompt Elsie and provide positive reinforcement before the pledge begins, or the teacher can ignore Elsie and provide positive reinforcement to classmates who also ignore Elsie's inappropriate behavior. Another intervention could involve assigning the paraeducator to stand near Elsie as a proximity prompt; or physical prompting could be provided by placing an arm on Elsie's back, or patting her on her back, to encourage her to engage in appropriate behaviors.

- The sound of drumming fingers or loud hitting of Leslie's hands against her body bothers others in the class and is not acceptable behavior. An intervention would involve the teacher determining what could be substituted for the finger drumming and leg slapping that would provide similar sensory input. One intervention would be to allow Leslie to drum on something soft so it would not make noise, or teach Leslie to rub her fingers or hands against an object that provides similar sensory input.

After the function of the behavior is determined, an intervention should be developed to modify the environment or other antecedents or to modify the consequences. In Tom's case, the teacher can either move Tom away from Millie during an exam or help Tom with his math. The teacher could also confer with the parents to help Tom at home or ask Millie or another student to serve as a peer tutor.

When modifying the antecedents, strategies such as shaping, prompting, modeling, time delay, and chaining are used. When modifying the consequences, teachers will use strategies to either increase or decrease the target behavior. If a teacher chooses to increase a behavior, reinforcement will be provided. If a teacher chooses to decrease a behavior, strategies such as differential reinforcement, extinction, response-cost, time-out, and presentation of aversive stimuli can be used. These strategies will be discussed in the following section.

Step 5: Evaluate the Intervention

After an intervention has been applied, the teacher must conduct an evaluation of its effectiveness. Many behaviors will change quickly; however, behaviors that have been ongoing for a longer time period will be more difficult to change. Data must be collected and compared to the initial baseline data. A trend in the desired direction will be evident if the intervention technique is effective. If the behavior change is not in the desired direction, or the change is not to the expected criteria level, then the teacher should consider changing the intervention strategy. However, sometimes the teacher will continue with the initial intervention to allow more time for the behavior change to occur.

Strategies for Increasing Behaviors

Positive Reinforcement

Positive reinforcement is the contingent presentation of a consequence after a behavior is exhibited that increases the likelihood that the behavior will recur. Simply stated, the teacher gives the student something he or she wants after the student performs a behavior that the teacher desires. Reinforcement is a naturally occurring phenomenon, but if we look around in our personal lives we can see that we receive and give to others very minimal amounts of positive reinforcement. We expect people to say nice words, be polite, and engage in "good" activities, but we more often tend to recognize and respond to the bad things that individuals do. If we want to increase behaviors, we need to provide positive reinforcement for those specific behaviors. However, when we reinforce unwanted behaviors, they too will increase. When individuals engage in desirable behaviors and we want these behaviors to be maintained, we need to provide positive reinforcement. If we want the behaviors to increase, we also need to provide positive reinforcement.

As stated previously, what one individual finds reinforcing (pleasurable) may not be the same as what another individual finds reinforcing. Therefore, it is important to determine what items are positive reinforcers for a specific individual (several methods were discussed earlier in this chapter). When we select reinforcers, we can choose from several different categories, all of which are classified as either primary or secondary. *Primary reinforcers* are innately motivating and satisfy our basic human needs (e.g., food, drink, sleep, shelter, and sex); they are unlearned, natural, and unconditioned. Both edible and sensory reinforcers are primary reinforcers. The most commonly used edible reinforcers are sips of soda or juice, small candies, cereal, or water. Sensory reinforcers provide access to visual, auditory, tactile, olfactory, or kinesthetic stimuli; they provide stimulation to our sensory organs. Examples include flashing lights, a fan blowing air, music, stroking or brushing with different textured material, different aromas, or swinging in a hammock.

It is important to remember that primary reinforcers are most effective when the individual has been deprived of that specific edible reinforcer or sensory input. A food reinforcer is most effective when the child is hungry (right before lunch) and least effective when the child is full (immediately after snack time or lunch). However, highly cherished reinforcers may even be effective without severe or prolonged deprivation (many children cannot resist the smell of popcorn, many adults cannot resist a delicious dessert even after a full meal). If the child has reached the state of satiation, the reinforcer is no longer effective. Satiation occurs after consumption of a large amount of a particular reinforcer or after prolonged exposure to the reinforcing stimulus. (Sometimes, after eating a large holiday dinner, no one is immediately ready to eat dessert.) Both edible and sensory reinforcers are more frequently used with individuals who have low cognitive functioning levels, who are young, or who are initially learning a task. Older or higher functioning individuals do not need primary reinforcement and are often insulted by their use. However, with any individual, the teacher should consider that primary reinforcers are temporary measures and should move to secondary reinforcement.

Secondary reinforcers are conditioned reinforcers; they initially have no value to us in our existence, but they acquire value. This value is learned by pairing a secondary reinforcer with a primary reinforcer. When we continually present the secondary reinforcer with a primary reinforcer that the student already values, we eventually teach the student to be motivated only by the secondary reinforcer. Secondary reinforcers may be categorized as social reinforcers (smiles, thumbs-up sign, proximity, praise and feedback), tangible reinforcers (stickers, stamps, certificates), privilege or activity reinforcers (homework pass, class line leader, computer time, access to music), and generalized reinforcers (points, tokens).

Social reinforcers (demonstration of approval or attention) are the most natural of the secondary reinforcers and are often used unconsciously and unsystematically. Social reinforcement is often the only type of reinforcement found in the natural general education environment and the community. Therefore, we want students to respond to social reinforcers because it will assist them in integrating into these natural settings. Sitting next to the teacher during story time or sitting by a friend during a group discussion demonstrate the use of proximity as a reinforcer. Praise is another social reinforcer; to be most effective, it must be contingent upon the student completing the specified behavior, it should detail the specific behaviors exhibited, and it should be sincere. The feedback should be affirmative but also constructive and informative. For example, "You did an excellent job writing the heading on your paper; you included your name, the date, and the activity" versus "Wow, what a great job you did!"

Teachers frequently use tangible reinforcers because they are easily accessible and they satisfy the desires of different students. There are a wide variety of stickers, stamps, and small trinkets that appeal to students, and teachers can unobtrusively distribute them to students when a specific positive behavior occurs. One concern, however, is the cost associated with tangibles. Many students who are either adolescents or members of families that have higher socioeconomic status may desire only larger, expensive items. It is impractical for a teacher to obtain these items as reinforcers; however, often the teacher can collaborate with family members to use these more expensive items as tangible reinforcers. A contingency contract can be written in cooperation with the student, teacher, and family to access these tangible reinforcers.

Activity reinforcers are used very effectively in the classroom environment and are often referred to as the Premack Principle (1959), or Grandma's Law. The Premack Principle states that when an individual does X, then he or she can engage in Y. When an individual does a low-frequency, less desired behavior (X), then the individual can engage in the high-frequency, more desired behavior (Y). For example, "As soon as you clear the table, you may go outside and play with your friends." Several concerns in using activity reinforcers have been identified:

1. The effectiveness of the reinforcer is diminished if the activity is not accessible immediately following the target behavior.
2. There is a lack of flexibility in distributing a portion of some reinforcers (a field trip is either earned or not earned).
3. The activity may interrupt the flow of instruction (it would be impractical to have a student "shoot a basketball" after every correct response).
4. Should the student's performance be monitored as the student engages in the activity (what if the student engages in unacceptable behavior such as cursing during the activity)? The teacher needs to address these concerns before using activity reinforcers.

A generalized conditioned reinforcer is an object that may be exchanged for something of value; it provides access to a variety of either primary or secondary reinforcers. Money is an example of a generalized reinforcer that is used in our natural community environment, whereas in the classroom setting we use token reinforcers or a point system. Tokens or points are acquired for one or several behaviors and can be exchanged at later times for valued reinforcers. It permits the teacher to immediately provide consequences for a behavior and then provide reinforcement at a later time, facilitating delayed gratification. To implement a token system, the teacher must engage in the following decisions:

- Identify the token
- Identify back-up reinforcers
- Establish the token exchange-purchase value
- Establish the time and place for exchanging tokens
- Determine response cost

To successfully implement this system teachers must do the following:

- Consistently and contingently deliver the tokens
- Use backup reinforcers that are valued by the students
- Create tokens that cannot be counterfeited or stolen
- Establish a system for collecting tokens
- Warn students in advance of the next exchange period when the cost of items will be changed
- Decide whether tokens can be saved and how many can be banked

Establishing a system of generalized reinforcers is a timely task and is typically completed for a class or a small group of students rather than for one student. These systems are versatile because they can be used for several behaviors, implemented in several settings, and used by several individuals. Due to these factors, a token or point system assists in the process of generalization to more natural environments.

Regardless of the type of reinforcement that is delivered to students, the teacher must establish a schedule of reinforcement. When an individual is acquiring a new skill or behavior, reinforcement should be delivered on a continual schedule, after every correct response. Once the behavior has been learned, an intermittent schedule of reinforcement should occur. This will facilitate generalization of the skill or behavior to a more natural setting. Intermittent reinforcement is provided for the number of correct responses (ratio schedule) or after a period of time has elapsed (interval schedule), and the schedule can be fixed or variable. With a fixed ratio schedule, a reinforcer is delivered after the student has performed the task or behavior for a specific number of times. With a variable ratio schedule, a reinforcer is delivered after the student has performed the task or behavior on the average of a number of times. A behavior on a fixed ratio 3 (FR3) schedule would be reinforced after every three correct responses. A variable ratio 3 (VR3) schedule indicates that the student would be reinforced on the average of every three correct responses. A variable schedule increases the fluency and consistency of student responses. With a fixed interval schedule, the student is reinforced after he or she provides a correct response after a specified amount of time has elapsed. In a fixed interval 3 (FI3) schedule, after 3 minutes have elapsed, the student will be reinforced immediately after performing the target behavior. With a variable interval schedule, the time intervals vary.

The student is reinforced after he or she provides a correct response after a variable amount of time elapses. A behavior on a variable interval 3 (VI3) schedule would be reinforced on the average of every 3 minutes.

Acquisition of a new behavior typically requires a consistent reinforcement schedule. However, once the behavior is learned, thinning the schedule of reinforcement will decrease the student's dependence on artificial reinforcement and facilitate transition to more natural reinforcers. In thinning, the teacher moves from a dense, continual schedule to a more sparse, or variable, schedule. This process cannot occur too quickly, or the desired behavior will not be maintained. The process of thinning should follow the sequence of continual reinforcement, intermittent fixed ratio or interval, intermittent variable, and nonscheduled delivery of reinforcement.

Negative Reinforcement

Negative reinforcement is often confused with punishment. However, negative reinforcement is a technique used to increase a behavior, whereas punishment is used to decrease a behavior. Negative reinforcement is the contingent removal of an aversive stimulus immediately following a response that increases the likelihood of the occurrence of the behavior (Alberto & Troutman, 1999). This technique is effective because the student wants to escape or avoid the aversive stimulus. The teacher is using negative reinforcement when he or she states, "John, you must stay inside during recess and finish your homework; you can go out when the work is completed." The aversive condition of remaining in the classroom to finish homework will be removed when the homework is complete. The negative reinforcement should increase the probability that in the future John will complete his homework before coming to school. Punishment, in this example, would be the following: "John, you will go to detention for fooling around instead of doing your work."

Teachers sometimes use negative reinforcement inadvertently and the goal of increasing the student's appropriate behavior is not accomplished. For instance, when Elise is bothering others during independent seat work, a teacher might sometimes allow her to do something else and stop doing the assigned work, so that other students will not be bothered and they can do their work. However, Elise learns that engaging in disruptive behavior allows her to escape the assignment; bothering others results in her being allowed to stop the independent seat assignment that she doesn't want to do. This often results in the continuation and sometimes even an increase of the inappropriate behavior. This example of negative reinforcement does not encourage or increase appropriate behavior, and the teacher's goal is not accomplished.

Contracting

A behavioral or contingency contract is a written agreement between two parties. One or both parties agree to engage in a specified level of the target behavior, with an identified consequence contingent on the occurrence or nonoccurrence of the behavior. The contract is a form of public commitment to change one's behavior, and it is visual reminder of the desired behavior change. Typically, in the classroom teachers develop a one-party contract, whereas two-party contracts are more often utilized in the home or work environment with people who have a relationship with each other (e.g., child-parent, parent-parent, or coworkers). In a one-party contract at school, the teacher identifies a target behavior and contingencies, and the contract manager or teacher arranges and implements these contingencies. The contract manager must implement the contingencies as written and must not gain to benefit monetarily or with products from the contract. In a two-party contract, both parties identify specific target behaviors to perform. The behavior change of one person can serve as the reinforcer for the behavior change in the other person, or a separate contingency can be identified, with another reinforcer for each party.

The parties involved in the behavioral contract must negotiate it so that it is acceptable to everyone. In a one-party contract, the teacher, as contract manager, will work with the student to agree on an acceptable level of the behavior, the consequences, and the time frame for the contract. The contract manager should make every attempt to establish criteria that are attainable, therefore increasing possibilities for reinforcement and subsequently increasing the occurrence of the target behavior. There are five components that are essential in developing the behavioral contract:

- Identify the desired target behavior
- State how the behavior will be measured
- State when the behavior must be performed
- Identify the contingency (preferably reinforcement)
- Identify the person to implement the contingency

In addition to the five components, it is important that all parties involved clearly understand the terms of the contract (DeRisi & Butz, 1975). A two-party contract is more difficult to negotiate. Often, one party wants the other party's behavior to change but does not recognize the need to change one's own behavior. Because the contract must be negotiated so that it is acceptable to both parties, each party must realize the benefit of each person's behavior change.

Contracts are frequently used in the classroom environment. It is recommended that the contracts state positive contingencies and use positive reinforcement rather than punishment. Maximum student involvement in the development of the contract is recommended.

Prompting

Prompting is the addition of a stimulus that increases the likelihood that the correct response will be exhibited at the right time. Teachers prompt students to respond to questions rather than wait for them to exhibit a correct or incorrect answer. Actors on movie or stage sets are also prompted when learning their lines or when they have forgotten their part. Prompting can occur as either verbal, visual, gesture, model, or physical cues and it is important for the teacher to use the least-intrusive prompt that the student needs. In other words, the teacher should provide the minimal assistance that the student requires to exhibit the appropriate behavior.

Verbal prompts are generally considered the least intrusive. They may be in the form of rules, instructions, or hints. When providing the directions "Let's walk to the cafeteria," the teacher may verbally state the rule "When we walk in the hallway, we walk quietly without disturbing other classes," the instructions "Keep your lips together and keep your hands at your sides," or the hint "Shh, remember, walking quietly means not talking to your friends as we move down the hall." For students who have difficulty completing lengthy, more involved tasks, the teacher can tape-record instructions (verbal prompts) for the student to follow.

Visual prompts may be in the form of words, pictures, diagrams or photographs. They provide a visual representation or visual directions that the student can follow. As adults, we provide ourselves with visual prompts when we make grocery lists, "to-do" lists, use self-stick notes, and write down telephone numbers to call (rather than rely on our memory), so it may be a natural skill. Teachers often post directions, instructions, or reminders on the wall of their classrooms or on bulletin boards so that students can follow them. Examples include paper heading rules, rules for grammar and punctuation, rules for behavior, picture schedules, and a chart of the ABCs. Students with significant disabilities will be more successful if the visual prompt is an actual photograph (e.g., a picture of children eating as a prompt that it's time to move to the cafeteria).

Gestures are another form of prompt that may be used very unobtrusively in the classroom and in the natural environment. Depending on the situation, they are often less intrusive than other visual prompts. A gesture is a physical action involving a portion of the body. For example, when it is time to line up at the door, after the directive is given, the teacher might gesture "pointing to the door." The "thumbs-up" sign is also a gesture that indicates to the student that he or she has done a good job.

Modeling, or providing a demonstration of the desired behavior, is another type of prompt that is very useful in the classroom setting. Modeling can be provided by either the teacher or other students, but students will most likely follow the model when the model is similar to the students, is competent, and has prestige (Sulzer-Azaroff & Mayer, 1986). A demonstration may occur with or without verbal directions, but when they are combined, the students receive a multisensory approach to teaching. A teacher may provide verbal directions while physically demonstrating the task; as the teacher states the steps in tying a shoe, for example, he or she is manipulating the laces. This is typically more effective than only verbal directions or a demonstration of the task. Teachers may reinforce other students' behavior and promote their acceptable behavior. However, they should use tact so as to not embarrass the student models or intimidate the onlooking students.

Physical guidance is the most intrusive prompting procedure. Another individual (teacher or trainer) physically guides the student through the task. Full physical guidance occurs when the teacher provides hand-over-hand assistance to guide the student through the entire task until completion. Partial physical guidance occurs when the teacher provides initial assistance to begin the task and then allows the student to independently complete the task. A physical prompt is often used in physical education activities, as the student is guided through "bowling a ball" or "hitting a softball with a bat"; but physical guidance may also be used to sort silverware in a vocational task, to clean a sink in a domestic task, to solve a math problem in a cognitive task, or for any other teaching task that permits physical manipulation.

Prompting is very effective as a teaching strategy; however, prompts should be faded. In fading, the prompt is gradually lessened across learning opportunities and eventually removed or no longer provided. The amount of assistance is systematically reduced. Fading should occur only after the behavior has been learned and the student demonstrates it consistently. As teachers, we often fade the prompts too soon and then get frustrated because the student no longer completes the task or demonstrates the behavior. If a student demonstrates the behavior consistently when provided with a prompt (e.g., partial physical), the teacher will fade to a less intrusive prompt (e.g., modeling). When the student again demonstrates the behavior with the modeling level of prompt, the teacher will fade to a lesser intrusive prompt (e.g., gesture). This process will continue until prompts are no longer necessary for the student to complete the task. This method is termed *decreasing assistance* or *most to least prompting*. The method of *time delay* can also be used to fade prompts. The teacher provides a directive and then waits a designated number of seconds before providing the prompt. This allows the student to process the directive and organize a response. The time delay can be constant or progressive. As the wait time increases, the likelihood of needing the prompt is lessened. *Increasing assistance* is a method for fading prompts whereby the teacher initially provides the least intrusive prompt and then provides more intrusive prompts if the student does not respond with the desired behavior. *Graduated guidance* is another technique for fading physical prompts. Here the teacher reduces full physical guidance to either touching the student lightly at a distance from the body part that is engaged in the behavior or shadowing (following the movement but not touching the student's body part).

Shaping

Shaping is a technique that is used to teach students new tasks by reinforcing successive approximations of the task until the desired target behavior is exhibited. The teacher systematically shapes an existing response into the desired behavior. Shaping occurs very naturally as children begin to learn developmental tasks such as walking, speaking in sentences, or eating with silverware. As a child pulls up to stand, the parents reinforce the upright posture and encourage the child to step to the adult's outstretched arms. Every attempt is positively reinforced through verbalizations, clapping, and physical hugging. As the child continues to make the stepping attempts (and is reinforced), the steps become steadier and longer, and posture becomes more upright until the child can walk unassisted for a few steps. This is the process of shaping a child's walking behavior. The teacher clearly delineates steps in the shaping process, and the number of steps will depend on the specific task and the child's abilities. Each step should be a closer approximation to the task than the previous step.

To begin the process of shaping, the teacher identifies an existing behavior that is an approximation of the target behavior. This behavior is reinforced and, as a result, the student more often exhibits this behavior. Once the teacher lessens the reinforcement, novel behaviors begin to appear. The teacher reinforces a novel behavior that is a closer approximation to the target behavior. This pattern continues until the desired target behavior is exhibited. Although the teacher must choose a starting behavior to begin this process, shaping can be used to teach a novel behavior, reinstate a previously exhibited behavior that is no longer occurring, or change a dimension of an existing behavior.

Strategies for Decreasing Behaviors

Teachers and parents often have little difficulty identifying child or student behaviors that they want to decrease. Annoying and undesirable behaviors are readily observable and identifiable. Often, however, we decrease a behavior without considering what behavior the child has in his or her repertoire to replace the target behavior or serve the same function. As we seek to decrease a behavior, identification of a replacement or an alternative behavior is critical. A fair-pair behavior must be identified. Students must receive an equal amount of reinforcement for the alternative behavior that was received for the original target behavior, if we expect the replacement behavior to continue.

There are several strategies that are useful for behavior reduction. Many parents and professionals use punishment and aversive consequences because they seem simple and often quickly stop the behavior. Parents and other adults frequently model aversive techniques when disciplining children. These behaviors are imitated by the children and eventually become reflexive actions. Then the adults wonder where the children learned these aggressive behaviors. Often, adults don't realize how aversive some of the techniques are and do not consider alternative strategies. There are several alternatives to punishment that may be equally effective in reducing behaviors, and they have fewer side effects and provide models for acceptable behavior. Alberto & Troutman (1999) provide a hierarchy of procedural alternatives for behavior reduction that is useful for teachers. We suggest that this hierarchy be followed, using the least intrusive alternative before more aversive techniques. Teachers should make databased decisions to move to a more intrusive strategy for a particular child, and we should substantiate the ineffectiveness of the previous procedures. We need to obtain permission to use a more intrusive procedure; consult with other teachers, a supervisor, parents, and the child; and conduct a review with a committee to obtain agreement on the intervention program.

Differential Reinforcement

Differential reinforcement procedures provide a positive reinforcement approach to reducing behaviors. The teacher differentially reinforces appropriate behaviors while reducing inappropriate behaviors. There are three types of differential reinforcement procedures that will be explained: differential reinforcement of lower rates, of other behaviors, and of alternative or incompatible behaviors.

In *differential reinforcement of lower rates of behavior* (DRL), the teacher provides reinforcement if the student exhibits the target behavior at a rate less than or equal to the prescribed rate. It allows the student to progressively adjust to exhibiting successively lower rates of the behavior. Full-session DRL compares the total number of responses in an entire session to a prescribed criterion, whereas interval-session DRL divides the session into segments and compares the number of responses during that segment to a preset criterion. Interval DRL is useful when the teacher determines that a more gradual approach to changing the behavior is warranted. With the DRL procedure, the goal is to decrease the student's behavior but not necessarily extinguish it (e.g., frequency of incidents talking to a peer during independent seat work, walking around the room to sharpen a pencil). To implement a DRL procedure, the teacher must identify the behavior, record baseline data, establish time segments (if implementing interval DRL), and establish the criteria for reinforcement to avoid too frequent or too infrequent reinforcement.

Zena could not control her catty remarks to peers who could not afford to dress in style. She constantly ridiculed her peers and soon discovered she had few friends. She asked her teacher for help. Together they charted the frequency of catty remarks during the school day. Zena's friend Angela also helped to count the incidents. Every morning they charted the behavior, and Zena could observe the target behavior decrease. Each day that the number of incidents was less than the day before, the teacher and Angela praised Zena.

Differential reinforcement of other behavior (DRO) involves providing a re-inforcer if the student does not exhibit the target behavior within a pre-scribed amount of time. DRO reinforces zero occurrences of the target behavior within a specified time period. The teacher reinforces a student as long as the target behavior doesn't occur; however, inadvertently the stu-dent may be reinforced for other behaviors that are also inappropriate and occur during the specified time period. The teacher does not want these other behaviors to increase, nor is it ethical for the teacher to allow the student to demonstrate an increase in these inappropriate behaviors. The teacher may design several DRO procedures to operate at one time or may initiate other consequences for these behaviors.

To conduct a DRO, the teacher must take baseline data to determine the frequency of the behavior. In accord with the baseline data, the teacher determines that the reinforcement will be contingent on the nonoccurrence of the behavior throughout the entire time period or during a smaller time segment. Implementing an interval DRO will increase the likelihood of the student receiving reinforcement if the behavior is occurring at a fairly high frequency. With interval DRO, when the student reaches criteria for several days, the time within each segment will be increased. With full-session DRO, when the student reaches criteria, the goal for behavior reduction has been reached.

Differential reinforcement of incompatible behaviors (DRI) involves reinforc-ing a behavior that is topographically incompatible with the target behavior, while *differential reinforcement of alternative behaviors* (DRA) involves reinforc-ing the occurrence of an alternative behavior. Both procedures require the teacher to determine a functional alternative to the behavior that he or she wants to reduce. With a DRI, the teacher must determine a new behavior that is physically impossible to do while doing the target behavior. When the child is reinforced for completing the incompatible behavior, the origi-nal target behavior should decrease or disappear. When determining an al-ternative behavior, the chosen behavior should be standard or appropriate behavior that addresses the function of the inappropriate behavior. The stu-dent should be able to frequently gain reinforcement for this alternative behavior. To implement either procedure, the teacher selects a behavior to replace the target behavior, records baseline data, and selects a schedule of reinforcement.

Extinction

Extinction reduces a student's inappropriate behavior when the teacher actively ignores the target behavior. The teacher abruptly withdraws posi-tive reinforcement, which had previously been maintaining the student's behavior. Therefore, this technique is most effective when the function of the behavior is teacher attention. It is also most effective when the teacher reinforces other more appropriate behaviors, thus providing attention for desired behaviors. Although this process seems quite simple, it is very difficult to ignore annoying, aggravating behaviors that a child exhibits. There are many reasons that make this strategy ineffective. Extinction typically does not immediately reduce the behavior, and the rate of the behavior often increases before it finally decreases. Sometimes the teacher does not have the patience or stamina to continue to ignore the behavior. Also, the student may replace the target behavior with an aggressive or more outlandish behavior in an attempt to get the teacher's attention, and it is difficult for the teacher to ignore this new, dangerous or aggressive behavior. It is also difficult to control the attention that peers might be paying to the target student when he or she exhibits the behavior; sometimes the peers imitate the behavior. Additionally, spontaneous recovery, a recurrence of the original behavior, might occur after the behavior has been extinguished. Finally, even when extinction is effective in one environment, its application to other environments is often limited.

Rena constantly raises her hand and blurts out the answer to Mrs. Ramirez's questions. At first, the teacher acknowledges Rena, but the behavior accelerates. Next, the teacher states, "Rena, put your hand down and give the other students a chance," but Rena appears to enjoy the negative attention. Mrs. Ramirez next decides to use extinction. She ignores Rena's blurting out and only acknowledges her directly when she raises her hand. At first, Rena's behavior accelerates, but gradually she raises her hand discreetly and responds when called upon.

Removal of a Desired Stimulus

The following strategies are considered to be punishment procedures. *Punishment* is the contingent presentation of an aversive consequence or the removal of a reinforcing consequence that makes it less likely for the behavior to occur in the future. A punishment decreases the behavior it follows: Therefore, if the behavior does not decrease, the consequence is not functioning as a punishment. In general, there are many misconceptions about the term *punishment*, and the technical definition above is different from the common view of many people.

Punishment may work quickly, but there are several problems associated with each of its strategies (Miltenberger, 1997):

- It may produce aggression or other emotional problems.
- It may result in the child developing escape or avoidance behaviors.
- It may be overused because it serves as a negative reinforcer for the teacher.
- We are modeling aggression.
- There are ethical issues related to punishment.

Response-Cost

Response-cost is a punishment procedure that reduces behavior by removing a desired reinforcer after it has been earned, contingent on the demonstration of the target behavior. The teacher withdraws a reinforcer because the child exhibits a specified target behavior. Response-cost is often compared to a system of levying fines. Most frequently, this strategy is used in concert with token economy or point systems. The student earns tokens or points for demonstrating appropriate behavior, and then is fined or loses tokens or points each time the inappropriate target behavior is demonstrated.

Response-cost programs have been used very effectively in school environments; however there are several problems associated with this strategy. A primary issue is that the teacher must be able to remove the reinforcer. Difficulties arise if the reinforcer is edible (it is probably gone!) or if the student has the ability to hide or conceal the reinforcer. Sometimes the student is unwilling to give it back and will engage in aggression to keep it. Another issue is that the teacher must levy the fines fairly. How much should a student lose for specific behaviors? This must be carefully calculated in advance. There is also the possibility that all of the reinforcers will be withdrawn, so that when a behavior problem occurs the student will not have any tokens or points that can be taken away. This might occur if the student is having an especially bad day. However, the teacher can develop alternatives to avoid most of these issues.

Time-Out

Time-out is considered to be "time out from positive reinforcement." Inherent in this definition is the idea that time-in is very important: the student wants to be involved in the class activity, the activity is reinforcing or external reinforcement is provided, and the student wants the reinforcement that is provided during class time. Time-out is a punishment procedure and should not be utilized until the teacher has tried strategies of differential reinforcement and extinction or has justified their nonuse. The least intrusive type of time-out occurs when a teacher manipulates the environment to deny reinforcement to a child. The teacher may remove materials from a child, have the child move to the edge of the activity, or have the child put his head down on his desk. These are forms of *contingent observation*. The child is aware of the class activities but is denied participation in them.

A more intrusive type of time-out is sometimes referred to as exclusionary time-out, whereby the student is removed from the educational activity and cannot receive reinforcement but remains in the classroom. The teacher may remove the child to another area of the room, put him behind a screen, or have her sit in a study carrel. The most intrusive type of time-out is when the individual is removed from the classroom after exhibiting a target behavior. The student may go to a supervised area or to a seclusionary room. Teachers ineffectively use time-out when they remove the child from the classroom and have him or her sit in the hallway or go to the principal's office as punishment. Although this is removing the student from classroom reinforcement, unfortunately there are often activities that occur in the hallway or the office that the student finds reinforcing. The environment outside the classroom actually provides reinforcement to the student; thus the inappropriate target behavior continues to occur at other times so that the student gains access to the reinforcers in the hallway or in the principal's office. Some schools have designated time-out rooms (seclusionary time-out) that are available for students who are consistently disruptive or engage in physically aggressive behaviors. Teachers must follow specific rules and regulations if they choose to use this intrusive and restrictive punishment procedure.

Presentation of Aversives

Presentation of aversives is popularly termed "punishment." We often think of corporal punishment as an example of an aversive, but aversives can also include any stimulus that results in physical pain or discomfort to the individual or any stimuli that an individual learns to associate with disdain, dislike, or physical or psychological pain. Yelling and verbal reprimands, strategies that some teachers frequently use to manage student behavior, are aversives. Coaches who require students who misbehave to run laps or complete extra push-ups or sit-ups are using aversive punishment.

There are many problems and ethical issues associated with the presentation of aversives. Teachers should be encouraged to use the other levels of behavior reduction and only pursue aversives when they have attempted strategies in all other levels. The authors of this text do not believe that corporal punishment should ever be used in the school setting.

Overcorrection

Overcorrection involves having a child repetitively complete the correct form of a task that she did incorrectly, or restore an environment that he disturbed to an immaculate state. An example of *restitutional overcorrection* is that if a child is caught chewing gum, and she quickly sticks it under her desk, the punishment is that the child must clean under her desk and all the other desks in the classroom. An example of *positive practice overcorrection* is if a student incorrectly ties his shoes so he can hurry out to recess, the teacher makes him tie his shoes correctly five times before he can go out to play with his friends.

Punishment Versus Discipline

Many traditional schools have equated punishment with discipline. Punishment and discipline are not the same. They are not synonymous terms. In the long run, punishment is not effective. Table 6-2 (Crawford, Bodine, & Hoglund, 1993) contrasts punishment with discipline. It provides a guide to help teachers sort out their own practices and attitudes toward these techniques. When a particular discipline measure is not successful, but it meets the guidelines for good discipline practice, it is important to avoid resorting to punishment. *Punishment is not the backup plan for failed discipline practices.*

TABLE 6-2. PUNISHMENT AND DISCIPLINE

PUNISHMENT	DISCIPLINE
Expresses power of an authority; usually causes pain to the recipient; is based upon retribution or revenge; is concerned with what happened (the past).	Is based on logical or natural consequences that embody the reality of a social order (rules that one must learn and accept to function adequately and productively in society); concerned with what is happening now (the present).
Is arbitrary—probably applied inconsistently and unconditionally; does not accept or acknowledge exceptions or mitigating circumstances.	Is consistent—accepts that the behaving individual is doing the best that he or she can do for now.
Is imposed by an authority (done to someone), with responsibility assumed by the one administering the punishment and the behaving individual avoiding responsibility.	Comes from within, with the behaving individual desiring and assuming responsibility; presumes that conscience is internal.
Closes options for the individual, who must pay for a behavior that has already occurred.	Opens options for the individual, who can choose a new behavior.
As a teaching process, usually reinforces a failure identity; essentially negative and short term, without sustained personal involvement of either teacher or learner.	As a teaching process, is active and involves close, sustained, personal involvement of both teacher and learner; emphasizes developing ways to act that will result in successful behavior.
Is characterized by open or concealed anger; is a poor model of the expectations of quality.	Is friendly and supportive; provides a model of quality behavior.
Is easy and expedient.	Is difficult and time consuming.

cont.

Focuses on strategies intended to control the learner's behavior.	Focuses on the learner's behavior and the consequences of that behavior.
Rarely results in positive changes; may increase subversiveness or result in temporary suppression of behavior; at best, produces compliance.	Usually results in a change in behavior that is more successful, acceptable, and responsible; develops the capacity for self-evaluation of behavior.

Application of Behaviorist Principles

The Village of Boys Town, Nebraska, founded by Father Flanagan in 1917, uses many of the principles of applied behavior analysis discussed in this chapter to increase the success of students with behavior and/or learning problems, as well as with court-adjudicated youth (Connolly et al., 1995; Dowd & Tierney, 1995). The technology used in this model finds its origins in the teaching-family model (Phillips, et al., 1972). A basic premise of this program is that teaching skills, building relationships, and developing self-discipline are the heart of success for students in school and for individuals functioning as adults in the community. Teachers, administrators, and support personnel continue efforts to teach life skills, help students to develop relationships, and learn self-discipline. The more a group home, a shelter, or a classroom in a school creates a family environment, the more likely it is for skills, relationships, and self-discipline to be learned.

Because the program emphasizes adult skills that produce a warm, nurturing environment, the Girls and Boys Town Program is known as the Family Home Program. Teaching and child-care skills—such as praise, empathy, the delivery of personally beneficial rationales when instructing youth; or the delivery of behavioral specificity when teaching social skills to youth—are known as "quality" components within the Family Home Program. They are the contextual variables that help to build the kind of relationships that foster youth happiness and satisfaction in educational and treatment settings (Wilner et al., 1977). These skills, in addition to program quality components such as youth self-government, peer management, and weekly family outings, develop environments that enhance the effectiveness of more traditionally known behavioral principles and technologies. These quality components form the contextual backdrop for implementing principles such as reinforcement and negative reinforcement, or for implementing technologies such as token economies or school notes.

The Girls and Boys Town Family Home Program also employs a number of "effectiveness components"—elements more traditionally recognized in behavior analysis circles. Some of the more prominent effectiveness components of the Family Home Program are teaching interactions, motivation systems, crisis teaching, and problem-solving techniques.

Teaching interactions combine praise, behavioral specificity for skill learning, rationales, positive or negative point exchange, and behavior rehearsal in combination to promote skill acquisition and skill use. Teaching interactions are the primary method used to promote skill learning in the program. They are used to teach basic skills such as greeting or complex skills such as assertiveness or asking for help. There are two types of teaching interactions: proactive teaching (teaching skills at a controlled time) and corrective teaching (helping a student to problem solve and move on).

The *motivation system* is a flexible token economy in which children can earn or lose points based upon their behavior. In the Family Home Program an emphasis is placed on point earnings for learning and using new skills and strategies that are taught youth through the teaching interaction component. The point earnings and losses provide motivation to use and learn new behaviors and to refrain form using maladaptive behaviors. The token economy has multiple levels. There is a daily system that provides 20 or more teaching interactions per day and backup privileges acquired daily. There is a less structured weekly system that provides 10 or more teaching interactions per day and a backup privilege menu that is exchanged weekly. The motivation system is faded as students progress to the third level, the achievement system, to promote generalization. In the achievement system privileges are not earned through point exchange but are negotiated, as they would be in most families.

A third effectiveness component is *crisis teaching*, which comprises a variety of adult skills (empathy, calm tone of voice, target behavior and not content) and a variety of youth self-control skills (voluntary time-out, relaxation, cognitive rehearsal). Crisis teaching has two functions: to de-escalate strong emotional and behavioral episodes and to teach new, adaptive behaviors to youth for dealing with conflict and disappointment.

The fourth effectiveness component, *problem-solving techniques*, is an individualized behavioral and cognitive strategy aimed to help youth cope with life problems, ranging from independent living to job choice to academic decisions.

Research on the Family Home Program documents a relationship between program components and youth happiness and satisfaction (Friman et al., 1996); improved youth behavior (Friman et al., 1997); and program effectiveness, defined as long-term positive effects on both academic attitudes and performance (Dowd & Tierney, 1995).

Summary

This chapter has provided an overview of applied behavior analysis and the strategies that are most applicable for teacher use. The emphasis has been the structure that is necessary to systematically apply behavior modification principles. Applied behavior analysis provides a five-step framework that should be followed when teachers address moderate to severe behavior problems. This framework is not necessary to develop an overall classroom management system or to manage typical inappropriate student behaviors that routinely occur in the classroom. Rather it is most useful for intervening with individual students who are exhibiting moderate to severe problems and require one-on-one intervention. Although some of the strategies can be used for overall classroom management (e.g., token economy), most of the strategies are suggested for one-on-one student intervention.

Proactive management strategies were discussed as general strategies that teachers can use to maintain a positive classroom climate. Manipulating the environment (e.g., physical environment, teacher behavior, student-teacher interactions, and curriculum) allows the teacher to establish a climate that facilitates learning and appropriate behavioral control.

Five steps were addressed to implement applied behavior analysis in the classroom environment. Within each step, procedures were provided that the teacher should employ to work toward managing student behavior. The five-step process has tight boundaries: When a teacher chooses to implement applied behavior analysis, this process should be consistently applied to all situations. However, there is flexibility in the strategies that a teacher can choose to implement this behavior change process. Strategies should be chosen based on whether the child's behavior is to be increased or decreased. If increasing a behavior, the teacher should use strategies of reinforcement, contracting, prompting, or shaping. If decreasing a behavior, the teacher should follow the hierarchy of least intrusive intervention. Strategies to decrease behavior include differential reinforcement, extinction, response-cost, time-out, presentation of aversives, and overcorrection. Corporal punishment should not be considered an option for use by teachers.

Fading reinforcers is an important component of applied behavior analysis. Students must be encouraged not to depend on constant external reinforcers. An optimal goal and end result is for each student to acquire self-regulation skills and exhibit appropriate behavior without adult intervention.

Activity 1: Contracting

Read the following guidelines on how to develop a contingency contract, and write a contract to modify a student's behavior. Develop a scenario and a contract to modify a problem behavior.

10 Basic Rules

The reward for following the contract should be immediate. It is important that the presentation of the reinforcer be contingent only on the adequate performance of the behavior. The reinforcer must be unique and be unavailable to the student under ordinary circumstances.

1. Initial contracts should call for and reward small approximations of the desired behavior.

2. Contract for a behavior that approaches the desired behavior. Determine whether the behavior was executed according to contract. Reward the behavior.

3. Reward frequently and consistently with small amounts of the reward.

4. The contract should specify the desired behavior and reward accomplishment rather than obedience.

5. Reward the performance after is occurs.

6. The contract must be fair to both teachers and students. If the contract is written to reward "not fighting," and the student eliminates the fighting behavior but uses a curse word, the reinforcer should not be withheld. In such a case a contract to eliminate cursing should be developed.

7. The terms of the contract must be clear. Be specific in stating how much performance is expected and mutually agree on the reward.

8. The contract must be treated seriously and carried out according to the terms specified by both teacher and student.

9. The contract should be stated in positive terms when possible.

10. Contracting as a method must be used systematically. The following conditions are crucial:

    a. The teachers have identified and broken down the target behavior into specific terms (e.g., instead of "fighting" say "kicking, pulling hair, scratching, punching, or spitting"; instead of "disrespect" say "using curse words, shouting, ignoring the teacher's directions").

    b. The parties specify the desired behavior(s) and agree on a criterion for evaluating the behavior (e.g., Tom will reduce interrupting his teacher by 30% during the next week).

    c. Determine what really reinforces the student. Ask the student and the parents and observe the student. What reinforces one student may not be reinforcing to another.

    The contingency contract should:

    a. Be negotiated and freely agreed to by both student and teacher

    b. Include the desired behavior and the specific criteria by which it is evaluated

    c. Consistently deliver the reinforcers in accordance with the terms of the contract

    d. Include a time for review and renegotiation

Example: Tricia, a third-grade student, has become aggressive with her peers ever since her baby brother was born a month ago. Tricia insults her peers by using abusive language and engages in physical fights on the playground. She was always fairly assertive and occasionally had to be reprimanded, but her recent behavior has worried her parents and her teachers. Tricia is gifted athletically and enjoys sports. At a parent-teacher conference, it was decided to write a contract to modify Tricia's behavior.

CONTRACT

I, Tricia Ryan, will use only "positive talk" (no curse words or shouting) and will get along (no hitting, biting, punching) with my classmates 100% of the time by January 14. When I succeed in getting along I will (1) be allowed to join the community girls soccer team, and (2) be given tickets for myself and two friends to the upcoming national soccer matches at the astrodome.

Signed: _____

Activity 2: Reinforcers

Divide in small groups and develop a menu of reinforcers for your particular classroom. The following is an example of reinforcers.

Consumable Food Reinforcers	**Social Reinforcers**
Fruits	Hugs
Candies	Smiles
Snack foods	Pat on the back
Popcorn	Handshake
Cookies	High five
Cake	Special attention
Milk	Special compliments
Soda	
Juice	
Special Treat	

Token Reinforcers	**Tangible Reinforcers**
Stars	Pens, pencils
Chips	Toys
Play money	Pad of paper
Checkmarks	Badges
Points	Art supplies

Reinforcing Activities

Reading or looking at books, magazines, comic books, catalogs

Watching television	Getting additional playtime
Getting free time	Using the computer
Caring for a class plant	Listening to music
Playing a computer game	Playing a board or table game
Participating in organized sports	Participating in extracurricular activities
Erasing the board	Getting leadership responsibilities
Receiving a positive parent note	Spending time with a favorite teacher or coach

Recognizing achievement (such as a student of the week award)

Activity 3: Role-Play—Charting

Pair participants and inform the student participant to use the word OK in a one-minute conversation with his or her partner (the teacher participant). Direct the teacher participant to count and record the student's use of OKs. Repeat this procedure three times. Both participants record the number of the three uses of OKs as baseline. They chart and display the results in a line graph. During the intervention period, the teacher and student decide on a strategy to reduce the annoying OKs. This could involve the student making a mark on paper every time he or she says OK. Repeat the exercise three times, and purposefully reduce the number of OKs each time. Chart the results on the same graph.

Activity 4: Leveling Charlie

Charlie was identified as having a behavior disorder. He was noncompliant (would not follow school rules or teacher directions, and refused to stay on-task), aggressive (kicking and punching peers and sometimes the teacher), and prone to displaying temper tantrums (he would throw himself on the floor kicking and shouting). His individual education plan (IEP) placed him in a general education reading class for one period per day. The special education and the general education teachers decided to develop a level system for Charlie. Develop a five-level plan to modify Charlie's aggressive behaviors.

References

Alberto, P. A., & Troutman, A. C. (1999). *Applied behavior analysis for teachers* (5th ed.). Upper Saddle River, NJ: Merrill.

Burke, J., (1992). *Decreasing classroom behavior problems: Practical guidelines for teachers.* San Diego: Singular.

Crawford, D., Bodine, R., & Hoglund, R. (1993). *The school for quality learning: Managing the school and classroom the deming way.* Champaign, IL Research Press.

DeRisi, W., & Butz, G. (1975). *Writing behavioral contracts.* Champaign, IL: Research Press.

Connolly, T., Dowd, T., Criste, A., Nelson, C. & Tobias, L. (1995). *The well-managed classroom: Promoting student success through social skill instruction.* Boys Town, NE: Boys Town Press.

Dowd, T., & Tierney, J. (1995). *Teaching social skills to youth: A curriculum for child-care providers.* Boys Town, NE: Boys Town Press.

Durand, V. M. (1988). The Motivation Assessment Scale. In M. Hersen & A. S. Bellack (Eds.), *Dictionary of behavioral assessment techniques.* New York: Pergamon Press.

Friman, P. C., Jones, M., Smith, G., Daly, D., & Larzelere, R. (1997). Decreasing disruptive behavior by adolescents in residential placement by increasing their positive to negative interactional ratios. *Behavior Modification, 21,* 470–486.

Friman, P. C., Osgood, D. W., Shanahan, D., Thompson, R. W., Larzelere, R., & Daly, D. L. (1996). A longitudinal evaluation of prevalent negative beliefs about residential placement for troubled adolescents. *Journal of Abnormal Child Psychology, 24,* 299–324.

Miltenberger, R. (1997). *Behavior modification: Principles and procedures.* Pacific Grove, CA: Brooks/Cole.

O'Neill R. E., Horner, R. H., Albin, R. W., Sprague, J. R., Storey, K., & Newton, J. S. (1997). *Functional assessment and program development for problem behavior: A practical handbook* (2nd ed.). Pacific Grove, CA: Brooks/Cole.

Phillips, E. L., Phillips, E. A., Fixsen, & Wolfe, M. (1972). *The teaching-family handbook.* Lawrence, KS: University of Kansas Achievement Place Project.

Premack, D. (1959). Toward empirical behavior laws I: Positive reinforcement. *Psychological Review 66,* 219–233.

Sulzer-Azaroff, B., & Mayer, G. R. (1986). *Achieving educational excellence.* New York: Holt, Rinehart & Winston.

Touchette, P. E., MacDonald, R. F., & Langer, S. N. (1985). A scatter plot for identifying stimulus control of problem behavior. *Journal of Applied Behavior Analysis 18,* 343–351.

Watson, J. B. (1926). *Behaviorism.* New York: Norton.

Wilner, A. G., Braukmann, C. J., Kirigin, K. A., Fixsen, D. L., Phillips, E. L., & Wolf, M. M. (1977). The training and validation of youth-preferred social behaviors of child-care personnel. *Journal of Applied Behavior Analysis, 10* (2), 219–230.

Wright, H. (1960). Observational study in P. H. Mussen (Ed.), *Handbook of research methods in child development.* New York: Wiley.

Chapter 7

Discipline With Flexible Boundaries

Overview

Democratic Discipline
   Reality therapy
   Control theory
   Quality schools

Social Models
   Adlerian theory
   Goals of misbehavior
   Consequences versus punishment, encouragement versus
     reinforcement

Rational Emotive Therapy
   A (event), B (interpretation), C (reaction or emotion),
     and D (new reaction to B)

Cognitive Behavior Modification and Self-Management
   Self-determination
   Self–goal setting
   Self-instruction
   Self-recording
   Self-evaluation
   Self-reinforcement

Judicious Discipline
   Democratic and Constitutional rights
   Adapted strategies

An Ecological Approach
   Child-environment interventions
   Milieu therapy

Summary

Activities

QUESTIONS

This chapter will help you to answer the following questions:

1. According to William Glasser, what steps should teachers take to deal with misbehaving students?

2. Does control theory imply that teachers should be in control? Explain.

3. What qualities does a teacher need to be a lead-teacher?

4. How can a teacher detect the cause or goal of students' misbehavior?

5. What are the four causes or goals of misbehavior?

6. What is the difference between consequences and punishment, and encouragement and reinforcers?

7. What are two important reasons why students need to learn self-management skills?

8. What three strategies did judicious discipline borrow from other models of behavior?

9. Why is self-reinforcement preferable to teacher-administered reinforcement?

10. In what ways does your thinking affect your feelings and behavior?

11. How does the student's total environment influence his or her behavior?

12. What is meant by milieu therapy?

Overview

Emotions, mental states, motivation, personality types, genetic predisposition, and attitudes influence behavior, as do pressures from other people and from the environment. Although teachers need to consider and understand internal causes of behavior, they should not overlook the behavior itself and must hold students responsible for their actions.

In this chapter, we will examine strategies advocated by several authorities that emphasize empowering students to take control of their behaviors. Unlike discipline with loose boundaries, discipline with flexible boundaries encourages placing definite boundaries until students demonstrate responsible behaviors. The students' emotional state and environmental conditions are considered, but so are their actions. This model proposes a democratic approach to allow students to develop responsibility and freedom and to own up to the consequences of their choices and decisions. They must face natural or logical consequences when they invade the rights of others or violate rules necessary for the good of the group. A discipline with flexible boundaries allows authority figures to set limits; however, the ultimate goal is to eventually transfer this control to the students.

William Glasser believes that we choose to behave in a way that gives us control over our lives. A coercive and authoritarian type of discipline is threatening, often results in anger or avoidance, and does not teach self-regulation. When adults set limits, children do not learn to set their own limits. We must teach children skills that they will use for a lifetime, such as setting standards, evaluating their behavior, and making choices. Rudolph Dreikurs submits four causes, or goals, of antisocial behavior: attention getting, power, revenge, and control. He suggests that teachers examine why students misbehave and respond in a way that will diffuse the student's goal. For instance, if the student's goal is power, the teacher can refuse to engage in a power struggle, because it takes two to engage in a conflict.

Albert Ellis proposes strategies that can help students to understand a rational way to think and self-analyze and to develop rational, commonsense thoughts. Rational emotive therapy (RET) teaches people how to think so that they can feel and behave rationally. Our emotions are made up of our perceptions, thoughts, beliefs, and feelings. When we have an emotion, we first perceive something. Next we think and believe something about our perceptions. By checking our thinking we can change our irrational thoughts and thereby change our feelings and subsequently our actions.

Teaching students self-management means guiding them to set their own standards of behavior and empowering them to take control of their lives. Self-management skills empower students to set goals for themselves, and to self-record, self-evaluate, and self-reinforce. Teachers are then able to lessen their control and expand the boundaries. The climate in which the behavior is occurring impacts greatly on the response of the students. Adults interacting with the students must be aware of how they are perceived and whether their behaviors and attitudes are drawing positive or negative responses. Teachers are encouraged to be sensitive to the ecology of the classroom and to arrange the physical and emotional climate to provide children with successful experiences.

Democratic Discipline

Changes in society resulting from court actions and federal legislation have extended many democratic rights to students and their parents. Parents are no longer bystanders and are encouraged to participate in their children's education. Numerous schools across the nation are including parents as decision makers in many issues concerning instructional as well as noninstructional school activities. Only recently have we placed such emphasis on children's rights. The past 30 years have witnessed a gradual change from a coercive type of discipline to a more democratic one. Prior to these changes, school principals and teachers held unquestionable authority in their schools. Parents rarely challenged this authority and in most cases supported whatever punishment their children received. Expelled students had no legal resources and, unlike adults, had no Constitutional rights or input in their education. The doctrine of *in loco parentis* ("in place of parents") gave educators the right to treat children as their parents would treat them. Teachers did not have to justify actions taken against youngsters who had violated school rules. Now, as a result of numerous litigation and legislation, students' and their parents are entitled to certain rights and privileges such as due process and access to personal records.

Reality Therapy

Does this mean that students are not accountable to authority and control? Not quite, says William Glasser (1990). This psychiatrist and educator believes that a social community, such as a school community, cannot exist without rules; however, these rules should be reasonable. They should be flexible and change when conditions change; whenever possible they should be decided upon jointly by faculty and students; and they should be enforced. Glasser also believes that when students are involved in their behavior management program, they are more likely to accept the consequences of their actions. His numerous books have influenced the discipline methods employed in many public and private schools.

William Glasser encourages teachers to become personally involved with their students by considering their individual needs. Students need to feel empowered and in control of their lives; however, when power is given without responsibility, students cannot develop self-imposed boundaries and respect for the needs of other people. On the other hand, if we want students to become disciplined and learn the value of obeying reasonable rules and regulations, then students must believe that they are a valuable and integral part of the group. Responsibility can be taught to enable students to fulfill their needs in a way that does not deprive others of fulfilling their needs. In his book *Reality Therapy*, Glasser (1965) explains that past experiences of individuals influence but do not necessarily determine their present functioning. In his latest book, *Choice Theory* (1998), Glasser explains that children choose to behave in a way that gives them control over their lives. A coercive and authoritarian type of discipline is threatening and often results in hostility or avoidance behaviors. For progress in human relationships, Glasser believes that teachers must eventually give up punishing and exerting external control over their students.

However, students must be held accountable to logical consequences whenever they violate established rules. Glasser does not condone using reinforcers with students. He uses the term *encouragement* to promote self-reinforcement and a desire to do well. For example, instead of saying, "I like the way you are cooperating," the teacher might say, "How does it feel to get along so well? It's great that you are able to do it." He cautions teachers to be caring and sensitive to their students and to encourage a warm and inviting classroom climate where students feel wanted. Glasser maintains that for a school to be effective, it must be a good place where students want to be. He believes that a good school allows students' input in developing rules. However, rules must be consistently enforced but flexible enough to be changed when needed. Glasser suggests the following 10 steps as guidelines for managing students' behaviors:

1. *Care.* Make friends and be personally involved with your students. Create an atmosphere of sociability and convey to your students that you are concerned about their misbehavior because you care. Example: "Tina, I really care about you, and that is why I am concerned about your fights." Not "Tina, you are such a trouble maker."

2. *Awareness.* Make the student aware of his or her behavior. Ask "What are you doing?" Use "what," "how," and "who" questions. Limit the "why" questions. Example: "What you are doing?" Not "Why are you doing this?"

3. *Value Judgment.* Lead the student in evaluating the behavior and in making a value judgment. Ask "Is what you're doing against the rules?" If the student refuses to answer your questions, then describe exactly what the student was doing. "I saw you stick the gum on Tracy's hair, and that is against the rules, because your behavior shows that you are not respecting Tracy."

4. *Plan.* Together with the student, make a plan to change the behavior. Start with a minimal plan at first, which will eventually lead to a larger plan. The student must have input into the plan.

5. *Commitment.* Get a commitment to the plan. Shake on it or, better still, develop a written contract when possible. The contract should specify the behavior and the consequence.

6. *Excuses.* Do not accept excuses. The student must accept responsibility for the behavior. Do not assume the student's responsibilities. Do not argue or preach, or the student will tune you out.

7. *No Punishment.* Glasser does not believe in punishment, but he believes in enforcing logical or natural consequences. Punishment is inflicted to decrease a behavior. Although punishment is effective in terminating or weakening a behavior, it can also lead to aggression and hostility. A natural consequence is the result of a good or a bad choice. If I choose to touch a hot stovetop, I will get burned. When natural consequences are not available, logical consequences are then imposed.

8. *Thinking Time.* If the student is extremely agitated and is not

listening to you, steps 2 through 7 will be ineffective. The next step is to provide a "cooling off" spot in the classroom or school where the student can gain composure and think. Unlike the time-out procedure, it is not regarded as a punishment. The teacher informs the student to cool off and think of a plan to resolve the conflict.

9. *Home-Based Exclusion.* If the student becomes a danger to self or to others, call the parents and send the student home until the student calms down and the problem can be resolved.

10. *Professional Help.* Some students have deep-seated problems and may need medical or psychological help. If the behavior is extreme, persistent, and lasts over an extended period of time, teachers should seek support and collaborate with other professionals such as the school counselors, school psychologists, and social workers. The family must also be involved to cope with the situation.

Glasser recommends that teachers constantly evaluate their own behavior in relation to the student's behavior. He advocates making a list of currently used interventions and being honest in listing the behaviors even if they include yelling, scolding, threatening, ignoring, sarcasm, and spanking. He advises teachers to keep the following in mind:

1. Reflect on your past behavior with the student.
2. Start with a fresh new approach. If your past actions were not successful, why do you think they will work in the future?
3. Expect a better tomorrow. Your optimism may be "contagious" and rub off on your students.

Glasser proposes class meetings to teach decision making, social responsibility, and cooperation. He feels that such meetings can keep a class together because the more and the less capable students are on equal standing in contributing suggestions; in such a meeting, no one fails. One person's opinion is just as good as another's; there is no right or wrong answer. By treating the class as a unit, a spirit of cooperation can be developed. These meetings can assist in eliminating failure, accepting each student's input, and allowing students to think for themselves. The first type of meeting is a problem-solving meeting; this should define and solve problems and provide fair and impartial mediation. The second type of meeting is an open-ended forum, which allows teachers and students to present problems they wish to discuss with the group. These meetings are conducted in a democratic climate to discuss and develop classroom rules. When students feel part of the school community, they are more likely to experience success and feel less like failures.

Control Theory

On the cover of his book *Control Theory in the Classroom,* Glasser (1986) states,

> We are mistaken if we believe that discipline, dropouts and drugs are
> what is wrong with today's schools. Serious as these are, they are
> symptoms of a much larger underlying problem, which is that far too
> many capable students make little or no effort to learn.

He describes his control theory as "payoff—what we need as human beings to be satisfied." Glasser bases his concepts of control on the premise that basic internal needs drive us to behave the way we do. Everything we do, think, and feel is generated by what happens inside us. We have a vast album of pictures in our minds of the way we see things and the way things "should" be. We are a control system, and it is painful to lose control when things happen that contradict our expectations. We cannot hold on to the "pictures" in our "albums." For example, let us examine Calvin's situation.

Calvin uses illegal drugs and is noncompliant with the teacher's instructions. He comes to class but sleeps on his desk during most of the class period. The teacher's "picture" of Calvin is to get him to comply, do his work, and to stop him from taking illegal drugs. Calvin has a different picture for himself. He wants to be a musician. He has intellectual potential but finds school boring and irrelevant. He is not in control of his needs, so he takes illegal drugs to help him tolerate school. To help Calvin regain control, the teacher needs to find a way to empower Calvin. Maybe the teacher can use his love of music as a starting point. Together, his teacher, the music teacher, and Calvin might develop activities that can motivate him and teach him responsibility. Punishing Calvin will not make him change his behavior but will only further his alienation.

Glasser believes that schools use criticism much too freely and manipulate students with grades to control them. Instead, the students must perceive teachers as need-fulfilling persons. Students will learn and behave appropriately when they feel motivated and include learning in their "picture album." Glasser proposes that successful schools teach information that is relevant to students' interests and experiences. Control theory can help students to take and keep charge of their lives, and to make more effective choices.

Quality Schools

In his book *The Quality School: Managing Students Without Coercion,* Glasser (1990) applies his theories of reality therapy and control theory to a quality system. The three cornerstones of quality schools are: (a) focusing on and promoting quality education, (b) eliminating coercion, and (c) changing from total teacher evaluation to student self-evaluation. Glasser believes that "education is the process through which we discover that learning adds *quality* to our lives" (p.174). When we are motivated to learn, we raise our proficiency to fulfill one or more of our basic needs. In addition to the basic needs of survival and sexuality, we also have needs to belong and love, to gain power, to be free, and to have fun. We all aspire to give and to experience love, and many students come to school needing affection and caring. The home should be the primary place where children can fulfill their need for belonging and love; however, this is not always the case. A quality school is a caring school where youngsters feel they are accepted and can develop self-confidence to succeed in the world. In addition to love and belonging, students need to be empowered. A feeling of powerlessness leads to apathy, hostility, or rebellion. Students cannot satisfy their need for power when they constantly receive low grades or are constantly punished for misbehaving. They will eventually feel helpless and overpowered in what they perceive as a coercive classroom atmosphere. A caring classroom allows students to be free to make choices, to enjoy learning, and to belong to their school community. Students are responsible for their behaviors and for satisfying their own needs. Teachers can facilitate this process by being caring and involved.

Glasser believes that educators use far too many coercive measures to elicit compliance from students. He compares the coercive management of schools to the coercive management of the business industry and refers to the role of W. Edwards Deming, the industrial managerial theorist, in Japan's democratization of its industry. Deming presented his democratic principles through a lead-management approach rather than a boss-management approach. Glasser suggests that schools should adopt a nonpunitive lead-management approach, starting at the state superintendent level and ending with the classroom teacher. Lead-managers involve the workers and consider their input. They guide workers in examining their product with an understanding of how to produce high-quality work. Lead-managers show and model what needs to be done. They are facilitators and not dictators, and they run the system in such a way that workers realize that it is to their benefit to do quality work. Lead-management teachers encourage their students to be creative in solving problems and promote collaboration within cooperative group arrangements. Lead-management teachers foster need-satisfaction and help students to achieve their need for love and belonging, for power, and for freedom and fun.

In contrast, boss-managers are autocratic and more concerned with the needs of the boss than the needs of the workers. They tell the workers what to do, and they punish them if the work is not done. They basically do not trust their workers, and they believe in "running a tight ship" with the manager at the helm. They do not include the workers in evaluating the work, and they use a strict uniform criterion in the evaluation process. Glasser admits that many boss-managers do not operate in a totally coercive manner, and that lead-managers sometimes use persuasion to obtain compliance. He adds that the "essence" of good managing is caring and hard work. He urges teachers to develop their own lead-management style and to refrain from using coercive tactics to obtain compliance.

The third cornerstone of a quality school is a change from total teacher evaluation to student self-evaluation. Glasser regards the grading system as damaging to students' motivation, self-concept, and cooperative spirit. In many schools, students who make Cs and Ds are considered inferior to the ones who make As and Bs. In other schools, where their peers do not value high grades, students who make As and Bs are referred to as "dorks," "teacher's pets," and are often intimidated. Glasser maintains that in quality schools there are no bad grades and that the coercive Cs, Ds, and Fs should be completely eliminated. He maintains that the evaluation process should be changed and that students can be taught to self-evaluate their work. When Glasser first suggested alternative evaluations, educators' reactions were skeptical if not negative; however, performance-based and alternative assessments are steadily gaining interest and acceptance. Regardless of this interest, the emphasis on standards and norm-referenced testing remains, and principals communicate their anxiety to teachers, who in turn communicate their anxiety to students. What can teachers do that is practical but still meets the students' needs? In addition to the traditional grading methods, teachers may consider alternative performance-based strategies to determine mastery, such as asking the student to write a poem or perform in a play.

Social Models

Adlerian Theory

Alfred Adler (1948) was a Viennese psychiatrist who disagreed with his colleague, Sigmund Freud, about what drives human beings. In Adler's view, we are driven by a need for security, escape from inferiority, and personal and social competence. Adler believed that humans are social beings who yearn to belong and be accepted in society. We belong to a species that needs close contact with others of its kind. He admitted that our environment is a forceful influence on our attitudes and behaviors; however, it's our attitude to the environment that shapes our character. Adler believed that most problems stem from the discrepancies we observe between our goals in life and our feelings of inferiority. Adlerian theory emphasizes that all behavior occurs in social situations, and when individuals feel powerless in those situations, they become instinctively aggressive, striving for psychological stability and balance. On the other hand, individuals who give up trying to reach their goals eventually feel inadequate, defeated, and helpless. Adler believed in the social equality of all human beings and in the development of a social conscience. He practiced what he preached, and his interest in human relationships and interactions characterizes both his theories and his practice. As a teacher, Adler was available and helpful to all his students and accepted poor people among his clients, which reflected his humanitarian views. Adler believed that teachers must invest in relationships that will result in success for all students (Dreikurs, 1953). An understanding of social theory can help teachers to grow in their relationships with students.

Goals of Misbehavior

Rudolph Dreikurs (1964), a prominent psychiatrist, adopted several Adlerian concepts in his discipline philosophy. He maintained that all behavior is purposeful or goal-directed, and that when individuals behave antisocially, they do so to achieve one of four goals: (a) to seek attention, (b) to seek power, (c) to seek revenge, or (d) to display inadequacy.

Attention Seeking

Attention seeking is the most common goal for most young children. They want to be the center of attention at all times, and when they are ignored they misbehave because being ignored is worse than punishment. Attention seeking can also be observed in the behavior of older children and in many adults. Dreikurs (1982) proposed that teachers pay attention to students' appropriate behaviors and ignore the misbehavior. Active attention seekers can be a major show-off nuisance in any classroom. The behavior can be distracting and annoying; students may interrupt, contradict, whine, or make strange noises. They may wear outrageous clothes or use vulgar language to get attention. Passive attention seekers operate on slow speeds. They are the last to get their book out of their desk or begin their work. Their pace eventually drives the teacher "insane." In confronting an attention seeker, the teacher may feel annoyed and think, "I wish Kathy would not bother me, she gets on my nerves. I'm at my wit's end." Students exhibiting attention-seeking behavior may have been showered with too much attention or given too little attention. In some instances parents and teachers may have paid more attention to the misbehavior, or children were not taught how to ask for appropriate attention (Dreikurs & Cassell, 1971). The following example illustrates an attention-seeking behavior.

Anthony was the only child of parents who had previously given up having children. He was a "miracle" baby and his parents showered him with attention. When he started school, he expected the same kind of attention. Anthony's mother was a school volunteer when he was in kindergarten and first grade, so he continued to receive a great deal of attention. However, when he entered second grade, his mother became pregnant and had to stop her volunteer work. Suddenly Anthony was not the center of attention anymore, and his cute childish ways were not so cute after all. Ms. Strictson, his teacher, felt annoyed at his immature behavior, and his constant questioning and interrupting drove his peers crazy. Ms. Strictson tried to ignore him at first, but Anthony accelerated his annoying behavior. She then punished him by sending him to the time-out chair behind a partition, but he became louder and argumentative, which made it difficult for the teacher to teach and the students to learn. We recommend the following interventions (Albert, 1989; Dreikurs, 1982):

- *Discuss the goal.* Discuss the attention-seeking behavior and make Anthony aware of how his behavior is perceived by others. Discuss the impact of the behavior on the teaching and learning situation.

- *Decrease the attention.* Ignore Anthony's interruptions or give him a secret signal (a signal decided in private) when he begins to interrupt. Walk away from Anthony and do not look in his direction.

- *Give I-messages.* Discuss privately with Anthony how you feel: "Anthony, whenever you interrupt, I cannot teach, and that makes me feel very upset." Show Anthony that you care about his feelings. In private say, "Anthony, I understand that you need attention, but we also need to continue the lesson."

- *Make a plan.* Tell him "Anthony, how can we work out a plan that would be satisfactory to you, to me, and to your classmates? How many times do you wish to be noticed during this period?" Agree on the number of "attention getters" and follow through.

- *Stop and relax.* When Anthony interrupts, stop; remain calm and relaxed. Do not look at him. When he stops interrupting, nod and thank him and continue the lesson.

- *Focus on the behavior.* Make a lesson out of behavior. Find stories in children's literature that portray behaviors similar to Anthony's. Use a bibliotherapy technique (see chapter 5) to discuss the story without embarrassing him.

- *Distract the student.* Ask a direct question: "Anthony, what do you think will happen if you keep interrupting?" Ask a favor: "Anthony, do me a favor. I don't want to lecture too long. Let me know when 15 minutes are up." Change the activity.

- *Accentuate the positive.* Watch for opportunities for giving attention to positive behavior. Walk over to Anthony and casually thank him for not disturbing.

- *Use logical consequences.* Tell Anthony beforehand that if his behavior is disruptive to the class, he will be removed. Send Anthony to in-class or out-of-class time-out to think about his behavior.

Power and Control

The second goal of, or reason for, misbehavior is power and control. Dreikurs explains that students often engage in "power struggles" to control situations and people. We all want to feel empowered; however, power-seeking individuals use their power to dominate others. Teachers who believe in autocratic methods (boss-managers) have difficulty refraining from engaging in power struggles with students. They quickly punish students to prevent them from realizing their power goal. In such situations there is no winner; the teacher ultimately loses because the development of a positive relationship with the student is frequently destroyed. In dealing with a power seeker, a teacher may say, " Who is running this show? I *am* the teacher, after all; I'll show him who is the boss." Dreikurs reminds teachers that it takes at least two people to engage in a power struggle; therefore, teachers can choose to sidestep the struggle and diffuse the situation. By using power to counteract power, teachers are modeling the value of force and may drive students to seek revenge. Behaviors of active power seekers include temper tantrums, lying, rebellion, and aggressive acts. They are disruptive, confrontational, and openly verbalize their defiance. Power seekers may also behave passively. Passive power seekers avoid confrontations and challenge authority in underhanded activities. They are often stubborn, lazy, and noncompliant and appear pleasant on the surface but will resist submitting to authority. The following example illustrates a power and control behavior.

Zeena was a born leader. She emanated power and a zeal for domination. Unfortunately, she used her power to control a group of four followers in her gang. The gang targeted and harassed certain students who received superior grades. They would rip their jackets, steal their belongings, and write crude remarks on the bathroom walls. Of course, nobody could prove that they were guilty, and nobody was inclined to do so. Zeena decided to take on the new teacher, Ms. Timidson, to prove her power. One day Ms. Timidson assigned a class project that involved working in cooperative groups of five students. She assigned students to five groups and separated Zeena and her followers. Zeena was furious. She told Ms. Timidson that her friends were always part of her group, they refused to be separated, and they would not cooperate with members of their assigned group. Ms. Timidson knew that Zeena and her followers would sabotage the work of each group and felt beaten and intimidated. What should she do?

- *Discuss the goal.* Discuss the power-seeking behavior and make Zeena aware of how her behavior is perceived by others. Discuss the impact of the behavior on the teaching and learning situation.
- *Avoid a power struggle.* Acknowledge Zeena's power. Remove the audience, take Zeena aside to talk. Table the matter and postpone the cooperative group assignment. Discuss the problem at a prearranged conference. Agree with Zeena and assign the five students to one group.
- *Separate the Powers.* Send Zeena to an out-of-class assignment (e.g., to help the librarian stack books) and assign the followers to separate groups.
- *Accent the positive.* Assign successful experiences, encourage and show Zeena how she can use her leadership abilities constructively.
- *Use time-out.* Send Zeena to a thinking time-out period out of the classroom.
- *Use logical consequences.* Set consequences beforehand for disruptive behaviors. Send Zeena to in-class or out-of-class time-out to

think about her behavior. Implement loss or delay of activity and the loss of favorite equipment (e.g., use of computer). Deny interactions with other students, and require interactions with school personnel, such as the counselor or school psychologist. Require a conference with parents to discuss the problem. If Zena becomes violent, require police intervention. If Zeena destroys materials, require restitution: repair of objects, replacement of objects.

Revenge

Dreikur's third goal explains the behavior of students who are motivated by revenge. These students have given up every hope of being accepted and view the world as cold and uncaring. They have decided that attention getting and power struggles will not bring them notice or empowerment. They experience pain and so seek revenge by hurting others. Teachers have difficulty with a revengeful student, and their first inclination is to retaliate and punish. They may say, "How mean can Herbie be? How can I give him a taste of his own medicine?" Dreikurs proposed that teachers need to build a caring relationship with these students and teach constructive avenues for the expression of hurt and hostility. Behaviors of active revenge seekers include physical and psychological attacks. They can be argumentative, stubborn, vindictive, noncompliant, and contrary. They are hurtful to teachers and peers. Students who lose the "revenge war" keep their anger within them and eventually displace it or may give up, withdraw, and project self-defeating and helpless behaviors. The following illustrates a revengeful behavior.

Ravi was absolutely furious. He was expelled from school because he started a fire in his classroom's trash can, but instead of spending the time at home, he was to attend an alternative school for the rest of the school year. His parents enforced the school's decision, so there was nothing he could do: It was either the alternative school or a boarding school in another state. He would go, but he was angry and resentful. His teacher, social worker, and school psychologist at the new school all represented the school system, and he was angry at all of them. Stupid people, he thought. He didn't intend to burn the school down. What's a little trash can fire? It was put out with one little glass of water! Those people had no sense of humor or excitement. He'd show them, he'd show all of them!

Of course, Ravi conveniently did not recall that this was his third fire. He was especially resentful of the school psychologist, Dr. Freudson, who reminded Ravi of the school principal in his original school. He was such a busybody, asking personal questions. At the end of one school day, as Dr. Freudson was approaching his car, he noticed that his two front tires had been slashed. He also noticed a red bandana behind one of the tires, which he immediately recognized as Ravi's. Ravi always tied this red bandana to his belt and used it to wipe the sweat off his face. Dr. Freudson felt hurt and disappointed. He thought he had been making headway with Ravi.

Which of the following interventions would you advise Dr. Freudson to use?

- *Understanding and caring.* Dreikurs advises not to retaliate. Seek to understand and care for the revenge seeker. The teacher can assist Ravi in realizing that people are not out to get him, that it is his behavior and not him as a person that people resent.

- *I am my brother's keeper.* Build a caring relationship with Ravi. Help him to express hurt and hostility in a nonviolent way. Invite Ravi to talk when he is upset.

- *Setting consequences*: Establish consequences for destructive behaviors. Present and follow through with the consequences. Implement a restitution plan (e.g., Ravi will have to pay for two new tires or mow Dr. Freudson's yard until he makes up the value of the tires).

- *Involvement of significant others.* Involve parents and other school personnel. In the case of uninvolved parents, ask Ravi who on the faculty could act as an unofficial surrogate parent. Allow Ravi to spend some quality time with this individual.

Display of Inadequacy or Learned Helplessness

Dreikurs warns that when students feel defeated, they give up hope of ever succeeding. They acquire what is known as *learned helplessness* and accept their condition with abandoned resignation. They feel unworthy and undeserving of love and caring. They want to be left alone and want nothing expected of them. By avoiding participation and by keeping a low profile, they assume that they can avoid humiliating and embarrassing situations. Teachers may initially attempt to reason with these students. However, when the students withdraw even more, teachers often feel overwhelmed and give up trying. These students may appear to be pseudo-stupid, indolent, lethargic, inept, and antisocial. When interacting with such students, teachers feel helpless, defeated, and "at the end of their rope." They may think, " I don't know what to do with Sara, I can't do anything with her." Dreikurs suggests that teachers refrain from criticism and highlight the students' strengths and accomplishments. They can teach students to think positively and to help them build confidence by engaging them in experiences that highlight their strengths. The following illustrates a helpless behavior.

Everybody said that Helen was "born shy." She never volunteered for anything in school, and at home she allowed her sister Jena to take the lead. Her mother emphasized perfectionism and verbally expressed her pride in Jena and her disappointment in Helen. Jena was in the gifted program; Helen was classified as having a learning disability and received instruction in a special education resource room. At first Helen tried to get her mother's attention by fighting with Jena, but she soon gave up that behavior after

Jena beat her up a couple of times. She tried pleasing her mother by setting the table but clumsily dropped her mother's precious china and was punished. At school she tried to make friends, but she stopped when a classmate called her a "dyslexic retard." She hated going to the resource room and found the instruction boring. Eventually she gave up, withdrew, and spent a lot of time by herself. During cooperative group activities, Helen refused to participate; she sat with the group but did nothing. One day, her teacher tried to involve her by assigning her the role of the heroine in the holiday pageant. She helped Helen with her lines, but Helen developed laryngitis the day before opening night. Her mother was very upset with her because she had told all her friends that Helen was the star attraction.

Which of the following interventions would you advise the teacher to use?

- *Don't criticize, please modify.* Modify Helen's assignment to allow successful experiences. Use age-appropriate material geared to Helen's readability level. Teach to Helen's learning style and allow her to take the lead in a planned activity.

- *Provide tutoring.* Give Helen extra help. Adult volunteer tutoring and peer tutoring can help to relieve the teacher from time to time. Use computer-assisted instruction, cooperative learning, and integrated thematic learning

- *Teach positive self-talk.* Teach Helen to talk to herself in a whisper and eventually covertly. Post positive classroom signs. Require two "put-ups" for every put-down. Encourage Helen to use positive self-talk before beginning tasks.

- *It's OK to make mistakes.* Tell Helen that mistakes are great teachers and that we can learn from mistakes. Making a mistake is OK and indicates that we at least made an effort. Minimize the effects of making mistakes, and ask Helen, "What have you learned?"

- *Build an "I can" attitude.* Focus on Helen's improvement and notice contributions. Build on Helen's strengths and convey an attitude of faith and trust. Acknowledge the difficulty of a task, but tell Helen that many famous people, like the singer Cher, were diagnosed with dyslexia. Provide Helen with books on celebrities who overcame their difficulties.

- *Focus on past successes.* Assist Helen in keeping a portfolio and show her how to analyze her progress. Analyze past successes and repeat them.

- *Make learning tangible.* Show Helen how to keep a checklist of skills and a flowchart of concepts. Assist her in keeping a self-regulation sheet and graph how many times a day she took the initiative to interact with a peer or how many times a day she volunteered a response in class.

- *Recognize achievement.* Recognize Helen's achievement with a "student of the week" award. Display a poster with Helen's picture and her achievements. Since Helen enjoys being alone, give her positive time-out when she does interact with others. Helen's introverted personality type may need some quiet time by herself.

A problem with Dreikurs' system is determining which goal is causing the misbehavior. The fourth goal, inadequacy, is easily identifiable; however, a teacher may have difficulty distinguishing the other three goals. Dreikurs proposed that teachers ask themselves the following questions and honestly examine their feelings to determine the precise goal.

Does the student want to be noticed? Do I feel annoyed? Then the goal is attention getting.

Is the student a bully and domineering? Do I feel beaten and intimidated? Then the goal is power.

Is the student aggressive and vindictive? Do I feel defensive and hurt? Then the goal is revenge.

Is the student withdrawn? Do I feel unable to reach him or her? Then the goal is helplessness.

Consequences Versus Punishment, Encouragement Versus Reinforcement

Both William Glasser and Rudolph Dreikurs propose that adults use natural or logical consequences instead of punishment to enforce the social order. Let's consider the following example of a natural consequence.

Mrs. Helm, the second-grade teacher, reminded her class to follow the class rule, which was to walk (not run) down the hall. She told her class that this rule was especially important today because the janitor just cleaned up mud tracks, and the hall was still damp. Nevil was in a hurry to get to the cafeteria and started to run down the hall. He slipped and fell, bruising both his knees and his elbows. On the way to the nurse's office, Mrs. Helm reminded him of the rule and its consequence. Punishing him for running would have added insult to injury.

When natural consequences are not the direct outcome of behavior, then the teacher can develop logical consequences. The teacher must establish a relationship between the consequence and the behaviors. Consequences must be discussed with the students and understood and accepted by them. Once this has occurred, the teacher must enforce the consequence. Consider the following example of Mr. Cortez, Elizabeth, and Margarita.

Mr. Cortez and his seventh-grade student body agreed on a class rule that required students to respect each other's property. They also agreed on a consequence if that rule was violated. Elizabeth was not a chronic discipline problem but was very envious of Margarita, who always wore the latest fashion in jeans and sweaters and was very popular with the boys. One day after a physical education class, as Margarita pulled her sweater out of her locker, she discovered, to her horror, that it was torn to shreds. A sixth-grade student who was in the dressing room before the class identified Elizabeth as the culprit. Elizabeth admitted tearing the sweater and was truly contrite. However, contrition was not enough; she had to pay the consequences of her behavior. The teacher and the girls agreed to a specific consequence; Elizabeth had to replace the sweater and, in addition, perform a positive service to Margarita. The two students and the teacher also decided on the nature of the service; Elizabeth would pay for Margarita's lunch the next day, join her at lunch, and discuss how they could improve their relationship.

A problem with externally reinforcing students for appropriate behavior is that it builds a dependency on reinforcers. Students expect something in return for their behavior, and they do not learn "to do good because good is good to do." In addition, some students become desensitized to praise and satiated with certain reinforcers. Teachers often find it difficult to find the appropriate reinforcers for certain students. However, encouragement conveys respect, trust, and a belief in students' abilities. Encouragement builds on students' strength and promotes self-esteem and self-management skills. The following illustrates how Mrs. Deveraux encouraged Pierre to be less overbearing and domineering.

Pierre was bossy and dominated the cooperative group project. The members of the group were fed up with him, and the situation always disintegrated into name-calling and off-task behaviors. Mrs. Deveraux had a private talk with Pierre and told him that she admired his leadership qualities but that an effective leader was democratic and allowed input from every member of the group. She gave Pierre a book to read on lead-management and told him that she would be observing him. The next day, she told the group that she was assigning Pierre as leader of the project because she believed that he could be democratic and welcome participation from the group. The members sighed and reluctantly accepted the teacher's decision. The teacher privately told Pierre, "I know you can do it, go ahead and show them." To everyone's surprise, Pierre did not interrupt and he invited every member's input. Later, the teacher told Pierre, "How does it feel to be a democratic leader, Pierre? Your group got a lot accomplished today." Pierre grinned and said, "This democratic stuff really is cool."

Rational Emotive Therapy

Although Dreikurs is adamant about following through with consequences, he is also concerned with the feelings of students. Albert Ellis (1969) takes this one step further and explains that our behavior is the result of how we interpret our feelings.

Most inappropriate behaviors are the results of how we feel. Feelings are hard to control; they seem to come from nowhere, and they are hard to change when they are full-blown. Feelings appear to be causative when it comes to behavior; we feel a certain way and we act upon the feeling, but feelings do not have a life of their own. Feelings result from the way we think about or interpret a particular situation or event. If you want to change your behavioral reaction to something that has happened, then you must change the way you feel about it, and you can only change the way you feel about it by changing the way you think about it. You must change the negative thought to a more rational, positive, or neutral thought rather than interpreting what you have experienced in a negative way. Negative feelings are often the result of irrational interpretations of events and things.

In presenting this theory, known as rational emotive therapy (RET), Ellis (1969) teaches that people are distressed not just by events in their lives but by their beliefs about those events. It is not just what happens to people that may be upsetting, but rather what they think it means. Ellis uses the letters A, B, and C to show how his theory works. A is the antecedent event—meaning whatever has happened that a person may feel upset about. B is the person's interpretation of that event, and C is the consequence or reaction.

He explains that most people believe that A causes C: that the event itself creates the bad feeling or distress that the person feels. However, that is not true in Ellis's view. Rather it is B, the person's self-talk or interpretation about what has occurred, and not the situation itself, that causes the distress. In between the event and the consequent reaction or emotion is either rational or irrational self-talk. The self-talk about the event gives shape and form to the emotions. If the self-talk or interpretation is positive, the emotion may be joy, peace, calm, or other good feelings of well-being. If the self-talk is negative, it may result in anxiety, anger, or depression. Each person has control of his or her own self-talk and interpretation of events. People in general have many irrational beliefs about their world. To change their emotional response, they have to change their beliefs through positive self-talk.

A	B	C
Event	**Interpretation**	**Reaction or Emotion**

RET emphasizes the importance of reviewing beliefs about a situation before becoming upset. For example, when a friend fails to telephone as promised, a person may feel distress, thinking the friend does not care, or he or she may think that the friend is angry or bored with the friendship and does not want to continue the relationship any longer. Despite the fact that there may be circumstances that could prevent the friend from calling, the person may choose to interpret the situation in a negative way before the facts are in. Because of that mistaken belief, much pain may be caused by an idea that has no reality to it. The resulting feelings, such as disappointment, rejection, fear, anxiety, anger, or shame, are not the result of the antecedent. Rather, they are the result of the person's *interpretation* of A, the antecedent event. Therefore, to change the feelings (which may cause a person to react inappropriately), it is necessary to change the interpretation. Students are encouraged to review their individual belief systems with the expectation that many painful situations may be caused by beliefs not rooted in reality.

There are times when our beliefs, even though negative, may be correct, and the pain caused by both the events and our beliefs about them are unavoidable. However, even then rational self-talk can reduce the elements of pain. Often students may experience unnecessary pain when they interpret the happenings in their lives negatively. Some RET proponents add a D component to Ellis's ABCs. D is the new response to B after the person, through self-talk, has reinterpreted the A rationally and positively. Consider the following example.

Billy, a middle school student, stares at Steve, a classmate. Steve gets angry but pauses to think about what he is feeling. Steve realizes he is angry and asks himself, "When did I get angry?" The answer is "When Billy looked at me." Next he asks himself, "Why did I get angry?" The answer is "Because he "dissed " me." Steve got angry because he interpreted Billy's stare negatively. That is, he interpreted it through negative self-talk, thinking that "Billy 'dissed' me."

After RET training Steve uses self-talk to ask himself, "Is the fact that Billy is looking at me causing my anger?" The answer is "No! It is my interpretation of Billy's action. I may be wrong in my interpretation that Billy 'dissed' me. Perhaps Billy is looking at me because he likes my clothes, because he has nothing better to do, or because he thinks I am about to say something. He may be daydreaming and not really paying attention to what he is focusing on visually, and I happen to be the thing that caught his attention." Steve is now choosing to interpret Billy's action positively or neutrally. As a result, Steve pays no further attention to the fact that Billy sometimes stares at him. He develops a new response to Billy's habit of staring. He ignores it and goes about his work. As a result, Steve's anger dissipates and a new feeling takes its place. The new response, D, is a result of the reinterpretation of the antecedent behavior, A.

Cognitive Behavior Modification and Self-Management

Cognitive behavior modification is a system that teaches individuals to manage their own behavior. It is based on internal control instead of external control. The best person to manage your behavior is yourself. Students who practice self-control learn to be self-reliant and to behave appropriately without outside supervision. They are also able to generalize their appropriate behaviors to various settings and situations. The goal of any behavior management program is to teach students to regulate their own behavior and develop self-discipline. We decided to include the concepts of cognitive behavior modification within the domain of discipline with flexible boundaries because we believe that behavior change can occur when teachers are willing to be flexible and allow students to assume an active role in changing their behavior. In most schools, students have few choices; school district personnel set the curriculum, teachers select the instructional materials and activities, and administrators pick the discipline rules.

As students grow older, it is important that they master self-management for internalizing social behaviors, generalizing skills, assuming responsibility, and achieving independence. Students who need constant external control cannot set and achieve goals for themselves, and they usually blame others or the environment for their failings. They are weak in emotional intelligence, have difficulty setting goals, and frequently lack persistence and motivation to pursue scholastic accomplishments. Eventually, these students assume a negative self-concept and display various antisocial behaviors.

To teach self-management, teachers must at first establish firm boundaries and be prepared to adjust the limits as students demonstrate steps toward the change process. Students must be taught how to monitor their own behavior, be allowed to participate in the educational goals, and be shown how to select interventions that will correct and reinforce the new behavior. In this section, the self-management strategies we describe include self–goal setting, self-instruction, self-recording, self-evaluation, and self-reinforcement. To achieve these self-management goals, a person must first be intrinsically motivated and self-determined.

Self-Determination

Parents and teachers frequently blame students' uninterest in school and their disruptive behavior on lack of motivation. Attempts to directly motivate students through punishment or reward generally fail, because when students lose their fear of punishment or their desire for the reward, the motivation ceases. Self-determination is based on intrinsic motivation. We are usually intrinsically motivated for tasks that cause us to feel successful and reinforced. Self-determined people base their actions on their own decisions, abilities, and interests; they are autonomous. This does not imply that they are egotistical or arrogant. Self-determination also involves a realistic attitude and a self-awareness of personal strengths and weaknesses. Michael Wehmeyer (1996) describes people who are self-determined as self-regulated and realistic. Understanding their strengths and weakness, they "act as the primary causal agent in one's life free from undue external influence or interference" (p. 22). Our first reaction to such a description is that self-determination is not easy to achieve even for adults, and it is certainly an impossible dream for schoolchildren. Self-determination is indeed a mature, adult outcome; nevertheless, schools should promote this outcome by offering training and support in self-management skills early in a student's educational years.

Self–Goal-Setting

Teaching students to select and set goals are important steps toward self-management. An important point to bear in mind is that goal setting is not necessarily goal realization. However, when goals are not attained, students can be guided to analyze the entire goal-setting process and implement and develop another set of goals. Teachers can guide students in developing goals that are within the student's reach and potential. Students must show motivation and a willingness to attain the goal. Visible signs of attainment of the goal provide encouragement and determination. In addition, the goal must be specific and discrete. Too many goals may lead to discouragement and failure.

Chad, a ninth grader, had a problem with frequent cursing. He used inappropriate language with people and would blurt out curse words to express strong feelings. His teacher, Mrs. York, decided to deviate from the usual punishment (in-school suspension, which didn't work anyway) and involve him in setting goals to change the cursing behavior. Mrs. York and Chad had a long talk, and Chad indicated that he had wanted to stop cursing since he became attracted to Trudy, who didn't approve of it. He also indicated that he had difficulty doing so, because cursing had become such an ingrained habit that it became second nature to him. However, he agreed to try to reduce the number of curse words until he completely stopped using them. He would ask Trudy to go to the movies when he achieved 80% of his goal. With his teacher, Chad wrote his goal in specific and measurable terms: "I will reduce the number of curse words until I completely stop using them." Next, he specified the starting date and the completion date: "I will reduce my use of curse words as of today, March 9, and completely eliminate cursing by April 10." Mrs. York gave Chad a wrist counter and directed him to record every time he used a curse word. At the end of each day he would plot the number of curse words on a line graph. She taught him how to use the graphics section on the computer to chart his progress and provided support and encouragement. Chad's progress was slow at first, but he became more aware of his cursing behavior when he had to visually track his progress. He reached 80% 3 weeks later and was pleased at his success. He asked Trudy to go to the movies and felt like a winner.

Self-Instruction

Verbal mediation, or self-talk, is an important component of self-instruction. Self-talk is thinking aloud, and we engage in this practice daily, whether overtly or covertly. Teaching students to think aloud helps them to sort out and rationalize their thoughts and feelings. Self-instruction strategies are useful to guide students in analyzing and directing their own behavior. Donald Meichenbaum and James Goodman (1971) developed four sequential steps for teaching self-instruction:

1. *State the problem.* "Here comes Kate, the first lady of cheerleading. She always says something nasty about my weight, my clothes, and the way I look. I would like to rearrange her looks, but I know I'll get in trouble, and she would love that."
2. *State a possible solution to the problem.* "I'll say something nice about

last night's cheerleading performance before she has the chance to open her mouth. If she responds with a nasty comment, I'll ignore her and walk away."

3. *Evaluate the response.* "I caught her off guard, and it worked. She did not dare reply with a nasty comment in front of the other cheerleaders."

4. *Verbally self-reinforce.* "Keeping my cool worked. Great plan. I'm great."

Students can use self-instructional strategies independently; they do not need constant supervision or reinforcement when they eventually learn to use their verbal behavior to solve problems. They must be taught, however, to use overt language unobtrusively and eventually switch from talking aloud to talking silently (thinking). Self-instruction strategies can be used to guide students' academic and social performances. The following five steps provide systematic teaching for both academic and social behaviors (Meichenbaum, 1975):

1. The teacher performs the task (or models the behavior), self-instructing aloud, while the student observes. (I know the answer to the teacher's question, but if I blurt out again, I'll get into trouble, so I'll raise my hand this time.)

2. The student performs the task while the teacher instructs aloud. (Correct, raise your hand.)

3. The student performs the task while self-instructing aloud. (I'll raise my hand, I won't interrupt.)

4. The student performs the task while whispering.

5. The student performs the task while self-instructing silently.

Self-Recording

Teaching students self-recording increases awareness of certain behaviors and provides a rationale for needed change. By simply keeping self-records, students can eliminate, reduce, or increase certain behaviors. Self-recording requires students to identify the behavior, to self-observe, and to self-record the occurrences or time spent performing these behaviors. The second step is to provide a recording strategy for evaluating the results. In the preceding example of Chad, the student was taught to use a computer program to graph his cursing incidents. Chad had a visual representation of his behavior and was reinforced by the decrease in cursing. Teachers can teach simple graphing as a motivator as well as an aid for self-recording. Self-recording aids include wrist counters, grocery store counters, journaling, golf counters, or paper and pencil. The following scenario illustrates a second grader's self-recording plan.

Amy was diagnosed as having Attention Deficit Hyperactivity Disorder (ADHD). She had difficulty remaining on-task for even 3 minutes at a time.

She was constantly out of her seat and, in many instances, interfered with the other students' concentration. Her teacher, Mrs. Wisener, took Amy aside and showed her a 3-minute sand timer. She allowed Amy to play with the sand timer to become familiar with the way it worked. Mrs. Wisener then showed Amy a picture of a plain flower with eight petals and a center. The teacher explained why staying on-task was important and how the sand timer and the picture could help Amy finish her work. She told Amy that she could keep the sand timer on her desk, and for every 3 minutes she stayed on-task (as indicated by the sand timer), she would be allowed to color one of the flower's petals and eventually the flower's center. The flower picture served as a graph indicating 27 minutes of on-task behavior. Amy was pleased with herself for coloring the entire picture, and she increased her time on-task to 6 minutes before coloring a petal, then to 9, 12, and 15 minutes.

Self-Evaluation

Self-evaluation provides students with immediate feedback without adult supervision. When teachers cannot provide immediate feedback, inappropriate behavior is more likely to accelerate. Self-evaluation is especially useful with students who have had a history of academic or behavior problems. It can serve several purposes. When students learn to self-evaluate, they provide themselves with immediate feedback and an opportunity to self-correct without adult interference. They feel empowered because they are in control. Students are more prone to self-correct without "losing face" when they fail. The visual progress indicator, such as a graph, serves as a reinforcer and an incentive to continue to improve or to strive for improvement. We have adapted Cecil and Ann Mercer's (2001) suggestions for teaching self-evaluation:

1. The teacher provides the students with the rationale for self-evaluation. Discuss the importance of evaluating one's work. Stress the notion that self-evaluation enables one to determine if the performance is satisfactory. Teach students that performance must meet some criterion or standard. Discuss social as well as academic behavior standards.

2. The teacher demonstrates and models self-evaluation. In this step the teacher selects a self-evaluation form that requires students to mark a scale from 0 to 2. The 0 to 2 instrument corresponds to a grading scale of poor progress (0), some progress (1), and good progress (2). Teachers may also use a scale from 1 to 5, which allows more latitude and indicates smaller steps toward progress. A score of 1 indicates no progress (I must try again); 2, some progress (I am making a little headway); 3, a 50% improvement (I'm halfway there); 4, acceptable progress (I'm good); and 5, great progress (I'm great).

3. The students practice self-evaluation with feedback from the teacher until proficiency is achieved.

Self-Reinforcement

Most of us like to receive compliments for our performance, looks, or efforts, and that's OK. However, reliance on external reinforcement does not encourage autonomy or independence. Teachers have been taught to change behavior through systematic presentations of positive or negative reinforcement. Rewards can be costly, may not be reinforcing to some students, and when delivered at the wrong time may actually increase an inappropriate behavior. The impact of the positive reinforcer will depend on the degree to which the students have been deprived of the reinforcer, and many students have access to many material goods. Students may easily become satiated and unresponsive to praise and stickers and other tangible reinforcers. Even grades are not reinforcing to students who have developed an apathetic attitude and learned helplessness.

Self-reinforcement was advocated by Albert Bandura (1977), who proposed that behavior can be maintained without consistent reinforcement from others; students learn to develop internal reinforcement and rely less on external reinforcement.

Prior to implementing a self-reinforcement program, teachers must teach students to determine standards of performance for the earning of reinforcers. In the Chad scenario, he needed to reduce his cursing by at least 80% before he could ask Trudy to go to the movies. The next step is to select a reinforcer. Chad knew what he wanted—a date with Trudy. The last step is to examine the self-recording data and the self-evaluation analysis to determine whether to self-reinforce. Chad examined his graph, and when it indicated 80% success, he asked Trudy for a date. The teacher can continue to provide support and corrective feedback until students become competent in their self-management skills.

Self-recording, self-evaluation, and self-reinforcement should be used concurrently to produce the best results. By involving students in their own management, teachers decrease their role as controlling agents. Self-management strategies may take time to teach; however, when learned, they provide students with valuable skills that will help them to grow emotionally and discover their self-worth.

Judicious Discipline

Democratic and Constitutional Rights

The United States is democratic in its political structure but still very autocratic in its social structures, such as in the home and schools. Glasser, Dreikurs, and many other authorities propose democratic approaches in schools and families to prepare students for democratic living in an adult world. The Bill of Rights of the Constitution of the United States includes provisions for justice, equality, and freedom for all citizens. The First, Fourth, and Fourteenth Amendments include the rights to free speech, free assembly, protection against illegal searches and seizures, and the right to due process. Violation of these students' rights have been challenged in courts of law, and in many cases the courts have ruled in favor of the students.

Forrest Gathercoal (1991) has adapted Constitutional rights into a discipline model he termed *judicious discipline*. This model elaborates on democratic ideals and presents a discipline approach based on a set of principles recognizing human rights. The foundation of judicious discipline is to create a common language based on the principle of equal rights and responsibilities. Responsibility lies with teachers as well as with students, and teachers must model in word and deed democratic values in daily living. Teachers begin by presenting to their students the concepts of freedom, justice, and equality and the dangers of prejudice, intolerance, and inequality. Freedom, however, has limits and is not permissible at the expense of others. The good of all must be considered as well as the rights of the individual. Freedom of speech is a democratic right, but not when it can cause havoc and destruction. McEwan, Nimmo, and Gathercoal (1999) explain that no one has the freedom to yell "fire" in a crowded theater. Students learn to resolve conflict through negotiation and mediation instead of violent acts. Classroom rules are reasonable and reflect what would be considered reasonable in any other social setting. For example, many schools conduct the lunch period as a prisonlike atmosphere in which no talking is allowed. However, schools using judicious discipline would allow talking in soft tones so as to encourage friendships but do not permit loud talking because that would interfere with someone else's conversation.

Judicious discipline incorporates self-monitoring procedures to teach students to critically examine their behavior and consider its consequences. These procedures are similar to the cognitive behavior modification strategies of self-management. Judicious discipline cautions not to set consequences that would humiliate or hurt but that redirect and teach students social skills. Strategies include discrimination training to help students generalize behavior and to explore their manner of behavior in relation to time and place. It is OK to yell on the playground, but not in the classroom. Students learn to resolve conflicts through negotiation and mediation instead of through spite or violence. Group meetings, such as those proposed by Glasser and Dreikurs, may take place to elicit students' involvement in discussing problems or to reconsider rules and regulations.

Adapted Strategies

The judicious discipline model does not offer specific discipline strategies but relies on techniques borrowed from other models with a democratic orientation. It requires commitment from all teachers and administrators in a school for its success. Teachers who rely on rigid behaviorist practices must be willing to change their behavior and adopt a new style that allows students rights and responsibilities. Many adolescents with behavior problems may have difficulty responding to the new freedoms, and many may react negatively. Teachers must be trained to consider all discipline problems relative to democratic rights and sanctions. They must be allowed the time and the support to train their student-citizens in developing classroom Constitutional rights and amendments. The student government may appoint peer mediation teams to assist in resolving conflicts and to take action against students who willfully break the rules or take away the rights of others by their behavior. The judicious discipline approach adapts its boundaries as students grow in responsibility and maturity.

An Ecological Approach

An ecological approach suggests that both internal and external factors must be recognized in dealing with deviant behavior. In other words, students' outward behaviors are the result of internal disposition, personality type, cognitive ability, medical condition, and emotional state combined with external factors in the environment. Problems occur when there is a misfit between the behavior of students and the social expectations of the environment. Therefore, both the child's behavior and the environment must be modified to bring about positive change. We have included the ecological approach within discipline with flexible boundaries because even though we should establish firm boundaries around deviant behaviors, we must also be flexible in changing the surroundings as well as our own behavior. In this section we will focus on two groups of environmental frameworks for understanding the notion of "goodness of fit": (a) Child-environment interventions, which emphasizes the student, the environment, and the interactions between the two (Rhodes & Gibbens, 1972; Rhodes & Tracy, 1972), and (b) milieu therapy, a concept that proposes manipulation of the environment to change students' behavior (Long, Morse, & Newman, 1980; Morse & Smith, 1980).

Child-Environment Interventions

Child-environment interventions examine the influence of the environment on the child. Several factors in the environment cause children to behave socially or antisocially. In this section we will examine the influences of family, community, classroom, and school.

Family Environment Interventions

The family environment plays an important part in how a student behaves in school. Many teachers complain, "What can I do? Hagan comes from a dysfunctional family, and I can't change that." Many teachers are frustrated when children come to school hungry and with visible signs of abuse. Several families are indeed dysfunctional in many ways, and children bear the brunt of this dysfunction, but schools can be instrumental in helping parents and children. Home and school collaboration programs frequently result in positive outcomes. Parental involvement pays off. Schools can involve parents by encouraging them to visit the school and by making them feel welcome any day and not just on "parent day." An increasing number of schools are expanding their social work programs to help parents change their physical and psychological environments. Schools can offer parenting classes and family counseling and can involve parents in their children's academic programs and behavioral plans. A growing number of schools include home newsletters, family homework assignments, classroom observations, and cafeteria lunch invitations. Family members can also actively participate as instructors, co-instructors, or as mentors of individual students or groups of students. Parent volunteers work in the cafeterias, in the libraries, on the bus, and in school offices. Schools can make parents equal partners by allowing them a voice in school decisions. Educators are not likely to earn the respect and cooperation of parents by assuming a cold, businesslike demeanor. Parents respond more readily to an informal, personal, warm approach. Parents feel connected when they know their children's school (Rasmussen, 1998).

The Title I federally funded programs originated to help students from low-income families. The program supports a component that strongly encourages parent partnerships and involvement in their children's education and behavior management. Title I money may be spent on many types of parent involvement activities, such as family literacy, transportation, child care, parent resource centers, and materials. The Individual With Disabilities Education Act (IDEA) requires parental participation in their child's individual education plan, including involvement in social goals dealing with behavior problems. Section 504 of the Vocational and Rehabilitation Act of 1973 provides support for disabilities not covered by IDEA. Part of this support could focus on parents' cooperation in planning interventions to change their children's disruptive behaviors. There is a growing need for parenting skills in the early secondary grades as a result of the increasing number of teenage pregnancies. Many untrained young parents often resort to physical discipline with their children. Children raised in violence will eventually become violent themselves. Many schools are implementing instruction in child rearing and offer medical and psychological support to young parents.

Community Environment Interventions

School is not "apart" but rather "a part" of the surrounding community, and therefore the community needs to be connected to the schools. *Community* means business enterprises; physical, psychological, social, and health institutions; religious organizations; law and order agencies; institutions of higher education; the media (newspaper and television); and other community establishments. Prevention programs work best when members of the community join schools in collaborative efforts to implement positive activities to prevent violence. For example, 40 Beacon School-Based Community Centers in New York City were formed based on the recommendation of a task force to develop antidrug strategies for New York City. Of these community centers, 75% are open 12 to 14 hours a day, 7 days a week, and offer sports, recreation, arts, culture, educational opportunities, vocational training, and the opportunity for community meetings and neighborhood social activities (Beacon School-Based Community Centers, 1998). The Edmonds school district north of Seattle involved various aspects of the community in the work of schools by hosting community forums and considering the recommendation of a Citizen Advisory Committee regarding instruction, drug prevention, discipline, and other matters impacting the education of students (Soholt, 1998). We recommend the following partnerships:

- Between secondary schools and community organizations to provide training and part-time jobs to potential dropout students.
- Between needy schools and community organizations to provide material resources and financial aid to economically disadvantaged students.
- Between schools and community organizations to release employees (social workers, psychologists, police officers, and lawyers) to assist in counseling troubled youth.
- Between schools and universities to offer professional assistance in consulting with the school district on discipline plans and to provide inservice workshops for practicing teachers.
- Between schools and religious organizations (churches, synagogues, mosques) to provide afterschool homework programs and youth leisure-activity programs.

Classroom Environment Interventions

The classroom environment is an important antecedent to students' behaviors. Both physical arrangement and classroom procedures influence the actions of the students and the teacher. The classroom organization will typically reflect the teacher's psychological type characteristics. For instance, teachers with a sensing/judging (SJ) preference are generally task oriented, conservative, sensible, and practical. They are organized and adhere to rules and regulations. Although their classrooms are usually neat and organized, they may appear sterile, unmotivating, and boring to many students. When bored, these students may misbehave and cause disruption. On the other hand, sensing/perceiving preference (SP) teachers are spontaneous, flexible, and adaptable. While their classrooms may be decorated and creative, they may also be a cause for distraction and discipline problems for some students. What, then, is the solution? The most important consideration in an effective classroom environment is to create an atmosphere in which teachers and students are involved in planning effective physical arrangements and developing class rules and procedures. Teachers must initially present the boundaries that are not negotiable and then allow students to work within those restraints.

The physical arrangement of the classroom should adapt to the student body and to the delivery of instruction. If instruction includes cooperative learning, then areas for such grouping need to be designated. Teachers must ensure that all students in the classroom have access to teaching materials and supplies and that organizing systems are in place for students to store and organize their school gear. Classroom seating arrangements should allow each student to participate in the teacher's instruction. A few individual learning carrels can be included for students who need an occasional private space.

William Glasser (1969) believes that when students are subjected to too many rules, they become angry, frustrated, and problematic; however, rules of behavior are needed to keep peace and order. Rules should be few in number, stated positively, and communicate expectations. Students are more likely to follow the rules if they are involved in their development. Rules should be reviewed periodically and changed through discussion and consensus. Classroom rules are in addition to, and not instead of, the school rules. To develop classroom rules, teachers should hold class meetings in which the students and teacher can discuss the needs of the group and the individuals. Teachers can lead the class in brainstorming rules while recording suggestions on the board or on an overhead projector. After the brainstorming session, the list is further discussed, prioritized, and reduced to the minimum requirements. Consequences for rule violations follow a similar procedure as rule establishment. The following should be included when setting rules: The teacher has certain needs to be able to teach, and these needs must be considered in the final composition of the rules. Every individual in the classroom has the right to learn and to feel safe. Every individual in the classroom deserves respect for self and for property. Once established, the rules and the consequences for breaking them must be consistently enforced.

School Environment Interventions

The information age is rapidly changing the school environment and society at large. In addition, the cultural and ethnic composition of students is increasingly becoming more diverse. Progress in medical diagnosis has enabled us to understand why some students lack the ability to pay attention, behave impulsively, or exhibit bizarre behaviors. In the past, many of these students were considered "bad" and were subjected to repeated physical punishment. As a result of recent litigation and legislation, children have received certain rights they previously were denied. Issues concerning gender, race, ethnicity, religion, and disabilities are changing the school environment. In addition, concerns that were not common in past generations, such as drugs, possession of firearms, gangs, sexual activities, and single-parent families, have become increasingly worrisome. We present the following suggestions for school environment interventions:

- Provide an ongoing inservice teacher training program to keep up with the rapid change in school environments.
- Give teachers the tools and the support to deal with misbehaving students.
- Make parents feel welcome. Contact them when their son or daughter had a good day. Traditionally, we waited until students were in trouble before contacting parents.
- Use technology to link parents to the classroom. Send e-mails when the disruptive student is behaving, as well as to seek the parents' help when the student is not.
- Schools must examine their discipline interventions. Twenty-three states in the United States still allow corporal punishment. Suspensions and expulsions are consistently being used for infractions, and in many cases with the same students. If 12 suspensions didn't change the student's behavior, the 13th one will not do it, either.
- Alternative schools for very difficult students can be an option. However, these schools must offer the services and support to enable students to return to their home school.

Milieu Therapy

Milieu is a French term meaning more than just the surroundings; it also indicates the social climate, value systems, and beliefs of an individual. The milieu of any setting—whether the home, the school or the community—influences the response of an individual (Morse & Smith, 1980). The term milieu was coined by August Aichorn in 1925 in the book *Wayward Youth*. Dr. Aichorn tried to use psychoanalytic methods to treat delinquent youngsters but soon found out that talking therapy was not effective for his young patients and that the total environment had to be manipulated to change the child's behavior. Numerous residential facilities for troubled youth include milieu therapy in their treatment plans. In addition, some special programs remove children from their environment and place them in totally different surroundings, such as camp, wilderness settings, or sea settings, for an extended period of time. Many concepts of milieu therapy can also be implemented in special education and general education classrooms. We have adapted several concepts of milieu therapy to fit the classroom setting.

1. Consider the needs of others in addition to the needs of the particular student.
2. Facilitate open communication among the student, faculty members, and administrators.

3. Include students in behavior management plans.

4. State behavioral expectations and agreements in a clearly written contract.

5. Examine the antecedents and modify factors that contribute to the student's behavior.

6. Support formal and informal group activities to promote sharing, cooperation, compromise, and leadership.

7. Examine your own behavior, attitude, opinions, and mode of communication in your relationship with the student; you may need an attitude adjustment.

8. Ensure proper supervision of the student's activities.

9. Include persons close to the student—parents, siblings, extended family members, friends—in the behavior plan, whenever possible or relevant.

10. Plan strategies with the student to avoid negative outcomes.

Fitz Redl (1959) identified the following 11 components as important to the milieu: social structures; value systems; routines, rituals, and regulations; impact of group processes; impact of the individual's psychopathological characteristics; personal attitudes and feelings; overt behavior; activities and performance; space, equipment, time, and props; limits and enforcement; and program responsiveness. The following are simplified definitions of Redl's interpretation of the milieu.

Social Structures

This element examines the positions and functions of certain people in relation to children and to each other. Parents' system of discipline and the relationship between parents and children greatly affect the children's actions in any environment. In addition, the quality of parent communication or lack of communication with school personnel can determine the outcome of a conflict. The relationship between students and teachers impacts on how teachers perceive students, and vice versa. How teachers and students feel toward each other also impacts the relationship and the behaviors of all concerned. Is there a helpful working agreement among the parent, teacher, school administrators, and the child? Are support personnel, such as the school counselor, social workers, and the school psychologists, involved with the student and with the teacher?

Value Systems

Values bear a strong influence on our behavior. They impact our moral and character development. Our value systems can also determine our attitudes toward people. For example: A society that values male dominance over females will consider women as inferior. This negative type of value system can be directed toward individuals of different cultures; ethnicity, races, disabilities, religions, and sexual orientations. Conflicting values have caused group conflicts in many schools: racial problems, ingroups versus outgroups, "jocks" versus "nerds," and so on. Teachers need to communicate a type of value system that teaches empathy, tolerance, acceptance, and democratic ethics. The level of teachers' expectations is also an important consideration. A self-fulfilling prophecy is bound to be realized sooner or later unless teachers change such attitudes.

Routines, Rituals, and Regulations

Individuals respond differently to routines, rituals, and regulations, and the reasons differ with every individual. Students with a J preference (judging) have a deep commitment to the standards of society; they live by the rules and welcome routines and regulations. Students with a P (perceiving) preference live according to the situation of the moment; they dislike routines and rituals and believe in a variety of legitimate standards. Rules and regulations can facilitate or frustrate individual students.

Impact of Group Processes

This element examines the influence of certain groups on individual students and on subgroups. Gangs, sports teams, religious groups, racial groups, and the like impact the school climate. Teachers need to examine individual students outside the group as well as within it.

Impact of the Individual's Psychopathological Characteristics

The behaviors of others impact our behaviors. Individual students respond to teachers' behaviors and to the behaviors of other students in the environment. Negative behaviors usually beget negative behaviors, whether they are aggressive or passive.

Personal Attitudes and Feelings

A positive school climate is one in which faculty members interact constructively with each other and with the student body. The attitude of the school leader can produce a productive or a destructive milieu. When the principal is a boss-manager, his or her management style will permeate each classroom and produce autocratic rather than democratic situations.

Overt Behaviors

The overt behaviors of faculty members as a group and the overt behaviors of the student body can be supportive and helpful or harmful and vindictive. In schools where autocracy rules, an "us" (faculty) against "them" (student body) mentality is demonstrated in overt dissent.

Activities and Performance

Learning activities are intended to help students understand and learn different academic concepts. However, many school activities are boring, tedious, and considered as busywork by many students. Students are more likely to misbehave when they do not perceive the activities as relevant and personally meaningful. They become unmotivated and frequently rebel and take out their frustrations on others.

Space, Equipment, Time, and Props

A new teacher was assigned to teach seven students with behavior disorders in a self-contained classroom at a junior high school. Due to lack of space in the building, her classroom was a small dressing room surrounded by mirrors off the stage. The teacher resigned two weeks later. Lack of space can be a serious antecedent to misbehavior. Adequate space must be provided to conduct the program's activities. Teachers must coordinate the material with the instructional and interest level of students. Time is also an important element. Is the teacher trying to cram too much or too little instruction in the appropriated time? Props can be helpful to hold students' attention and concentration. Lectures without props can be boring and give rise to behavior problems. Teachers can use overhead projectors, pictures, or concrete props when lecture is the instructional media.

Limits and Enforcement

Teachers, even lead-managers, must establish boundaries for student behavior. These limits must be enforced; however, they must be reasonable and subject to change according to the students' self-management abilities.

Program Responsiveness

This element examines the structure of the milieu. Is it flexible and responsive to permit and encourage changes to meet the individual needs of students? Administrators and faculty members can safeguard a healthy milieu when the program is monitored, discussed, evaluated periodically, and directed to the welfare of all students.

Summary

The emphasis of discipline with flexible boundaries is on teaching and empowering students to take control of their lives. That does not imply unlicensed freedom and permissiveness. Boundaries are set and enlarged as students learn responsibility and self-regulation. Self-discipline means making decisions and accepting the consequences of the decisions, whether good or bad. Glasser has been referred to as a behaviorist, a charge that he quickly denies. He endorses a caring, democratic atmosphere free from fear and punishment. Likewise, Dreikurs believes in children's rights, but he also supports the rights of parents and teachers. Permissiveness can be just as dangerous as punishment, and he urges adults to discipline children without authoritarian control. Discovering the students' goals for misbehaving can prevent power struggles with students and facilitate interactions. Both Glasser and Dreikurs believe that caring relationships between teacher and student are essential.

Ellis proposes that we can change our feelings by reviewing our beliefs and our thinking about a situation. Students will frequently project blame for their feelings on other people or on circumstances. Teachers can guide students in understanding that nobody or anything can "make" you sad, you have a choice to feel the way you do by rationally examining the facts. Cognitive psychology teaches that our cognitive processes such as our perceptions, memory, and inferences influence our emotions and our behaviors. We can teach self-management skills to students by modeling self-talk and thinking through a problem to find solutions.

Judicious discipline applies a set of legal principles based on human rights and democratic values. Teachers teach concepts of freedom, justice, and equality and provide experiences for students to grow in responsibility and autonomy. Students are part of a total environment, and we cannot expect our students to change their behaviors if conditions in the environment remain the same. Sometimes teachers have to change themselves in order to actualize changes in their students. An ecological intervention includes the student, the family, the school, and the home environment as well as social structures, value systems, and personal attitudes and feelings. A discipline with flexible boundaries upholds democratic principle and the rights of students, teachers, and families.

Activity 1: Management Styles

Change the following boss-management statements to lead-management statements:

1. I don't want to hear another word or sound; and you will do as I say because I say so.

2. I will not tolerate disobedience, you were told to come straight to your classroom after P.E.

3. What is the matter with you, can't you take an order? I said put away your coloring books.

4. I am the teacher, and my rule says you may not look at each other's papers, that's cheating.

5. Who said you two could work together? Did you get my permission? I don't think so.

6. Listen up and pay attention. Anyone cursing in my classroom will get detention.

Activity 2: Praise and Encouragement

Study the difference between praise and encouragement in the first three examples and supply an encouragement statement opposite the praise statement. Phrases of encouragement include: You do a good job of . . . You have improved in . . . I like you, but I don't like what you do . . . You can help me by . . . So you made a mistake, what have you learned . . . Let's try it together . . . Keep trying, don't give up . . . I think you can do it . . .

PRAISE	ENCOURAGEMENT
You made the only A on the final.	You did very well on the final exam.
I'm so proud of you, you're so smart.	Its great to see that you enjoy science.
You're the best math student I've ever had.	You seem to grasp math work very easily.
I like when you talk nicely, no swearing today.	
Great! Isn't cooperating better than fighting?	
You did such a great job organizing the shelf and cleaning the room. You're the best.	
Your work is perfect. You stayed on task.	
You have such a great personality, you can get along with others when you try.	
You're the best dressed student in the class, you have such good taste in clothes.	
You are so good, you didn't interrupt me, not once. You can do it when you want.	

Activity 3: Consequences

Indicate natural consequences and apply logical consequences to the following behaviors. Indicate whether natural (N) or logical (L). Remember that logical consequences are guided, arranged, discussed, understood, and accepted by the students.

BEHAVIOR	CONSEQUENCES
Jim does not ties his shoelaces.	He trips and falls. (N)
Kim spills Lori's paint on purpose.	She cleans the mess. (L)
Gretchen kicks Tara.	She is required to make reparation to Tara. (L)
Dorian runs down a slippery hallway.	
Cora uses the "F" word in class.	
Jose spits his food at Tanya.	
Mike stuffs his mouth and tries to swallow.	
Maria is oppositional and refuses to do her work.	
Lennox disobeys his mother and does not use sunblock before lying on the beach.	
Ricardo trips Refuggio in the gym.	
Dino does not prepare for the exam.	
Madison hits a vicious dog.	
Griffen steals $20 from the teacher's purse.	
Saphire is not paying attention to directions.	

Activity 4: Goal of Misbehavior

Decide the goal of misbehavior. Ask yourself the following questions: Do I feel annoyed? (Goal: attention getting) Do I feel intimidated or browbeaten? (Goal: power) Do I feel hurt or maltreated? (Goal: revenge) Do I feel unable to help the student? (Goal: inadequacy learned helplessness)

1. Mr. Smith is teaching a Spanish lesson. He pronounces a Spanish word the way it is pronounced in Spain and is quickly corrected by his student Jose. Mr. Smith explains that this word is pronounced differently in Argentina, but Jose won't let up; he says his parents, who were born in Argentina, speak perfect Spanish and taught him the correct way to pronounce words. The argument continues.

   Jose's goal is _____. Mr. Smith should

   _____.

2. Mr. Hughes is calling roll. Whenever he calls a girl's name, Stan lets out a soft whistle that produces giggles and comments of exasperation.

   Stan's goal is _____. Mr. Hughes should

   _____.

3. Abdullah, a ninth-grade student, refuses to participate because some classmates have ridiculed his Egyptian accent. Ms. Dionne tells Abdullah to ignore the hurtful comments and praises his Egyptian heritage. However, Abdullah does not respond to her encouragement.

   Abdullah's goal is _____. Ms. Dionne

   should _____.

4. Jacqueline is disqualified from the cheerleading team because she failed math and English. Mrs. Cano, the math teacher, and Mr. Lazaro, the English teacher, find their yards trashed with garbage.

   Jacqueline's goal is _____. They should

   _____.

Activity 5: Rational Thinking

Read and notice the difference between Mr. Woodmark's irrational and rational thinking. Write two irrational thoughts in the blank spaces, then change them to rational thoughts.

Rational thinking is true: Tell it like it is.

IRRATIONAL/FALSE THINKING	RATIONAL/TRUE THINKING
Irrational thought has nothing to do with objective reality; it's a lie.	Rational thought is based on objective reality; it's true.
Dancy is a savage beast. I hate the way he fights and pushes his weight around.	Dancy is not a beast, he is a human being, and how can he "push" his weight around.
Lila is always getting into trouble. I've tried everything earthly possible. I give up.	Lila does get into trouble, but not always. I have not really tried everything earthly possible. How can I give up?

Activity 6: Internet

This activity requires access to the Internet. Surf the Net to find out what ecological interventions are developed in the country, your state, and your community. Divide into small groups and search the Net for information on the following:

1. "School-to-Work"

The School-to-Work Opportunities Act of 1994 (Public Law 103-239) was passed to establish a national framework for the development of school-to-work opportunities systems in all states. It provides federal funds through grants to local school districts. School that have implemented school-to-work programs have witnessed a reduction in discipline referrals, detentions, suspensions, and expulsion. Learn more about the school-to-work programs by searching the Internet.

2. "Alternative Schools"

Alternative schools were established to help youngsters who could not find success in the conventional school setting. These are not separate special education schools in the traditional sense; however, students classified to receive special education may be eligible for placement in alternative schools. The last time we searched the term "alternative schools," we came up with 6,697 searches. A good place to start is to go to the Minneapolis alternative schools at <tomas@Mpls.k12.mn.us>. The Minnesota Department of Education also has another Web site on preventing violence: http://www.cytc.umn.edu/Other/unlearning.html.

3. "Community-School Projects"

Management plans for students with discipline problems are more likely to be successful when there is shared responsibility among school, family, and community. Each component must reinforce the importance of social behavior and learning. The Title I programs emphasize parental participation and community involvement. In many localities, communities and religious groups are involved in combating alcohol, drugs, and violence in schools and neighborhoods. Find out what is happening in the country, your state, and your community. Information on community-school projects can be obtained on the Web: http://www.ed.gov/pubs/SafeandSmart.

References

Adler, A. (1948). *Studies in analytic psychology.* New York: Norton.

Aichorn, A. (1925). *Wayward youth.* New York: Viking Press.

Albert, L. (1989). *A teacher's guide to cooperative discipline: How to manage your classroom and promote self-esteem.* Circle Pines, MN: American Guidance Service.

Bandura, A. (1977). Vicarious and self-reinforcement processes. In R. Glasser (Ed.), *The nature of reinforcement.* New York: Academic Press.

Beacon School-Based Community Centers (1998). *Beacons of hope: New York City's school-based community centers.* [On-line.] Available: http://www.ncjrs.org/txtfiles/beacons.txt.

Dreikurs, R. (1953). *Fundamentals of Adlerian psychology.* Chicago: Alfred Adler Institute.

Dreikurs, R. (1964). *Children: The challenge.* New York: Dutton.

Dreikurs, R. (1982*). Maintaining sanity in the classroom* (2nd ed.). New York: Harper & Row.

Dreikurs, R., & Cassell P. (1971). *Discipline without tears: What to do with children who misbehave.* New York: Hawthorne Books.

Ellis, A. (1969). A cognitive approach to behavior therapy. *International Journal of Psychotherapy 8*, 896–900.

Ellis, A., & Bernard, M. (1983). *Rational emotive approaches to the problems of childhood.* New York: Plenum Press.

Gathercoal, F. (1991). *Judicious discipline.* Davis, CA: Caddo Gap Press.

Glasser, W. (1965). *Reality therapy: A new approach to psychiatry.* New York: Harper & Row.

Glasser, W. (1969). *Schools without failure.* New York: Harper & Row.

Glasser, W. (1984). *Control theory.* New York: Harper & Row.

Glasser, W. (1986). *Control theory in the classroom.* New York: Harper & Row.

Glasser, W. (1990). *The quality school: Managing students without coercion.* New York: Harper & Row.

Glasser, W. (1993). *The quality school teacher.* New York: Harper & Row.

Glasser, W. (1998). *Choice theory.* New York: Harper & Row.

Long, N. J., Morse, W., & Newman, R. (1980). *Conflict in the classroom* (4th ed.). Belmont, CA: Wadsworth.

McEwan, B., Nimmo, V., & Gathercoal, P. (1999). Application of judicious discipline. In J. Freiberg (Ed.), *Beyond behaviorism.* Needham, MA: Allyn & Bacon.

Meichenbaum, D. (1975). Self-instructional methods. In F. H. Kanfer & A. P. Goldstein (Eds.), *Helping people change.* New York: Pergamon Press.

Meichenbaum, D., & Goodman, J. (1971). Training impulsive children to talk to themselves: A means of developing self-control. *Journal of Abnormal Psychology, 77,* 115–126.

Mercer, C., & Mercer, A., (2001). *Teaching students with learning problems* (6th ed.). New York: Merill-Macmillan.

Morse, W., & Smith, J. (1980). *Understanding child variances.* Reston, VA: Council for Exceptional Children.

Rasmussen, K. (1998). Making parent involvement meaningful. *Association for Supervision and Curriculum Development Education Update 40* (1), 1–7.

Redl, F. (1959). The concept of the life-space interview. *American Journal of Orthopsychiatry 29,* 1–18.

Rhodes, W., & Gibbens, S. (1972). Community programming for the behaviorally deviant child. In H. C. Quay & J. F. Werry (Eds.), *Psychopathological disorders in childhood.* New York: Wiley.

Rhodes, W., & Tracy, M. (1972). Interventions: Conceptual projects in emotional disturbance. In W. C. Rhodes, & M. L. Tracy (Eds.), *A study of child variances* (Vol. 2). Ann Arbor, MI: University of Michigan Press.

Soholt, S. (1998). Public engagement: Lessons from the front. *Educational Leadership 56* (2), 22–23.

Wehmeyer, M. (1996). Student-directed learning and self-determination. In M. Agran (Ed.), *Student directed learning: Teaching self-determination skills*. Pacific Grove, CA: Brooks/Cole.

Chapter 8

Accommodating Behavioral Diversity: Matching Discipline Models to Individual Differences

Overview

Individual Differences
    Review of personality preferences
    Temperament
    Teacher and student expectations—a gap

Modifying Strategies With Flexible Boundaries
    Psychological Type (personality) differences—implementing
        Glasser's Steps
    Class meetings

Modifying Strategies With Loose Boundaries
    The NP teacher
    The SJ teacher
    NP and SJ students
    SP students
    NJ students

Modifying Strategies With Tight Boundaries
    Reinforcement and type
    Individual attention
    Other type differences
    Assessment and planning for behavioral diversity
        and regularity control

Situational Leadership
    Empowering teachers—essential elements
    Position power versus personal power
    Maturity levels, situations, and power
    Management styles

Summary

Activities

QUESTIONS

This chapter will help you to answer the following questions:

1. Do discipline practices normally employed in classrooms reflect a teacher's psychological type (personality)?

2. Is a school with well-defined lists of behavioral expectations and clearly stated consequences for violators expected to have fewer discipline problems?

3. Should the consequences be the same for two students who break the same rule?

4. Should discipline practices vary according to differences in students and also according to a teacher's personality? Can such practices be considered fair?

5. How can a teacher accommodate personality differences when disciplining students in a class of 25 students?

6. How can teachers adapt their personality type to accommodate students of personality types unlike their own?

7. How does the situation and maturity of students affect the selection of a discipline strategy?

8. What role does power play in selecting an appropriate strategy with which to address the misbehavior of a student?

9. How does the situation and the maturity level of students impact the selection of a behavior management style?

10. Which management style is more likely to elicit compliance from students with a low maturity level? From students with a high maturity level?

Overview

Chapter 3 explained how personality or psychological type affects student and teacher behavior in the classroom. Building on those concepts, this chapter reviews the discipline strategies presented in chapters 5, 6, and 7 and gives examples of how students with different personality preferences and maturity levels might respond to particular strategies. We review personality type characteristics and why teachers or students might respond differently to a particular discipline method. The same exercise might be done using an overlay of learning style characteristics, Multiple Intelligences, or any other ability, interest, type, or environmental condition to explain differential responses.

One example of the role that personality differences and the social skills that accompany them play in the classroom can be found in the oft-touted need for more individual attention in the classroom. Is that attention to be given in the form of individualized personal tutoring in a one-on-one relationship between the teacher and the students? Or does it carry with it the usually unstated belief that individual attention includes an expression of personal caring and a relationship of personal communication between teacher and student? Smaller class size can encourage personal caring and warmth only when the teacher considers personality factors and other variables involved in the life of individual students.

Moving beyond the individual classroom to examine larger issues related to discipline leads to consideration of schoolwide and districtwide policies. Discipline strategies are often adopted by entire schools or even districts. Those in authority who undertake the adoption of such policies appear to believe and expect that all children will respond in similar ways to the strategies chosen. Many teachers are aware of the shortcomings of a "one size fits all" approach to academics and understand its impact on behavior management as well. The reasons that a uniform approach to discipline does not work is explained in chapter 3.

The present chapter also explains how different situations and maturity levels affect the behaviors of students and teachers. Situational leadership presents various options in selecting seven power bases and four leadership styles a teacher can use to elicit compliance: (a) *coercive power*, based on the ability to provide punishment or consequences for not conforming to the wishes of the leader, (b) *connection power*, based on a connection with another power, which can bring about obedience, (c) *reward power*, based on the ability to give desired rewards, (d) *legitimate power*, based on the rightful position of the leader in the organization, (e) *referent power*, based on the teacher's personal traits, (f) *information power*, based on information others need from you, and (g) *expert power*, based on the teacher's skills and knowledge.

In addition to a developmental approach, Situational Leadership examines how the situation affects the maturity level of students. Teachers can help students to progress in their developmental socialization process by carefully choosing the correct discipline procedure. A telling and selling leadership style can eventually be replaced by a delegating and participating style to empower students to take control of their lives.

Individual Differences

Review of Personality Preferences

A quick review of the personality preferences will help in understanding the connection between personality type and the selection of behavior management procedures. For more in-depth explanation, the reader is referred back to chapter 3. The four preference indexes as described by Myers and McCaulley (1985) are as follows:

Extraversion (E) _____ Introversion (I)

Sensing (S) _____ Intuition (N)

Thinking (T) _____ Feeling (F)

Judging (J) _____ Perceiving (P)

The E–I index indicates the focus of people's attention and energy in their environment. Extraverts are energized by doing things and being with people. Introverts are more concerned with thoughts and ideas. Introverts prefer to learn through quiet reflection and are more reserved, whereas Extraverts learn through verbalization and interaction with others.

The S–N index focuses on the way people perceive and assimilate information. Sensing people acquire information through the five senses. They are practical, realistic, sensible, and sequential. They concentrate on the here and now and tend to rely on facts. Individuals who prefer intuition appear to trust a "sixth sense." They are interested in "why" and "what if" type of questions; they are creative, comfortable with theory and abstractions, and future oriented. They prefer a global perspective, depend on their instincts or intuition, and often take risks.

The T–F index focuses on how people prefer to make decisions. Individuals with a Thinking preference tend to decide in a rational, logical, and impersonal way. Decisions made by individuals with a Feeling preference are more personalized and are based on values, relationships, and the effect of their decisions on others.

The J–P index refers to how individuals determine their lifestyle. Those with a Judging preference are planned, decisive, orderly, and work for closure. People with a Perceiving preference are usually flexible and spontaneous. They are not oriented to time or deadlines, they like change, and they prefer events to be open-ended. There are 16 possible combinations of the 8 psychological type characteristics, usually shown as in Table 8-1.

TABLE 8-1. THE 16 PSYCHOLOGICAL TYPE COMBINATIONS

ISTJ	ISFJ	INFJ	INTJ
ISTP	ISFP	INFP	INTP
ESTP	ESFP	ENFP	ENTP
ESTJ	ESFJ	ENFJ	ENTJ

Temperament

Temperament is defined in chapter 3 and may be identified by combining type preferences. There are four temperament types: SJ (Stabilizers), SP (Artisans), NT (Innovators), NF (Idealists). The four psychological types that include the letters S and J are said to have an SJ temperament. Those psychological types with an SJ temperament are ISTJ, ESTJ, ISFJ, ESFJ and are described as responsible, dependable, and dutiful. The SP temperament group includes ISTP, ISFP, ESTP, and ESFP and is described as performers, adventuresome, and playful. Those with an NT temperament are INTJ, INTP, ENTP, and ENTJ and are described as competent, objective, and logical. The NF temperament group includes INFJ, INFP, ENFP, and ENFJ and is described as empathetic, subjective, and concerned with values and harmony.

It is worthwhile for teachers to lay aside some of their own cherished agendas and work with students to help them build upon their talents in areas the students care about, areas in which students are willing to learn and grow. A child with a strong Thinking preference may never develop the deeply emotional response to poetry, art, and literature that a teacher who prefers Feeling may have. A free-flowing Perceiving child may never develop the personal habits of neatness and organization that serve a Judging teacher so well. A teacher who prefers Intuition may never strike the same kind of spark of creativity with a methodical Sensing student type. As schools become more accepting of these differences, and more honor is afforded the diversity found among children, success in school will increase, and discipline problems will decrease. For all of their lives students will be able to access their own unique strengths to support the life activities they choose. Helping students to develop these strengths and preferences is a choice to do the possible rather than waste time on the impossible.

Teacher and Student Expectations—A Gap

The following is the account of a bright and well-behaved junior high school boy named Lee. Lee is receiving failing grades in English class; however, he enjoys reading for recreation and reads far above his grade level. He is successful in other classes and has no other failing grades. Lee is bright and has creative ideas; he invests real effort to make his English assignments interesting and informative. Despite his best attempts, his composition grades are consistently low. A counselor's visit with the teacher makes the problem clear. During their conference, the teacher pulls out file after file of student compositions and leafs through them one by one. As she lays each student's work on the desk, she plants her pencil point firmly on the heading at the top of each page.

"There, you see," she comments emphatically with each paper, "the student's name is here, followed by the teacher's name on line 2 and the date on line 3. Name, teacher's name, date. One, two, three. Then the title is next, written in the center of the page, and the body begins here." Over and over she stresses the importance of this orderly arrangement of data in the heading. Her approach to evaluating the paper is very sequential. The first order of business is the first item on the paper; in this case, it was the student's name. The student's name is followed by the teacher's name and then by the date. Each mistake or omission found in those first three steps formed a barrier, in a sense, between the teacher and the content of the student's composition. When three barriers exist, it seems impossible for this concrete, sequential, planful teacher to get past them to look at the content of the paper. In her view, those three barriers are problems that must be solved first and in their proper sequence. When they have been dealt with, the teacher will consider the content of the paper. Because they were not dealt with, the body of the paper seemed to sink into oblivion. She engaged with the heading. She did not engage with the content.

The arrangement of the student's name and other information in the heading is so important to Lee's English teacher that it obscures the genuine effort of the student to write the composition. Lee is baffled when confronted by the teacher's criticism of his heading. Because he is an Intuitive Feeling Perceiving (NFP) type the details of the heading are so unimportant to him compared to the content of his compositions that he is mystified by the poor grades he receives.

"The teacher knows who she is," he commented with sincere puzzlement. "Why does she need to have her name at the top exactly between the date and my name? What difference could it possibly make which comes first?" He feels upset and believes that his ideas and work were "dissed." Clearly Lee needs to learn the importance of following the teacher's rules. They are simple enough, and failure to comply is costing him a great deal. On the other hand, Lee seems genuinely oblivious to feedback related to things that are not important to him. Students are much in need of information about psychological type, their own type and the teacher's type. Students need this information as much as the teacher needs it. And Lee also needs to have the high quality and originality of his compositions noticed and affirmed.

The student who works hard and turns in a perfect paper with every line of the heading correct, every word spelled correctly, and every detail of punctuation and grammar checked and double-checked will be looking for positive recognition for his performance. The student who includes an extra measure of interesting information and an interesting twist to the basic assignment will be looking for special notice from the teacher. What the two students are doing may look very different, but the attention-seeking motivation may be far more similar than different. If it is not forthcoming, the deficit in needed attention may sow seeds that result in some type of discipline intervention.

Personality type differences determine many of the expectations in each teacher's classroom that are important enough to become discipline issues. The example above demonstrates that each teacher's own personality preferences have the potential for causing conflict with students whose preferences are different. Highly structured teachers with a Judging preference may find themselves in conflict with students with a Perceiving preference, who resist structure and feel stifled by it. Teachers who prefer Thinking may be baffled by the tears or withdrawal of an upset student with a preference for Feeling, one who perceives the teacher as uncaring, perhaps even wounding (Keirsey & Bates, 1978). An Extraverted teacher may misinterpret an Introverted student's reflection before answering as uncertainty or unpreparedness. A Sensing teacher may leave an Intuitive student confused by a presentation of facts and details without a global overview upon which to build them. Psychological type differences are important for a teacher who wants to be effective with every child.

A teacher's own psychological type influences the point at which a decision is made to take a stand with a student. Type differences directly affect the potential for a tolerance break in the face of classroom confusion or the degree to which creative deviation from the specifications for an assignment will be acceptable. Teachers' personalities influence their preferences for one discipline strategy over another, and psychological type preferences also affect a teacher's ability to be successful in the use of particular techniques. Teachers reflect their type differences in the personal social skills they have chosen to acquire and learn to use over a lifetime. Each discipline strategy has its own set of skills that is required to make it effective.

Along a continuum of tight (teacher-directed), flexible, and loose (child-centered) boundaries, Sensing types of teachers prefer discipline models that establish tight boundaries and employ rules, behavior modification, reinforcement, modeling, physical intervention, and isolation. Teachers with a preference for Intuition lean toward discipline models that employ flexible boundaries and utilize contracts, questions, and reality models that are more confronting and direct. Moving on across the continuum, Intuitive teachers who are also Feeling (the NF teacher) prefer discipline models with loose boundaries that are relationship oriented, individually focused, and supportive (Meisgeier et al., 1994). Regardless of the teacher's psychological type preferences, efforts should be made to discipline students in ways that are compatible with each student's psychological type characteristics. Physical punishment is not appropriate for any psychological type.

Modifying Strategies
With Flexible Boundaries

William Glasser (1969) identifies three phases of discipline: (a) involvement, (b) counseling, and (c) time-out. He proposes 10 steps for the management of students' behavior. Discipline strategies affect students differently. The first four of Glasser's 10 steps will be examined as examples of how discipline strategies can be analyzed and modified in the light of psychological type differences. These four steps demonstrate the role of personality differences in determining the successful outcome of a particular strategy. They also help to explain why some teachers like and use a strategy successfully while others dislike it and have difficulty making it work. Additional adaptations a teacher might make to accommodate either the teacher or the student are considered. Space limitations will not allow for an analysis of all 10 steps or all the models in this category.

Psychological Type (Personality) Differences— Implementing Glasser's Steps

Step 1. Care

Glasser's first step suggests that teachers be personally involved by developing a relationship with the student. Most students will respond positively to adults who are concerned about them on a personal level. However, teachers vary markedly in their skills and their ability to personalize relationships with students.

Teacher Issues: Some teachers have the ability to be logical, rational, and impersonal (Thinking). Thinking types may have little inclination to create the kind of warm relationships that a person with a Feeling preference expects and needs. Thinking types are more direct and corrective. Thinking teachers, particularly those who prefer both Thinking and Judging, combine logical behavior with a need for order, closure, and adherence to schedules, plans, and rules. They tend to resist any kind of sentiment in a work setting. They value clear, objective criticism themselves and give that kind of feedback to students. TJ types may seem cold and even a little threatening to students with a Feeling preference. While teachers with a Thinking preference are less common in the elementary grades (Feeling types are more common), they form a majority in secondary schools and are more prevalent still in higher education.

If teachers have both Thinking and Judging preferences combined (TJ), they have high expectations for order, conformity, and excellence. Performance and adherence to standardized procedures will have a higher priority than the development of a personalized classroom climate. On the other hand, a teacher with a Feeling preference has no difficulty adapting to Glasser's first logical step to show care and concern. Most types who prefer Feeling have developed the skills necessary to do this as a natural part of their lifelong social development. This is particularly true when a Feeling preference is combined with Extraversion (EF). Teachers with an EF preference tend to personalize their relationships as a way of life.

Just as the effectiveness of a discipline strategy will vary from student to student because of personality differences, those same differences present among teachers will cause a teacher's proficiency in the use of a particular strategy to vary. There are differences from teacher to teacher in a willingness to use a specific strategy and in their effectiveness to implement it.

Student Issues: Students of all types require a certain measure of personal caring by a teacher. For some students it is an effective addition to the classroom, but for others it is essential to their ability to function well in school. Feeling types must believe that their personal relationships with both teachers and classmates are OK before they move into a work mode. If they are uneasy that a particular personal relationship is not OK, then the task of repairing it may take precedence over learning tasks. The anxiety generated by uneasiness about a relationship produces behaviors that often look like problem behavior. Students behave inappropriately in pursuit of problem resolution in relationships with both teacher and classmates. Friends may write notes, form them into little airplanes, and sail them to one another when the teacher's back is turned. An anxious student troubled by the teacher's disapproval may hover around the teacher's desk in an annoying way, seeking reassurance when the rest of the class is on-task. These are students with a feeling preference; they will respond positively to a teacher who is warm and friendly and in touch with the emotional climate of the classroom.

Thinking types of students (particularly the STJs) may not respond to teachers who try to be too friendly or personal. They may be distrustful of approaches that are not straightforward cause-and-effect presentations. This is true of academic instruction and discipline as well. Students with Feeling preference may resist being on task until the personal relationship is clarified, but Thinking types resist involvement in the personal aspects of a relationship until factual issues are defined and settled—and often not until the task at hand is completed. Even then, they may resist relationships if they are interpreted as carrying affective baggage. The Thinking type's resistance sometimes evolves into a discipline issue for a Feeling type of teacher, who may view the Thinking student's questions, arguments, and other behavior as hostile or a personal attack. Sometimes what appears to be rebellion or disagreement is, in reality, an expression of type differences.

It is important to consider how to address the differences of Thinking and Feeling Preferences students as part of the implementation of Glasser's first step. Below are examples of how a teacher might initiate a discussion about a behavior problem with a Thinking or a Feeling type of student.

> *Thinking type:* Tom, I want to discuss your behavior and the rules regarding that behavior in our school. (This approach is simple, direct, and largely impersonal.)
>
> *Feeling type:* Tom, I like you. You are a special person and I am concerned about you and the behavior that I've noticed today. If you want to be happy in this school, you will need to follow the same rules that others obey. I want to help you understand what they are and what we can do so that we all get along. Is there a special problem you might want to talk over with me?

Students with a preference for Extraversion will want the teacher to talk to them directly about the above issues. Introverts might prefer to receive a note from the teacher and talk about the matter alone at a later time. The above comments about the thinking or feeling preferences of teachers and students apply to all discipline strategies, which push particular personality type–related buttons. Those buttons are real for teachers as well as students.

Step 2. Awareness—Step 3. Value Judgment

There is a relationship between Glasser's steps 2 and 3, so we have combined them. Glasser's second step is directed toward making the student aware of his or her behavior. He suggests eliminating the *why* questions, preferring that the teacher ask, "What are you doing?" and related *how* or *who* questions. The various type preferences address the *what* and *how* and *who* questions in different ways. Glasser suggests limiting the *why* questions, which is often the first question that thinking or intuitive types of teachers would ask. Therefore, a thinking or intuitive teacher would have to stretch to replace *why* questions with Glasser's recommended *what, how,* or *who* questions. Glasser's step 3 focuses on helping the student to evaluate behavior and to make value judgments regarding the efficacy of the behavior.

Student Issues: Students with a Thinking or Intuitive preference will not settle for simply telling the teacher what they are doing. They will want to explain why they are doing it—and they often ask a teacher many *why* questions. Students with a Thinking preference will offer logical reasons for their behavior and defend both the behavior and the reasons for it. They will require logical, rational, impersonal reasons from the teacher as to why their reasoning is incorrect. It is often more workable to combine Glasser's step 2 (awareness) and step 3 (value judgment) and ask, "How did your behavior break the rule when you _____ ?" When making a value judgment about the behavior, Thinking types will consider and may even argue with the teacher about the logic and fairness of the rule and of the teacher's impartial enforcement of it. If they are Sensing Thinking (ST), they might go over in detail the specifics about how they did or didn't break the rule.

The value judgments made by Feeling types are often related to how the rule correlates with their personal value systems and its impact on their relationships. They also will consider the bad, or maybe even the good, outcomes of their behavior in terms of people rather than in terms of the most literal application of the rule. They will say things like, "But it didn't hurt anybody!" or "Nobody cares about that anyway!" or "Nobody was around who saw me, so what difference does it make?" or "I gave them answers when they asked because I didn't want to hurt their feelings" or "I didn't want her to fail." Feeling types tend to make judgments, decisions, and choices about their behavior that are based more on their concern for people or the impact of their behavior on others than on following the letter of the law.

Students may behave in similar ways in response to rules but for very different reasons. Students with both Thinking and Feeling preferences may choose to break a rule, but their reasons for doing so may be quite different. Thinking students may see a rule as illogical or unfair, so they do not feel compelled to obey it. Students with a Feeling preference may break a rule out of compassion or concern for another student, and that concern may outweigh the value of obedience. They may also break a rule to be accepted by a certain peer group. Their "showing off" is intended to get the attention and admiration of their friends. Both students and teachers with preferences for Sensing Judging (SJ) consider rules a solid foundation in their own right. Sensing types follow rules because they tend to trust someone who "knows the way." Intuitive types chafe at rules and may consider them to be a marvelous challenge to their ingenuity; they find ways to get around a rule without literally violating it. Thinking types will honor rules that they perceive as logical and rational in a given situation; and if they are sensing and judging as well as thinking (STJ), they will honor rules as fundamental to the stability of their social circle. Those who prefer Feeling may honor rules to please people they care about or because the rule affects how people are treated. In many cases, Feeling types value rules for their effectiveness in eliminating conflict and promoting harmonious relations, but for people who prefer Feeling, when a rule is pitted against a deeply held value, the value often wins.

Teacher Issues: When students press hard for answers to their questions that challenge the rules involved in a discipline issue, teachers may take offense for different reasons. For the Thinking type teacher, it may be viewed as a challenge to authority, knowledge, or competence. For Feeling types, such challenges often are interpreted as rude, uncooperative, or hostile. Rudeness and hostility tend to undermine the harmonious climate they strive to maintain. Feeling preference teachers experience the Thinking preference students' direct questions as personally confrontational and disrespectful, and they may become offended. A Thinking type student's natural tendency to challenge new ideas or requirements may be perceived as rebellious by Feeling preference teachers. In general, Thinking preference students may seem aggressive to others when that is not their intent at all. They may simply be driving toward the answers that their Thinking style requires of them before submitting to the control imposed by a rule or agreeing to a particular interpretation or decision.

Step 4. Plan

In their emotional strand, Dunn and Dunn (1978) identify Motivation, Persistence, Responsibility, and Structure as distinct elements of individual learning style. Differences in perseverance in completing work or in the implementation of a behavioral plan can be a reflection of psychological type issues as well. Rita and Kenneth Dunn also note learning style differences in Analytical and Global students. These learning style characteristics mirror marked psychological type differences and affect the way a student will respond to the use of a behavioral plan. Analytical students tend to be sequential in what they do. Students who are SJ types are also sequential, preferring to receive directions in a clear step-by-step order. They like to develop a plan and will follow it. It provides them with security and support. Students with preferences for Sensing, Thinking, Judging (STJ) may have questions about a plan that have to be answered to their satisfaction; but in general a plan is viewed as a road map designed to get to a goal and as such is acceptable.

For the Judging types, and particularly the SJ types, once a plan has been agreed upon, it probably will be considered an inviolable contract that lends comforting structure to their lives. SJ students will tend to accept a plan outlined by a teacher who has won their respect as the appropriate authority figure in the classroom. They will feel secure with a teacher who has clear rules and expectations and clear ideas about such things as behavioral plans. They will tend to be comfortable accepting the teacher's step-by-step directions for following the plan that is agreed upon.

By contrast, Perceiving preference students like the freedom to participate in the development of their own plans. They will tend to follow the steps necessary to implement it more willingly if they have ownership in deciding just what those steps will entail. For students with an Intuitive or Perceiving preference, plans in general are seen as setting the direction for getting started. But most Ps expect plans to be flexible and subject to change one or many times as the situation may warrant. In a sense, one type of person submits to being ruled by the plan that is agreed upon, whereas the other agrees with the plan as a mutually satisfactory starting place. Thus a jointly developed plan is an excellent way to approach the need for freedom and change in a student with a perceiving preference.

Glasser points out the importance of the student and teacher working together in making plans for student behavior change. In using the collaborative process, the SJ students will want to know that the teacher has a clear idea of what a good plan entails and how to implement it. For the Thinking type student, the plan and the consequences stipulated by it should be logical and fair. For a Perceiving preference student, any good plan allows for change when needed, and the presence of a rigid and inflexible attitude about it on the part of the teacher may cause the student's response to shift from cooperation to resistance. In a Perceiving type student's mind, extremely rigid rules and overcontrol represent a fundamental danger to the freedom that is the hallmark of their personalities. Anything that seems like stifling inflexibility on the part of the teacher may shift the Perceiving preference student's goal from the successful implementation of the plan to overt or covert resistance of the teacher's tight control. This kind of situation can escalate into an embarrassing war between the teacher and the student. At the very least, it prompts what may seem to SJ teachers to be baffling resistance from the student.

It is important to note again that Perceiving students (especially SP students) are fundamentally egalitarian. If any strategy for dealing with a Perceiving preference student, in either the academic or the behavioral realm, comes to seem repressive—meaning that all the power lies in the hands of the teacher—Perceiving type students may simply disengage. When they lose faith in the process, they may simply go through the motions to whatever degree the teacher has power to make them compliant without being committed to the process at all. A teacher must approach Perceiving preference students with genuine respect for the freedom and autonomy without which they do not function at their best and without which they have difficulty being compliant and cooperative.

Glasser stresses the importance of expecting students to accept responsibility for their own behavior and for coming up with their own plans for changing inappropriate behaviors. Glasser encourages the employment of logical and natural consequences as a part of the plan rather than teacher praise or punishment. His approach is precisely appropriate for the NTP student. Intuitive type students will want to consider a number of possibilities and probably integrate or synthesize several ideas into any suggestions the teacher may offer before arriving at a plan that seems right to them. All students could benefit from personal approval of the teacher, but the approval and personal affirmation of the teacher may carry extra weight as a reinforcer for some students. Feeling type students need an overall atmosphere of personal interest and affirmation wherever they are. Although such reinforcement may not find its way into a formal plan, it may be powerful in dealing with students who have a preference for feeling.

Praise from a teacher must strike the ear of an Intuitive Feeling student preference as sincere and authentic before it acquires real power as a reinforcer. When praise is genuine, it is a reward worth working to achieve. With all students, it is important to remember the old adage about "damning with faint praise." Unless praise is wholehearted, sincere, and based in reality, it is better omitted. Specific conditional praise often is more effective for Thinking or Judging type students. Extravagant and personally warm praise that tends to be unconditional may be more helpful with Intuitive or Feeling type students. As a matter of fact, the response that is normally lumped under the category of "praise" or a "compliment" might actually be considered something else because of type differences. Praising a student with a Feeling preference, particularly one who has an Intuitive preference might be considered a quick moment of quality time, shared by the teacher and the student in an experience of genuine personal relationship. In it they take time together to celebrate the success of whatever is being reinforced. Without that personal element, the praise loses much of its power to reinforce a student with a feeling preference. A Feeling type student may respond to a compliment with a tiny minute of warm personal relationship. A Thinking type student may view the same compliment simply as a pleasant transmission of a piece of data but not experience any sense of personal relationship in the moment the compliment is given.

Student Issues: For the Feeling preference student, a plan should acknowledge people's feelings and the importance of social impact. For the SP preference child, both the plan itself and the consequences for its violation will need to be developed cooperatively. During the planning process, it is helpful to minimize the one-up–one-down power differential normally prevalent between teacher and student.

Every behavioral plan developed for an SP type child should be short, concise, doable, and rooted in the here and now. It should not be spread out over several weeks or a month. If necessary, it can be renewed for short spurts of effort. The behavioral objectives should be spelled out clearly, and any agreed-upon reinforcement must be forthcoming in a timely manner.

When reinforcement for the SP preference students can be presented as a challenge that places them in a situation from which they emerge as "winners" in some way, it often strikes a responsive chord. Any way in which the plan could be construed as fun or a game will enhance its chance for success many times over.

Glasser recommends that teachers analyze their own behavior in relation to student behavior. One way to begin the process of looking at how teacher behavior may be affecting students is to consider the psychological type differences between the teacher and the students. Next, the teacher can determine which, if any, type characteristics may be influencing the positive or negative working relationship with a particular student or an entire class.

Class Meetings

An important aspect of Glasser's (1969) and Driekurs' (1982) approaches to discipline is class meetings. The purpose of these meetings is to teach decision making, social responsibility, and cooperation. The meetings have a problem-solving orientation. They focus on classroom rules and other issues as they emerge.

Teacher Issues: A teacher's response to class meetings may be similar to the responses of students with similar type or temperament. Extraverted type teachers enjoy the excitement of a good lively discussion. Introverted type teachers tend to have discussions move at a more controlled and quiet pace. Teachers who are the STJ type usually want to control the outcome of discussions and classroom interactions and often have very specific expectations for student responses. Teachers with a Feeling preference want a class meeting conducted with goodwill by all. They want students to be friendly and supportive of one another. Thinking type teachers want to discuss the issues in a more impersonal way. They like a good argument or a heated debate. They focus on the objective of the meeting and may not be sensitive to the need to protect students, particularly students with a feeling preference, from having their ideas and suggestions be discounted or attacked.

Teachers who prefer Judging often have a detailed agenda for the class meeting in their minds before it begins, and they may have difficulty allowing "free-wheeling" discussions. They tend to exercise strong control over the content and process of the meeting. It helps to plug into their agenda a specific item that allows for free discussion, which will be valued by a large segment of the class. Teachers who prefer Perceiving may be resistant to committing everyone to a final plan. As a result, important decisions may not be made. Teachers and students with a Judging preference press for closure. Sometimes they seek closure prematurely before the best decision is reached, but perceivers may resist closure even when it is needed.

Student Issues: All four type indexes have relevance to the effectiveness of class meetings. Extraversion and Introversion preferences certainly have a significant impact on the conduct of a meeting. Extraverted students like to work either in small groups or with the whole class. They enjoy the interaction that occurs. Introverted students are more private and reflective. They may or may not volunteer to offer a question or comment no matter how important it may be. In group activities such as class meetings, Introverts should be encouraged to participate in a number of ways. Before the discussion begins, suggest that the students write down their questions, comments, or proposals. This allows the Introverted type students the reflection time they need before they are ready for participation. Make it a point to let everyone know that each student will be asked for input. If Es monopolize the "air time," give each student three or four "speaking passes" and collect one each time a person speaks. When a student's passes are gone, that student must be quiet until given additional passes. This will allow time for the Introverts to speak and will create an atmosphere that may encourage them to do so. To ensure participation in a meeting, choose speakers from certain areas of the room or by row or by front or back. Choose boys or girls as a group, specifically, to speak. Designate that all the people wearing a particular color will be asked to comment next. The success of these meetings depends on active involvement by everyone in the class. Remember that public speaking usually stimulates an Extravert, but Introverts may not be as comfortable participating in group discussions.

Sensing type students prefer to focus on practical here-and-now kinds of concerns in class meetings. Alternatively, the Intuitive preference students may digress and range beyond the topic at hand. Thinking type students will be looking for weak points and flaws in everyone's logic. If they are Extraverts as well, they will point them out to the group. When they are Thinking Judging, they tend to be perfectionists wanting to set standards that may be unattainable. Feeling students will join in if there is goodwill and harmony in the discussion. Their issues will revolve around their idealistic, personal, and value-driven orientation.

In a discussion, Judging type students evaluate what is said in terms of the rules or conventions governing the situation. They will want a product from the discussion that is organized and that spells out expectations and consequences. Perceiving preference students always want more choices and less control. They are ready for new and different experiences. They will work to make the meeting and its outcome fun and interesting. They are adaptable with solutions when it comes to problem solving, but they resist proposals that impose rigid and stifling rules.

Modifying Strategies With Loose Boundaries

Psychological type principles are helpful in understanding strategies with Loose Boundaries. Discipline strategies in this category evoke both support and opposition from the public and from educators as well, more so than strategies with Flexible or Tight boundaries. These differences of opinion are in themselves a clear reflection of the psychological type preferences of both advocates and detractors. Meisgeier and colleagues, in a study of 91 prospective teachers, found that Intuitive (N), and especially Intuitive Feeling (NF), types of teachers preferred discipline strategies with loose boundaries. Teachers with Intuitive preferences tend to choose strategies with Flexible Boundaries. By contrast, teachers with a preference for sensing, including SJs and STs, preferred strategies with tight boundaries (Meisgeier et al., 1994).

The principles defining discipline strategies with loose boundaries that are child centered—open communication and negotiation, freedom to choose, self-concept, individual autonomy, individual empowerment, respect for differing gifts, and democratic principles—resemble specific personality type preferences. The type preferences most comfortable using strategies with loose boundaries are N, especially NP, NT, and NF. The personality types least compatible with loose boundaries are S, especially ST and SJ. The term *loose boundaries* for some is equivalent to "loose ends". The SJ type, both teachers and students, usually feels at loose ends in this kind of environment.

The NP Teacher

Intuitive perceiving (NP) type teachers create a learning environment in which students have a great deal of freedom to make choices and where individual differences are respected and accommodated as much as possible. They generally provide broad global overviews and guidelines for completing an assignment or project. They provide a wide playing area upon which students can use their unique skills and abilities to pursue their own particular interests. They tend to value democratic principles in a classroom and will allow students to vote or participate in planning and decision making that affects the class as a whole. Usually there are few rules, and when rules do exist, they provide students with a wide latitude in pursuing academic goals, in accommodating differences in working style, and in their social behavior. Rules in an NP classroom are often developed by class consensus as needed rather than being planned carefully by the teacher in advance. NP preference teachers usually believe in empowering their students by guiding them to manage their own work and learning and to access and use resources. In this way students are prepared to become productive, self-responsible, self-reliant adults with skills to match their initiative.

In the NP teacher's classroom, there is much activity, interaction, and movement. Although it may appear unstructured, much planning and preparation is required to provide a variety of options and to achieve a combination of freedom and meaningful activity leading to relevant learning. Students are given freedom but are expected to maintain appropriate working attitudes and on-task behaviors. Sometimes the NP preference teacher's classroom will tend to get a little out of control because of the flexibility and openness, signaling the teacher to deal differently with students who work better in a tight boundaries classroom or those who take advantage of the freedom they are given. Students are expected to be responsible for meeting standards of achievement in their work, but they are permitted to choose from among many pathways for reaching their goals.

Teachers with NP preferences are naturally quite comfortable with discipline strategies that fit into the category of loose boundaries. NP type teachers view practices that exert strong control or are coercive as interfering with the development of each student's full potential. NP type teachers view strong control as limiting. It is seen as interfering with the development of the self-management, responsibility, personal initiative, creativity, and self-esteem that are necessary for lifelong productivity.

The SJ Teacher

In contrast to the NP type teacher, who believes in individual autonomy, negotiating with students, and providing freedom in the classroom, the Sensing Judging (SJ) type teacher prefers a structured classroom with clearly established rules and routines for academic performance and behavior. SJ type teachers may allow their students to engage in experiential activities, but they expect them to follow set procedures. SJ type teachers prefer traditional discipline practices. They assume that every child will behave according to expectations. The rules and consequences for behavior are uniformly applied, with little adaptation or individual consideration given. The SJ type teacher may understand an excuse but feel reluctant to relax the rule for extenuating circumstances. Special accommodations, including the adaptations provided for special education students, may be viewed as unfair to the rest of the class. Justice and fairness dictate identical enforcement in most situations. The SJ preference teacher tends to have a quiet, orderly, and productive classroom in which the teacher is the clearly designated authority.

Both SJ type teachers and SJ type students prefer structure, order, and predictability. NP teachers and students prefer an atmosphere of freedom, autonomy, and flexibility. In some instances, a principal may elect to choose a "canned" behavior management program but soon discover that some teachers are successful in the implementation of the program and some are not. Clearly, both NP and SJ preference teachers are out of their comfort zones when asked to use discipline strategies that are not compatible with their own personality characteristics. By the same token, they tend to be less successful in disciplining students whose personality characteristics differ sharply from their own.

NP and SJ Students

Not all NP type students have the same intensity of need for autonomy and freedom, but for many it is quite strong. When these students are with an NP preference teacher, they thrive in a classroom that is compatible with their own values, needs, and preferences. The NP type student will tend to resist the structure and inflexibility associated with the rules and routines—and also the discipline practices—found in a classroom run by an SJ preference teacher.

Likewise, SJ type students are not comfortable in classrooms with loose structure and informal organization. They often feel uncertain about what is expected of them and uneasy that rules and discipline practices are not firm, predictable, and enforced. When SJ type students find themselves in classrooms with loose boundaries, they may begin to question the competency and authority of the teacher and push for structure and rules. They may think that there is no accountability at all in a system in which precise policies of rule enforcement are missing. This group may cause its own set of discipline problems in its drive to find the limits and clarify expectations.

SP Students

A semester may come and go for college professors doing research in psychological type without a single teacher preparation class that includes a student who prefers Sensing and Perceiving (SP). This information underscores a significant issue facing educators who try to individualize instructional and behavior management programs to accommodate the behavior diversity found in the schools.

Given the premise that teachers instinctively teach the way they themselves learn best, it could be assumed that SP type teachers would have special insight into the behavior management issues unique to SP preference students. SP type teachers would be expected to be natural advocates for the educational needs of SP type students. The problem is that SP types are not attracted to the teaching profession. It is difficult to identify the preferred discipline practices of SP preference teachers because few of them can even be found in the studies being done, but some inferences may be made.

Descriptions of the psychological type characteristics of SP type individuals do offer clues as to the strategies that would be effective in dealing with SP preference students. Distant goals and rewards are less effective as reinforcers than immediate ones. The freedom to make a game out of a learning task can serve as a reinforcer. Problem solving embedded in real-life kinds of activities sets the stage for learning concepts and skills that are useful in real time. Therefore, these activities have more power to engage SP preference students than material that may be useful later. A large dose of abstract information presented to passive students sets the stage for behavior problems. The SP type student needs to be actively involved in life and learning.

It is important to know something about the strategies that work best with the SP segment of the school population, because close to a third of the general population is believed to be SP. If that percentage is close to correct, then a huge number of children in school seldom if ever encounter a teacher who naturally creates a classroom that is as perfect a match for them as the SJ type teacher's classroom is for the SJ preference student, or the NF type teacher for the NF preference student, or the NT type teacher for the NT preference student.

SP preference students tend to be uninterested in considering strategies for dealing proactively with behavior problems and management issues that have not yet arisen. Intuitive type teachers and students alike naturally live in the land of future possibilities and enjoy considering them, so developing a democratic structure to deal with problems before they occur makes sense to them. SP individuals are likely to disengage from consideration of issues that are not immediate and important to them. However, they may be expected to engage in dealing with problems and have good input once they have occurred.

An NJ teacher is inspired by comprehensive goals and tends to be committed to moving the group toward them in an orderly and structured way. The process of moving groups toward large future goals may require a rather powerful effort on the part of a leader or teacher, so NJs tend to reach for strength and power in their leadership and teaching styles. Intuitive students, in general, are motivated by broad inspiring goals. Although NFs sometimes may be wounded by or shrink back from risking the censure or criticism that may accompany an NTJ's task-driven focus, NTs usually thrive. Significant achievements and student progress often result from the work of an NJ teacher. For the S students who have difficulty bringing future possibilities and global objectives into focus in the here and now of the classroom, an NJ teacher can learn to break down learning tasks into concrete step-by-step instructions and then make it a point to notice and reinforce the completion of each intermediate objective. Unlike the SJ teachers who significantly outnumber SPs in the classroom, NJ and NP teachers appear to be drawn to the teaching profession in roughly equal numbers, with the NJ teachers slightly more numerous.

Modifying Strategies With Tight Boundaries

This section focuses on the application of psychological type information to concepts and methods of reinforcement and tight-boundary rules, rewards, and punishment discipline model. According to behavior theory, reinforcement is a process in which a behavior is strengthened when it is followed by a desired consequence (Schloss & Smith, 1998). It is extremely important, when implementing an applied behavior analysis program, to determine the psychological type of the student and to make adaptations that are appropriate to it. Using reinforcers such as verbal praise, differential reinforcement of alternative behaviors, activity reinforcers, modeling, consequences, or antecedent control all should be done in the context of the psychological type of the student. Modifying interventions to fit the psychological type of the student will increase the likelihood that a particular program or intervention will succeed.

Reinforcement and Type

Discipline strategies with tight boundaries are under the control of the teacher. Since reinforcement is a key to these strategies, the focus of this section will be on an analysis of issues related to reinforcement. For the most part, reinforcers are determined by the teacher. Most people understand that rewarding good behavior tends to cause that behavior to be repeated. Reinforcement is far more than popcorn served on Friday afternoon, marbles in a jar to earn free time, or stickers on a sheet of paper for work completed. Reinforcement is affirming and rewarding the performance of each student in terms of the fundamental values that motivate that student. Praising students for things they do not really value may be pleasant, but it will not affect their behavior very much. Pinpointing and reinforcing the aspect of a student's performance that means the most to the student will afford him or her the greatest sense of success. Personality or psychological type theory helps us to identify some of the more important motivating factors for individual students.

Reinforcement or punishment, whether or not recognized, is occurring continuously throughout the day. The environmental conditions, the regularities, and even casual teacher-student interactions may be reinforcing to some students and punishing to others. Words are important. Words like *logical, competent,* and *outstanding* may be reinforcing for a student with a Thinking preference, while terms such as *sensitive, caring,* or *understanding* may be more reinforcing for a child with a preference for Feeling. Some students may disdain, while other students may value, specific reinforcement terms. At a more complex level, what students value and what is reinforcing to them may be strongly influenced by their individual personality preferences. Therefore, a teacher who plans to use behavioral reinforcement as a discipline strategy will find the insights offered by psychological type theory very helpful. The principles of applied behavior analysis are simple and straightforward: Any behavior that produces something pleasant and desirable generally will be repeated. Behaviors that result in outcomes that are uncomfortable or undesirable generally will not be repeated. Most teachers apply these principles and find they work very well with many students. Then a student appears in the classroom with whom they seem to be less effective. Why is this so? One answer may be found in a mistaken assumption on the part of the teacher about what is punishing or reinforcing to a student.

One of the most universally accepted truths about teaching is that each student will perform better if given more individual attention by the teacher. Of course that is true—if the individual attention given is experienced as positive, desirable, and helpful by the student. The kind of individual attention given by a teacher probably will reflect the teacher's own personality type. Unless taught to do otherwise, teachers give the kind of direction, help, and support that they themselves find most helpful. For the students that are most like them, a teacher's efforts to offer more individual attention will be helpful, but for students who are unlike them, some kinds of attention may be upsetting or even punishing.

Many elementary teachers are Extraverted, Intuitive, and Feeling (ENF) in their personality preferences. For a student who is also ENF, an opportunity to sit down and chat with the teacher or peers about wide-ranging ideas before writing a story or developing a special project would be both encouraging and helpful in a very practical way. It would provide an opportunity for examining any fragment of an idea that may come to mind and consider its value to the final product. But for Introverted preference types, the idea of having to talk about half-formed ideas would tend to be troubling. So despite a teacher's best intentions, a warm friendly talk with an Introverted type student who has not had time to put his or her ideas in order and think them through ahead of time might be more upsetting than helpful. When you talk with Introverted preference students, give them some time to think things over and let them know you will get back to them to discuss the matter further. Unless teachers preferring Extraversion possess extraordinary insight, they probably will not be aware of the inner turmoil their well-meant attention may produce in a student with a strong preference for Introversion.

Another example of well-intended "individual attention" that could prove to be counterproductive is found in differences between students with NP (Intuitive Perceiving) preferences and students who have SJ (Sensing Judging) preferences. A student who has embarked on a major project often needs periodic reinforcement by the teacher to maintain the persistent effort required to complete the work assigned. What kind of reinforcement will work best to encourage a student? What kind of personal, individual attention will produce the best student performance? A teacher who establishes specific goals, works out a clear schedule of intermediate objectives, and includes clear steps for reaching those objectives usually will give an SJ student a sense of solid support and clear direction, but teachers who sit down individually with an NP student and attempt to enforce the same kind of plan may find themselves faced with a student who is not yet ready to select a topic or finalize a plan. NPs generally prefer to select and develop their projects in their own way.

The kind of outwardly imposed schedule and structure that gives an SJ student solid footing and a foundation upon which to work may make an NP student feel uneasy and constrained. NP students may need some structure and time lines; however, they will require more latitude, and they may not readily accept strong external control. They perform better when given latitude to diverge while being carefully reminded of the broad goals, time lines, and presentation format. As the teacher begins to lay out a plan and schedule along with the development of a final goal, the NP student who wants to be compliant may disengage and relinquish the all-important global inquiry phase of planning that characterizes the NP working style. When that happens, the NP student has no conceptual framework upon which to build ideas, no substance with which to work. An NP student who is not inclined to be compliant may simply "check out" of the project altogether at that point. The resulting product tends to be superficial, not because NP students choose to be lax, but because they are without the cognitive "clay" from which to sculpt ideas. Many NP students walk through assigned steps with little personal ownership or interest because ideas and plans that are not the result of their own creative conceptualization tend not to engage their interest. Concepts that do not emerge from their own synthesis of ideas may be less than real to them. There needs to be room for NP students to approach learning in an atmosphere of freedom. Teachers should focus not only on formats and schedules but also on the originality and creativity of the performance. Even a well-defined and structured paper might be completed in a different format, one that would provide an outlet for the individuality and uniqueness of an NP student.

Individual Attention

It has become clear that students thrive when given individual attention if the attention given accommodates individual personality differences, learning styles, and multiple intelligence interests. When a student is working on a project that requires sustained effort over time, a wise teacher offers periodic reinforcement in the form of attention, encouragement, and praise. The form this intermittent reinforcement may take is best determined by the personality differences identified in the student. A brief scheduled conference between the teacher and an SJ student to discuss progress on the term project should include a review of the schedule and the plan. Encouraging the SJ student with praise and recognition for diligence, discipline, and meticulous care taken in following the steps outlined in the plan, along with commendation for the trustworthiness and reliability the student has shown, should prove reinforcing.

A teacher may take time to ask whether the NP students have any new ideas they want to talk over or whether there are any resources they need help obtaining. The responsibility for identifying the goal, outlining the steps, and planning the process can remain with the student with supportive guidance and unintrusive monitoring by the teacher. The most necessary point of guidance from the teacher working with an NP student often comes when the student needs to make a final choice from among a variety of possible themes and settle down to one clearly defined goal. In a positive way, the teacher needs to acknowledge the value of any number of possible goals and plans generated by the student, but insist that a final choice must be made and implemented. Along the way, the teacher may express confidence in the student's creative ability, interest in the various stages of development in the project, and then inquire about progress toward closure.

SJ students tend to prepare their assignments with careful attention to the instructions they have been given. They follow directions and honor deadlines. It is natural for them to do a beautiful job of tying up all the loose ends and taking care of all of the important details in a project. NPs often leave out details, but they have an excellent broad concept and good synthesis with other ideas. Thus, each of these two strengths deserve special recognition by the teacher who is reinforcing student performance by accommodating individual personality type. All else being normal, the SJ student will work steadily toward closure, which gives satisfaction and serves, in many cases, as its own reinforcer for SJ students and teachers alike. They cross the task off their "list" of assignments with satisfaction. Reinforcers by the teacher might include recognition for reliability and for completing the work neatly and as outlined and planned according to or even ahead of schedule as well as approval for the content.

Teachers in primary grades often use stars or stickers to recognize student performance. For SJ students, a star for completing work ahead of time or on time addresses the need for approval in a way that recognizes and reinforces them for things they value and work to accomplish. For the NP child, the star or sticker may be given for creativity, ingenuity, or inventiveness. The NP students should not be given special recognition only for reliability, trustworthiness, or following directions or work completed, but rather for the things they value most. This does not mean that a teacher does not expect NP students to complete projects on time or an SJ child to show ingenuity or inventiveness. It simply means that rewarding the NP student for timeliness of the work will not be reinforcing them for good work with the content of the assignment. A reinforcer will not increase a student's efforts to produce the desired behavior unless the student finds the reward reinforcing. That is the key. There are many type-related characteristics about each child that can be reinforced. Although this list is incomplete, a teacher who becomes sensitive to psychological type differences in students soon finds it easy to identify and reinforce the special aspect of a task or performance that is most valued by the child, thereby creating a positive learning environment in which many discipline problems are diminished.

An NP student often tends to be late in completing an assignment. Promptness in turning in work is its own issue. Strategies for changing unwanted behaviors such as procrastination and tardiness should not be confused with the need to reinforce the content of an individual student's classroom assignment or performance. Efforts by a teacher to punish lateness often have the unwanted consequence of punishing the quality and creativity of a child's work at the same time. The content and quality of the work submitted may be excellent and worthy of praise quite apart from issues related to following the correct format or completing the work on time. Issues of compliance with format requirements and lateness should be ongoing with NP students. Care should be taken not to extinguish the NP student's joy in new ideas, love of learning, and willingness to engage in the learning process by overlaying the strategy for reinforcing the content of the work with the strategy for extinguishing the unwanted lateness.

In contrast to the SJ student who is reinforced by completion of a project, an NP student may come to closure on the same project with a sense of disappointment and grief. For one thing, the final project is never as expansively wonderful as the creative flights of fancy with which the student initially envisioned it. The final product was produced only after a compromise with a whole array of many more wonderful possibilities that proved to be impractical. Next, the steady work that is done on any project stimulates a constant influx of new possibilities, and an NP student who is truly and fully engaged in the project may be reluctant to discard all the undeveloped ideas at the end of a lively, stimulating process. All of this adds up to the surprising conclusion that closure, when it comes at the end of a project, may evoke negative as well as positive responses.

A good look at the difference in response to closure between the SJ and the NP individual offers an excellent example of the general differences between them. When an SJ person goes shopping and the item is found and purchased, there is usually a sense of satisfaction in a completed task. For an NP type, there is a reluctance to make a final choice because all of the alternative choices must be given up. Closure for the SJ usually is a satisfaction and thus a reinforcer. Closure for an NP is usually a compromise and often produces uneasiness over the loss of all the other possible selections in that or other stores. Therefore, closure for an NP may produce uneasy rather than positive feelings and thus may not be reinforcing. The nature of the reinforcement given and the strength of the praise given for a task completed should take this into account. Special attention to reinforcement for the SJ student may be best given during the process—while the work is in process—because the completion of the task may tend to reinforce itself. This is reversed with the NP student, who may be enthusiastically engaged during the process but in need of reinforcement at the end. It also should be noted that other preferences, such as introversion and extraversion, will modify the behavior of both the SJ and the NP student.

Sometimes people who are trying to introduce new ideas or methods in a well-established system have observed that SJ individuals find it difficult and uncomfortable to "get out of the box" to consider doing things in new ways. By the same token, NP people find it difficult to permit themselves to be "put into a box." Fitting themselves into a firmly institutionalized social system—even a stable and time-honored one—and accepting all of its prescribed rules and methods can be punishing and uncomfortable for NPs. Schools fall into the category of social systems with prescribed rules and methods and schedules, down to and sometimes including dress codes, walking in silent lines, and sitting in straight rows and columns in the classroom. The regularities or structure of school establishes a comfort zone that predisposes one kind of teacher or one kind of child to optimum productivity. For other personality types, the very same social system may prove constrictive and punishing. As teachers become sensitive to personality differences among students and colleagues, it will be possible to approach students who behave inappropriately with knowledge and insights that contribute to healthy growth and learning.

Other Type Differences

Many qualities and characteristics contribute to the individual differences that make each person unique. Fortunately, we learn more all the time about some of the characteristics that make us alike and some that make us different. We have explored the differences between SJ students and teachers and NP students and teachers in some depth. Before leaving this topic, it might be helpful to touch briefly on other psychological type differences that express themselves in differing responses to discipline strategies. For a student preferring introversion, a time-out, though embarrassing, may prove to be a welcome period of quiet and disengagement from the intensity of classroom activities; the same period of disengagement may be excruciating for a strong extravert. For an introvert, the privilege of reading an essay in front of the class may be more punishing than reinforcing, whereas the same opportunity might be relished by an extravert. Being allowed to work in a group of fellow students may enhance the performance of extraverted students, but it can increase the level of stress for an introverted student. An intuitive child may be highly incensed when punished for a simple rule infraction, but a sensing child may feel reassured that the rules are firmly in place, comfortingly enforced, and that someone is "watching the store."

A thinking student appreciates the effort invested in detailed criticism of a piece of work even though some aspects of the criticism may be somewhat painful. Both the thinking teacher and the thinking student will tend to believe that a piece of work in which a teacher is willing to invest time and energy to offer criticism has worth and value. A child with a feeling preference often must have negative feedback mediated by accompanying positive comments and may be devastated—possibly immobilized—by feedback from a teacher who points out only the work that needs improvement or correction. Such immediate criticism maybe interpreted by F types personally—that the teacher doesn't like them.

Assessment and Planning for Behavioral Diversity and Regularity Control

The following procedures can be used to determine the extent to which classroom or school regularities should be modified to facilitate a student's academic or social learning.

1. Identify inappropriate behavior and the behavior desired to replace it.
2. Determine how the inappropriate behavior serves the child (attention, escape, excitement).
3. Does the problem respond to standard behavioral interventions, such as verbal redirection, contingency contracting, logical consequences, reinforcement of the appropriate behaviors, or reinforcement of incompatible, alternative, or other behaviors?

4. If the problem is chronic and unresponsive to standard interventions, compare the psychological type, learning style, and interests of the student and the teacher.

5. Are the instructional strategies, arrangement, materials, climate, and discipline strategies compatible with the type, learning style, and intelligences of the student?

6. Rule out family and neighborhood stressors.

7. Control the regularities to be certain the student is working in an enhancing, supportive environment.

8. Monitor progress and continue adjusting the regularities in response to the legitimate needs of the student as necessary.

Situational Leadership

Another option in selecting a behavior management model is a situational or developmental approach. Situational leadership (Hersey & Blanchard, 1998) is a model of management that considers both the situation and the maturity level of followers. It is based on various types of powers and styles and management to influence and gain compliance. Teachers are leaders and managers in their classroom, and students' compliance and cooperation are important attributes in developing an environment in which disruptive behavior is minimized and learning behavior is maximized. An understanding of the concepts of situational leadership can assist in selecting strategies from the three areas of discipline described in previous chapters: discipline with tight boundaries, discipline with loose boundaries, and discipline with flexible boundaries. Situational leadership integrates three essential elements to help teachers in developing behavior strategies: the use of the leader's power, the maturity levels of people who are being influenced, and the situation (Richardson, 1981).

Empowering Teachers—Essential Elements

We all need to feel empowered. Power gives us the ability to influence people and establish relationships. Through power we can earn the confidence and trust of people we are trying to convince. Individuals who know how to use power constructively are more effective than those who do not. Lack of power places us at a disadvantage; powerless individuals feel defeated and inadequate because they are ineffective in dealing with others. Despite its significance, the concept of power is often misunderstood and regarded as a negative. This view is supported by diverse cultural and religious values. "The meek shall inherit the earth," for instance, is usually interpreted to mean that it is better to be subservient than powerful. There are two sides to power; a positive, democratic, socialized side and a negative autocratic, tyrannical side. Both interpretations of power can be observed in every kind organization, extending from governmental to private organizations, to homes and classrooms. It is important to understand how power can be used constructively. Paul Hersey and Ken Blanchard (1998) described power as an influence potential—a resource that teachers can use to obtain compliance and commitment from students. These authors apply the use of power in a management system they identify as Situational Leadership. They defined seven different power bases that teachers can use to influence others.

Coercive Power

Hersey and Blanchard describe coercive power as based on the ability to provide punishment or enforce consequences for not conforming to the wishes of the leader. (I'd better behave or else the teacher will send me to detention.) Punishment must be used only with great caution and extensive understanding of its outcome. Punishment is temporarily effective and immediately stops the inappropriate behavior. A punitive action, such as physical restraint or isolation, can stop an out-of-control student. However, consistent punishment models a negative style of interaction and promotes power struggles between students and teachers. Teachers often diminish their coercive power by not following through on threats of punishment. Teachers can also become ineffective by constantly punishing and by failing to discriminate the type of punishment or consequences relative to the misbehavior. Coercive power has little or no impact when students believe that they will be punished regardless of their performance. Coercive power can also become ineffective when the punishment is excessive and produces hostility. Whenever coercive power is legitimized, it will produce less resistance and will more readily be accepted. For example, we may resent paying a speeding ticket, but we can accept this sanction if we were truly speeding. In chapter 6, we discussed the difference between punishment and negative reinforcers and between punishment and consequences. It is important that when using coercive power that we do not choose punishment and, when needed, consider negative reinforcment and consequences. It is important that teachers teach an appropriate behavior when coercive power is used.

Connection Power

This power is based on a connection with another power that can bring about obedience. (I'd better behave or the teacher will tell my parents and I'll be grounded again.) Connection power is effective only when the connection is able to follow through and support the teacher. However, teachers must be cautious when using connection power, and they should become familiar with the consequences imposed by the connection. Example: A teacher, bound by a discipline program's requirements to communicate with parents, sent a note home describing the student's unruly behavior. The next day, the student came to school with signs of physical abuse, which he had received on account of the teacher's communication with the parent.

Reward Power

This power is based on the ability to give desired rewards. (If I behave and finish my work, the teacher will let me play a game on the computer.) Reward power has a positive attraction if the reward is truly reinforcing. When students value the reward they are more likely to decrease resistance and increase compliance and motivation. A disadvantage of rewarding students is that it may promote external dependence on the reward and does not teach self-management skills.

Legitimate Power

This power is based on the rightful position of the leader in the organization. (I'd better behave; after all, Mr. Carver is the teacher and has the right to tell me what to do.) Legitimate power gives teachers the "right to rule." This power is eroded when parents or school principals do not support teachers, or when teachers are intimidated by the students' behavior. Students will accept the teacher when they accept the teacher's legitimate position. Students are more likely to comply in cultures where teachers evoke great respect and teaching is viewed as a noble and revered position.

Referent Power

This power is based on a teacher's personal traits. Popular teachers have influence over people who like and admire them. (I will behave because I like Ms. Dionne and want to please her.) Referent power has clear advantages over the other power bases, especially when the situation calls for a high relationship need. Referent power is also more effective in changing cognition and in causing students to internalize social behaviors. Teachers can obtain referent power by personalizing relationships with students and by creating a caring and supportive class climate. Confidence, trust, and caring are important elements for influencing people.

Information Power

This power is based on information that others need from you. Students look to their teachers for information to improve performance or to get something they want or need. ("If I behave, the coach will be more likely to tell me what I need to do to make the team". "When the teacher thinks I work hard, I get more individual information when applying for admission to college".) Unlike with expert power, the information does not necessarily need to be based in some area of expertise. Information power is founded on perceived access to information. For instance, Teacher A may comply with Teacher B to obtain some juicy gossip, or Teacher A may comply with the principal's secretary because she believes that the secretary has some inside information on salary raises.

Expert Power

This power is based on the teacher's skill and knowledge, attributes that are necessary for the students. (If I behave, the teacher will be more likely to give me individual instruction to make passing grades, and I can continue to be on the cheerleading team.) Students who are motivated are more likely to be influenced by expert power. Extracurricular activities such as cheerleading and playing sports can motivate misbehaving and reluctant learners to seek their teacher's expertise to achieve their goals.

Position Power Versus Personal Power

Hersey and Blanchard (1998) define coercive, connection, reward, and legitimate powers as *position power*, and referent, information, and expert powers as *personal power*. It is not only essential for people to perceive us as having power, we must also be able and willing to use it. Consider the following example.

Mr. Ammons, the seventh-grade teacher, is upset at Hilda's fighting behavior. He warns her, "Hilda, your fighting is unacceptable. This is your second fight this month. I'm really upset. You have no choice, you either learn to get along with your peers, or I will have to send you to the principal's office. Three strikes and you're out." Two weeks later, Hilda instigates and participates in another fight. Mr. Ammons uses his connection power, and warns, "Hilda, I know how strict your parents are in dealing with fighting. You will be grounded for weeks if I tell them how you are behaving." However, Mr. Ammons does not contact the parents. This scenario occurs several times, and Mr. Ammons attempts to use various power bases with no results. Hilda has learned that Mr. Ammons, who has the power to get her suspended from school and grounded at home, will not use his power. Power is a matter of perception, and if you do not use it, you will lose it.

Maturity Levels, Situations, and Power

When selecting and implementing discipline strategies, teachers need to consider the maturity levels of their students. The maturity level may be defined as the willingness and the ability to follow the wishes of the leader. In chapter 4, we described stages in the areas of social and emotional growth, interpersonal development, and moral progression of human beings. Many immature individuals lacking the qualities needed to function at the high end of these areas may respond differently to power bases. Situational Leadership suggests that individuals at the lower end of the maturity scale are more likely to respond to coercive power, connection power, and reward power. As individuals move from lower levels to higher levels of maturity, they will respond to legitimate power, referent power, information power, and expert power.

In addition to recognizing levels of maturity and levels of power, Situational Leadership also considers the situation and how it influences maturity level. Circumstances may trigger immature behavior in otherwise mature students. Under stressful circumstances, teachers must have the sensitivity and flexibility to recognize when a student needs a firm hand, or a kind ear and an understanding heart.

Consider a teenage student, usually task oriented, who comes to school in a bad mood and cannot concentrate on her algebra assignment because she just broke up with her boyfriend. In situational behavior management, active listening is initially used to determine what happened to bring on this situation and why the student is despondent. This is not the time to use coercive power. The teacher may need to use referent power and take time to convey a caring message to the student. She or he can also use reward power to engage the student in school-related activities.

Management Styles

Situational Leadership describes four management styles: telling, selling, participating, and delegating. Teachers initially *tell* low-maturity students what to do. As students grow in maturity, teachers *sell* their expectations through discussions and explanations. When students accept responsibility, they are able to *participate* in decision making. Teachers are able to *delegate* responsible tasks to those students who reach high maturity levels. This approach considers all the models of behavior management from different viewpoints. The situation and maturity levels of students will determine the strategy. Numerous teachers, unfortunately, persevere at a telling style of leadership. In order to move from a telling to a selling management style, teachers must lead students to higher levels of character development and moral reasoning. Teaching students social and emotional skills, such as those described in chapter 4, can help students to raise their emotional quotient (EQ). Students do not instinctively learn how to read and how to do math. Neither do they learn how to empathize, relate to others, or resolve conflicts automatically.

Traditionally, teacher training programs have provided the knowledge base needed in developing various behavior management strategies. However, beginning teachers usually succumb to the influence of the school district's philosophy on discipline. In the United States, most schools follow a strict behavioral approach, and many of them use coercive procedures, including physical punishment. Teachers who consistently use punishment and reward power are not helping students to internalize and generalize social behaviors. With the constant use of the three lower power bases (punishment, connection, and reward power), students are not provided with opportunities to develop their maturity. Initially, teachers may implement behavioral strategies to correct the inappropriate behaviors of immature students. They must, however, gradually use strategies from the other models of behavior management to guide their students in achieving higher levels of character development, moral reasoning, and self-discipline.

Through an understanding of the principles of situational leadership, the various models of behavior management, and the development of moral reasoning, teachers can personalize the discipline procedures they select. They can adapt their leadership styles and wisely use their power bases to influence and assist their students. As teachers consider the relationship between these three variables, they may want to shift from reliance on power bases that induce compliance and concentrate on those power bases that convey influence. In addition, teachers can gain valuable insight into their own maturity levels in their choice of power bases. By addressing their own personal growth, they can also intervene in advancing their students' maturity level.

TABLE 8-2. IMPLICATIONS OF SITUATIONAL POWER BASES FOR SELECTING A DISCIPLINE STRATEGY

Power Bases	Teacher Characteristics	Student Response	Model of Discipline	Teacher Direction	Discipline Strategies
Expert	Education, experience, competence	Respect	Loose	Delegating	Group 1
Information	Access or possession of information	Need to know	Loose Flexible	Delegating Participating	Group 1, 2
Referent	Good personal relations	Admiration or identify	Flexible	Participating	Group 3
Legitimate	Position, status, job	Acceptance of status	Flexible Tight	Telling Selling	Group 2, 3
Reward	Access to reinforcers	Desire for reward	Flexible Tight	Telling	Group 4*
Connection	Association with influence	Fear or pleasure	Tight	Telling	Group 3, 4
Coercive	Potential sanction or punishment	Avoidance of punishment	Tight	Telling	Group 4

Group 1: Active Listening—I-Messages—Analyzing TA Ego States
Group 2: Glasser's Steps—RET—Self-Regulation Strategies
Group 3: Determining and Dealing with Goals of Misbehavior—Contracting—Meetings
Group 4: Positive and Negative Reinforcement—Enforcing Consequences
* Omit negative reinforcement and enforcing consequences for reward power.

Summary

In the past, educators have expected all students to respond alike to a given strategy. The differential response of students to a particular strategy has seemed random and unpredictable; in many cases it was attributed to the overall stubbornness of the student and strengthened a teacher's or an administrator's determination to obtain student compliance. The insights afforded by psychological type theories cast new light on old practices that presumed one strategy would work with all children and also on the once mysterious reactions of those students with whom they failed to work.

To be effective, every discipline strategy used in the classroom must take into account the individual characteristics of the student being disciplined. Student characteristics to be considered in the selection of a discipline strategy include psychological type and individual learning style, abilities and interests, extent of family support, cultural background, emotional and social maturity levels, and any other aspect of the student's life that may make him or her unique. The behavioral diversity that exists in any classroom, school, or family must be recognized and accommodated when selecting or applying different discipline measures. The need to individualize discipline practices is fully as important as the need to individualize instruction. Classroom regularities such as general climate, curriculum, and teaching strategies must be continually analyzed to determine their relationship to discipline problems. The role played by classroom regularities in both the creation and elimination of discipline problems cannot be overstated.

Discipline strategies employed by teachers or parents are experienced differently by each individual child. A "one size fits all" approach should never be employed. For some, justice seems to demand that discipline be administered with a fair and even hand to all students. However it has become clear that the same discipline actions may affect students in significantly different ways. For that reason justice would seem to demand that individual circumstances be addressed and accommodated in ways that permit each student to be comfortable and successful in school. The measure must be not what is absolutely fair and equal for all students as a group but rather what will work and be effective in accomplishing the desired outcome for each student as an individual.

Understanding the process of the use of power is important in keeping a well-managed classroom. Teachers who are reluctant to use their power often lose the respect of their students. Conversely, teachers who use their power indiscriminately may face a group of hostile students. Hersey and Blanchard integrated the concept of power with their theory of situational leadership. They suggest that leaders may rely on some combination of power bases when seeking compliance. Power bases can be organized into a definite hierarchy corresponding to the maturity level of followers. Situational leadership also considers how specific situations impact on the maturity level of an individual at a particular time and place.

All new insights into the individual differences found in students will probably help to explain why a discipline strategy that is very effective with one student may prove to be totally or partially ineffective with another. This fundamental understanding of the importance of differences should remove the fear of failure from any teacher who is having discipline problems and stimulate, in its place, a search for the key to success with each child.

Activity 1: Psychological Type

Direct participants to complete a personality inventory found on the Internet, or have them guess their type by studying the personality review at the beginning of the chapter. Form type-alike groups by organizing small groups of Extraverts and Introverts for the first activity, then Sensing and intuitive preferences for the second, and so on. Ask each type-alike group to discuss the following issues in light of its own type characteristics. Discuss each issue as it relates to students who are the opposite type. Record the ideas generated by the group. Then report back to the large group and have each group compare its ideas for dealing with like students and then with unlike students.

The E Student	**The I Student**
Disciplining the E child	Disciplining the I child
Reinforcing the E child	Reinforcing the I child
Punishing the E child	Punishing the I child
Supporting and loving the E child	Supporting and loving the I child
Motivating the E child	Motivating the I child

The S Student	**The N Student**
Disciplining the S child	Disciplining the N child
Reinforcing the S child	Reinforcing the N child
Punishing the S child	Punishing the N child
Supporting and loving the S child	Supporting and loving the N child
Motivating the S child	Motivating the N child

The T Student	**The F Student**
Disciplining the T child	Disciplining the F child
Reinforcing the T child	Reinforcing the F child
Punishing the T child	Punishing the F child
Supporting and loving the T child	Supporting and loving the F child
Motivating the T child	Motivating the F child

The J Student	**The P Student**
Disciplining the J child	Disciplining the P child
Reinforcing the J child	Reinforcing the P child
Punishing the J child	Punishing the P child
Supporting and loving the J child	Supporting and loving the P child
Motivating the J child	Motivating the P child

Alternative activity: E & I

Form E and I type-alike groups. Develop a reinforcement menu that would work for Extraverts and another that would work for Introverts. Compare and contrast the two menus. Record conclusions. Rejoin the large group. Present conclusions and submit them to the opposite group. React and discuss.

Activity 2: S & N

Form type-alike groups of Sensing and Intuitive types. Discuss things that are reinforcing and things that are punishing for each one. Note how they might be alike for both groups and how they might be different. Record conclusions. Rejoin the large group. Present conclusions and submit them to the opposite group. React and discuss.

Things that are reinforcing for Ss and Ns:

Things that are punishing for Ss and Ns:

Activity 3: T & F

Form alike groups of Thinking and Feeling types. Discuss issues related to giving love and support to T children and to F children. Consider how the issues might be alike for both types and how they might be different. Record conclusions. Rejoin the large group. Present conclusions and submit them to the opposite group. React and discuss.

Love and support to Ts:

Love and support to Fs:

Activity 4: J & P

Form type-alike groups of Judging and Perceiving types. Discuss issues related to motivation. Poll the group to look for common threads in what motivates the members of the groups. Discuss possible ways to motivate students who are different. Consider how teachers could try to motivate Js and Ps differently. Record conclusions. Rejoin the large group. Present conclusions and submit to the opposite group. React and discuss.

Motivating Js:

Motivating Ps:

Compile the suggestions that were agreed upon from all four activities and duplicate them as a handout that participants can take with them.

Activity 5: Strategies

Discuss in small groups the use of the different power bases and management styles for the following scenarios. Consider the student's maturity level and the situation in your decision.

Scenario 1: Victor did not turn in his homework for the 10th time this month. He's been late for school and does not seem to care about his failing grades anymore. He does not have the grades to be promoted to the next grade. He has also been involved in a couple of fights. After-school detention does not seem to work. Last year, Victor was on the honor roll, was class president, and was involved in several extracurricular activities. His family life took a drastic change six months ago. His parents are getting a divorce, and he is living with his father and his sister is living with his mother. Should the situation be considered in determining whether to fail or pass Victor to the next grade?

Scenario 2: Matthew, a 13-year-old, aces all standardized tests. He scored at the 99th percentile in the state-mandated test but is failing because he seldom completes his home assignments. His excuse is "I already know this stuff, this is just busywork." He is the class clown and has received several detentions because of "off-color" remarks in class and for making insensitive remarks about the weight and appearance of certain peers. In addition, he is constantly grounded at home. His teachers and parents are at their wits' end. Matthew has been diagnosed as having attention deficit disorder and is gifted. His teachers realize that basically Matthew is a caring, sensitive, intelligent, young man but a rebel at heart. He participated in accelerated classes for a time but failed because he would not turn in his work. Besides, he did not want to be considered a "dork" by his friends. What power do you think would turn Matthew around?

References

Briggs, K., & Myers, I. (1987). *The Myers-Briggs Type Indicator.* Palo Alto, CA: Consulting Psychologists Press.

Carbo, M., Dunn, R., & Dunn, K. (1991). *Teaching students to read through their individual learning styles.* Needham Heights, MA: Allyn and Bacon.

Dreikurs, R. (1982). *Maintaining sanity in the classroom.* (2nd ed.). New York: Harper & Row.

Dunn, R., & Dunn, K. (1978). *Teaching students through their individual learning styles.* Reston, VA: Prentice-Hall.

Glasser, W. (1969). *Schools without failure.* New York: Harper & Row.

Hersey, P., & Blanchard, K. (1998). *Management of organizational behavior: Utilizing human resources* (4th ed.). Englewood Cliffs, NJ: Prentice-Hall.

Keirsey, D. (1998). Please understand me II: Temperment, character, intelligence. Del Mar, CA: Prometheus Nemesis Books.

Keirsey, D., & Bates, M. (1978). *Please understand me.* Del Mar, CA: Prometheus Nemesis.

Meisgeier, C., & Murphy, E. (1987). *Murphy-Meisgeier Type Indicator for Children.* Palo Alto, CA: Consulting Psychologists Press.

Meisgeier, C., Swank, P., Richardson, R., & Meisgeier, C. (1994). Implications of psychological type to educational reform and renewal. In M. U. Fields (Ed.), *Orchestrating educational change in the '90s: The role of psychological type.* Gainesville, FL: Center for Applications of Psychological Type.

Myers, I. B., & McCaulley, M. (1985). *Gifts differing.* Palo Alto, CA: Consulting Psychologists Press.

Richardson Coombs, R. (1981). Ego development and power base reliance of school principals. *Dissertation Abstracts International* No. AAI-8125886, Page 2421.

Richardson Coombs, R., & Thompson, B. (1982*). Ego development and power base reliance of school principals.* (ERIC Document Reproduction Service. No. ED 216 444)

Schloss, P. J., & Smith, M. A. (1998). *Applied behavior analysis in the classroom.* (2nd ed.). Boston: Allyn & Bacon.

Chapter 9

Aggression and Violence in Schools

QUESTIONS

This chapter will help you to answer the following questions:

1. Who bears the responsibility for addressing the problem of aggressive and violent students in public schools?

2. What are the indications of violent behavior of young children that would necessitate interventions?

3. How does desensitization occur and what is its role in the present culture of violence?

4. In what ways can bullying lead to violence?

5. How is bullying "socialized"?

6. What is the connection between social and economic conditions and gangs?

7. Why has violence escalated among female students?

8. According to the DSM-IV-TR, how is a student with a behavior disorder different from a mischievous student?

9. Is the special discipline provision for students with disabilities fair and equitable?

10. In your opinion, is isolating students in alternative schools a viable solution in the prevention of violence?

Overview

Most discipline problems in schools are minor disagreements; however, violent behavior in schools has increasingly become lethal, accelerating to shooting sprees and mass killings of students. These incidents are not limited by geographical boundaries, socioeconomic conditions, or racial or cultural determinants. They occur in rural as well as in urban schools and have dominated nationwide as well as worldwide headlines, causing shock and alarm. The last three years of the 20th century witnessed a barrage of school killings from Pearl, Mississippi, to West Paducah, Kentucky, to Jonesboro, Arkansas, to Edinboro, Pennsylvania, to Springfield, Oregon, to Notus, Idaho, to Littleton, Colorado. The first three months of the new millennium witnessed a killing of a first grader by a peer in a Mount Morris, Michigan, school; in Lisbon, Ohio, a student armed with a gun held his classmates and teacher hostage until he was disarmed by another teacher. These shocking events evoke outrage, causing parents, educators, law enforcers, policy makers, and citizens to look for reasons and solutions. Although these tragedies are a constant source of discussion on news programs, in homes, and in the workplace, it is teachers and school personnel who are ultimately responsible for the children in our nation's schools. It is teachers who must make decisions and take action in response to violence in the schools.

Before television, children did not have to deal with live up-to-the-minute images of violence from all over the world. Today they are as much a part of family life as the evening meal. Weapons are easily accessible and more sophisticated, and in spite of growing opposition to firearms, antigun legislation is decried as unconstitutional. Exposure to violence as a daily occurrence has been normal for most children living in inner cities. Americans kill one another about eight times as often as people from other industrialized countries. America has a long history of violence. Violent behavior is everywhere in society, but violent acts in schools have an abhorrent effect on the public because schools, like homes, are perceived as safe havens. In spite of random school violence, schools are still relatively safe. Nevertheless, too many youngsters experience and witness murders and assaults. A 1994 Gallup poll revealed that two-thirds of teenagers reported that they knew someone who had been physically harmed in a period of a year. However, in spite of this report, another study by the National Center for Education Statistics found that 92% of high school sophomores felt safe in their schools; an increase of 12% since 1980 (National Center for Health Statistics, 1996).

Is violence a result of environmental conditions, or are some children more genetically or biological predisposed to violence? Are males more violent than females? Is violence more predominant among certain racial or ethnic groups? What are the risk factors leading to violent acts? This chapter will explore such issues and will also examine the factors contributing to violence proposed by the American Psychological Association (APA). Suicide is the ultimate act of violence against the self. The APA lists warning signs of violence against the self. They include themes of death, morbid thoughts, isolation, depression, feelings of hopelessness, deep psychological pain, and threats of committing harm to the self. Teachers need to react swiftly to suicide threats and report them to the appropriate individuals.

Bullying and hurtful teasing are behaviors that may cause students to turn to violence. Schools must be mindful of such behaviors and institute proactive measures to stop and avoid such demeaning and offensive behaviors. Educators must become sensitive to the issues of violence in schools but must also realize that suspending and expelling disruptive students without providing help will not solve the problem, and in many cases the disruptive behavior will accelerate to violent behaviors.

American children must be taught the skills necessary for the perpetuation of a democracy. Democracy is a form of self-government that can exist only if each generation of its citizens renews its commitment to a peaceful and nonviolent society, and the role of the schools in this process is vitally important. Today's children must also be taught how to survive and function in a social, political, and entertainment climate that exposes them to violence rather than protecting them from it. Violence is illustrated by the media, by athletes, by the military, and even by activists behaving in the name of righteousness. For some, violence is accepted as a way to right an injustice.

Parents, teachers, counselors, psychologists, and others need to participate in the process of teaching children how to handle conflict and how to deal with feelings of rage, anger, hopelessness, frustration, powerlessness, and alienation. These issues lie at the heart of violent behavior in society. Many communities may not have formal programs that address these underlying causes of violence, but all schools teach how to handle violence nonetheless—often as incidental (or accidental) learning. It is taught by what we do or do not do in the face of all the large and small incidents of rudeness, roughness, harassment, discourtesy, and bullying that occur in the life of any school.

Traditionally, the typical response of schools to aggression and violence has been first to suspend the students involved and then to expel them from school, or to turn offending students over to law enforcement officials. Being expelled from school amounts to excommunication from life for many children, who never find another pathway to adult success. Where will they go if not to school? Is this policy the result of the fact that counselors and other school personnel do not have the time or the expertise to deal with such students? Counselors in secondary schools often complain that their job description does not involve what they were trained to do; counseling and helping students. Is the pressure for improved academic performance so intense that it leaves no time or energy to implement programs in social and emotional learning? Not everyone believes that schools should teach children about interpersonal relationships and other psychologically oriented topics. Many parents fear that these topics may be contrary to home values and religious beliefs, and they believe that this type of training should take place in the home. The ideal may be that parents bear this responsibility and teach and model such values as peace, love, and understanding; however, this is not happening in many homes, and students come to school lacking social skills. All of us need to become more sophisticated in our understanding of conflict resolution and dealing with feelings of anger and alienation.

According to a report by the National Center for Education Statistics (1998), patterns of criminal behavior are established by the age of 15. Approximately 20% of 70 million young people in the United States will be arrested before they are adults. The report indicates that an estimated 525,000 assaults, shakedowns, and robberies occur in senior high schools in an average month. In the 1997–98 year, 3,000 children either were murdered or committed suicide. Of those deaths, 44, or 1.4%, occurred in school. Youths between the ages of 12 and 18 reported that they were victims of 253,000 incidents of serious crimes, such as robbery and rape, in schools. Nearly double this number were victims of serious crimes outside school. Despite these high numbers, the chief school-related concern of students is reported to be the daily disruptive behavior of their classmates.

Intimidation by fellow classmates is a long-standing and pervasive problem, and 15% to 20% of students are victims of schoolyard bullying. Replacement and repair costs resulting from school crime exceed $600 million yearly, according to the national PTA (Stephens, 1997). Student misconduct interferes with teaching for 44% of teachers. Cheating on tests, stealing from employers, and keeping money that does not belong to them are actions viewed as normal by 25% to 40% of students. The presence of gangs is reported by 15% of students. Alcohol and marijuana are easily obtained near school for 30% of students. Nearly two-thirds of teenagers have used illegal drugs before they finish high school (National Center for Education Statistics, 1998).

Causes of Violent or Antisocial Behavior

Current public interest in the problem of youth violence seems focused on the need to establish blame. The media has devoted extensive programming time to consideration of the problem. Almost no group is immune to scrutiny by the media as they focus effort to identify those who are or should be held responsible. Following dismay and disbelief, attributing blame is a natural response to shock and horror. In the aftermath of the major incidents of school violence seen in the United States, those efforts have focused in turn on parents, teachers, schools, law enforcement, media, and others. Who is to blame? Everyone is looking for someone to blame.

In the case of violence in the schools, it is very unlikely that any one issue will prove to be the sole cause of the problem or that a one-dimensional solution will be enough to correct it. It is becoming clear that school violence cannot be laid at the doorstep of any single cause. Violence in children is a vastly complex issue that involves many segments of society. The solution will require significant changes in parenting, schooling, and the social, business, and political environments in which our children grow up.

The American Psychological Association (1999) suggests that people commit violent acts because they *are unable to express out-of-control emotions* appropriately, or because they *want to control,* or because they are *seeking retaliation.* According to the APA, the following primary factors contribute to violent behavior:

- Peer pressure
- Need for attention or respect
- Feelings of low self-worth
- Early childhood abuse or neglect
- Witnessing violence at home, in the community, or on the media
- Easy access to weapons

The authors would add two more items to the APA list: neurological impairment and continuous exposure to harassment (sexual, racial, or other). It is unusual for violence to occur where prior indicators have not been present. These indicators may not always have been noted or responded to appropriately, but they are there nonetheless. The following signs of potential violence should alert those who work with young people to take action, according to the APA:

- Loss of temper on a daily basis
- Frequent physical fighting
- Significant vandalism of property
- Increase in use of drugs or alcohol
- Increase in risk-taking behavior
- Detailed plans to commit acts of violence
- Announcing threats or plans for hurting others
- Enjoying hurting animals
- Carrying a weapon

The APA reports that the potential for violence exists when the following conditions are present:

- A history of violent or aggressive behavior
- Serious drug or alcohol use
- Gang membership or strong desire to be in a gang
- Access to or fascination with weapons
- Threatening others regularly
- Trouble controlling feelings like anger
- Withdrawal from friends and usual activities
- (Evidence of) feeling rejected or alone
- Having been a victim of bullying
- Poor school performance
- History of discipline problems
- (Evidence of) feeling constantly disrespected
- Failure to acknowledge the rights or feelings of others

The APA recommends that children and others who observe these warning signs should report them to a responsible adult. Everyone in school—both children and adults—must understand how such reports are made.

Violence to Self

Ken froze as he read the note he found near his friend's body. It read, "Life is worthless. I cannot live without Jolee." As he dialed 911, visions of Harold's spells of depression flashed before him. Harold and Jolee had been a couple since middle school. Everyone expected the relationship to last forever; however, in their senior year, Jolee called it off. She was planning to attend medical school

and received a scholarship at a prestigious university in another
state. Harold was devastated and began to drink heavily and take
drugs. His grades were suffering and he frequently skipped school.
He withdrew from his friends and often commented, "Life sucks,
I want out."

Child suicide is relatively rare; however, the risk of suicide increases in
adolescence. After the age of 10, suicide becomes a leading cause of death.
Suicide ranks as the fourth leading cause of death in the 10- to 14-year-old
age group after accidents, cancer, and homicide. Suicide ranks as the third
leading cause of death among 15- to 24-year-olds after accidents and homicide (National Center for Injury Prevention and Control, 1998). Suicide is
the ultimate act of violence against the self. Threats of suicide must always
be taken seriously and, as with other forms of violence, there are warning
signs. Unlike violence toward others, the warning signs of violence against
the self revolve around generally dark themes of death, morbid thoughts,
isolation, depression, feelings of hopelessness, and deep psychological pain.
Sometimes violent behavior toward others stems from suicidal impulses in
which the child expects to die or to be killed at the conclusion of the
vengeful acts.

The APA (1999) lists the following warning signs of violence against
the self:

- Previous suicide attempts
- Significant alcohol or drug use
- Threatening or communicating thoughts of suicide, death, dying,
  or the afterlife
- Sudden increase in moodiness, withdrawal, or isolation
- Major change in eating or sleeping habits
- Feelings of hopelessness, guilt, or worthlessness
- Poor control over behavior
- Impulsive aggressive behavior
- Drop in quality of school performance or interest
- Lack of interest in usual activity
- Getting into trouble with authority figures
- Perfectionism
- Giving away important possessions
- Hinting at not being around in the future or saying goodbye

Suicide in school-age youngsters has a hysterical, copy-cat component.
It often occurs in clusters after the death of hero figures, role models, or
peers. According to the APA, the foregoing warning signs are particularly
noteworthy when related to (a) a recent death or suicide of a friend or
family member, (b) a recent breakup with a boyfriend or girlfriend, (c) con-

flict with parents, or (d) news reports of other suicides by young people in the same school or community

An April 2000 issue of *Time Magazine* published a follow-up report on the Columbine massacre. Jodie Morse described a new computer threat-assessment program called "The Mosaic 2000" being field-tested in 42 school districts throughout the nation. It has a battery of 42 questions and is purported to provide a rough prediction of whether a child is at risk of becoming violent. The article also lists a set of indicators that the FBI believes can help to identify children at risk for committing violence. Some of these indicators are: a hurtful or negative event that can lead to depression, thoughts of suicide and killing, a history of mental health treatment, a dislike of popular students or bullies, verbal threats to kill others, cruelty to animals, setting fires, wetting the bed, and a fascination with firearms.

School personnel should be alert to these signs and immediately report them to the attention of counselors, the school nurse, or other designated mental health workers. As previously stated, referral procedures for obtaining help for any student exhibiting signs of aggression or violence toward others or self must be outlined clearly for all teachers and school personnel.

Desensitization to Violence and Aggression

Violence and aggression are learned responses and therefore can be unlearned. Slaby (1995) reasons that children must be taught alternatives to aggression, and teachers must provide opportunities to practice new behaviors until they are internalized. Sautter (1995) proposes that schools examine their culture and discipline methods in the sensitization of students. Are they promoting a climate of aggression and extreme competition, or are they providing a climate that encourages a spirit of belonging and cooperation? Are they turning the "troublemakers" out in the streets through expulsion and suspension, or are they providing intensive needed assistance? Are they encouraging dropping out of school by demanding that students repeat grades when they fail to pass rigid standardized tests, or are they providing alternative methods of assessment and assistance (Sautter, 1995)?

Causes and Influences

As early as kindergarten, teachers recognize the insensitivity of some children toward the feelings of others, and toward their own feelings as well. Children can become desensitized to others by being subjected to abuse, neglect, deprivation, or by witnessing repeated images of violent behavior. Through actual or simulated experiences, many children experience constant exposure to violence during the early years of their lives. Children are especially vulnerable to television viewing. By the time they reach their teenage years, they have seen untold hours of every form of violent behavior. Violent television programs and films have the potential to influence aggressive behaviors in some children (Macbeth, 1996). Repeated exposure to violence in musical lyrics and in computer games compound the inclination to perceive violent behavior as normal or acceptable.

The process of desensitizing children to aggression and violence begins in infancy as babies watch and experience verbal and physical abuse in the home. Although fewer than 5% of parents inflict serious brutal abuse on their children, an overwhelming majority will use corporal punishment with their children by hitting, slapping, whipping, shaking, and punching, often accompanied by cursing, shouting, raging, or out-of-control behaviors such as slamming doors and throwing or smashing household articles. What is the effect of harsh or violent treatment upon children? Young children usually comply with demands that are accompanied by harshness; therefore, adults who inflict it are reinforced for being aggressive or passive aggressive. At the same time, children learn that aggressive behavior gets results and that it is socially acceptable.

Corporal punishment has negative effects on children. Researchers at the University of New Hampshire Family Research Laboratory (FRL) report that children who are spanked score lower on cognitive abilities tests. The FRL says that children who are spanked are more likely to display antisocial behaviors such as lying or bullying, suffer from low self-esteem and depression, and be involved in abusive relationships later in life (Kaufman-Kanter & Jasinski, 1996). Despite these findings, violent responses are very much a part of ordinary family life for many children in this country. The process of desensitization to aggression begins for many children early in life as they watch cartoon characters violently attack one another. It continues through thousands of hours of violent images on television dramas, video games, movies, and in increasingly violent computer games. Children who grow up in a culture that makes heroes of people whose success is based on aggressive behavior learn to be aggressive. Aggression works. They may see little kindness appreciated. They see aggression in operation more often than kindness and often misinterpret kindness as weakness. Kindness is not taught, and opportunities to see it modeled are few. Aggression is taught, modeled, and often reinforced. Children learn that it is "natural" to turn to aggressive behavior when a need arises. Since their lives often reflect neediness in many forms, they may become preoccupied by aggressive thoughts. Anger and hostility may displace their own feelings of pain and provide a welcome respite from their own negative feelings.

Children who experience a preponderance of rejection, fear, hopelessness, and other negative feelings develop a variety of addictive patterns that serve them by helping to suppress or deny their own pain. Often anger is allowed to displace other unwanted emotions. In time, many begin to lose touch with their own feelings as they become unresponsive to the feelings and needs of others as well. This process is often allowed to proceed unchecked because too many adults grew up experiencing the same desensitizing process themselves. They adopt the attitude that painful experiences and fighting among children is normal and believe that learning to handle exposure to youthful aggression is a normal part of growing up. All too often that conclusion is correct. It is "normal" but it is not desirable. Early intervention must occur with these children. We cannot shield children from every exposure in their environment, but we can teach them skills that can minimize the influence of violence. We can teach young children the differences between television and real-life violence and the inhumanity and consequences of violent acts (Kirkman, 1997). We cannot place the blame for violence and aggression on a single factor (the media, entertainment, or environmental causes), but we must teach children conflict management, anger management, empathy, and respect for others. This responsibility rests on the schools as well as on the home.

Desensitization in Schools: Corporal Punishment

The fear of violence and the public's perception of undisciplined schools have caused an outcry for sterner measures of discipline. This urgency has compelled many schools to reinforce punishment, including corporal punishment, as a viable solution. The public school system is the only institution that legally supports corporal punishment of its clients. This practice is forbidden in the military, in prisons, and with employees in the work force. Paddling students legitimizes violence and conveys the message that a violent approach is needed to solve problems. Violent students are frequent recipients of paddlings.

Corporal punishment of students is prohibited in the schools of many developed countries of the world, except in 27 states of the United States, in South Africa, and in parts of Australia and Canada (Hyman, 1997). Advocates of paddling children often quote from the Book of Proverbs when justifying their punitive actions. They adhere to a "spare the rod and spoil the child" philosophy and believe that the rod of correction must not be spared and a good whipping will suppress a child's inherently evil nature (Hyman, 1990). Corporal punishment is supported by decisions of the Supreme Court, which has ruled that such disciplinary procedures are not in violation of Constitutional rights. In addition, it was ruled that the Eighth Amendment ban on cruel and unusual punishment does not apply to corporal punishment in public schools (*Baker v. Owen*, 1975; *Ingraham v. Wright*, 1977).

While the administration of corporal punishment temporarily suppresses undesired behaviors, it also legitimizes violence. Moreover, it does not teach appropriate behaviors, nor does it teach logical problem-solving skills. When inflicting corporal punishment on students, adults in authority are modeling resolving conflict through violence. Corporal punishment in schools discriminates against students from certain sociocultural groups. Minority and poor White students receive paddlings four to five times more frequently than middle- and upper-class White students (Richardson & Evans, 1992). Corporal punishment can result in hostility, posttraumatic stress, and displaced aggression.

The following incident was witnessed by one of the authors of this book. A man in his 30s walked into a high school carrying a baseball bat and headed straight for the gym. He was looking for a coach, not a particular individual, just a coach. He found one sitting on a bench waiting for his class to arrive. The man struck the coach repeatedly with the baseball bat. The coach was seriously hurt and the man arrested. The police questioned his motives and discovered that throughout his school career, the man had been repeatedly hit by his coaches. He accepted his punishment because his parents justified the school spankings by repeating the beatings at home. He continued this cycle of spanking with his own children but lost control one day when his son came home from school with red swollen buttocks from being whipped by his own coach. This incident is an isolated case, and the great majority of coaches are responsible teachers, but corporal punishment can result in posttraumatic stress and violent behavior. Aggression that is passive in nature is equally devastating to children when it comes in the form of rejection, isolation, or the withholding of love, care, acceptance, or refusal by parents or caregivers to notice or speak to their children. Recently, the American Academy of Pediatrics renewed its opposition to spanking and other forms of corporal punishment and published a report on the harmful effects of such discipline on children. They called for state laws to abolish corporal punishment of children. Many school districts forbid the use of corporal punishment (Committee on School Health, 2000).

Setting Boundaries

Everyone who has observed the behavior of a small child with a pet realizes that children are not born sensitive to the feelings of other living creatures. Pulling the cat's tail or pounding a pet dog with a toy truck are common behaviors. Even baby brothers and sisters must be watched to protect them from injury by older siblings who have not yet been sensitized to the feelings of others. Children are patiently taught to think about how their actions will affect others. Those lessons are best taught by loving parents and caregivers during the early years, but that does not always happen, and the fact remains that they are lessons that have to be learned. If they are not taught at home as toddlers, then something must be done to teach them later.

Parens (1987), in the book *Aggression in Our Children,* emphasizes that it is the parents' job to begin to set boundaries for children at about 6 months of age, and to help them understand the consequences of their actions. Parens believe that undesirable social behavior should not be allowed. Older children must be helped and taught to express feelings of hostility in reasonable and acceptable ways. Parents should help children to express feelings such as anger, sadness, frustration, fear, and disappointment in appropriate ways. Children must learn that behavior such as hitting others, being verbally abusive, or making vulgar or prejudicial statements are not acceptable and will not be tolerated. If children are not taught appropriate ways to express their feelings, and if they do not understand appropriate limits in their expression, then hostility may result in aggressive behaviors. Young children do not have the ability to understand the consequences of their actions without help. Children may be yelled at for doing things that annoy parents and others, but in many cases appropriate teaching does not accompany the reprimand. The job of teaching these principles and behaviors sits squarely on the shoulders of teachers. In the early grades, this may be more important than the academic instruction. If students are not able to meet these basic behavioral expectations, their potential for success in life will be reduced.

If children are not sensitized to the feelings of others by parents or primary caregivers during the early years, they will have to be taught another way. Our society accepts the need for schools to teach some children about toothbrushes and dental and personal hygiene along with nutrition and other basic lessons that we might expect parents to teach at home. There are times when the lessons that should have been learned at home have to be taught at school. Sensitizing children to the feelings of others, teaching them to respect others' personal rights and boundaries, and helping them to learn how to deal with anger, rejection, and conflict must be given the same attention and care devoted to the teaching of anything else that is important in life.

Escalating Violence: Access to Weapons and Poisonous Weeds

The presence of weapons provides the final precondition for extreme violence. Most adults can remember children from their high school years or earlier who were insensitive, angry, withdrawn, or prone to violence, but they did not have the ready access to weapons that children have today. There are more guns in society now than ever before, and an American child today is 15 times more likely to be killed by gunfire than a child in war-ravaged Northern Ireland during the Protestant-Catholic hostilities (Sautter, 1995). Over a 2-year period across the nation, 6,000 students were found bringing weapons to school. Society has never been confronted with a situation in which guns have been so readily available to children (Goldberg, 1994). Although there have always been people who desired revenge, only recently have they had access to weapons to shoot their classmates or teachers, and access to the knowledge and materials required to blow up the schoolhouse. The Internet has made recipes for building bombs readily accessible to anyone.

In the great classic *The Republic of Plato,* written more than 2,000 years ago, the philosopher considered the issues involved in reshaping society so that humanity could be its best. He recognized the importance of children and their upbringing for the future society. He wrote that care should be taken not to raise children "in fields of poisonous weeds." He defined *poisonous weeds* as those social influences that contaminate children's thinking and behavior, thus suppressing their social and moral growth. Plato made the case that society has an obligation to prevent poisonous weeds from growing. Many in our society realize that poisonous weeds are plentiful. These weeds produce cruelty, violence, and revenge. The varieties of poisonous weeds found in modern society include:

- An entertainment industry obsessed with pushing the limits of normal decency beyond the norms of the majority of our society
- Leaders who are more occupied with finding someone to blame and punish for what is amiss than with addressing root causes
- Parents who create dysfunctional families and allow children to grow up unloved, undisciplined, or unnurtured
- Laws that protect people or things that are hateful, deviant, extreme, vulgar, or mentally, spiritually, or physically harmful to children
- A media that presents powerful images of violence, hate, and deviant behavior and then asks, "Shouldn't parents control what children watch?"
- A society that forces the knowledge and experience of adulthood on children who are ill-equipped to handle global issues like nuclear holocaust, adult sexuality, violence, deviancy, and instant media coverage of every crisis that occurs anywhere in the world.
- Those schools that, with a detached benevolence, teach every child the same way, provide no accommodation for individual differences and needs, and set the stage for underachievement by many
- Policies that put teachers into the classroom without adequate resources to help children who are at risk
- Small numbers of teachers who are uncaring, detached, uncommitted, who ridicule students, who permit themselves to become adversarial toward students, who look the other way when bullies are at work or ignore indications of parental neglect and abuse
- Small groups of children who have acquired license to be mean to one another, who are rude to teachers and adults, who prey upon other children with ridicule, rejection, mocking, and contempt—and with threats of physical violence
- Access not only to guns used for recreation, but to powerful guns and instructions for creating other weapons of death and destruction
- A social attitude that conveys a belief that children must be tough to survive—an attitude that unrelenting pressure and firm

treatment prepares children for the "real" world of competition

- Schools that are forced by economic constraints to ignore the research that presents effective teaching practices but costs money, and schools that ignore research that shows better ways to teach because they do not wish to make the changes necessary to implement new methods

- Talk show hosts and programs that foster a victim mentality and sow seeds of hatred, revenge, and dissatisfaction with the social contract upon which democracy is based

- Communities where drug pushers, crack houses, and gangs are present on every corner, where violence is the norm, and no safe haven exists

- Communities that use public funds for sports stadiums or spend hundreds of millions of dollars for projects such as rail lines to convey tourists to those stadiums but vote down public funds to build and improve school facilities or provide teachers with salaries adequate to care for and educate their own families

These are examples of poisonous weeds that grow in the environment in which our children live. They pose a danger to children, interfering with their normal growth and development. Changing the violent climate in which children grow and develop is not a simple task. The above list presents some of the variables that allow troubled children to trouble their world.

Children who grow up with early and continuous adult support that helps them to sort through what is normal and what is abnormal will develop adequate ego strength as teenagers and adults. They generally make it through the fields of weeds. They will overcome and heal from the damage done to them. Those without that support and without ego strength are like children with a compromised emotional immune system. They will be affected by the poison. Some will fall by the wayside. Some will act out with violence and destruction. As students or later in life as adults, they will act out with spouse or children, with coworkers or strangers, blowing up buildings, or in eruptions such as drive-by violence or road rage.

The Price of Violence: The Impact of Violence on Learning

The human toll of violence in schools is great. Its detrimental effects are far-reaching. The physical and emotional scars of bereaved families, friends, and survivors will remain long after media interest has faded. Individuals witnessing violence or even those in attendance in schools in which it occurs are often traumatized and remain fearful for years. Many are prone to carry weapons for self-defense, thus setting the stage for further tragedy. A few years ago one of the authors taught youngsters in an urban middle school and experienced the following dilemma. Kenita, a student in the sixth grade, was found to be carrying a switchblade knife. Immediately school personnel demanded that she turn it in, but she begged to keep it. She protested and pleaded, explaining that it was her "protection" and that without it she would surely be raped on her way home from school. Kenita lived in an inner city housing project where gang fights, shootings, and rape were not infrequent. Despite her pleas, her knife was confiscated. No protection was offered to her in place of the knife. No action was taken in response to the threat of rape. The violent attack she feared occurred that very afternoon. She was raped on her way home from school. The fear that walked with that young girl on her way to and from school was a constant part of her life. It culminated in a terrifying and violent trauma. The effect her experience may have had on her life is incalculable. Its effect on her ability to learn and to function—either short term or long term, in school or in life—is not known.

Violent acts in schools interfere with learning. Precious instruction time is devoted to dealing with inappropriate behavior. Teachers cannot devote time to teaching when they have to attend to constant physical and verbal altercations. Faculty and students are distracted. Violence creates a climate in which students feel unsafe or traumatized, emotional states that certainly preclude most academics. These factors not only interfere with learning, they also demoralize experienced teachers and scare off prospective ones because neither group is willing to work in dangerous or disruptive situations. A great society is an educated society. Simply stated, violence in school is antithetical to learning. Illiteracy breeds contempt, despair, and economic failure. We all eventually pay a price for scrimping on the programs needed to solve the problems of violence in the schools.

Other Determinants of Violence

Is violence solely the result of environmental conditions, or are some children more genetically predisposed to violence than others? Are males more violent than females? Is violence more predominant among certain racial or ethnic groups than others? What are the risk factors leading to violent acts? Factors affecting the neurochemistry of the brain may cause individuals to behave impulsively or ignore the consequences of their actions. Brain dysfunction can be genetic or the result of head trauma or exposure to alcohol or other toxic substances during the early prenatal period.

Scans of the brain of some violent individuals seem to indicate several abnormalities. Dr. Daniel Amen (1999), a neuroscientist, notes that the cingulate gyrus (CG), which curves through the middle of the brain, is abnormal in the brain of murderers. This part of the brain acts like a transmission controlling one thought to another. An impaired CG causes people to get stuck on one thought and if that thought happens to be a violent one, it is likely that a violent behavior could follow. Lesions in the frontal lobe may cause apathy and distorted judgment and emotion. Researchers have found that the prefrontel cortex (the brain's "referee") of 50 murderers was dysfunctional. Factors affecting the neurochemistry of the brain can also cause individuals to behave impulsively and ignore the consequences of their actions. On a positive note, Debra Niehoff (1999), in her book *The Biology of Violence*, explains that in spite of damage, the brain has many blank pages, a "tabula rasa" that can record positive experiences and learning. Brain dysfunction does not necessarily predict violent behavior. Behavior is the interaction between our brain and our experiences. Brain pathology and genetic vulnerability are only small components that may cause individuals to commit violent acts.

Dr. Stanton Samenow (1998) a specialist on the discipline of "difficult" children, believes that, from a very early age, noncompliant and irresponsible behavior follows a pattern that can be readily identified. Samenow says that these children require different discipline strategies than other children. Dr. Samenow recommends a firm, consistent but nurturing approach for teaching children with antisocial behaviors to be responsible and to accept the consequences of their behavior. Antisocial children may exhibit some or all of the following behaviors. They try to control others, try always to prevail, are uncompromising, impose their will by intimidation or brute force, blame others no matter what occurs, have no fear of consequences, have no concept of injury to others that may be caused by their behavior, and see themselves as victims when anyone tries to hold them accountable for their own behavior. Samenow suggests that these patterns may indicate a neurological pathology. The behavior of these children often leads to a diagnosis of antisocial personality when they become young adults. Brain pathology and genetic vulnerability are only small components of the configuration of events that may cause individuals to become antisocial and violent.

Bullying and Teasing

Bullying is such a pervasive problem in schools that it must be given special attention. Bullying in schools is commonplace. Being a victim of the aggressive behavior of classmates is high on the list of concerns for many schoolchildren. Most adults would not tolerate threatening, bullying behavior by colleagues in the workplace, yet it occurs constantly in the lives of children. Schools cannot be insensitive to the fear and intimidation experienced by children at the hands of bullies from elementary grades all the way through high school. Because of the pervasiveness of bullying in the nation's schools, it is important to examine some aspects of this problem in detail. Nearly everyone, no matter how old, can remember experiencing or observing a bully at work. In the United States it is believed that 15%–20% of all children are directly involved in bullying, as either a bully or a victim (Batsche & Knoff, 1994). Many more are indirectly involved by witnessing the bullying incident. It is estimated that in a given month, 285,000 students are attacked by other students (Wilczenski, 1994). Sadly, bullying usually lasts a long time, often for years or for a lifetime (Marano, 1995). It is not a problem that sorts itself out. Bullies and victims are in frequent contact, often with no adults around (Wilczenski, 1994). The effect on the life and development of the victims and the offenders, often over long periods of time, is frightening to consider. The problem exists in both rural and urban settings (Batsche & Knoff, 1994).

One common misconception is that bullying is normal, tolerable, pecking-order behavior. In the early 1900s, it was recommended that children be permitted to fight in play. In the 1950s, teaching children to fight was considered a legitimate educational aim. As recently as the 1980s, some psychologists suggested that it was unwise to intervene in fights between children because children fight to get attention. They thought nonintervention would lead to a more peaceful atmosphere (Wilczenski, 1994). The problem is that nonintervention presumes that children involved in a conflict are physically, cognitively, socially, and emotionally equal, and if left alone they will eventually find a better way of solving problems. This is not the case for bullies and their victims. Rather, it is important that children develop effective conflict resolution skills. Violence brings a kind of success for the bully in elementary school, and therefore bullying is reinforced, but the older a bully gets, the less successful and the more costly this method of problem resolution becomes. A child who is busy perfecting the skills and techniques necessary to be a successful bully is not learning more appropriate conflict resolution and problem-solving skills.

What Is Known About Bullies

Bullies see and experience their own aggressive behavior as being very effective. They are often rewarded for their aggression, even by adults. We know the following about bullies:

- Most children are not bullies or victims.
- The aggression starts early.
- It takes a unique series of experiences to create a person who can start fights, threaten, intimidate, and actively inflict pain on others.
- The bully may also suffer feelings of jealousy, low self-esteem, and even guilt.
- Bullies are on a downward spiral. Their behavior interferes with learning, friendships, work, intimate relationships, income, and mental health.
- Bullies turn into antisocial adults and are far more likely than others to commit crimes, batter their spouses, abuse their children, and produce another generation of bullies. (Marano, 1995)
- Bullies often are victims at home. (Olweus, 1995)

- Bullies perceive provocation where there is none. They generally attribute a hostile intent to others. They endorse revenge. (Marano, 1995)
- Bullies have a favorable attitude toward violence and the use of violence to solve problems. They believe or come to believe that aggression is a good way to resolve conflict.
- Bullies have a strong need for affiliation. (Wilczenski, 1994)
- Bullies do not feel empathy. They do not relate well to others. (Marano, 1995)
- Bullies generally have a good opinion of themselves and do not realize what others truly think of them. (Marano, 1995) They may be blind to what others think or feel about them; however, they are very much in tune with the effect of their bullying. They know where and when to bully.

Although aggression is one method of gaining dominance, it is not the only method. In our civilized society, it is not even the most successful method. Over time, as the bully grows older, aggression is less and less effective. Verbal skills are much more important in gaining status and success. Most individuals who are bullies at a young age remain bullies as they grow up. Marano (1995) reports the findings of a long-term study of bullies. Sixty percent of those identified as bullies in Grades 6 to 9 had at least one criminal conviction by 24 years of age. They had more driving offenses, more convictions, more alcoholism, more drug addiction, and more diagnosis of antisocial personality disorders. It was found that bullies were more abusive to their spouses and children, often producing another generation of bullies. Marriages tended to be unsuccessful for bullies. They were troublesome among peers and disruptive at work as adults. Bullies seemed able to associate only with others like themselves. Bullies were marginally skilled, had more accidents, had shorter and less productive lives, and paid less in taxes. In summary, bullies do not succeed socially, economically, intellectually, professionally, or emotionally. These findings indicate that the bullies identified in school are on a downward spiral and their problems will only grow worse over time (Marano, 1995).

Girls as well as boys can be violent; however, there is a form of bullying that seems exclusive to girls. It is relational aggression (Marano, 1995). Relational aggression involves hurting the victim through damaging or manipulating their relationships with others. This aggression may include persuading others to stop being friends with someone they are bullying, and using social exclusion to control others (such as using threats to withhold invitations to social events if the victim does not comply with the bully's demands). Female bullies tend to be passive-aggressive rather than actively aggressive by giving the victim "the silent treatment" and making sure she knows she is being excluded from the social interactions of the group.

Bullying can also take the form of sexual harassment. Power-dependent relationships in the family, such as a dominant father and submissive mother, can be a model for bullying. Cross-gender bullying is often dismissed as flirtation, and this fact raises the question: What is the message when a girl is told that abusive behavior toward her is equated with liking her (Wilczenski, 1994)? Boys too may experience cross-gender bullying. Boys who have been bullied by girls may have trouble relating to women later. Many love-shy adults reported being victimized by the opposite sex as a child. Bullies typically come from homes in which there is a lack of firm, consistent discipline. Usually there are relationship difficulties between the parents and also with the children. Financial and social problems often exist in the family. There is a cold emotional environment with little family structure and few if any consistent rules. There is often social isolation as a family and disengagement from community life. Parenting is ineffective and aggression is positively reinforced, while social nonaggressive behavior is neither rewarded nor actually punished. Child rearing is usually rigid, domineering, and authoritarian. There may be excessive physical punishment and angry emotional outbursts (Olweus, 1995).

What Is Known About Victims of Bullies

Bullies shop around until they find a victim (Marano, 1995). Bullies are usually strong, and they seek out individuals who are not well equipped to fight back. The victims are more sensitive, cautious, and quiet. They avow a negative view of violence, and they withdraw from confrontation. Victims are more submissive and nonassertive, and they are likely to give in to a bully's demands. Often they are forced to hand over their belongings and thus reward the bully for his behavior. Victims are often not popular students and so experience loneliness. The rejection of others keeps victims from developing the social skills they need to relate well to others—or to deal with the intimidating tactics of a bully. They hate going to school and their grades often suffer. Victims internalize the negative view that others have of them and develop a low opinion of themselves. They may believe that they deserve the harsh treatment they receive at the hands of a bully; others around them may share that opinion also. Victims often suffer from headaches, stomachaches, and other somatic illnesses. Some are driven deeper into the world of books and excel in school work (Marano, 1995). Victims may perceive asking for help to be risky because there may be a negative or incompetent response to the request (Wilczenski, 1994). Victims tend to have close, enmeshed relationships with their parents and tend to come from overprotective families. They are ill-prepared to handle the world on their own and have little confidence in their own abilities (Marano, 1995). Victims may also develop learned helplessness, particularly if they are victimized by a sibling with no parental intervention. There are basically three kinds of victims: (a) those who are passive and anxious victims, neither provoking others nor defending themselves, (b) provocative victims who are anxious but will retaliate when attacked, and (c) a victim who voluntarily assumes the role in order to gain acceptance (Wilczenski, 1994). Teachers are sometimes the victims of bullies, and in other cases teachers bully students. In a survey of teachers, a majority of the respondents reported seeing a teacher bully a student (Olweus, 1995).

Heroes and Bullying

The May 24, 1999, issue of *Newsweek* magazine reprinted a letter to the editor under the headline "The Lessons of Littleton." It points out an aspect of bullying that has been common in schools for generations (Bagley, 1999). Nothing done to them could justify the two students' acts of carnage at Columbine High School, but until we address the ethos of arrogance associated with the "jockocracy," both in America's schools and in our society at large, at least one of the important roots of such violence will continue to do its damage, as it has for generations. How much pain has been and is being suffered by countless children who are emotionally tormented and physically brutalized by their peers on a regular basis at school—a place where they are supposed to be safe? This significant issue will never get the attention the massacre did, simply because it is not as visible.

Lorraine Adams and Dale Russakoff (1999) wrote in an article that at Colombine High School, the state wrestling champion regularly parked his $100,000 Hummer in a 15-minute parking space. Adams and Russakoff indicated that a football player "teased a girl about her breasts in class with no fear of retribution by the boy's teacher who was also his coach." Sports trophies were prominantly displayed in Colombine's front hall, and student artwork was down a back corridor. Adams and Russakoff described a culture at Colombine High School in which upper-class wrestlers twisted the nipples of freshmen wrestlers until they turned purple and the homecoming king was "a football player on probation for burglary." The article described how parents and students alike were beginning to examine parts of the culture of Colombine that might have provoked the incident. A special task force was set up to look into this issue 2 weeks prior to publication of the article. Members of the task force said that "discipline, harassment, and special treatment for athletes must be dissected without defensiveness." The article goes on to describe numerous incidents of special treatment of athletes, harassment and bullying of others, and "a climate in which many students walked the halls in fear."

Bullying is a severe problem. It affects a massive number of children and, eventually, society as a whole. Bullying is a problem that does not go away when ignored. Students are not able to deal with the problem on their own. It is, however, a problem that can be dealt with and reduced through intervention programs. The extent of the problem of bullying needs to be assessed in every school, and intervention programs must be introduced on a schoolwide basis. These programs should involve students, faculty, administrators, and parents. Those who are the victims of bullying are subjected to ongoing fear, anxiety, and misery; moreover, the bullies themselves are on a road to failure. If this problem is not dealt with, the loss to victim, offender, and society will continue. Somewhere in the future, will we begin to see litigation seeking to make someone accountable for providing children with the protection they need?

Can Bullying Be Stopped?

Bullies generally do not stop bullying on their own. Intervention is usually required (Marano, 1995). An environment in which aggressive behavior is not tolerated must be established. Such an environment can be created by increasing the knowledge of the staff, having the "watchers" or "silent majority" set the positive values of the school, and having specific program components set up to intervene directly with victims, bullies, parents, staff, and students (Garrity, 1994). The focus should be shifted from fear to positive regard and respect for all students. Batsche and Knoff (1994) propose the following intervention plan to counter bullying.

1. Educating about bullying
2. Dispelling inappropriate beliefs about aggressive behavior, such as the belief that aggression is a normal part of growing up
3. Conducting a schoolwide assessment of bullying
4. Developing a student code of conduct and involving students in the process
5. Providing counseling services for bullies and victims
6. Involving parents in the intervention process
7. Implementing intervention strategies specific to aggressive children
8. Establishing accountability and evaluation of the programs and services provided

Children need to be able to ask for help when they are being bullied at home or at school. There must be respect for all students, and there should be a clear message that oppression will not be tolerated. Encouraging empathy through victim-centered socialization strategies encourages the victim to ask for help. However, care should be taken that "victimhood" is not glorified or given high status or visibility. The experiences necessary to teach negotiation and compromise skills should be provided (Wilczenski, 1994).

Multicultural Issues

We often form expectations of individuals based on cultural generalizations even though it is erroneous to believe that all members of a group have the same traits. Cultural misunderstanding and stereotyping can negatively impact a society. The melting pot theory has hurt many subcultures who simply cannot assimilate even if they wanted to because of racial features, skin color, or language. Stereotypes generally reinforce our beliefs, especially when we are conditioned by the media portraying poverty and violence as conditions of race and ethnicity. Readers are cautioned to bear in mind that stigmatizing, categorizing, and generalizing about abilities, personality characteristics, and learning styles can limit individuals and groups of people (Griggs & Dunn, 1989). Nevertheless, awareness, understanding, and acceptance of differences can positively affect interactions and learning.

The United States, among other countries, is becoming increasingly multicultural, and it is not unusual to hear several languages and dialects spoken in large urban city schools. Teachers are encountering first-generation Black immigrants from African countries and Latinos from Central and South America and Caribbean nations. These students' experiences and traditions are unlike second-generation or more African and Hispanic Americans.

The four main minority groups in the United States—Africans, Asians, Hispanics, and Native Americans—largely belong to collectivistic cultures and are faced with the challenge of adapting to the expectations of anglophilic individualistic cultures. In families of collectivist cultures, group goals are more important than individual goals, and family members often display shared concern for one another. Many times these collectivist values continue after a family breaks down or is no longer viewed as being able to protect a child or help a child to reach certain goals. The same values are carried over and transferred from the family to the gang. The impact of family values on social behaviors cannot be minimized; the influence of the family is an important variable contributing to the development of the socialization process. Behavior control based on cultural philosophical beliefs and values may range from swift punitive discipline to gentle lecturing.

Gender and Antisocial Behavior

Traditionally, many cultures have deemphasized aggression in female behavior, expecting women to be submissive to male domination. Gwendolyn Cartledge (1996) notes that society socializes females to be nurturers and caregivers. Males are believed to be more physically aggressive, and females to be more relationship oriented. Social norms allow girls to be more sensitive and open with their feelings, whereas boys who openly express emotions may be ridiculed. In schools, most aggressive and violent acts are committed by male students, and the rash of school shootings and killings of the late 1990s are attributed exclusively to male students. Males commit more murders and are more involved in the gun culture than are women. However, violent behavior among females has escalated in the past decade. These infractions include petty theft, physical assault, truancy, burglary, illicit sexual activity, drug use and sale, and gang activity. Alcoholism among female students has escalated, as has the use of marijuana (Sheldon, Tracy, & Brown, 1996).

In recent years female students have become more assertive. However, many females, like males, have resorted to destructive aggressive behaviors, including roles in sexual conduct that result in pregnancies. Membership in an antisocial gang will probably result in unwanted pregnancies, injury, drug abuse, a criminal record, incarceration, and possibly death. The number of teenage pregnancies is steadily decreasing in areas where sex education (abstinence or the use of contraceptives) is implemented. Schools must continue to provide programs not only to discourage young girls from gang membership but also to provide a system of support and assistance.

Girls join gangs for the same reason boys do. Goldstein (1991) reports that most female gang members come from economically deprived homes and live with a single parent. In many cases their need for love and belonging is not met in their home life. Other reasons for joining gangs are poor self-image, peer pressure, excitement, fear, threats, and intimidation. Female street gangs consisting of girls ages 9 to 19 are violent in nature, often reflecting the culture of their members' schools and the neighborhoods studied in Toronto, Los Angeles, and Milwaukee. Gangs of girls engage in criminal activities in much the same degree as their male counterparts (Sheldon et al., 1996). In general, female students have become more aggressive in their behavior, and while assertiveness should be taught and encouraged, aggressive behavior must be discouraged and redirected.

Environmental Regularities and Social Learning

Lack of appropriate modeling or high exposure to inappropriate modeling are high risk factors for violence along with a lack of family guidance in moral instruction. Children are not born with a social conscience. To a large extent, they acquire the morality of their social environment. Children are taught the expectations of their society and the importance of conforming to them in order to be an accepted part of the larger community. In gangs, those expectations often include participation in violent behavior and criminal activities, with an emphasis on suppression of feelings of fear or compassion. Children need to be guided to internalize the "traditional" mores of a democratic society, such as obeying the law, honoring individual and cultural differences, and respecting the rights of others. They also need to be valued as individuals and recognized for their individual talents, achievements, or attempts to achieve a task or goal. Adults convey their expectations to their students, and students inevitably meet these expectations. In many cases, adults do not expect students with problems to succeed, and their self-fulfilling prophesies are realized.

Teenagers have a need to belong to a community, and when it is unavailable elsewhere they will find it in the gang culture. The gang "family" promises to fulfill their needs. With membership in gangs comes exposure to gang value systems and behavior expectations, both of which include violence. Gangs teach their members gang values and dispense harsh discipline for noncompliance. Such teaching is necessary for gangs to survive and operate. The same principles apply to schools and indeed to democratic societies. They must teach value systems and their behavioral expectations and then insist on compliance if they are to survive and function. How is it that schools seem unable to accomplish what gangs do so well?

For many children, the stage is set very early for rejection of standard societal norms and reliance upon cliques, subgroups, gangs, and the ability to be personally intimidating to meet their needs. If schools do not offer genuine respect, care, and acceptance to all students, the students will seek it elsewhere. If schools do not offer protection, children will seek it elsewhere. If schools do not convey a feeling of belonging, children may well find acceptance offered by a peer group or gang. Schools simply cannot avoid participating in the moral development of children. If that participation is not deliberate and purposeful, learning occurs anyway, and it will be the unanticipated and random learning that comes from the most powerful teacher of all, modeled behavior.

Schools that are uncaring teach children to be uncaring. Schools that choose not to notice the pain people are experiencing model denial, rationalization, and minimization of the needs and concerns of others for their students. Schools that permit bullying and intimidation to go unnoticed demonstrate lip service to the need to be law abiding and respectful of others, and do little to enforce such standards and rules. If the overall climate of a school is detached, impersonal, and uncaring, then detached, impersonal, and uncaring behavior becomes the model for a child's social and moral development. If there is no appeal, no way to seek mercy or present a case for extenuating circumstances in times of stress or problems, a child will not learn mercy, empathy, or compassionate problem solving. If power is held and wielded without gentleness or responsiveness to individuals, then this way of behaving is presented as society's norm. Everything a school does in response to its students is teaching moral development, whether intended or not. Treatment of individual children and groups of children must conform to the principles of respect, honor, and compassion, without which a democracy cannot work.

Children need to be taught acceptance of others, not punished for lack of acceptance. They must be *taught* to refrain from ridiculing peers who look or dress different—or for any other reason. They must be taught to value peace and how to resolve the conflicts that inevitably arise in any group. In the context of conflict resolution, many of the vital issues related to how to handle our feelings of hurt, loss, rage, and hatred can be addressed. It is vital that schools accept responsibility for teaching children how to recognize, name, and handle their feelings. Such vital subjects are as important as the matching of subject and predicate or any other grammatical principle.

The response to major problems in a school often produces a tack-on or pilot program of some kind supported with, and often shaped by, special funding. These projects, even successful ones, usually are add-ons that may not affect anyone except those who are directly involved in the project. Therefore, they do not bring about the fundamental and widespread system changes that are needed. When the funding runs out, the projects die. Students need an environment that is emotionally supportive for learning and the development of appropriate social behavior. Consider the following example:

A public school teacher was trying to help a fellow teacher deal with a problem learner. It was clear that the child's learning style was different from the teaching style of the teacher seeking help. As those differences were discussed, the child's teacher flatly stated that she did not care about how the student learned. That student was simply going to have to learn the way she was taught! Such an attitude sets the stage for frustration and anger.

Special Cases

The Diagnostic and Statistical Manual of Mental Disorders, Fourth Edition (DSM-IV-TR) (American Psychiatric Association, 2000) provides a comprehensive description and classification of mental disorders used by mental health practitioners throughout the United States. The manual cautions that the term *mental disorder* also includes much that is "physical," just as what is "physical" includes much that is "mental." The manual classifies mental disorders into types that have specific defining features. Students who are identified and have been classified with DSM-IV-TR labels generally require more help than a regular class teacher may be able to provide. The children who have been so classified should have a certified practitioner supervising their treatment and training. The teacher's role is to assist, facilitate, and collaborate with other professional personnel who are working with the child. Specialists, such as psychologists or counselors, must devise a specific behavioral plan for the child and provide backup support and consultation to assist the teacher and the child in a regular classroom setting.

The DSM-IV-TR identifies a number of disorders that are evident in infancy, childhood, or adolescence. While many of these have a behavioral component that may need to be addressed by educators, only the disorders specifically related to disruptive behavior will be described here

Conduct Disorder: The main characteristic of conduct disorder is persistent violation of the rights of others or of societal norms or rules. The behaviors can be aggressive, such as threats of physical harm to others or animals, nonaggressive conduct dealing with property loss or damage, deceitfulness or theft, and serious violation of rules. The DSM-IV-TR indicates that children or adolescents with this disorder

> often initiate aggressive behavior and react aggressively to
> others…display bullying, threatening, or intimidating behavior;
> initiate frequent physical fights; use a weapon that can cause serious
> physical harm (e.g., a bat, brick, broken bottle, knife, or gun); steal
> while confronting a victim (e.g., mugging, purse snatching,

> extortion, or armed robbery); or force someone into sexual activity.
>
> Physical violence may take the form of rape, assault, or, in rare
>
> cases, homicide. (p. 86)

The disorder includes destruction of property, vandalism, fire setting, frequent lying, conning others, and the violation of rules. The pattern usually begins before age 13 and includes staying out late at night, running away from home, truancy, or absence from work.

Oppositional Defiant Disorder (ODD): The DSM-IV-TR describes the main feature of this disorder as "a recurrent pattern of negativistic, defiant, disobedient, and hostile behavior toward authority figures." It is characterized by

> losing temper, arguing with adults, defying or refusing to comply
>
> with requests or rules...doing things that will annoy other people,
>
> blaming others for his or her own mistakes or misbehavior, being
>
> touchy or easily annoyed by others, being angry or resentful, or
>
> being spiteful or vindictive. (p. 90)

The DSM-IV-TR indicates that in order to meet the criteria of this disorder, the occurrence of these behaviors must be more frequent than those that might be observed among peers of comparable age and developmental level and must lead to social, academic, or occupational impairment. Negativistic and defiant behaviors are expressed by persistent stubbornness, resistance to directions, and unwillingness to compromise, give in, or negotiate with adults or peers. They may exhibit low self-esteem, unstable moods, low frustration tolerance, and conflicts with others. Children with ODD view their behavior as a reasonable response to the unreasonable demands of others upon them. ODD is prevalent in families that are harsh, inconsistent, and neglectful and is commonly associated with ADHD.

There are behavioral implications for children diagnosed with substance-related disorders, psychotic disorders, and schizophrenia, mental retardation, autism, ADHD, and so forth, as described by the DSM-IV-TR. These disorders may have implications for noncompliant, aggressive. or violent behaviors in schools. For example, more and more children are being diagnosed with a bipolar disorder in which there are mixed episodes of depression and manic behavior. Adults diagnosed with an antisocial personality disorder often have a long history or symptoms of conduct disorder before the age of 15 years. Children with DSM-IV-TR classifications should always have a physician, psychologist, or psychiatrist supervising their treatment.

Discipline for Students With Disabilities

For years disciplining students with disabilities has caused concern for teachers and school administrators. The 1997 Amendments of IDEA do not allow cessation of special services even for dangerous and chronically disruptive students. The IEP team can place these students in an alternative education setting or in suspension for not more than 10 days in a given school year. If a student brings a weapon to school or school functions, or possesses, uses, or sells illegal drugs, the IEP team may utilize an alternative setting for not more than 45 days without parental consent. During that period, the IEP team, including the parents, may opt to change the student's permanent placement (Council for Exceptional Children, 1998).

Laws protecting students with disabilities are necessary to prevent capricious suspensions and to keep these students in school. Before 1975, students with disabilities were not receiving an appropriate education. Students with behavior and emotional disorders were especially vulnerable to suspensions and expulsion and were routinely excluded even as late as the 1970s. These students were (and still are in some school districts) subjected to corporal punishment, resulting in high dropout rates. Consequently, they often were pushed into society without appropriate skills, and their antisocial and often violent behavior continued to threaten the public. To this day students with emotional and behavioral disorders present problems and challenges to educators, parents, and the community. According to U.S. Department of Education statistics, this group of students has alarming indicators in school absenteeism, dropout rate, low grade-point average, and a low rate of employment.

Discipline provisions were included in Public Law 94-142, the Education for All Handicapped Children Act (1975), to stop abuses and to grant students and their parents the right to challenge exclusionary practices. In the landmark case *Honig v. Doe* (1988), the Supreme Court ruled that the expulsion of dangerous students for more than 10 days is indeed considered a change of placement. School administrators felt that their authority was being challenged, and procedures to determine whether the behavior was related to the exceptionality were time-consuming, nebulous, and restrictive. In addition, numerous court cases ruled in favor of students and sent a message that no matter what antisocial behavior students with behavior or emotional disorders displayed, their behavior was related to their exceptionality. It is no wonder then, that prevalence of students classified with behavior disorders or emotional disturbance is relatively low. It is surprising that the percentage of school-age population in this category varies widely across states. Prevalence figures range from a high range of 1.69% in Connecticut to a low of 0.03% in Mississippi. A possible explanation for the low prevalence is the discipline factor (National Center for Educational Statistics, 1998). School officials may hesitate to increase the number of students in this category because it is more difficult to prove that their disruptive behaviors are not caused by their condition. Other explanations for the disparity could be attributed to more obvious factors such as a definition that is subjective, conflicting viewpoints concerning the nature of this exceptionality, the negative social connotation associated with the label, the decreased self-concept caused by the label, the loss of popularity among peers, and low expectations and self-fulfilling prophecies. The following scenario is an example of preconceived expectations of teachers toward students labeled as behavior problems. The incident involved a student with a behavior disorder in a large high school. Two teachers were staring at a young student labeled emotionally disturbed who was getting his books out of his locker. Their eyes wandered from the student to a large clock on the wall. Feeling uncomfortable at their stare, he approached them and said, "What are you looking at?" One of the teachers replied, " We were wondering how long it would take you to make a complete fool of yourself." The student was enraged, cursed at the teachers, and slammed the locker door, knocking it off its hinges. Of course, he was punished for cursing the teachers and for destroying school property. We believe that this is not the norm, and a great majority of teachers are compassionate and caring; however, labels do seem to fuel self-fulfilling expectations.

In addition to educators' dilemmas, parents of general education students often perceive the discipline code for students with disabilities as unfair and discriminatory. Consider the following example. Two students are involved in a physical fight; one is a student with a behavior disorder, and the other is a general education student. The general education student is suspended from school, while the student with the disability is not. A behavior disorder is an "invisible disability" that does not necessarily evoke understanding or compassion. To many onlookers these students are often described as "troublemakers" who need firm discipline with no exceptions. Special concessions are often regarded as unfair and only serve to reinforce inappropriate behaviors.

Alternative Schools

In the 1960s, alternative schools were developed to segregate rebellious students who could not succeed in a regular program. These schools were considered as one last chance prior to expulsion or incarceration. Students classified as having behavior or emotional disorders were placed in self-contained alternative schools or in mental health institutions. Many school districts had an alternative school for unmanageable students. Students who did not qualify for special education programs were considered at risk and also placed in alternative schools. Many came from minority groups and disadvantaged homes. Typically, the programs in these alternative schools included in-school suspension, cooling-off rooms, and extended placement for habitually disruptive and violent students. Mental health institutions provided psychological and drug treatment, and the stay in these institutions could stretch for years. Discipline management in these alternative settings was strictly based on a behavioral model, and level systems and contingency contracting were used extensively. Instead of cooperative learning, students were isolated in individual carrels to perform the exact work demanded by the curriculum they left behind in their previous school. The environment was intensively structured to avoid disruption and other discipline problems. The teachers were in control, and students were given few choices in their education.

We do not advocate segregating students in alternative schools. However, some situations call for a temporary separation to allow time to work out solutions. Alternative schools for students who engage in antisocial behaviors have reemerged with a difference, and many can be considered models for reform in all education. Contrary to the isolationist strategies of the past, the curriculum of new alternative schools is designed to empower and engage students in their education. Gold (1995) discusses two key components of a successful alternative school for at-risk youth. The first component is to keep students from failing and the second is the caring attitudes of teachers who provide interpersonal support. This requires a compassionate staff willing to be involved and to focus on both the academic and the social-emotional growth of each student. It also requires a staff knowledgeable in behavior management techniques willing to work with difficult students. These requirements call for retraining teachers in methodology and skills needed to redirect students in their social behaviors and teach self-regulation skills. Alternative schools, contrary to traditional schools, have the luxury to be innovative and nontraditional. Teachers in alternative schools are allowed to be creative in their assignments and deviate from traditional expectations yet meet accountability to improve student performance in both their academic and social skills. Strategies employed in alternative schools can serve as models and be implemented in general education to deal with disruptive and violent students.

Summary

Teachers often express frustration that the social skills they attempt to teach and model are lost when students return to a dysfunctional home or when they are strongly influenced by peers. However, teachers can light that necessary spark that might lead students to search further and reach for a productive life. No matter what, teachers must treat all students with the kindness and respect we want to see students express toward one another and toward us. Modeled behavior is a powerful teacher, and the way we treat our students teaches them how to behave toward us and others.

In spite of the violence experienced in schools, we must remember that schools are relatively safe and that students are learning so much more than their parents and grandparents. They are also much more aware of injustice, prejudice, and environmental hazards. The majority of young people are not violent, and many more are involved in community work than ever before. Numerous schools are encouraging students to become involved in service to others. In Maryland, students must complete 75 hours of service as a graduation requirement. The school district provides opportunities for students to develop civic values by engaging in some form of work in the school or in the community (Ernst & Amis, 1999). Schools, not only in the United States but all over the world, are experiencing a merging of cultures, and differences often spawn conflict. We must learn to live peacefully, and schools are in a prime position to teach this very important value.

To counteract violence, educators can include strategies to address five crucial issues:

1. Specific methods and procedures for conflict resolution must be taught and employed on an ongoing basis.

2. The nature, process, and skills of affective development in children must be taught with the same attention and care afforded the physical and intellectual development of our children. Such programs will need to teach children to recognize and name feelings in themselves and others and offer children practical suggestions and experiences for dealing with their own feelings and those of others. They will need to provide truly open and welcoming support services for students who feel unable to cope with their feelings alone.

3. Specific methods and procedures must be used for teaching stress management.

4. Programs must be implemented to provide students and staff personal with referral services to put students in touch with community services that might be needed by the students.

5. Proactive planning should enforce zero tolerance for hazing, sexual harassment, ridicule, bullying, and other unacceptable behaviors among students.

In general, teachers are second only to parents in the amount of time they spend with students. Sometimes they have more control with students than the parents have. When students have no personal and meaningful interaction with adults, they seek peer groups that will give them a sense of belonging. The gang serves as their "security blanket," and the emotional arousal that is transferred from the group encourages each individual member to behave in ways that he or she would not behave without the influence and support of other gang members. Each school must engage in constructive communication with students, parents, and other community organizations and institutions to create safe schools.

Activity 1: Dealing With Violence

1. Survey a local school system (or systems) to determine whether a curriculum for teaching social skills, moral development, and management of aggression has been adopted. If one is in place, identify the instructors, the grade level, and the amount of time allotted to it. If social skills are not formally taught, try to

determine why such a program has not been included in the curriculum. If a program is in operation, determine what training is given to teachers and counselors regarding the management of aggressive or potentially aggressive or violent students.

2. Interview counselors from elementary, middle, and secondary schools to determine their role in dealing with aggressive children, bullies, cliques, and victims of physical or verbal abuse and sexual harassment. Identify referral procedures and obtain a comprehensive list of available services.

3. Contact your city and/or county law enforcement to determine the extent of local gang activity. Determine whether programs are in place to counteract gang activities and growth. Make a list of signs, symbols, clothing, and initiation rites of local gangs. Develop a profile of a typical gang member in your area.

4. Invite a law enforcement person who works with gangs to speak at a teacher's meeting.

5. In small groups, discuss examples of poisonous weeds. Discuss specific ways that schools and teachers might reduce the impact of these negative influences.

6. Form small groups. Draw an outline of a lifesize figure on 8 feet of wrapping paper that has been taped to the wall. Discuss the characteristics of students in your school who are or might have the potential to become aggressive or violent. Label, list, draw, or symbolize the characteristics of these children on the paper with the outline. Present your aggressive child profile to the larger group and discuss.

Activity 2: Poem

Divide into small groups and read the following poem by Rita Coombs-Richardson. Help each other to compose a poem in rhyme or prose expressing what a student with a behavior problem might feel. Write your poem on a flip chart and share with the entire group.

Who Am I?

I'm always acting like a fool
I have no friends, I can't be cool
Deep inside I feel so sad
So helpless, frustrated, and so mad

I rant and rave, I fume and rage
I'm like a tiger in a cage

Violence is the world I know
Outrage I must surely show

I cannot fit your situation
I'll live up to my reputation
My world you cannot understand
In your environment I cannot bend

I need someone to reach my soul
To listen, to care, but not control
Please do not ridicule
I really want to stay in school

Rita Coombs-Richardson

Activity 3: Resources

Locate and contact centers in your community that are engaged in violence prevention. Or select a center from the provided list. Share the information you receive with your faculty.

List of Resources for Counteracting School Violence

Biblio alert: Focus on Firearms, New Resources for Preventing Injury and Violence, Children's Safety Network, National Center for Education in Maternal and Child Care, 2000 15th St. N., Suite 701, Arlington, VA 22201-2617. Tel. (800) 899-4301.

A Comprehensive Strategy for Serious, Violent, and Chronic Juvenile Offenders: U.S. Department of Justice, Office of Juvenile Justice and Delinquency Prevention, Washington, DC 20055. Tel. (800) 638-8736.

Educational Resources for Violence Prevention. A list of curricula, videos, and other materials. CSN Adolescent Violence Prevention Resource Center, Education Development Center Inc., 55 Chapel St., Newton, MA 02158. Tel. (617) 969-7200 ext. 2374. Cost: $3.00.

Juveniles and Violence: Juvenile Offenders and Victimization Fact Sheet: U.S. Department of Justice, Washington, DC 20055. Tel. (800) 638-8736.

National Teens, Crime, and the Community Program Center: 1700 K Street, N.W. Second Floor. Washington, DC 200056. Tel. (202) 466-6272.

Connecticut Collaborative for Education Against Gun Violence. P.O. Box 523, Department P., Southport, CT 06490.

Sexual Harassment in Schools: What It Is, What to Do. A report on steps to understand the legal and educational aspects of sexual harassment, and recommendations for state action and ways to help students. National Association of State Boards of Education, 1012 Cameron Street, Alexandria, VA 22314. Tel. (800) 220-5183.

References

Adams, L., & Russakoff, D. (1999). Spoiled sports: Athlete injustices bothered many Columbine students. *Houston Chronicle 98* (244), 1A & 8A.

Amen, D. (1999). *Change your brain, change your life: The revolutionary, scientifically, proven program for mastering your moods, conquering your anxieties, obsessiveness, anger, and impulsiveness.* New York: Amazon.

American Psychiatric Association. (2000). *Diagnostic and Statistical Manual of Mental Disorders, Fourth Edition, Text Revision.* Washington, DC, American Psychiatric Association.

American Psychological Association. (1999). *Warning signs.* [On-line] Available from http://www.helping.apa.org/warningsigns/reasons.html.

Bagley, S. (1999, May 24). Why the young kill. *Newsweek,* pp. 32–35.

Baker v. Owen. (1975). 423 U.S. 907, 96 S. Ct. 210.

Batsche, G., & Knoff, H. (1994). Bullies and their victims: Understanding a pervasive problem in the school. *School Psychology Review 23* (2), 165–174.

Canada, G. (2000). Understanding youth culture: Raising better boys. *Educational Leadership, 57* (4), 14–17.

Cartledge, G. (1996). *Cultural diversity and social skills instruction.* Champaign, IL: Research Press.

Collins, M. (1992). *Ordinary children, extraordinary teachers.* Charlottesville, VA: Hampton Roads.

Committee on School Health. (2000). Corporal punishment in schools. *Pediatrics 106* (2), 343.

Council for Exceptional Children. (1998). IDEA—Let's make it work: Behavior and discipline sections 613 and 615. *Teaching Exceptional Children 30* (4), 32–35.

Ernst, D., & Amis, B. (1999). Service learning: A growing movement. *ASCD Infobrief 19,* 1–8.

Garrity, C. (1994). *Bully-proofing your school: A comprehensive elementary curriculum.* Paper presented at Safe Schools, Safe Students: A collaborative approach to achieving safe disciplined and drug free schools conducive to learning conference, Washington, DC. (ERIC Document Reproduction Services No. ED 383 956)

Gold, M. (1995). Charting a course: Promise and prospects for alternative schools. *Journal of Emotional and Behavioral Problems 3* (4), 8–11.

Goldberg, S. (1994, February 27). Juvenile justice "fails massively": Crime is an "after-school sport" for some. *San Francisco Examiner,* p. 1A.

Goldstein, A. (1991). *Delinquent gangs: A psychological perspective.* Champaign IL: Research Press.

Goldstein, A., & Kodluboy, D. (1998). *Gangs in schools: Signs, symbols, and solutions.* Champaign IL: Research Press.

Goley, E. (1992). United States: Native Americans. In L. Miller-Lachmann (Ed.), *Our family, our friends, our world.* New Providence, NJ: Bowker.

Griggs, S., & Dunn, R. (1989). The learning style of multicultural groups and counseling implications. *Journal of Multicultural Counseling and Development 17* (4), 146–155.

Hammond, W., & Yung, B. (1993). Psychology's role in the public health response to assaultive violence among young African American men. *American Psychologist 48* (2), 142–154.

Honig v. Doe (1988). 484 U.S. 305, 108S. Ct. 592, 98. Ed. 2d 686.

Howell, J. C. (1997). *Youth gangs in the United States: An overview.* Report prepared for the U.S. Department of Justice, Office of Juvenile Justice and Delinquency Prevention. Tallahassee, FL: National Youth Gang Center.

Hyman, I. (1990). *Reading, writing and the hickory stick: The story of physical and psychological abuse in American schools.* Lexington, MA: Heath.

Hyman, I. (1997). *School discipline and school violence.* Boston: Allyn & Bacon.

Ingraham v. Wright, 525 F. 2nd 248 (5 Cir. 1977).

Kaufmann-Kanter, G., & Jasinski, J. (Eds.). (1996). *Out of the darkness; Contemporary research perspectives on family violence.* New York: Sage.

Kirkman, J. (1997). Murder and media: What elementary teachers can do about violence. *McGill Journal of Education 32* (3), 231–247.

Knox, G. (1993). *An introduction to gangs.* Berrien Springs, MI: Vande Verde.

Macbeth, T. (1996). *Tuning in to young viewers: Social science perspective on television.* Thousand Oaks, CA: Sage.

Marano, H. (1995 September/October). Big, bad, bully. *Psychology Today,* pp. 50–61.

Morse, J. (2000, April 24). Looking for trouble. *Time, 155,* p. 16.

National Center for Education Statistics. (1998). *Digest of education statistics.* Washington. DC: Department of Education. Also available online: http://nces.ed.gov/fastfacts/display.

National Center for Health Statistics. (1996). *Vital statistics of the United States.* Hyattsville, MD: DPHS.

National Center for Injury Prevention and Control. (1998). *Scientific data, surveillance and injury statistics.* Atlanta, GA: Centers for Disease Control and Prevention. [Also available from http://www.edc.gov/ncipc/osp/mortdata.htm.

Niehoff, D. (1999). *The biology of violence: The brain, behavior, environment, and violence.* New York: Free Press.

Olweus, D. (1995). *Bullying at school: What we know and what we can do.* Blackwood, NJ: Blackwell.

Parens, H. (1987). *Aggression in our children: Coping with it constructively.* Northvale, NJ: Jason Aronson.

Ramirez, O. (1989). Mexican American children and adolescents. In J. T. Gibbs, L. N. Huang, (Eds.), *Children of color.* San Francisco: Jossey-Bass.

Richardson, R., & Evans, E. (1992). *African-American males: An endangered species and the most paddled.* Paper presented at the Seventh Annual Conference of the Louisiana Associations of Multicultural Education, Baton Rouge.

Ridgeway, J. (1995). *Blood in the face: The Ku Klux KLan, Aryan Nations, Nazi skinheads, and the rise of a new white culture.* New York: Thunders Mouth Press.

Samenow, S. (1998). *Before it's too late.* New York: Time Books.

Sautter, C. (1995). Standing up to violence: A Kappan special report. *Phi Delta Kappan 76* (5), K1–K12.

Sheldon, R., Tracy, S., & Brown, B. (1996). Girls and gangs: A review of recent research. *Juvenile and Family Court Journal, 47* (1), 21–39.

Short, J. F., Jr. (1996). *Gangs and adolescent violence.* Boulder, CO: Center for the Prevention of Violence.

Slaby, R. (1995). *Aggressors, victims, and bystanders.* Newton, MA: Education Development Center.

Soriano, F. (1993). Cultural sensitivity and gang intervention. In A. P. Goldstein & C. R. Huff (Eds.), *The gang intervention handbook.* Champaign, IL: Research Press.

Stephens, R. (1997). (Ed.). *Safe schools and quality schooling: The public responds.* Washington, DC: National School Safety Center.

UNICEF. (1994). Annual deaths by homicide per 100,000 aged 15–24. *Health Promotion 6* (6), 407.

Wilczenski, F. (1994). *Promoting "fair play": Interventions for children as victims and victimizers.* Paper presented at the annual meeting of the National Association of School Psychologists, Seattle. (ERIC Document Reproduction Services No: ED 380 744)

Index

Author Bios

Dr. Rita Coombs-Richardson was born in Alexandria, Egypt of European origin. She completed a British education through high school and received her higher education degrees in the United States. She earned a Bachelor of Arts degree from Dominican College, a Master of Education degree from the University of Houston and a Doctorate of Philosophy degree from the University of New Orleans. Dr. Coombs-Richardson has taught in parochial and public schools in Louisiana and in Texas in both general and special education.

Dr. Rita Coombs-Richardson has published extensively in professional journals and has presented at numerous national and international conferences. She received the Chancellor's teaching excellence award from the University of Texas and Southmost College in brownsville, Texas. She has authored four volumes on teaching students social and emotional skills entitled *Connecting with Others: Lessons for Teaching Social and Emotional Competence.*

Dr. Coombs-Richardson is presently a professor at Southeastern Louisiana University where she is instructing graduate level courses in Special Education. She is the author and director of Project Inclusion, a state funded grant designed to assist general educators in teaching of students with special needs. She has previously held teaching positions at the University of Louisiana at Lafayette, Prairie View A & M University in Texas, and at the University of Texas at Brownsville. She resides in the northwest section of Houston, Texas.

Dr. Charles Meisgeier, nationally recognized educator and author, has developed programs used throughout the nation that are designed to address school behavior problems and accommodate individual differences. He was coordinator of the Special Education Administration program at the University of Texas. He was founding chair of the Educational Psychology Department and currently is Coordinator of the Special Education program and professor of Educational Psychology at the University of Houston. He has served as consultant to schools, colleges and agencies and has conducted workshops and training programs in the US and in Europe. Meisgeier has been a teacher, principal, and was administrator in charge of psychological services, special education, and special teacher training programs for the Houston Independent School District where he pioneered mainstream special education and developed the nation's first large prototype "mainstream" program. He headed the program for mental retardation at the U.S. Office of Education. He has been Director or Principal Investigator of many research and development grants. He is a tireless advocate for programs that increase the power of schools and teachers to accommodate individual differences in the classroom. Meisgeier has authored more than 125 publications and is a frequent presenter at national professional conferences. Consistently on the cutting edge in his field, he originated the Content Mastery Program, the Synergistic Social Behavioral Program, and the Synergistic Reading Fluency program used in Texas, Louisiana, and other areas of the Southwest. He is a leader in the identification and accommodation of personality type in children and has generated a significant body of research in this area.